Accounting in the Hotel and Catering Industry

Fourth Edition

Richard Kotas

B.Com., M.Phil., A.C.I.S.
Senior Lecturer in Accounting
Department of Hotel, Catering and Tourism Management
University of Surrey

INTERNATIONAL TEXTBOOK COMPANY

Published by
International Textbook Company Ltd
a member of the Blackie Group
7 Leicester Place
London WC2 7BP

First published 1966
Second edition 1969
Third edition published 1972
Fourth edition 1981
Reprinted 1986

British Library Cataloguing in Publication Data

Kotas, Richard
Accounting in the hotel and catering industry.
—4th ed.
1. Hotels, taverns, etc.—Accounting
2. Caterers and catering—Accounting
I. Title
657'.837 HF5686.H75

ISBN 0-7002-0279-X

Printed by Thomson Litho Ltd, East Kilbride, Scotland.

Preface to the Fourth Edition

It is now fifteen years since 'Accounting in the Hotel and Catering Industry' was first published in 1966. This fourth edition leaves the basic structure of the volume unaltered, but introduces several new elements which reflect changes in current hotel and catering accounting practice.

Chapter 14, *Accounting for Limited Companies*, has been completely re-written and incorporates the recent changes introduced by the Companies Act, 1980. Some new text has been added to explain the principles of funds flow statements and VAT. Chapter 6, *Mechanized Accounting*, has been replaced by a completely new chapter entitled *Revenue Accounting*. The new chapter explains the technique of profit sensitivity analysis, and should be particularly useful to students planning to take up employment in the market-oriented sector of the hotel and catering industry.

Since the publication of the third edition, the general level of prices has continued to show an upward trend. The opportunity has, therefore, been taken to update all numerical examples and illustrations.

R.K.

By the same author

Book-keeping in the hotel and catering industry (3rd edition)
Published by International Textbook Company Ltd

Food and beverage control (with Bernard Davis) (3rd edition of **Food cost control**)
Published by International Textbook Company Ltd

Management accounting for hotels and restaurants
Published by Surrey University Press

Managerial economics for hotel operation
Published by Surrey University Press

Market orientation in the hotel and catering industry
Published by Surrey University Press

Labour costs in restaurants
Published by International Textbook Company Ltd

An approach to food costing
Published by Barrie and Jenkins

Management accounting problems in hotels and catering
Published by New University Education

Contents

Page

Page

CHAPTER 1

Theory and mechanics of double entry

Nature of business transactions

In the course of any one day, a business will make a number of transactions. It will buy provisions, wines, and spirits from its suppliers; sell meals, drinks, and accommodation to its customers; pay business expenses such as rent, rates, wages, and salaries; and buy china, cutlery, and equipment.

All such transactions result in a transfer of money (or money's worth, value, or benefit) between two parties; the giver and the recipient of value. Thus, when a hotel buys provisions from its supplier; the giver of value is the supplier and the recipient of value is the hotel. When wages are paid by the hotel, the hotel is the giver and the employees are the recipients of money. When a meal is served to a customer, the hotel is the giver and the customer the recipient of value.

Hence, it may be said that *every business transaction has two aspects: the yielding of a benefit and the receiving of that benefit*, and it is impossible to think of one without the other.

The ledger

In order to have a systematic record of all transactions, it is necessary to keep what is known as the ledger. This is the principal book of account and contains a number of ledger accounts, each of which will be ruled as in Figure 1.

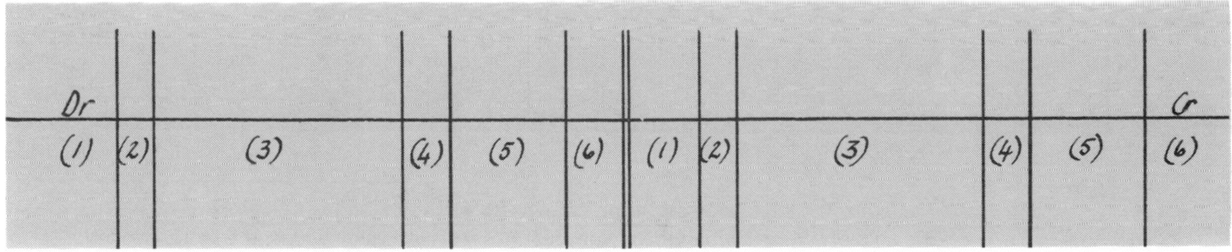

Figure 1

It will be observed that the ledger account is divided into two identical parts. The left-hand side of the account is known as the *debit side* (abbreviated to Dr.), and the right-hand side of the account is known as the *credit side* (abbreviated to Cr.).

The columns numbered (1) – (6) are used as follows:

(1) The month;
(2) the day of the month;
(3) particulars;
(4) folio (a folio is a page in a book of account; the pages of the ledger are numbered consecutively and each ledger account appears on a different page; the folio column is used to cross-reference the double entry of a transaction);
(5) – (6) money columns for pounds and pence respectively.

Principle of double entry

In order to have a complete record of all transactions, each transaction must be entered in the ledger twice: once on the debit and once on the credit side of an account. The receiving of value is entered on the debit side and the giving of value on the credit side, as in Figure 2.

Dr.									Cr.
		VALUE RECEIVED					VALUE GIVEN		

Figure 2

The following examples show how the principle of double entry is applied in the recording of transactions.

(a) On 1st January, 19. ., a hotel pays wages of £1 000

Dr.		Wages A/c							Cr.
19.. Jan.	1	Cash	1,000	00					

Dr.		Cash A/c							Cr.
					19.. Jan.	1	Wages	1,000	00

Figure 3

Note: The cash account of the hotel has given value and is, therefore, credited; the wages account (representing the employees) has received value and is, therefore, debited.

(b) On 4th February, 19. ., a restaurant borrows £10 000 from X Finance Company.

Dr.		Cash A/c							Cr.
19.. Feb	4	X Finance Co.	10,000	00					

Dr.		X Finance Co. A/c							Cr.
					19.. Feb	4	Cash	10,000	00

Figure 4

Note: The cash account of the restaurant has taken value and is therefore debited; the finance company has given value to the restaurant and is therefore credited.

(c) On 3rd April, 19.., a motel buys furniture on credit from Motel Furnishers Limited for £5 000

Dr — Furniture A/c — Cr

			£	p				£	p
19..									
April	3	Motel Furn. Ltd	5,000	00					

Motel Furnishers Ltd. A/c — Cr

			£	p				£	p
					19..				
					April	3	Furniture	5,000	00

Figure 5

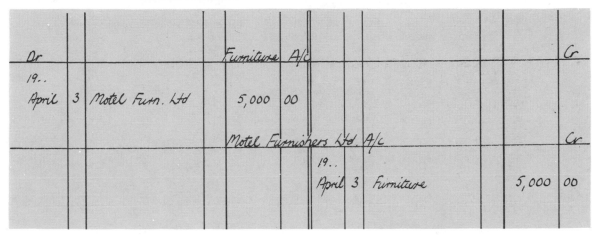

Note: The suppliers of furniture have given value and their account in the ledger must be credited accordingly; the corresponding debit entry must therefore be in the furniture account of the motel.

(d) On 7th September, 19.., a hotel receives rent of £500 in respect of sub-let premises.

Dr — Cash A/c — Cr

			£	p				£	p
19.. Sept.	7	Rent Receivable	500	00					

Dr — Rent Receivable A/c — Cr

			£	p				£	p
					19.. Sept.	7	Cash	500	00

Figure 6

Note: The cash account of the hotel, having received value, is debited; the corresponding credit entry must therefore be made in the rent receivable account.

A consideration of the examples given will show that:

(1) By applying the principle of double entry it is possible to ensure that *both aspects of each transaction* are reflected in the books of a business;
(2) a separate account is used for every type of transaction; as a result, at the end of any one period the ledger contains *a systematic and classified summary* of all the transactions for the period concerned; and

(3) as there is a debit and a credit entry in respect of each transaction, *the sum total of debit entries must be equal to the sum total of the credit entries in the ledger.*

A second illustration is given below, showing how the principle of double entry is applied within a particular business.

On 1st March, 19.., A. Caterer started in business with a capital in cash of £50 000. During March his transactions were as follows:

March	2	Paid quarterly rent	£2 500
,,	4	Purchased furniture for cash	5 000
,,	6	Bought equipment on credit from H. & C. Ltd	3 000
,,	8	Paid wages	500
,,	11	Bought provisions on credit from B. Blake & Son	1 000
,,	14	Sold meals for cash	750
,,	18	Paid wages	600
,,	22	Sold meals for cash	450
,,	26	Paid wages	650
,,	29	Paid H. & C. Ltd	1 000
,,	31	Sold meals for cash	300

(a) A. Caterer's transactions to be entered in his ledger.
(b) The accuracy of the ledger entries to be checked as at 31st March, 19...

Dr — Cash A/c — Cr

19.. Mar	1	Capital	50,000	00	19.. Mar	2	Rent	2,500	00
"	14	Sales	750	00	"	4	Furniture	5,000	00
"	22	-do-	450	00	"	8	Wages	500	00
"	31	-do-	300	00	"	18	-do-	600	00
"					"	26	-do-	650	00
					"	29	H & C Ltd	1,000	00

Dr — Capital A/c — Cr

					19.. Mar	1	Cash	50,000	00

Dr — Rent A/c — Cr

19.. Mar	2	Cash	2,500	00					

Dr — Furniture A/c — Cr

19.. Mar	4	Cash	5,000	00					

Dr — Equipment A/c — Cr

Date		Particulars		Amount		Date		Particulars		Amount	
19.. Mar	6	H & C Ltd		3,000	00						

Dr — H & C Ltd. A/c — Cr

Date		Particulars		Amount		Date		Particulars		Amount	
19.. Mar	29	Cash		1,000	00	19.. Mar	6	Equipment		3,000	00

Dr — Wages A/c — Cr

Date		Particulars		Amount		Date		Particulars		Amount	
19.. Mar	8	Cash		500	00						
"	18	-do-		600	00						
"	26	-do-		650	00						

Dr — Purchases A/c — Cr

Date		Particulars		Amount		Date		Particulars		Amount	
19.. Mar	11	B. Blake & Son		1,000	00						

Dr — B. Blake & Son A/c — Cr

Date		Particulars		Amount		Date		Particulars		Amount	
						19.. Mar	11	Purchases		1,000	00

Dr — Sales A/c — Cr

Date		Particulars		Amount		Date		Particulars		Amount	
						19.. Mar	14	Cash		750	00
						"	22	-do-		450	00
						"	31	-do-		300	00

Figure 7

The most important check of the accuracy of the entries in the ledger is the agreement of the total of debit entries with the total of credit entries. In order to find out whether or not there is this agreement, it is necessary to extract what is known as the *trial balance*. This is done by extracting a list of ledger accounts, showing the total of the debit entries and the total of the credit entries in each account, as follows:

Trial balance as at 31st March, 19..

	Dr. £	Cr. £
Cash account	51 500	10 250
Capital account		50 000
Rent account	2 500	
Furniture account	5 000	
Equipment account	3 000	
H. & C. Ltd account	1 000	3 000
Wages account	1 750	
Purchases account	1 000	
B. Blake & Son account		1 000
Sales account		1 500
	£65 750	£65 750

In practice, instead of showing the total of the debit side and the total of the credit side of an account only the difference between the two sides is shown. Thus, whether we show that the H. & C. Ltd. account has a debit total of £1 000 and a credit total of £3 000 or show the difference, i.e. £2 000, in the credit column of the trial balance has no effect on its agreement. We would thus re-write our trial balance as follows:

Trial balance as at 31st March, 19..

	Dr. £	Cr. £
Cash account	41 250	
Capital account		50 000
Rent account	2 500	
Furniture account	5 000	
Equipment account	3 000	
H. & C. Ltd account		2 000
Wages account	1 750	
Purchases account	1 000	
B. Blake & Son account		1 000
Sales account		1 500
	£54 500	£54 500

Balancing: nature of balances

The difference between the two sides of an account is known as the *balance*. A *debit balance* arises when the total of debit entries exceeds the total of credit entries. A *credit balance* arises when the total of credit exceeds the total of debit entries.

The method of balancing the account is shown below.

Dr.				Cash A/c							Cr.
19.. Jan.	1	Capital		20,000	00	19.. Jan.	4	Rent		3,000	00
"	16	Sales		1,500	00	"	9	China		2,000	00
"	29	-do-		3,500	00	"	14	Wages		2,000	00
						"	31	Furniture		10,000	00
						"	31	Balance	c/d	8,000	00
				25,000	00					25,000	00
19.. Feb.	1	Balance	b/d	8,000	00						

Figure 8

Note: It will be observed that:

(a) The total of the debit entries in the cash account is £25 000 and the total of the credit entries £17 000, giving a debit balance of £8 000.

(b) In order to balance the cash account (i.e. make both sides of the account equal) it is necessary to place the balance on the credit side of the account.

(c) Both money columns are then totalled and the balance is entered as the figure brought down on the debit side.

The abbreviations c/d and b/d stand for 'carried down' and 'brought down', respectively. When a balance is carried from one page of the ledger to another or from one accounting period to another it is said to be 'carried forward', hence the abbreviations c/f and b/f are then used.

A debit balance may represent one of two things. It may be an asset, e.g. furniture, china, cash, etc., or an expense (or loss), e.g. wages, rent, purchases. Similarly, a credit balance may represent one of two things. It may be a liability, e.g. an amount owing to suppliers, or a gain (or income) such as sales, as is indicated in the chart below.

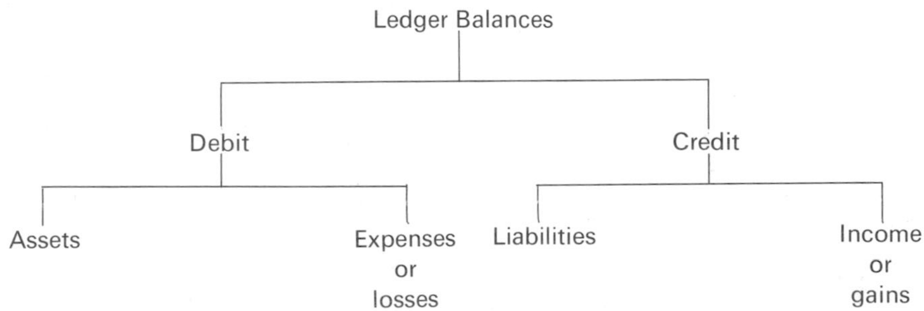

The main purpose of the present chapter is to explain and illustrate the principle of double entry. In the next few chapters we will consider the more practical aspects of book-keeping, an important feature of which is the keeping of books other than, and subsidiary to, the ledger.

Problems

1 Explain what is meant by the principle of double entry.

2 What do you understand by: (a) the ledger; (b) debit balance; (c) credit balance?

3 From the following information, write up V. Goodfellow's cash account and balance it as at 7th March, 19..:

March	1	Balance b/d	Dr. £31 520
,,	1	Received from B. Smythe	260
,,	2	Paid rent	5 500
,,	3	Paid for stationery	130
,,	4	Sold meals for cash	3 120
,,	4	Paid wages	1 660
,,	5	Paid Hotel Suppliers Ltd	2 000
,,	6	Paid electricity account	960
,,	6	Sold meals for cash	3 270
,,	7	Paid Wm. Grocer & Sons	550
,,	7	Paid for advertising	220

4 On 1st January, 19.., J. Robinson started as a café proprietor with a capital in cash of £50 000. His transactions in January were:

January	1	Purchased premises for cash	£30 000
,,	3	Paid for kitchen utensils and equipment	2 500
,,	5	Paid for furniture	3 750
,,	10	Paid wages	370
,,	12	Purchased provisions for cash	1 250
,,	14	Sold meals, etc. for cash	560
,,	16	Paid insurance	200
,,	18	Paid wages	390
,,	19	Sold meals, etc. for cash	630
,,	21	Bought provisions on credit from M. Mann & Co.	350
,,	23	Paid for cleaning materials	120
,,	25	Paid wages	380
,,	27	Sold meals, etc. for cash	450
,,	29	Purchased provisions for cash	270
,,	31	Purchased additional equipment for cash	1 000

Enter the above transactions in Robinson's ledger, extract a trial balance as at 31st January, 19.., and balance his cash account.

5 On 1st July, 19.., W. Gravett started in business as a snack bar proprietor with a capital in cash of £1 000. His transactions in July were:

July	1	Borrowed £20 000 from City Finance Co.
,,	5	Bought premises for £60 000 and settled the purchase price as follows: paid a deposit of £5 000 and obtained a mortgage for the balance due (£55 000) from the Stable Building Society
,,	9	Purchased furniture on credit for £7 500 from Oak Furnishing Co.
,,	13	Paid in cash £6 000 for china and equipment
,,	18	Bought provisions on credit from B. Baker & Sons for £800 and from S. Fish & Co. for £950
,,	24	Sold meals for cash £1 050
,,	28	Paid wages, £500
,,	29	Sold meals on credit to Midland Motors Ltd £500 and B. M. Dining Club £750
,,	30	Borrowed from A. Lender £5 000
,,	31	Paid Oak Furnishing Company £500

Enter Gravett's transactions in his ledger, extract a trial balance as at 31st July, 19.., and balance the cash account.

CHAPTER 2

Accounting for cash

Due to the varying circumstances of each business it will be found that the actual arrangement and layout of books of account vary somewhat from one business to another. We thus find many kinds of cash accounts (cash books, as they are usually called).

Single column cash book

This is the simplest form of cash book and has already been illustrated in Chapter 1. It takes the form of a ledger account. The debit side is used for the recording of money (coin, notes, cheques, postal orders, travellers' cheques, etc.) received; the credit side is used for money paid.

Example The following cash transactions are to be recorded in the cash book of the Milano Restaurant; the cash book balance brought down as at 31st January, 19..:

January	1	Debit balance b/d	£10 000
,,	2	Paid wages	1 250
,,	7	Cash sales	4 200
,,	11	Paid to A. Supplier	450
,,	16	Received from B. Brown	800
,,	21	Paid wages	1 250
,,	26	Cash sales	4 300
,,	31	Paid for linen	300

Cash Book

				£	p					£	p
19.. Jan.	1	Balance	b/d	10,000	00	19.. Jan.	2	Wages		1,250	00
"	7	Cash Sales		4,200	00	"	11	A. Supplier		450	00
"	16	B. Brown		800	00	"	21	Wages		1,250	00
"	26	Cash Sales		4,300	00	"	31	Linen		300	00
						"	31	Balance	c/d	16,050	00
				19,300	00					19,300	00
19.. Feb.	1	Balance	b/d	16,050	00						

Figure 9

Double column cash book

Consideration of the single column cash book will indicate that it is inadequate in some respects. First, the majority of businesses keep most of their cash in a bank account and some 'office cash' on the premises. Second, though some payments are made by cheque others are in cash. Hence it is necessary to have a cash book which will distinguish between the two separate funds of cash (i.e. bank account and office cash) and thus differentiate between payments made by cheque and those in actual cash.

The double column cash book has two money columns, headed 'cash' and 'bank', on the debit side, and two money columns, also headed 'cash' and 'bank', on the credit side. The cash and bank columns are used as follows:

Debit side All amounts paid into office cash are entered in the 'cash' column and all amounts banked in the 'bank' column.

Credit side All amounts paid out of office cash are entered in the 'cash' column and all payments by cheque in the 'bank' column.

Any amounts of cash transferred from the bank to the office should be credited in the bank column and debited in the cash column; any transfers of cash from the office to the bank should be credited in the cash column and debited in the bank column. Any transfer of cash from the bank to the office, or *vice versa*, is shown in the cash book by means of a 'contra entry'. The term contra entry means that both the debit and the credit entry are to be found in the same account; contra entries are denoted by the sign ¢.

Example The following transactions are to be entered in the cash book of the Chelsea Luncheon Club, and the cash book balanced as at 28th February, 19..:

February	1	Bank balance b/d	Dr. £20 000
,,	1	Balance of office cash b/d	200
,,	2	Paid by cheque for furniture	2 500
,,	4	Paid by cheque to A. B. Manning	450
,,	5	Paid for stamps—cash	30
,,	7	Banked cash sales	2 150
,,	9	Paid wages by cheque	820
,,	11	Paid by cheque H.C.I. Supplies Ltd	1 150
,,	13	Received from B. Naylor and banked	250
,,	15	Paid manager's travelling expenses—cash	60
,,	18	Banked cash sales	2 450
,,	20	Paid wages by cheque	920
,,	22	Paid for stationery—cash	50
,,	23	Paid for flowers—cash	20
,,	24	Withdrew from bank for office use	200
,,	25	Banked cash sales	1 900
,,	26	Paid by cheque to M. Cooper & Sons	650
,,	27	Paid for stamps—cash	30
,,	27	Paid cleaner's wages—cash	50
,,	28	Paid wages by cheque	860

Cash Book

Date		F	CASH	BANK	Date		F	CASH	BANK
19..					19..				
Feb. 1	Balances	b/d	200	20,000	Feb. 2	Furniture			2,500
" 7	Cash Sales			2,150	" 4	A.B. Manning			450
" 13	B. Naylor			250	" 5	Stamps		30	
" 18	Cash Sales			2,450	" 9	Wages			820
" 24	Bank	¢	200		" 11	H-C-I Supplies Ltd			1,150
" 25	Cash Sales			1,900	" 15	Manager's Trav. Exp.		60	
					" 20	Wages			920
					" 22	Stationery		50	
					" 23	Flowers		20	
					" 24	Cash	¢		200
					" 26	M. Cooper & Sons			650
					" 27	Stamps		30	
					" 27	Cleaner's Wages		50	
					" 28	Wages			860
					" 28	Balances	c/d	160	19,200
			400	26,750				400	26,750
19..									
Mar. 1	Balances	b/d	160	19,200					

Figure 10

Petty cash book In hotel and catering establishments it is often necessary to make numerous payments of small amounts for various expenses. Where this is so, it may be convenient to have a main cash book and a separate petty cash book. The main cash book would be in the charge of a senior clerk or the head cashier, whereas the responsibility for maintaining the petty cash book would be delegated to a relatively junior clerk.

Petty cash books are usually analysed and kept on what is known as the *imprest system*. This operates as follows. At the beginning of a period a fixed amount of cash, say £200, is advanced to the petty cashier. At the end of the period the petty cashier balances his petty cash book, and the total amount expended by him (and represented by appropriate vouchers) is refunded to him by the person in charge of the main cash book. Thus, at the beginning of each period, the petty cashier will start with the same fixed float of cash.

For example:

	£
Petty cashier's cash float on 1st January, 19..	200
,, ,, weekly expenditure (total vouchers)	160
,, ,, balance of cash on 7th January, 19..	40
Therefore (i) cash refunded to him on 7th January, 19..	160
(ii) his cash float on 8th January, 19..	£200

The above payments should be recorded and, assuming that the total of expenditure is refunded, the petty cash book balanced as at 7th July, 19...

It will be observed that every petty cash payment is recorded twice: once in the total column and once in one of the analysis columns: consequently, the sum of the analysed totals should be equal to that of the total column.

In the folio column are recorded the numbers of the petty cash vouchers. These would be numbered consecutively and presented to the head cashier when requesting a refund in respect of payments made.

V.P.O. stands for 'visitors' paid outs'. This is a column often added in the petty cash book of a hotel. Payments made on behalf of guests staying in the hotel are recorded in this column. As soon as a payment of this kind is made, a copy of the appropriate voucher should be passed on to the reception office (bill office, in a larger hotel) to ensure that the charge is debited to the guest's account in the visitors' ledger. In many hotels the total of V.P.O. from the petty cash book is checked against the total of debits in the V.P.O. column of the visitors' ledger to ensure that all charges have been posted.

The petty cash book, though physically separated from the ledger, is a ledger account: as a result, every entry made in it counts for double entry purposes. It is also a *subsidiary book* in that it collects and analyses detailed transactions and enables totals to be posted to the ledger.

Example The petty cash book of the Wessex Hotel is kept on the imprest system. On 1st July, 19.., the petty cashier's balance is £200. His expenditure during the first week of July was:

July	1	Paid for postage stamps	£22.50
,,	2	Paid for guest's telegram (Room 64)—Jones	7.50
,,	3	Paid manager's fares	27.50
,,	3	Bought flowers for guest (Room 87)—Brown	15.00
,,	4	Paid for postage stamps	17.50
,,	5	Gave tip to delivery man	2.50
,,	5	Bought bill pads for restaurant	25.00
,,	6	Paid chef's fares	7.50
,,	7	Paid donation to local charity	5.00
,,	7	Bought pencils and ink	2.50

PETTY CASH BOOK

16

Dr.		Date		F	TOTAL		POSTAGE		STATIONERY		TRAVELLING EXP		V.P.O.		SUNDRY EXP	
200	00	19.. July 1	Balance	b/d												
		" 1	Postage Stamps	1	22	50	22	50								
		" 2	Guest's Telegram Rm 64 – Jones	2	7	50							7	50		
		" 3	Manager's Fares	3	27	50					27	50				
		" 3	Guest's Flowers Rm 87 - Brown	4	15	00							15	00		
		" 4	Postage Stamps	5	17	50	17	50								
		" 5	Tip to Delivery Man	6	2	50									2	50
		" 5	Bill Pads	7	25	00			25	00						
		" 6	Chef's Fares	8	7	50					7	50				
		" 7	Donation to Charity	9	5	00									5	00
		" 7	Pencils and Ink	10	2	50			2	50						
					132	50	40	00	27	50	35	00	22	50	7	50
		" 7	Balance	c/d	67	50	L/29		L/31		L/45				L/47	
200	00				200	00										
67	50	July 8	Balance	b/d												
132	50	" 8	Cash Received													

Figure 11

Double entry in respect of petty cash items is completed as follows:

(a) Any amounts drawn by the petty cashier are credited in the main cash book and debited in the petty cash book.

(b) Petty cash payments are credited (individually) in the petty cash book and debited in total in the appropriate account in the ledger. Thus the total of the postage column, £40, would be debited in the postage account as in Figure 12.

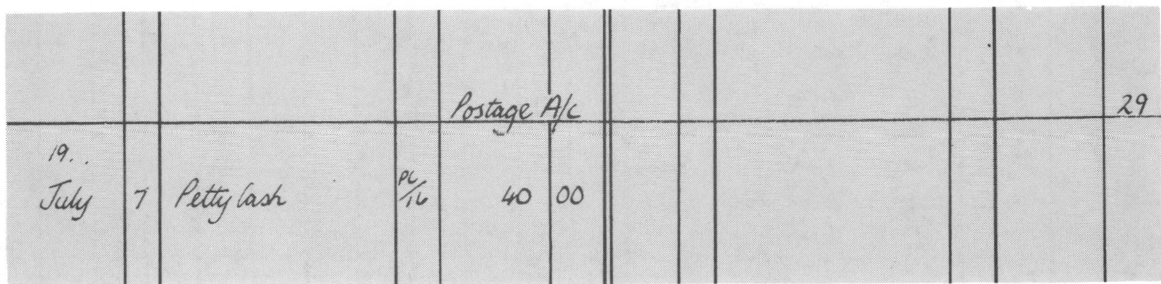

Postage A/c — 29

Date		Particulars	F	£	p
19.. July	7	Petty Cash	PC/16	40	00

Figure 12

Note that the totals posted to the ledger are cross-referenced as follows:

(a) Under the analysis totals of the petty cash book the page number of the relevant ledger account is given. In the illustration, L/29 means that the corresponding double entry is in the postage account which is on page 29 in the ledger. The ledger folio column shows the relevant page number of the petty cash book.

(b) The V.P.O. items, as already explained, are debited individually in the visitors' ledger. Hence the total of the V.P.O. column is left in the petty cash book.

Treatment of discounts received

Many suppliers of hotel and catering establishments offer cash discounts. A cash discount is a deduction allowed from the amount due to the supplier, provided that payment is made within a specified time. Thus, if a hotel owes A. Supplier £1 000, and the latter allows a discount of five per cent, provided that the payment is made within the specified time £50 may be deducted from the amount due, and only £950

Cash Book

Date		F	Detail	Bank	Date		F	Discount Received	Bank
19..					19..				
Jan 1	Balance	b/d		12,000 00	Jan 3	Wages			2,200 00
Jan 2	Sales:				" 4	A. Supplier	L/45	50 00	950 00
	Restaurant		2,000 00		" 4	X. Tabacco Co.		100 00	2,200 00
	Bar		1,200 00		" 5	Rent			3,500 00
	Sundries		200 00	3,400 00	" 6	Insurance			300 00

Figure 13

need be paid. It may be seen, therefore, that the main object of cash discounts is to encourage prompt payment.

In order to facilitate the recording of cash discounts received, many hotel and catering establishments add a discount received column on the credit side of their cash book. The layout of a cash book with a discount received column is illustrated in Figure 13.

The discount received column is described as a memorandum column. It is there for convenience and does not count for double entry purposes. Double entry in respect of discounts received is completed as follows. Debit both the cash paid and the discount received in the account of the supplier. Credit the periodical (usually monthly) total of the discount received column in the discount received account in the ledger.

Assuming that the total of discounts received from suppliers by the end of January, 19.., is £500, the entry in the discount received account would be:

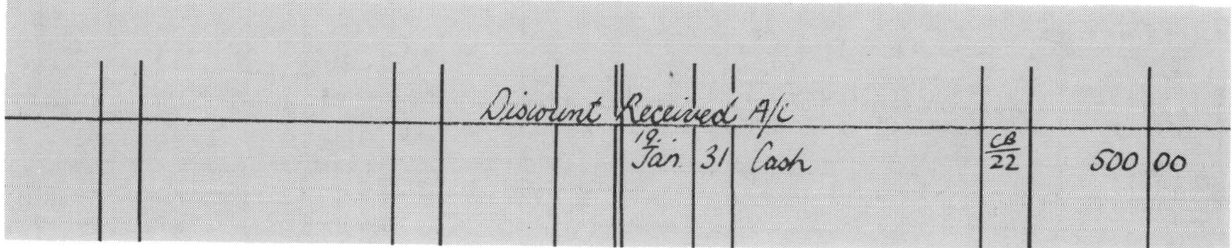

					Discount Received A/c					
					19.. Jan.	31	Cash	CB 22	500	00

Figure 14

The amount paid to A. Supplier would be posted to his account as in Figure 15.

				A. Supplier A/c						45
19.. Jan.	4	Cash	CB 22	950	00	19.. Jan.	1	Balance	b/d.	1,000 00
"	4	Discount	CB 22	50	00					
				1,000	00					1,000 00

Figure 15

The purpose of the detail column on the debit side of the cash book is twofold: to indicate the sources of any cash banked, and to facilitate an easy cross-reference to the ledger account concerned.

Cash received book

Many hotels maintain, in addition to the main cash book, a cash received book. This is kept in the reception office and usually acts as a subsidiary book to the main cash book. A typical cash received book is illustrated in Figure 16.

Cash Received Book — 21

Date	Name	Rm. No or Fol.	Visitors Led. Receipts		Sales Led Receipts		Deposits on Arrival		Total	
19..										
May 1	R. W. Brown, Mr.	Rm 106	226	00					226	00
" 1	Midland Motors Ltd.	S-L-56			185	00			185	00
" 1	A. V. Ewing, Mr. & Mrs.	Rm 117	85	00					85	00
" 1	S. P. Browning, Miss	Rm 36	100	00			100	00		
	etc.									
" 1	Total Trans. to Cash Book	CB/46	2,205	00	1,002	50	200	00	3,407	50

Figure 16

At the end of each day the cash received book would be balanced and the total of cash received debited in the main cash book, as shown in Figure 17.

The corresponding credit entries would be made as indicated below:

Visitors' ledger receipts—the individual amounts received from visitors would be credited in their accounts in the visitors' ledger.

Sales ledger receipts—these, again, would be credited individually in the relevant customers' accounts in the sales ledger.

CASH

Date		F	Sales: Meals		Sales: Bars		Sales: Tobaccos		Sales: Sundries		Bank
19..											
Jan 1	Balance	b/d									3,001
" 2	Sales		2,000	00	1,000	00	102	50	107	50	3,210
" 3	-do-		2,200	00	801	00	151	00	50	50	3,202
" 4	-do-		1,902	00	908	00	200	00	100	00	3,110

Figure 18

Deposits on arrival—any such deposits received would be credited in the guests' accounts in the visitors' ledger on their departure.

Cash Book										46
Date		F	Detail	Bank	Date		F	Discount Received	Bank
19.. May 1	Cash Received								
	Visitors Ledger	CEB/21	2,205 00						
	Sales "	CEB/21	1,002 50						
	Dep. on Arrival	CEB/21	200 00	3,407 50					

Figure 17

Multi-column cash book

Many hotel and catering establishments, particularly canteens and clubs, keep multi-column cash books. The main purpose of a multi-column cash book is to analyse, under appropriate headings, all receipts and payments and, in this way, facilitate the preparation of final accounts, as shown in Figure 18.

A multi-column cash book is particularly useful in smaller businesses, many of which do not keep a full set of books. In such circumstances the analysis columns for receipts and payments accumulate data which may be used in the preparation of final accounts.

OOK

ate		F	PURCHASES				WAGES & SALARIES	OTHER EXPENSES	BANK
			Food	Drink	Tobaccos	Sundries			
2	H. C. I Supplies Co.				301 00	104 00			405 00
3	Wm. Brown & Sons		500 00						500 00
4	Eastern Supplies Co.			1003 00					1,003 00
5	Wages						2,502 50		2,502 50

Kinds of bank accounts

Reference has already been made to *the* bank account. In fact, there are two kinds of bank account that may be opened by a business: a current account and a deposit account.

A current account is an account into which payments are made and on which cheques are drawn. The balance of a current account will, therefore, vary continually.

A deposit account is an account into which money is paid with the intention of leaving it in the bank for a period of time.

The main differences between a current account and a deposit account are:

(1) Withdrawals from a current account may be made at any time, but (usually two weeks') notice of intention to withdraw from a deposit account must be given to the bank.

(2) Interest is paid by the bank on the balance standing to the credit of a deposit account; no interest is allowed in the case of a current account.

(3) Unlike a current account, a deposit account cannot be drawn upon by means of a cheque. The usual procedure is to write a letter (signed by the persons authorized to withdraw funds) to the bank informing the bank of the intention to withdraw funds from a deposit account.

Transactions affecting the current account are recorded in the bank columns of the main cash book. Any amounts lodged with the bank will be debited in the bank column; any payments by cheque will, of course, be credited in the bank column.

Before any amount is paid into a current account particulars of the cash to be banked must be entered in a *paying-in book* supplied by the bank. This usually consists of a number of paying-in slips bound together in book form. The bank cashier detaches one copy and keeps it; the other copy of the paying-in slip, having been stamped and initialled by the cashier, remains in the book for reference. A specimen paying-in slip is shown in Figure 19.

________19__

Cash________

£

Cashier's stamp
and initials

Date______

BANK GIRO CREDIT

CODE No.

BANK

BRANCH

ACCOUNT

Paid in by

£5 Notes & over
£1 Notes
50p coin
Silver
Copper

Total cash
Cheques
PO's etc.

£

Figure 19

Any amounts transferred from a current account to a deposit account will be credited in the main cash book and debited in a deposit account opened in the ledger. Any amounts withdrawn from the deposit account will be credited in that account and debited in some other account.

Example On 1st February, 19. ., the main cash book of the Bryton Hotel shows a debit balance of £37 520. On that day the amount of £1 500 is transferred to a deposit account opened by the hotel. This will be recorded as in Figure 20.

Cash Book (37)

19.. Feb.	1	Balance	b/d	37,520	00	19.. Feb.	1	Deposit A/c	L 59	15,000	00

Deposit A/c (59)

19.. Feb.	1	Cash	CB 57	15,000	00						

Figure 20

On 15th November, 19. ., £14 000 is withdrawn from the deposit account to pay for new kitchen plant. The necessary entries will then be: Cr. deposit account and Dr. kitchen plant account as shown in Figure 21.

Deposit A/c (59)

19.. Feb	1	Cash	CB 37	15,000	00	19.. Nov.	15	Kitchen Plant	L 87	14,000	

Kitchen Plant A/c (87)

19.. Nov.	15	Deposit A/c	L 59	14,000	00						

Figure 21

Cheques Bankers supply two form of cheques:

(1) Bearer cheques—a bearer cheque is worded: 'Pay . . . . . . or Bearer' and would be paid to the person presenting the cheque. Bearer cheques are not as safe as order cheques and are, therefore, used infrequently.

(2) Order cheques—an order cheque is worded: 'Pay . . . . . . or Order' and is payable to a specified person or to such person as the payee may order to receive the money. A specimen of an order cheque is shown in Figure 22.

16th May 19 82 16-17-73

EASTMINSTER BANK LIMITED
13 GREEN LANE, CHISWICK, W4

Pay Catering Suppliers Ltd. or Order

One hundred pounds fifty pence £100 - 50

J. BROWN

John Brown

754717 16–17–73 80115118

Figure 22

The parties to the cheque are:

Drawer—the person who signs the cheque (John Brown)
Drawee—the banker on whom the cheque is drawn (Eastminster Bank Limited)
Payee—the person to whom the cheque is payable (Catering Suppliers Ltd)

A cheque which is not crossed is known as an *open cheque*, and cash may be obtained for it from the banker on whom it is drawn. In practice, in order to secure a measure of protection against fraud, nearly all cheques are *crossed cheques*. A crossed cheque has two parallel lines drawn across the face of it. Sometimes the words 'and Co.' are written between the lines, but they are not essential to the crossing. When a cheque is crossed the banker will not pay cash over the counter. The payee must hand the cheque to his own banker who will collect it for him and credit his account.

Crossings A general crossing consists of two parallel lines with or without (i) the words 'and Co.', (ii) 'not negotiable'.

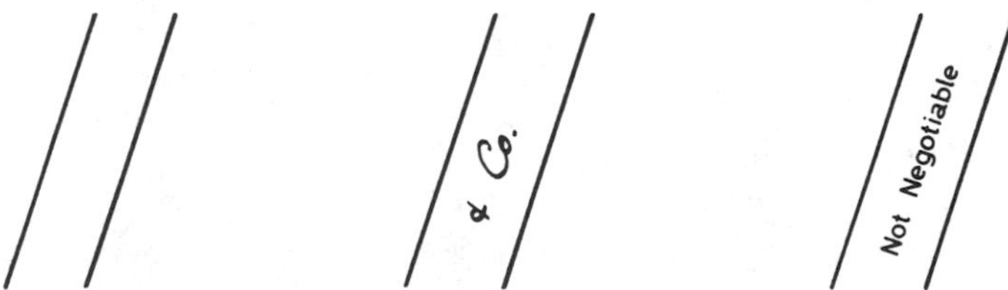

A special crossing consists of the name of the banker written across the face of the cheque with or without (i) the parallel lines, (ii) the words 'not negotiable'. The effect of a special crossing is to instruct the paying banker to pay only the banker named in the crossing. If a banker disobeys a crossing, he becomes liable to the true owner of the cheque for any loss caused thereby.

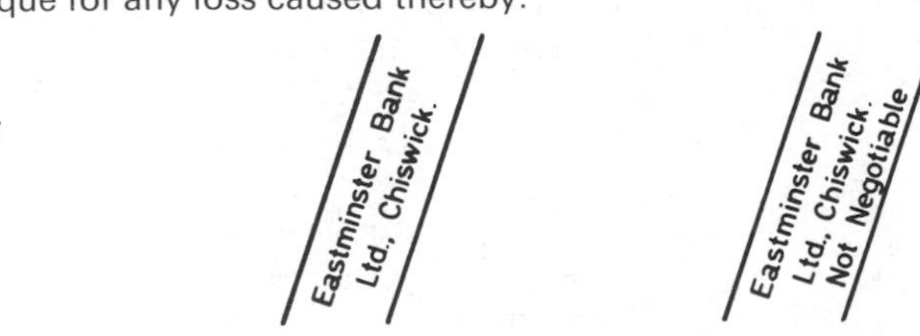

We must now explain what is meant by the *negotiability* of a cheque. A cheque is, in legal language, a 'negotiable instrument'. Therefore, if it is accepted by a person in exchange for value given, and in good faith, it becomes his property; his title to it cannot be disputed, provided that there is no previous forgery on it.

When a cheque is crossed 'not negotiable', it ceases to be a negotiable instrument. A person who takes a cheque so marked, takes it subject to all defects of the title of the person who gave it to him. If there is any irregularity of title, the drawer may refuse to honour the cheque and the holder of it will lose the money.

Sometimes cheques have to be *endorsed*. To endorse a cheque is to sign one's name on the back of it. Students should know when endorsement is or is not necessary. The present position is as follows:

Endorsement is necessary in the following cases:

(a) Cheques cashed or exchanged across the counter.

(b) Cheques tendered for the credit of an account other than that of the ostensible payee.

(c) Cheques payable to joint payees; these will require endorsement if tendered for the credit of an account to which all are not parties.

Endorsement is not necessary in the following cases:

(a) Cheques paid in for the credit of the account of the payee.

(b) Cheques paid in for the credit of a joint or partnership account.

Cheques are sometimes 'dishonoured' (returned by the banker unpaid) for various reasons, e.g. in the event of the drawer's death or bankruptcy, or where there are insufficient funds to meet the cheque. The bank will attach a slip to a cheque so returned. This is usually marked R/D (refer to drawer) and really means that there are insufficient funds to pay the cheque. When a cheque is returned for some technical reason the bank will usually indicate this by means of an appropriate wording, e.g. 'words and figures differ'; 'another signature required'; 'signature differs'; 'endorsement irregular'.

Bank reconciliation statements

Periodically, usually once a month, a business will receive a loose-leaf statement from its bank. This will show the balance of cash at the beginning of the period, any amounts paid in or withdrawn, and the balance of cash at the end of the period. The bank statement is a copy of the customer's account in the books of the bank and, in theory, should contain entries identical with those in the cash book of the business. In practice, it will be found that the balance shown by the bank statement and that in the cash book rarely agree, since:

(a) Cheques sent to suppliers and credited in the cash book may not have been presented for payment, and will not appear on the bank statement.
(b) Cheques, etc., received, debited in the cash book, and paid into the bank account may not have been credited by the bank.
(c) The bank statement may contain items which do not appear in the cash book, e.g. bank charges, interest, or standing orders.
(d) Errors may have arisen in either the cash book or (which is less likely) in the bank statement.

As the two balances rarely agree, it is usual to reconcile them by drawing up what is known as a bank reconciliation statement. Before this is done, it is usual to examine the bank statement and enter in the cash book all items of bank charges, interest, and standing orders. The bank reconciliation is then prepared and the cash book balanced.

Example Figure 23 shows the cash book of the Crown Hotel Ltd.

CASH BOOK

Date		F	Bank	Date		F	CHQ. No.	Bank
19..				19..				
Jan 1	Balance	b/d	10,000	Jan 2	Properties Ltd.		501	2,200
" 6	Sales		1,500	" 8	H&C Ltd.		502	500
" 11	-do-		2,000	" 9	B. Brown & Co		503	800
" 24	-do-		1,800	" 14	H.H. Smith		504	1,100
				" 19	V. May & Co.		505	300
				" 27	A.S. Foods Ltd.		506	400
				" 29	W. Cramer		507	600
				" 30	A. Grocer & Co		508	500

Figure 23

At the end of the period the bank statement in Figure 24 is received.

The bank reconciliation statement of the hotel would be prepared on the following lines.

Crown Hotel Ltd. 17 Hill Lane, W5		in Account with EASTMINSTER BANK LTD. 13 Uphill Drive, W5			
DATE	FOR CUSTOMER'S USE		DEBITS	CREDITS	BALANCE
ABBREVIATIONS:	BGC – Bank Giro Credit CH – Charges or Commission		IN – Interest SO – Standing Order		

Figure 24

The cash book shows a debit balance of £8 900 (the difference between the Dr. and Cr. totals of the cash book). An examination of the bank statement shows bank charges of £50. This would have to be credited in the cash book and debited in the bank charges account in the ledger. The cash book balance would thus be reduced to £8 850.

The next step is to reconcile the two balances, £8 850 and £10 450, i.e. to explain how the difference has arisen. This may be done by starting with the cash book balance and arriving at the balance per bank statement or *vice versa*. The second alternative will now be used.

Bank reconciliation statement as at 31st January, 19..

Balance per bank statement dated 31.1.19..		£10 450
Add Bank charges		50
		£10 500
Less Unpresented cheques		
B. Brown & Co. — 503	£800	
V. May & Co. — 505	300	
A. Grocer & Co. — 508	500	1 600
Cash book balance as at above date		£8 900

Had the bank charges been deducted from the cash book balance before drawing up the bank reconciliation statement, the latter would have been done as follows:

Bank reconciliation statement as at 31st January, 19..

Balance per bank statement dated 31.1.19..			£10 450
Less Unpresented cheques:			
	B. Brown & Co. — 503	£800	
	V. May & Co. — 505	300	
	A. Grocer & Co. — 508	500	1 600
Cash book balance as at above date			£8 850

Problems

1 Explain what you understand by the 'imprest system' as applied to the petty cash book. Give a specimen ruling of a petty cash book with five analysis columns.

2 B. A. Branson commenced business as a snack bar proprietor. His capital on 1st January, 19.., consisted of:

Cash at bank	£39 800
Cash in hand	200
	£40 000

The following were Branson's transactions in January:

January	1	Paid by cheque for provisions	£400
,,	2	Paid by cheque for:	
		cash register	1 200
		furniture	3 600
		kitchen utensils	2 600
,,	4	Bought provisions, paid by cheque	500
,,	6	Banked cash sales	750
,,	8	Cash payments:	
		cleaning materials	40
		stationery	50
		travelling expenses	10
,,	14	Banked cash sales	300
,,	16	Paid wages by cheque	450
,,	18	Paid by cheque for provisions	1 100
,,	21	Cash payments:	
		stationery	20
		vegetables	30
		postage stamps	20
,,	23	Banked cash sales	850
,,	24	Withdrew from bank for office use	200
,,	26	Paid water rates by cheque	300
,,	27	Paid wages by cheque	420
,,	28	Banked cash sales	350
,,	30	Paid for advertising by cheque	560
,,	31	Paid window cleaner in cash	40

Enter the above transactions in Branson's double column cash book, post to ledger, and extract his trial balance as at 31st January, 19...

3 Design a petty cash book to show expenditure under the headings of postage and stationery; travelling expenses; provisions; and miscellaneous expenses. Enter the following in your petty cash book and balance it as at 6th June, 19. .

June	1	Balance b/d	£100.00
,,	1	Bought postage stamps	10.50
,,	2	Paid messenger's fares	2.45
,,	2	Bought envelopes	3.10
,,	3	Paid for flowers	8.20
,,	3	Paid chef's fares	14.60
,,	4	Paid tip to delivery man	0.90
,,	4	Paid for coffee	4.45
,,	5	Paid for telegram	5.45
,,	5	Paid for strawberries	8.30
,,	6	Paid for blotting paper	1.20
,,	6	Bought cleaning materials	10.75

4 Explain how double entry is completed in respect of discounts received from suppliers.

5 Explain the difference between a current account and a deposit account.

6 Write short explanatory notes on each of the following: bearer cheque; order cheque; open cheque; crossed cheque; general crossing; and special crossing.

7 Explain the position with regard to the endorsement of cheques.

8 What is the object of a bank reconciliation statement? Draw up a bank reconciliation statement from the following information.

Cash book balances as at 31.3.19. .	£2 205
Bank statement ,, ,,	2 405
Unpresented cheques	585
Loan interest paid to bank, not entered in cash book	350
Amounts paid into bank, but not credited by bank until 3.4.19. .	735

9 From the cash book and bank statement given below prepare a bank reconciliation statement as at 31st January, 19. . .

CASH BOOK

			£					£
January	1	Balance	10 000	January	1	H. & C. Ltd	001	1 500
,,	3	Sales	2 000	,,	4	Wages	002	1 000
,,	7	B. Brown	1 000	,,	6	H. M. & Co.	003	500
,,	11	Sales	3 000	,,	10	Equipment Ltd	004	2 000
,,	16	G. Gray	1 500	,,	14	Wages	005	500
,,	21	Sales	4 000	,,	18	H. M. & Co.	006	1 250
,,	27	do	2 000	,,	22	Wages	007	1 000
,,	31	W. Green	1 500	,,	29	Catering Co.	008	250
				,,	31	H. & C. Ltd	009	1 000

BANK STATEMENT

Date....			Debit	Credit	Balance
			£	£	£
January	1	Balance			10 000
,,	3	001	1 500		8 500
,,	4	Cash		2 000	10 500
,,	5	002	1 000		9 500
,,	8	Cash		1 000	10 500
,,	10	003	500		10 000
,,	12	Cash		3 000	13 000
,,	15	005	500		12 500
,,	17	Cash		1 500	14 000
,,	20	006	1 250		12 750
,,	22	Cash		4 000	16 750
,,	23	007	1 000		15 750
,,	28	Cash		2 000	17 750
,,	31	Chgs.	50		17 700

CHAPTER 3

Accounting for purchases

From the accounting point of view the purchases of a business fall into two categories: cash purchases and credit purchases. When food, drink, etc., are purchased, for cash, there is an immediate exchange of cash for the commodities purchased: all that need be recorded in the books of the business is, therefore, the payment of the purchase price and the acquisition of the goods purchased.

When food, drink, etc., are purchased on credit, the business acquires the commodities concerned but the settlement of the purchase price (i.e. payment of the amount due) is delayed until several weeks (or sometimes months) later. In the meantime a debt exists from the business to the supplier of the goods (creditor) and this must be reflected in the supplier's account in the ledger.

Cash purchases

The treatment of cash purchases is simple. All payments made in respect of food, drink, tobaccos, etc., purchased for cash are credited in the cash book and debited in the purchases account. For example, if a hotel buys provisions worth £50 for cash, the double entry will be made as shown in Figure 25.

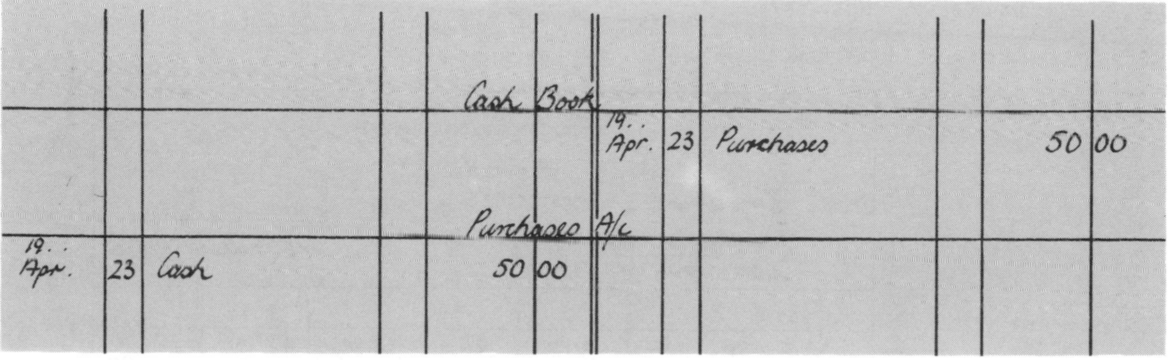

Figure 25

It will be observed that no entry is made in the personal account of the supplier. The transaction is fully settled and, thus, the identity of the supplier is of no consequence.

Credit purchases

When goods are purchased on credit, the payment of the amount due to the supplier does not take place until some time after the delivery of such goods. In the meantime, the supplier of the goods is a creditor to the business in that money is owing to him in respect of the goods with which he has parted. The debt due to the supplier is represented by a credit entry in his personal account. Double entry in respect of credit purchases is given in Figure 26.

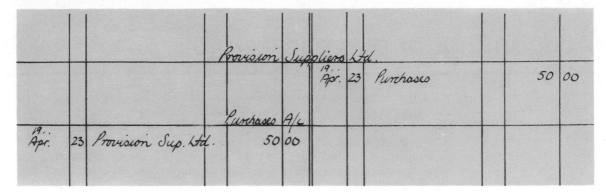

Provision Suppliers Ltd.

Date		Details	£	p	Date		Details	£	p
					19.. Apr.	23	Purchases	50	00

Purchases A/c

Date		Details	£	p	Date		Details	£	p
19.. Apr.	23	Provision Sup. Ltd.	50	00					

Figure 26

Whenever goods are purchased on credit the buyer receives, either together with the goods or a few days later, an *invoice*. This shows particulars of the goods, such as the quantity, price per unit, description, and the total amount due.

Hotel and catering establishments which are sufficiently large in size purchase from wholesalers rather than retailers. In such circumstances a *trade discount* is often allowed by the supplier. This is a deduction from the amount due and would only be extended to establishments buying sufficiently large quantities. Trade discount is *not* recorded in the books: all goods purchased are entered net, after deduction of trade discount.

A specimen invoice is given in Figure 27.

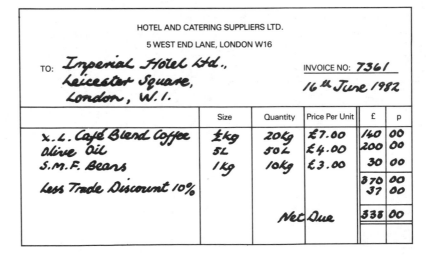

HOTEL AND CATERING SUPPLIERS LTD.

5 WEST END LANE, LONDON W16

TO: Imperial Hotel Ltd.,
Leicester Square,
London, W.1.

INVOICE NO: 7361

16th June 1982

	Size	Quantity	Price Per Unit	£	p
X.L. Café Blend Coffee	½kg	20kg	£7.00	140	00
Olive Oil	5L	50L	£4.00	200	00
S.M.F. Beans	1kg	10kg	£3.00	30	00
				370	00
Less Trade Discount 10%				37	00
		Net Due		333	00

Figure 27

As already mentioned, double entry in respect of credit purchases is completed by debiting the purchases account and crediting the account of the supplier. It will be appreciated, however, that the number of invoices received is usually very large; many hotel and catering establishments receive hundreds of invoices each month. It would, therefore, be inconvenient to debit each separate invoice in the purchases account and, also, unusual to show this amount of detail in the ledger.

Consequently, purchase invoices are recorded as follows:

(1) All invoices, having been numbered consecutively, are entered individually in a subsidiary book known as the *purchases day book*, and
(2) Double entry is completed by:
(a) crediting the invoices in the accounts of suppliers individually;
(b) debiting the periodical (weekly, monthly) total of the purchases day book in the purchases account.

In this way the number of debit entries in the purchases account is reduced considerably. As double entry is completed in the ledger, the entering of invoices in the purchases day book does not count for double entry purposes.

Example The following invoices are received by the Kensington Restaurant:

January	1	B. Baker & Sons	£550
,,	3	A. G. Grocer & Co.	250
,,	5	H. & C. Suppliers Ltd	200
,,	8	B. Baker & Sons	450
,,	11	A. G. Grocer & Co.	350
,,	14	Food Sellers Ltd	50
,,	17	H. & C. Suppliers Ltd	100
,,	20	B. Baker & Sons	150
,,	24	H. & C. Suppliers Ltd	500
,,	27	Food Sellers Ltd	300
,,	29	A. G. Grocer & Co.	200
,,	31	Food Sellers Ltd	250

The invoices are entered in the purchases day book (Figure 28) of the restaurant and posted to appropriate accounts in the ledger (Figure 29).

When posting, the folio number of the purchases day book is entered in the account concerned and the folio number of the purchases account is entered in the purchases day book.

		Purchases Day Book				27
Date			Inv. No.	Led. Fol.		
19..						
Jan.	1	B Baker & Sons	1	L 51	550	00
"	3	A. G. Grocer & Co.	2	L 53	250	00
"	5	H. & C Suppliers Ltd.	3	L 55	200	00
"	8	B. Baker & Sons	4	L 51	450	00
"	11	A. G Grocer & Co.	5	L 53	350	00
"	14	Food Sellers Ltd.	6	L 57	50	00
"	17	H. & C Suppliers Ltd.	7	L 55	100	00
"	20	B. Baker & Sons	8	L 51	150	00
"	24	H & C Suppliers Ltd.	9	L 55	500	00
"	27	Food Sellers Ltd.	10	L 57	300	00
"	29	A. G. Grocer & Co.	11	L 53	200	00
"	31	Food Sellers Ltd.	12	L 57	250	00
"	31	Transferred to Purchases A/C		L 106	3,350	00

Figure 28

		B. Baker & Sons								51
					19.. Jan.	1	Purchases	PB 27	550	00
					"	8	- do -	PB 27	450	00
					"	20	- do -	PB 27	150	00
		A. G. Grocer & Co.								53
					19.. Jan.	3	Purchases	PB 27	250	00
					"	11	- do -	PB 27	350	00
					"	29	- do -	PB 27	200	00

Figure 29 (a)

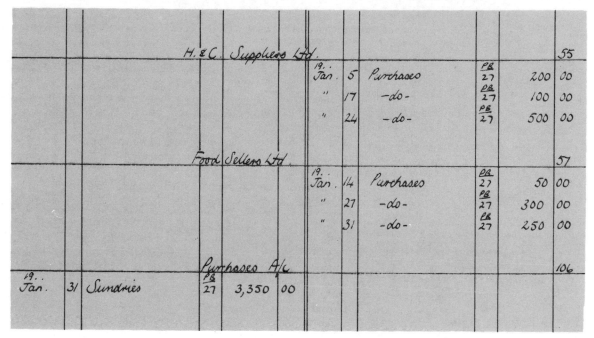

H. & C. Suppliers Ltd. 55

Date		Particulars	Fo.	£	p	Date		Particulars	Fo.	£	p
						19.. Jan.	5	Purchases	PB 27	200	00
						"	17	-do-	PB 27	100	00
						"	24	-do-	PB 27	500	00

Food Sellers Ltd. 57

Date		Particulars	Fo.	£	p	Date		Particulars	Fo.	£	p
						19.. Jan.	14	Purchases	PB 27	50	00
						"	27	-do-	PB 27	300	00
						"	31	-do-	PB 27	250	00

Purchases A/c 106

Date		Particulars	Fo.	£	p	Date		Particulars	Fo.	£	p
19.. Jan.	31	Sundries	PB 27	3,350	00						

Figure 29 (b)

Purchases returns

Sometimes goods which have previously been purchased have to be returned to the seller. This may be necessary when they are found to be defective in quality or damaged. Again, sometimes the seller over-charges for the goods. As a result, it often becomes necessary for a supplier to reduce the amount charged on an invoice already sent to a customer. This is done by means of a *credit note*.

A specimen credit note is shown in Figure 30.

HOTEL AND CATERING SUPPLIERS LTD.

5, West End Lane, London, W16

TO: Imperial Hotel Ltd.,
Leicester Square,
London, W.1.

CREDIT NOTE

29th December 1982

	£	p
By Overcharge per invoice dated 1·9·1982 Amount Charged – £20.00 *Less* Correct Charge – 15.00	5	00

Figure 30

Note: It is assumed that the invoice dated 1st September 1981, was not subject to a trade discount. Otherwise the percentage of trade discount would have to be deducted from the amount of the above credit note.

The accounting treatment of a credit note is as follows:

(1) All credit notes, having been numbered consecutively, are entered individually in a subsidiary book, called the *purchases returns book*.
(2) Double entry is completed by:
(a) debiting the credit notes in the accounts of suppliers individually;
(b) crediting the periodical (weekly, monthly) total of the purchases returns account in the ledger.

At the end of the accounting period the balance of the purchases returns account is transferred to the purchases account. The latter will thus show the net purchases for the year.

Example A hotel receives the following credit notes during the month of January, 19..:

January	6	Brompton Food Market	£30
,,	13	X.Y.Z. Wines Co.	50
,,	25	Brompton Food Market	10
,,	31	B.S.L. Grocers	25

The above credit notes are entered in the purchases returns book of the hotel (Figure 31) and posted to appropriate ledger accounts (Figure 32).

		Purchases Returns Book				32
Date 19..			C/N No.	Led. Fol.		
Jan.	6	Brompton Food Market Ltd.	1	L 77	30	00
"	13	X.Y.Z. Wines Co.	2	L 79	50	00
"	25	Brompton Food Market Ltd.	3	L 77	10	00
"	31	B.S.L. Grocers	4	L 81	25	00
"	31	Transferred to Purchases Returns A/c		L 109	115	00

Figure 31

				Brompton Food Market Ltd.							77
19..											
Jan	6	Returns	PR 32	30	00						
"	25	-do-	PR 32	10	00						
				X.Y.Z. Mines Co.							79
19..											
Jan	13	Returns	PR 32	50	00						
				B.S.L. Grocers							81
19..											
Jan	31	Returns	PR 32	25	00						
				Purchases Returns A/c							109
						19..					
						Jan	31	Sundries	PR 32	115	00

Figure 32

Suppliers' statements

Most suppliers who sell goods on credit send their customers a statement of account (usually monthly). This is a copy of the buyer's account in the books of the supplier and shows particulars of invoices and any credit notes sent to the customer, any cash received and, of course, the balance due to the supplier at the end of the period.

It is usual to check all suppliers' statements against their accounts in the ledger. Any cash discount offered should then be deducted before payment is made. The treatment of cash discounts was explained in Chapter 2. A specimen statement of account is shown in Figure 33.

Assuming that this statement is paid within one month (i.e. before the end of July), a cash discount of £11.00 would be deducted from the amount due and a cheque for £209.00 drawn in favour of the supplier.

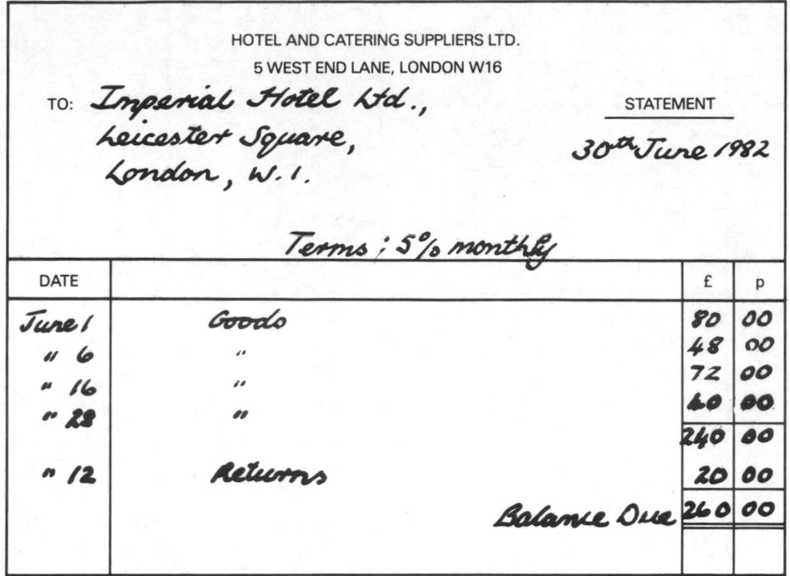

HOTEL AND CATERING SUPPLIERS LTD.
5 WEST END LANE, LONDON W16

TO: Imperial Hotel Ltd.,
Leicester Square,
London, W.1.

STATEMENT

30th June 1982

Terms ; 5% monthly

DATE		£	p
June 1	Goods	80	00
" 6	"	48	00
" 16	"	72	00
" 28	"	40	00
		240	00
" 12	Returns	20	00
	Balance Due	260	00

Figure 33

Example The following transactions took place between a hotel and Hotel Supplies Co.:

January 1	Goods purchased		£200
,, 4	,,	,,	150
,, 13	,,	,,	200
,, 21	,,	,,	250
,, 27	,,	returned	50
,, 31	,,	purchased	250
February 2	,,	,,	200
,, 10	Cash paid to supplier		950
,, 10	Discount received from supplier		50

The account of Hotel Supplies Co. is written up in the ledger of the hotel; and the account balanced as at the end of January. See Figure 34.

				Hotel Supplies Co.					
19.. Jan.	27	Returns		50 00	19.. Jan.	1	Purchases		200 00
"	31	Balance	c/d	1,000 00	"	4	-do-		150 00
					"	13	-do-		200 00
					"	21	-do-		250 00
					"	31	-do-		250 00
				1,050 00					1050 00
19.. Feb.	10	Cash		950 00	19.. Feb.	1	Balance	b/d	1,000 00
"	10	Disc. Received		50 00	-	2	Purchases		200 00

Figure 34

Problems 1 Distinguish clearly between cash discount and trade discount.

2 Write short notes on the purpose of invoice; credit note; and statement of account.

3 On 1st December, 19.., after eleven months' trading, Jack Mason had the following balances in his books:

Capital	£22 000
Sales	17 500
Purchases	6 200
Cash at bank	8 400
Premises	17 250
Wages	3 700
China and cutlery	800
Furniture	1 250
Insurance	150
Kitchen equipment	2 500
Gas and electricity	750
Creditors: V. A. Rigby	500
O. Kay	1 000

Arrange these in the form of a trial balance and enter balances in accounts.
Mason's transactions in December were:

December	2	Purchased provisions by cheque	£1 500
,,	6	Paid for kitchen equipment by cheque	500
,,	10	Paid amount due to O. Kay	1 000
,,	14	Banked sales to date	850
,,	16	Paid wages by cheque	600
,,	19	Paid rates by cheque	770
,,	23	Bought groceries on credit: V. A. Rigby	1 200
		A. M. Williams	600
,,	27	Paid by cheque for insurance to 31st March, 19..	150
,,	31	Banked sales to date	1 410

Enter these transactions in Mason's books and extract a trial balance as at 31st December, 19..

4 On 1st January, 19.., John Brown started in business with a capital in cash of £50 000. In January, his transactions were:

January	1	Paid by cheque rent for premises	£11 000
,,	2	Paid by cheque for furniture	2 000
,,	4	Paid by cheque for kitchen equipment	4 000
,,	6	Paid wages by cheque	650
,,	8	Credit purchases: F. W. Young & Co.	330
		V. Fatt & Son	220
		Jack Player & Son	160
,,	10	Banked cash sales	570
,,	14	Paid by cheque for provisions	360
,,	19	Paid wages by cheque	660
,,	22	Credit purchases: Jack Player & Son	130
		V. Fatt & Son	270
		F. W. Young & Co.	460
,,	23	Paid by cheque for stationery	120
,,	25	Credit purchases: F. W. Young & Co.	260
		Five Squares Ltd	150
		V. Fatt & Son	190
,,	26	Banked cash sales	2 190
,,	28	Paid wages by cheque	720
,,	29	Paid for advertising by cheque	500
,,	30	Received credit notes from: V. Fatt & Son	50
		F. W. Young & Co.	30
		Jack Player & Son	40
,,	31	Banked cash sales	1 160
,,	31	Paid by cheque for groceries	330

Enter the above transactions in appropriate books, post to ledger, and extract Brown's trial balance as at 31st January, 19..

5 Jack Lane commenced business on 1st January, 19.. as a café proprietor with £40 000 in the bank.

His transactions in January were as follows:

January	1	Purchased leasehold premises, paid by cheque	£27 000
,,	2	Purchased furniture, paid by cheque	1 000
,,	3	Withdrew for petty cash	400
,,	3	Paid by cheque for fruit and vegetables	740
,,	4	Received invoices from:	
		A.N.B. Grocers Ltd	700
		O.K. Provisions Ltd	840
		B. S. Fish & Sons	320
,,	7	Paid wages by cheque	780
,,	8	Paid by cheque for kitchen equipment	4 200
,,	9	Paid out of petty cash	
		Stationery	60
		Postage	40
		Cleaning materials	40
,,	10	Banked sales	2 500
,,	11	Invoices received from:	
		O.K. Provisions Ltd	240
		B.S. Fish & Sons	380
		Battersea Fruiterers	360
,,	14	Banked sales	2 720
,,	15	Paid wages by cheque	9 200
,,	17	Paid by cheque for groceries	420
,,	19	Invoices received from:	
		A.N.B. Grocers Ltd	520
		Battersea Fruiterers	260
		B.S. Fish & Sons	440
,,	21	Banked sales	3 520
,,	23	Paid out of petty cash:	
		Cleaning materials	60
		Postage	60
		Travelling expenses	20
,,	24	Credit notes received from:	
		O.K. Provisions Ltd	60
		A.N.B. Grocers Ltd	80
,,	25	Paid wages by cheque	940
,,	27	Banked sales	840
,,	28	Paid by cheque for electricity	1 720
,,	29	Petty cash payments:	
		Stationery	40
		Travelling expenses	20
,,	30	Credit notes received from:	
		Battersea Fruiterers	100
		B.S. Fish & Sons	80
,,	31	Paid wages by cheque	780

You are required to write up Lane's books in respect of the month of January, 19.., and extract his trial balance as at the end of that period.

CHAPTER 4

Accounting for sales

Cash sales

The sales of a business may be of two kinds: cash sales and credit sales. A cash sale takes place when food, drink, etc., are sold and the price is paid immediately. As soon as the price is paid by the customer, the transaction is fully settled. From the book-keeping point of view all that is needed is an entry in the cash book (to show that cash has been received) and an entry in the sales account (to show that something has been sold).

Hence, the double entry in respect of cash sales is:

Dr. cash book
Cr. sales account

Example On 1st April, 19.., the cash sales of a restaurant amounted to £425, and were paid into the bank the same day. This is recorded in the books of the restaurant (Figure 35).

Cash Book (12)

Date		Particulars	Fo.	£	p	Date		Particulars	Fo.	£	p
19.. Apr.	1	Sales	L 47	425	00						

Sales A/c (47)

Date		Particulars	Fo.	£	p	Date		Particulars	Fo.	£	p
						19.. Apr.	1	Cash	CB 12	425	00

Figure 35

Credit sales

The treatment of credit sales is different and may vary from one type of hotel and catering establishment to another. Within a particular business, e.g. a hotel, there may be several distinct methods of recording credit sales. In general, however, credit sales in hotels and catering establishments fall into three main categories.

First, there are *restaurant sales*. These include all food, drinks, etc., sold on credit to non-residents, paying their accounts periodically (usually monthly). Next there are *banqueting sales*: these include all the banqueting sales in respect of which there is no immediate settlement. Finally, there are short-term credit sales to the guests of a hotel recorded in the *tabular* or *visitors' ledger*.

Restaurant sales

The general method of recording the credit sales of a restaurant is the same whether these are sales to non-residents dining in a hotel or expense-account customers dining in a restaurant. Briefly, the procedure may be described as follows.

When the customer has been served, the waiter prepares a bill, usually in duplicate. This is signed by the customer, who takes the top copy of the bill, (Figure 36).

	No. 116	
BLUEBELL RESTAURANT 16 Second Avenue, London W1		
Table No. 9	Date 16·5·82	
Waiter No. 12	No. of Covers 2	
	£	**p**
2 × Crème de Champignons	1	20
Mixed Grill	3	60
Escalope de Veau	4	70
2 × Pommes Sautées		80
2 × Haricots Verts		80
2 × Fruit Salad	1	00
TOTAL MEALS	12	10
1 Bot: Nuits St. Georges	4	20
1 Tia Maria		60
TOTAL BEVERAGES	4	80
TOTAL	16	90

Figure 36

The second (carbon) copy of the bill is sent to the accounts department. Here, all such bills in respect of credit sales are numbered consecutively and entered in a subsidiary book, the *restaurant sales book*.

Double entry is completed by debiting each individual bill in a customer's personal account, and crediting the periodical (weekly or monthly) total of such sales in the sales account in the ledger.

Example The following are the credit sales of the Bluebell Restaurant:

January	1	Midland Motors Ltd	£30
,,	2	Business Promotions Ltd	40
,,	3	B. M. Blake, Esq.	50
,,	4	Midland Motors Ltd	120
,,	4	Business Promotions Ltd	60
,,	5	B. M. Blake, Esq.	20
,,	6	Midland Motors Ltd	80
,,	7	Business Promotions Ltd	100

The above transactions are entered in the restaurant sales book (Figure 37) and posted to ledger accounts (Figure 38).

Restaurant Sales Book — 36

DATE			BILL NO	LED. FOL.		
19..						
Jan.	1	Midland Motors Ltd.	1	L/101	30	00
"	2	Business Promotions Ltd.	2	L/103	40	00
"	3	B. M. Blake, Esq.	3	L/104	50	00
"	4	Midland Motors Ltd.	4	L/101	120	00
"	4	Business Promotions Ltd.	5	L/103	60	00
"	5	B. M. Blake, Esq.	6	L/104	20	00
"	6	Midland Motors Ltd.	7	L/101	80	00
"	7	Business Promotions Ltd.	8	L/103	100	00
"	7	Transferred to Sales A/c		L/201	500	00

Figure 37 (above)

Figure 38 (below)

Midland Motors Ltd. — 101

19.. Jan.	1	Sales	SB/36	30	00						
"	4	-do-	SB/36	120	00						
"	6	-do-	SB/36	80	00						

Business Promotions Ltd. — 103

19.. Jan.	2	Sales	SB/36	40	00						
"	4	-do-	SB/36	60	00						
"	7	-do-	SB/36	100	00						

B.M. Blake Esq. — 104

19.. Jan	3	Sales	SB/36	50	00						
"	5	-do-	SB/36	20	00						

Sales A/c

						19.. Jan.	7	Sundries	SB/36	500	

On receipt of the amount due from a customer, the cash book is debited and the account of the customer is credited. Thus, if Midland Motors paid the amount due on 31st January, 19 . ., their account would appear as in Figure 39.

Midland Motors Ltd.

19..						19..					
Jan.	1	Sales	SB 36	30	00	Jan.	31	Cash	CB	230	00
"	4	-do-	SB 36	120	00						
"	6	-do-	SB 36	80	00						
				230	00					230	00

Figure 39

Banqueting sales

From the point of view of the book-keeping involved, the treatment of banqueting sales proper is similar to that of the various functions such as wedding receptions, dinner parties, conferences, etc. We will, therefore, refer to all such sales as banqueting sales.

The arrangements with the client organizing the banquet may vary quite considerably. The organizer may agree to pay so much per cover for the meals only, in which event all drinks ordered by those taking part in the banquet would have to be paid for in cash. Any such drinks would be treated as bar cash sales.

Another common arrangement is for the organizer to agree to pay a given charge per cover for the meals and, additionally, request that a given number of bottles of wine be made available to members of the party. Then, both the meals and the wines are sold on credit.

Whatever the arrangements made, it is clear that a distinction should be made between what the organizer has agreed to pay for (credit sales) and any additional drinks, cigars, and cigarettes required by particular members of the party and supplied on a cash basis.

The nature of the book-keeping records kept in respect of banqueting sales depends on the volume of banqueting business done and on the frequency of banquets undertaken for particular clients.

Where the volume of banqueting is small, it is sometimes the practice to treat all banqueting sales as if they were cash sales. No entries would then be made until such time as the client settled his account. The cash book would then be debited and the sales account credited with the amount received.

It must be pointed out that this procedure is not in accordance with the best accounting practice, as the books of the business do not reflect the true financial state of affairs.

Where the volume of banqueting business is substantial, it is usual to open a separate *banqueting sales book*. Particulars of banqueting credit sales are recorded in the same manner as are restaurant credit sales in the restaurant sales book (see p. 46).

Clients making frequent use of the banqueting facilities of the hotel/restaurant would have a proper ledger account opened for them. All such accounts would be posted in the same way as those illustrated on p. 40. Clients using the banqueting facilities infrequently (e.g. wedding receptions, twenty-first dinner parties, association annual dinners) may have a composite account opened for them, Figure 40.

Banqueting Debtors A/c

Date		F	No of Covers	@		£	p	Extras	Total	Date		F	£ p
19..										19..			
May 1	Mr & Mrs T. Wedlock	61	20	15	00	300	00	100.00	400.00	May 6	Cash	CB	400 00
" 4	Miss D. F. Age	62	10	10	00	100	00	50.00	150.00	" 10	-do-	CB	150 00
" 9	X.Y.Z Association	63	100	10	00	1,000	00	500.00	1,500.00	" 16	-do-	CB	1,500 00
" 18	Mr & Mrs A. Wedmore	64	30	15	00	450	00		450.00				
" 22	Miss B. Bonar	65	15	10	00	150	00	50.00	200.00	" 29	-do-	CB	200 00
" 31	The '61 Society	66	50	15	00	750	00		750.00				

Figure 40 Banqueting debtors' account

Whenever a banqueting debtor settles his/her account, a debit entry is made in the cash book and a corresponding credit in the banqueting debtors account. The total amount of outstanding debts may easily be determined by reference to the banqueting debtors account. In the above specimen account this amounts to £1 200.

ROOM	1	2	3	4	5	6	7	8	9	10
NAME	Fenton	Black	James	Stein	Dewey	Saxton	Turner	Weston	Bentley	
NO OF VISITORS	1	1	2	2	1	2	2	1	1	
Balance b/f	35 00	67 00	76 00	19 50	23 00	89 00	98 00	143 00		
Apartments	15 00	15 00	25 00	25 00	15 00	25 00			15 00	
Breakfasts	2 50	2 50	5 00	5 00	2 50	5 00	5 00	2 50		
E.M. Teas	1 00			2 00	1 00					
Luncheons		6 00	15 50	17 00	7 50	18 00			7 00	
Afternoon Teas	1 50		3 00		1 50	3 00			1 50	
Dinners	8 50	9 50		21 00		22 50			8 50	
Liquors		6 00		8 00		12 00			2 00	
Telephone	50		5 00		50					
Miscellaneous	4 00				5 00				12 50	
Paid Out		1 50		4 00		18 00				
Total	68 00	107 50	129 50	101 80	56 00	192 50	103 00	165 50	46 50	
Cash								145 50		
Ledger							103 00			
Allowances					5 00					
Balance c/f	68 00	107 50	129 50	101 50	51 00	192 50			46 50	
Total	68 00	107 50	129 50	101 50	56 00	192 50	103 00	145 50	46 50	

DAILY SUMMARY	£	p
Balance b/f	550	50
Apartments	135	00
Breakfasts	30	00
E.M. Teas	4	00
Luncheons	71	00
Afternoon Teas	10	50
Dinners	70	00
Liquors	28	00
Telephone	6	00
Miscellaneous	21	50
Paid Out	23	50
Total	950	00
Cash	145	50
Ledger	103	00
Allowances	5	00
Balance c/f	696	50
Total	950	00

Figure 41 Hotel visitors' ledger (vertical type)

Hotel visitors' ledger

The most convenient way of keeping the accounts of hotel guests is to maintain a hotel visitors' ledger, also known as the tabular ledger.

Of all the accounting records kept by hotels this is certainly the one in most common use and, therefore, deserves a more detailed description. Because of its layout, many students find difficulty in understanding how it is compiled and how it fits into the general scheme of double entry. These two aspects of the hotel visitors' ledger will, therefore, be dealt with first.

Layout

The specimen visitors' ledger shown in Figure 41 may be divided horizontally into two sections: the upper section, including the totals, and the lower section, including the second line of totals.

The upper section contains the debit side of visitors' accounts, and is used to record the balances owing from visitors, brought forward from the previous day, and the charges made to visitors during the day concerned.

The lower section contains the credit side of visitors' accounts and is used to record any cash paid by visitors in settling their accounts; any transfers from the visitors' ledger to a personal account in the sales ledger; allowances, if any, made to visitors; and the balances owing from visitors at the end of the current day carried forward to the following day.

Vertically, the visitors' ledger may also be divided into two sections: the personal accounts of visitors on the left-hand side and the somewhat smaller 'daily summary section' on the right-hand side. The latter shows the daily totals of entries made in the individual accounts of the guests.

Double entry

Although different from a conventional ledger, the visitors' ledger is a proper ledger, consisting of the personal accounts of the visitors. In fact, each of the visitors' accounts could be re-written and presented as a conventional, double-sided account. Thus, Fenton's account could be re-written as in Figure 42.

Dr		Fenton – Room 1									Cr
19.. May	3	Balance	b/d	35	00	19.. May	3	Balance	c/d	68	00
"	3	Sales		15	00						
"	3	-do-		2	50						
"	3	-do-		1	00						
"	3	-do		1	50						
"	3	-do-		8	50						
"	3	-do-			50						
"	3	-do-		4	00						
				68	00					68	00
19.. May	4	Balance	b/d	68	00						

Figure 42

Charges debited to visitors are totalled in the last column of the visitors' ledger and, daily, transferred to the monthly summary sheet. This is totalled monthly and the individual totals posted to the appropriate accounts in the ledger. A specimen monthly summary sheet is given in Figure 43.

May, 19..

MONTHLY SUMMARY SHEET

DATE	APARTMENTS	B/FASTS	E.M. TEAS	LUNCHES	A/NOON TEAS	DINNERS	LIQUORS	TELEPHONE	MISCELLANEOUS	DAILY TOTAL	ALLOWANCES
May 1	150 00	32 50	6 00	113 00	21 00	96 00	49 50	16 50	9 50	494 00	7 50
" 2	130 00	35 00	3 50	86 00	17 00	81 00	31 50	3 00	16 00	403 00	
" 3	135 00	30 00	4 00	71 00	10 50	70 00	28 00	6 00	21 50	376 00	5 00
etc.											
TOTAL	4,400 00	800 00	200 00	3,000 00	400 00	3,800 00	1,500 00	450 00	600 00	15150 00	100 00

Figure 43 Monthly summary sheet

Note: (1) column headings in the monthly summary sheet correspond with the sequence of charges in the hotel visitors' ledger. (2) No column is provided for the paid outs because (a) monthly summary sheet is a summary of sales, (b) double entry in respect of paid outs is completed by crediting the petty cash book and debiting visitors' accounts in the visitors' ledger.

Assuming that by the end of May the total of apartments sales is £4 400, this would be posted in the ledger (Figure 44).

Sales A/c - Apartments

					19..				
					Jan.	31	M.S.S.	2,900	00
					Feb.	28	-do-	3,400	00
					Mar.	31	-do-	4,150	00
					Apr.	30	-do-	4,300	00
					May	31	-do-	4,400	00

Figure 44 Sales account—apartments

To sum up, double entry in respect of sales (charges) to visitors is completed by debiting the individual charges in the visitors' accounts in the visitors' ledger, and crediting the monthly totals from the monthly summary sheet in the appropriate accounts in the ledger.

Any allowances made to guests should be properly authorized by the management. As may be seen from the specimen visitors' ledger, these are credited in visitors' accounts (see Dewey, Room 5), entered in the allowances column of the monthly summary sheet and, at the end of each month, debited in the allowances account in the ledger.

The treatment of cash received from visitors is simple: the cash book is debited and the account of the visitor credited (see Weston, Room 8).

Sometimes a guest leaves the hotel without, for one reason or another, paying his account. When that happens there is, clearly, no point in keeping the guest's account in the visitors' ledger. The balance owing on the guest's departure is, therefore, transferred from the visitors' ledger to a personal account in the sales ledger.

In the specimen visitors' ledger given above, Turner left the hotel on 3rd May, 19.., without settling his account. Consequently, his account in the visitors' ledger is credited with £103.00. The corresponding debit entry in his account in the sales ledger would appear as is shown in Figure 45.

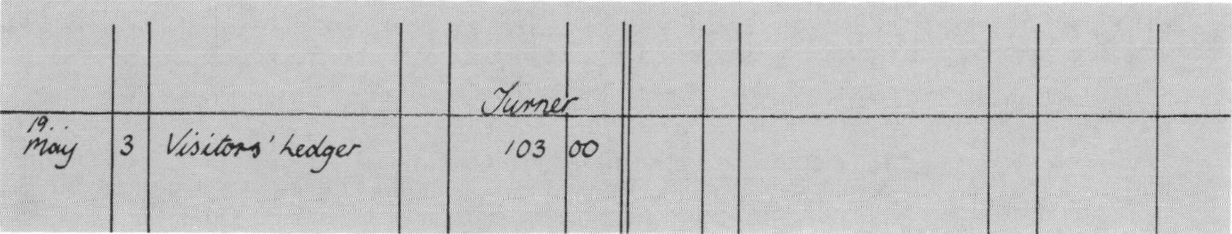

Turner

19.. May	3	Visitors' Ledger		103	00						

Figure 45 Turner's account

Assuming that a few weeks later Turner sends the hotel a cheque for £103.00 in settlement, this would be debited in the cash book and credited in his account, thus balancing the latter.

The monthly summary sheet (Figure 43) is fairly typical of those in actual use in hotels. It has, however, one serious deficiency: the allowances to customers are not analysed and, as a result, at the end of each month it is impossible to post figures of *net sales* to the ledger. *Gross sales* are posted to the credit of the various ledger accounts, and the total of monthly allowances to the debit of allowances account. In consequence, at the end of a trading period, it is impossible under this method to ascertain the exact amount of profit from any one department.

In order to remedy this, it is possible to maintain a monthly allowances sheet in conjunction with the monthly summary sheet. Under this method, allowances to visitors are analysed daily and totalled at the end of each month. They are then deducted from the gross sales in the monthly sheet. The resulting net sales are then posted to the ledger.

A specimen monthly allowances sheet is given in Figure 46.

MONTHLY ALLOWANCES SHEET — May 19..

Date	Apartment	Break-fasts	E.M. Teas	Luncheons	A/noon Teas	Dinners	Liquors	Telephone	Misc.	Total
May 1						4 00	3 50			7 50
" 3				2 50					2 50	5 00
etc.										
Monthly Total	20 00	10 00	15 00	5 00	5 00	20 00	15 00	5 00	5 00	100 00

Figure 46 Monthly allowances sheet

The monthly summary sheet shown in Figure 47 is a variant of the conventional type. Its main advantage is that it shows a figure of net sales for each section of the turnover.

It will be appreciated that when this type of monthly summary sheet is used there is no necessity for an allowances account in the ledger.

MONTHLY SUMMARY SHEET — May, 19..

Date	Apartments	B/fasts	E.M. Teas	Lunches	A/Noon Teas	Dinners	Liquors	Telephone	Miscellaneous	Daily Total	Less Allowances	Net Total
May 1	150 00	32 50	6 00	113 00	21 00	96 00	49 50	16 50	9 50	494 00	7 50	486 50
" 2	130 00	35 00	3 50	86 00	17 00	81 00	31 50	3 00	16 00	403 00		403 00
" 3	135 00	30 00	4 00	71 00	10 50	70 00	28 00	6 00	21 50	376 00	5 00	371 00
etc.												
Monthly Total	4,400 00	800 00	200 00	3,000 00	400 00	3,800 00	1,500 00	450 00	600 00	15,150 00	100 00	15,050 00
Less Allowances	20 00	10 00	15 00	5 00	5 00	20 00	15 00	5 00	5 00	100 00		
Net Total	4,380 00	790 00	185 00	2,995 00	395 00	3780 00	1,485 00	445 00	595 00	15,050 00		

Figure 47

Sources of charges The charges incurred by visitors may be numerous and arise in various parts of the hotel. The purpose of the present section is to explain where they originate and how they find their way to the visitors' accounts.

Apartments This basic charge is incurred by all guests who stay at least one night. The charge originates in the reception office and is determined by reference to the room list or room index or the terms book. The charge is debited to the visitors' account as soon as such an account is opened. On subsequent days the charge is usually debited to the visitor each evening for the coming night's stay. In the specimen visitors' ledger on p. 42, Turner (Room 7) and Weston (Room 8) left the hotel after breakfast. No charge for apartments is, therefore, debited to them. Bentley (Room 9) arrives before luncheon and is debited £15.00 in respect of the coming night's stay (3rd/4th May).

Meals This heading, for the purpose of the visitors' ledger, includes all meals and non-alcoholic drinks, such as teas and coffees. In respect of each such meal it is usual to raise a duplicate voucher (Figure 48), a copy of which is passed to the book-keeper for debiting a visitor's account. It is important, particularly in the case of transient hotels, that this is done as soon as possible. Otherwise a guest may leave the hotel before certain charges are debited. The second copy of such a voucher is usually passed on to the control office for checking purposes.

No:

DUPLICATE VOUCHER

Dept: .... Date: ....

....

....

....

....

....

Room No: .... Signature: ....

Table No: .... Waiter's No: ....

Figure 48 Duplicate voucher

Drinks This heading includes all alcoholic beverages and, usually, minerals. A charge in respect of drinks may originate in a dispense bar, a cocktail bar, or the lounge. The procedure adopted is the same as in the case of meals. It is usual for the person dispensing the drinks to price the voucher, though in some hotels this may be left to the book-keeper responsible for the visitors' ledger.

Sundry sales In addition to the three basic charges—apartments, meals, and drinks—there are numerous other charges (e.g. telephone, laundry, valeting, garage, etc.) that may be incurred by a visitor. Here again, the general rule is that a voucher in duplicate must be made out and a copy thereof sent to the book-keeper for debiting the visitor's account.

Visitors' paid outs This heading includes various amounts paid out by the employees of the hotel on behalf of visitors. Examples of such paid outs are theatre tickets, flowers, and payments for C.O.D. mail addressed to the visitors. Any such payments would be credited to the petty cash book. A duplicate voucher would then be made out and a copy of it passed to the book-keeper responsible for visitors' accounts.

It is important that a distinction be drawn between visitors' paid outs and sundry sales. The former is a recovery of the hotel's payments and is not a part of current revenue; the latter is, of course, as much a part of the hotel's revenue as meals, drinks, and other similar charges. It will be appreciated that what is a visitors' paid out (V.P.O.) in one hotel may well be regarded as a sundry sale in another. Thus where visitors' laundry is sent out, any charges made to them would normally be regarded as V.P.O. Where a hotel has a laundry of its own, any charges made to visitors would contain an element of profit and would, therefore, be regarded as sundry sales.

Guests' bills

In addition to opening an account in the visitors' ledger, the book-keeper will open a bill for each guest on his/her arrival. Guests' bills are written up daily from the duplicate vouchers which are debited in the visitors' ledger.

It will be appreciated that, as identical charges are entered in the visitors' ledger and in the guests' bills, when all vouchers have been posted all balances in the visitors' ledger will correspond with the balances shown by guests' bills. In fact, as soon as all charges have been posted it is usual to compare the two sets of balances. Any differences should be investigated and put right before carrying the balances to the following day. A specimen guest's bill is shown in Figure 49.

GRAND HOTEL LTD

TO: M. A. Jones, Esq. ROOM: 126

	2nd May		3rd May		4th May			
Balance b/f			76	00	129	50		
Apartments	25	00	25	00				
Breakfasts			5	00	5	00		
E.M. Teas								
Luncheons	37	50	15	50				
A/Noon Teas	3	50	3	00				
Dinners								
Liquors	6	50						
Telephone			5	00				
Miscellaneous Paid out	3	50						
Balances c/f	76	00	129	50	134	50		
Deposits/Allowances					-	-		
Amount Due					134	50		

Figure 49 A specimen bill

There are two main kinds of guests' bills: four-day bills (as illustrated here) and eight-day bills. The choice of the kind of bill used depends on the average length of stay of the guests. Thus transient and other short-stay hotels tend to use four-day bills, whereas resort hotels tend to use eight-day bills. There is, of course, no reason why a hotel should not use both kinds.

Treatment of deposits

It is customary in many hotels to require deposits in respect of any advance bookings made by guests. Even where that is not so, some customers will send a deposit to ensure that a room is properly booked for them.

It must be realized that advance deposits do not represent current revenue (sales) but must be regarded as amounts owing to guests. It is not until such time as the guest arrives and incurs charges in excess of the deposit that the latter may be treated as current revenue.

There are several different methods of recording such deposits in the books of a hotel. The two most popular methods are outlined below.

Under the first method the deposit received is debited in the cash book and credited in a personal account opened for the intending visitor in the sales ledger. On the visitor's departure, the balance from his personal account (i.e. the deposit) must be transferred to the credit side of his account in the visitors' ledger.

Under the second method, the treatment of advance deposits is the same except that a separate account is not opened for each deposit. Instead a composite account is opened for all deposits received. This is illustrated in Figure 50.

The credit balance of the advance deposits accounts represents the total amount of deposits received but not yet transferred to the visitors' ledger. Any deposits returned to guests, for one reason or another, would be credited in the hotel's cash book and debited in the advance deposits account.

Advance Deposits A/c

Date		Room No.	£	p	Date		Date of Arrival	£	p
19..					19..				
May 28	Visitors Ledger	116	50	00	Jan 29	Mr. & Mrs. Goode	May 21	50	00
					Feb 22	V. Browne	July 7	25	00
June 20	-do-	347	25	00	Mar 16	H. George	June 16	25	00
July 5	-do-	118	50	00	" 25	Mr. & Mrs. Fisher	June 29	50	00
					Apr 3	Mr. & Mrs. Henry	Aug 11	50	00

Figure 50 Advance deposits account

En pension terms

Many hotels, particularly resort hotels, offer *en pension* terms or terms inclusive of certain specified meals. There are two main methods of dealing with *en pension* terms in the visitors' ledger.

Under the first method, the procedure is as follows:

(1) The weekly inclusive charge is divided by seven to arrive at the daily charge.

(2) The daily charge is debited in the visitors' ledger in an *en pension* column (line). This additional column is usually placed between the 'balances b/f' column and the 'apartments' column.

From the visitors' ledgers the daily total of the inclusive charges would be transferred to an *en pension* column of the monthly summary sheet, in the same manner as all other charges to visitors. Similarly, at the end of each month the total of inclusive charges in the monthly summary sheet would be posted to the credit of the *en pension* account in the ledger.

Under the second method, the procedure is as follows:

(1) The weekly inclusive charge is divided by seven to arrive at the daily charge.

(2) The daily charge is divided into a number of component parts (e.g. apartments, breakfast, luncheon, dinner) according to what is included in the terms.

(3) Each separate component part of the inclusive charge is debited in the visitors' ledger in the usual manner.

Example The *en pension* terms of a hotel are £157.50 per week. On the basis of past experience the apportionment is: food—66⅔ per cent; apartments—33⅓ per cent.

Following the second method above:

$$\text{the daily charge is } \frac{£157.50}{7} = £22.50$$

Of the daily charge:

the charge for apartments = £7.50
the charge for food = £15.00

Assuming that the *en pension* terms include breakfast, lunch and dinner, the £15.00 charged for food might then be apportioned as follows:

Breakfast	£2.50
Lunch	5.50
Dinner	7.00
Total	£15.00

This second method is preferable to the first as, due to the analysis of the inclusive charge, all sales to visitors are recorded in a uniform manner. On the other hand, it is clear that the analysis of the inclusive charge is to an extent a matter of judgement, as there is no precise method of determining how much of the total should be credited to food and how much to apartments. It may be added that most hotels credit about one-third of the *en pension* charge to apartments and about two-thirds to food.

Where *bed and breakfast terms* are offered, either of the methods outlined above may be used.

Finally, it should be remembered that duplicate vouchers are not necessary in respect of meals included in *en pension* terms. Care must, however, be taken to ensure that a voucher is raised in respect of all other credit sales to *en pension* guests.

Functions Most smaller hotels record functions sales in the visitors' ledger. The procedure is as follows:

(1) All particulars of functions sales are entered in a vertical column, headed 'functions', specially provided for that purpose. Thus, if a function were sold, consisting of 20 dinners at £10.00 and drinks to the value of £100.00, in the 'functions' column we would enter £200.00 against 'dinners' and £100.00 against 'liquors'.

(2) All such functions sales will be totalled in the daily summary column and included in the daily transfers to the monthly summary sheet.

Any amounts remaining unpaid by the organizers of such functions would have to be noted. Often a special 'functions diary' is kept and any unpaid accounts noted down in it. The treatment of functions in the visitors' ledger is illustrated in the specimen on p. 55.

Chance trade Chance trade is a term applied to cash sales to non-residents. It follows, therefore, that the total of chance sales must be equal to the total of cash received. The treatment of chance trade is similar to that of functions, and may be described as follows:

(1) Particulars of all meals, etc., sold to chance customers are summarized, meal by meal, in what is known as the 'chance book'. This requires no special ruling and is kept for the sole purpose of summarizing all such sales prior to their entry in the visitors' ledger.

(2) The totals of chance luncheons, dinners, etc., from the chance book are then debited in the 'chance' column of the visitors' ledger.

(3) From the visitors' ledger the daily chance sales are transferred to the monthly summary sheet in the usual manner.

The 'chance' column should be balanced each day to ensure that the total of cash received and credited in the 'chance' column is equal to the sales debited therein. The treatment of chance sales is illustrated in the specimen given on p. 55.

Forms of visitors' ledger

So far we have considered one type of visitors' ledger. Several different kinds of visitors' ledger are, however, used in practice. Yet, it is possible to distinguish two main types of visitors' ledger, and these are dealt with below:

Vertical visitors' ledger This is the type already described and illustrated in Fig. 41. It is known as the vertical type because all charges to visitors are recorded vertically; also each visitors' account appears vertically— the upper portion being the debit and the lower portion the credit side of the visitor's account.

Horizontal visitors' ledger In this type of ledger all charges to visitors are recorded horizontally and the names of guests are recorded vertically. It will be realized that there is, in fact, little difference between the vertical and the horizontal types of visitors' ledger. The difference is one of layout only. A specimen example is given in Figure 51, and students should compare this with the vertical visitors' ledger in Figure 41. In order to facilitate comparison, identical information was used to write up both ledgers

Finally, there is a variant of the vertical type already described. The layout of this ledger is the same as that of the vertical type except that the daily sales are (a) accumulated monthly in the visitors' ledger, and (b) posted to appropriate ledger accounts at the end of each month.

It will be appreciated that, as a result, no monthly summary sheet is required with this type of visitors' ledger. A specimen is given in Fig. 52. Two additional columns 'functions' and 'chance trade' are inserted to illustrate the treatment of these sales in the visitors' ledger.

Some basic considerations

A review of the various methods of accounting for sales outlined in this chapter suggests that in each hotel and catering establishment there are several ways in which it is possible to record sales. It will not be out of place, therefore, to conclude this chapter with a few basic considerations that influence the actual sales accounting records kept.

An important decision that must be made in each hotel is whether the hotel visitors' ledger should be used:

(i) to record all the sales of the hotel, or
(ii) to record sales to guests only.

Most smaller hotels use the visitors' ledger as a record of all the sales. Large hotels, on the other hand, tend to use it as a record of sales to guests only. Other sales (banqueting, bars, dinner parties, etc.) are then recorded in separate books of account.

Secondly, it is necessary to decide on the type of hotel visitors' ledger to be used, i.e. vertical or horizontal. It seems that the vertical type is the more popular. Further, the layout of the vertical visitors' ledger is such as to enable the individual guest's account to be more easily balanced than is the case with the horizontal type. Similarly, at the end of the day when both the visitors' ledger and the guests' bills are written up, a comparison of the two sets of balances and the location of errors seems to be easier with the vertical type of visitors' ledger.

HOTEL VISITORS'

Room No	Name	Balances B/Fwd	Apartments	Breakfasts	E.M. Teas	Luncheons	A/Noon Teas	Dinners
1	Fenton	35 00	15 00	2 50	1 00		1 50	8 50
2	Black	67 00	15 00	2 50		6 00		9 50
3	James	76 00	25 00	5 00		15 50	3 00	
4	Stein	19 50	25 00	5 00	2 00	17 00		21 00
5	Dewey	23 00	15 00	2 50	1 00	7 50	1 50	
6	Saxton	89 00	25 00	5 00		18 00	3 00	22 50
7	Turner	98 00		5 00				
8	Uleston	143 00		2 50				
9	Bentley		15 00			7 00	1 50	8 50
		550 50	135 00	30 00	4 00	71 00	10 50	70 00

Figure 51 Hotel visitors' ledger (horizontal type)

Finally, the degree of analysis of charges and the degree of detail necessary should be considered. Thus, where there are numerous minor selling departments it is necessary to decide whether the sales of each such department should be recorded separately, or whether some of them may be lumped together and, for accounting purposes, treated as 'sundry sales'. A similar problem arises in the treatment of functions. The treatment of functions, as described in this chapter, is rather simplified, and many hotels prefer to record these in greater detail. A common arrangement is not to have just one 'functions' column in the visitors' ledger but to make several columns available for this purpose. The sales in respect of each function would thus be recorded separately.

Problems

1 Describe the two main types of the visitors' ledger.

2 Explain how double entry is completed in respect of the following: (a) charges to visitors; (b) allowances; (c) cash received from visitors; and (d) visitors' disbursements.

3 Write short explanatory notes on the book-keeping treatment of: (a) *en pension* terms; (b) advance deposits.

LEDGER (horizontal type)

Liquors	Telephone	Paid Out	Miscellaneous	Total Debits	Cash	Ledger	Allowance	Balance c/ Fwd	Total Credits
	50		4 00	68 00				68 00	68 00
6 00		1 50		107 50				107 50	107 50
	5 00			129 50				129 50	129 50
8 00		4 00		101 50				101 50	101 50
	50			56 00			5 00	51 00	56 00
12 00		18 00	5 00	192 50				192 50	192 50
				103 00		103 00			103 00
				145 50	145 50				145 50
2 00			12 50	46 50				46 50	46 50
28 00	6 00	23 50	21 50	950 00	145 50	103 00	5 00	696 50	950 00

Room No. / Name	1 Coles		2 Mills		3 Gordon		4 Bingley		5 Gallagher		6 French	
Balances b/f.	104	00	45	00	167	00	27	50	97	00	119	00
Apartments			20	00			20	00	35	00	35	00
Breakfasts	5	00	2	50	5	00	2	50	5	00	5	00
E.M. Teas	3	00			3	00	1	50				
Luncheons	20	00	7	50					17	50		
Drink	8	50			21	00	3	00			17	50
A/Teas			2	50			2	50				
Dinners					19	50						
Telephone	1	00							1	00		
Miscellaneous					5	00						
Paid Out			5	00							10	00
Total Debits	141	50	82	50	220	50	57	00	155	50	186	50
Cash	141	50										
Ledger					220	50						
Allowances									3	00		
Balances c/f			82	50			57	00	152	50	186	50
Total Credits	141	50	82	50	220	50	57	00	155	50	186	50

Figure 52 Hotel visitors' ledger (vertical type—alternative form)

4 Explain how the following charges to visitors originate and how they are debited in their accounts in the visitors' ledger: (a) apartments; (b) meals; (c) drinks; and (d) sundry sales.

5 Peter Fraine is a proprietor of a restaurant. The following balances appeared in his ledger on 1st January, 19 . . .

	Dr. £	Cr. £
Capital		120 000
Cash at bank	20 000	
Premises	60 000	
Furniture	15 000	
Equipment	20 000	
Food stocks	5 000	
	£120 000	£120 000

7 Davison	8 Hagen	9 Brown	10 Beeson	Chance Trade	Functions	Daily Total	Brought Forward	Carried Forward
55 00	58 50					673 00	612 00	1,285 00
20 00	20 00	35 00	20 00			205 00	195 00	400 00
2 50	2 50					30 00	27 50	57 50
	1 50					9 00	10 50	19 50
	12 50			100 00	180 00	337 50	362 50	700 00
		10 00		40 00	70 00	170 00	157 50	327 50
2 50	2 50			50 00	250 00	60 00	45 00	105 00
9 50		35 00	12 00	160 00		486 00	414 50	900 50
			3 00			5 00	15 50	20 50
2 50		2 50				10 00	5 00	15 00
						15 00	25 00	40 00
92 00	97 50	82 50	35 00	350 00	500 00	2,000 50	1,870 00	3,870 50
				350 00	500 00	991 50	787 00	1,778 50
						220 50	400 00	620 50
						3 00	10 00	13 00
92 00	97 50	82 50	35 00			785 50	673 00	1,458 50
92 00	97 50	82 50	35 00	350 00	500 00	2,000 50	1,870 00	3,870 50

Open the necessary accounts and enter the above balances.
Fraine's transactions in January were:

January	1	Food purchases—by cheque	£960
,,	2	Paid by cheque for advertising	500
,,	4	Cash sales—banked	870
,,	5	Credit sales: E.X. Dining Club	220
		Midland Cars Ltd	120
		City Banking Co.	260
,,	6	Paid wages by cheque	690
,,	9	Paid by cheque for new furniture	1 500
,,	10	Cash sales—banked	930
,,	13	Paid by cheque for fruit	100
,,	16	Credit sales: City Banking Co.	170
		E.X. Dining Club	120
		Midland Cars Ltd	390
,,	19	Paid wages by cheque	720
,,	22	Paid by cheque for fish and poultry	190
	26	Cash sales—banked	1 000
			c/f 8 740

			b/f £8 740
,,	27	Credit sales: Midland Cars Ltd	160
		E.X. Dining Club	190
,,	29	Paid for travelling expenses by cheque	120
,,	31	Paid wages by cheque	660

Write up Fraine's books in respect of January and extract his trial balance as at 31st January, 19...

6 Before business is commenced in the Hyview Hotel on 4th May, 19.., the cash book balance is £79.00 and the following balances are brought forward on the visitors' ledger from the previous day:

Room No.	1	2	3	4	5	Total
No. of visitors	one	one	two	two	–	six
Balance b/f	£25.00	£47.50	£39.50	£109.00		£221.00

During the day the business is as follows:

Breakfast:	all residents
Lunch	all residents in rooms 2, 3 and 4
Sherry:	Room 1 —£1.75
Departure:	Room 2—account paid in cash
Dinner:	Room 1; 1 only in Room 3, 1 only in Room 4
Wine:	one bottle @ £12.50 served in Room 3
Apartments:	charged to all residents

Hotel Tariff

Apartments	— £15.00 per person per day
Breakfast	— £2.00
Lunch	— £5.00
Dinner	— £6.00

MONTHLY SUMMARY SHEET MAY, 19..

Date	Apartments	Breakfasts	Luncheons	Dinners	Miscellaneous	Total
May 1	45.00	8.00	17.00	21.00	9.00	100.00
,, 2	60.00	6.00	8.50	21.00	2.00	97.50
,, 3	60.00	10.00	8.50	10.50	13.50	102.50

You are required:

(a) to write up the visitors' ledger for 4th May, 19.., in conjunction with a simple cash book;

(b) to balance the visitors' ledger and the cash book;

(c) to enter the day's business in the monthly summary sheet;

(d) to construct a trial balance as on 4th May, 19...

7 The following exercise on the visitors' ledger extends over three days. The following is the tariff of the hotel.

Bed and breakfast			*Rooms*
Single	— A	£15.00	1 — 6
Single	— B	£12.50	7 — 12
Double	— A	£27.50	13 — 18
Double	— B	£22.50	19 — 24

Extra child's bed in the room and breakfast	— £7.50
Early morning tea	— £0.50
Luncheon	— £4.00
Afternoon tea	— £2.00
Dinner	— £6.00
Coffee	— £1.00

Note: Breakfast is charged for whether taken or not.

First day

Arrivals a.m.	Room 1 — Mr J. Derbyshire
	,, 2 — Miss L. Smith
	,, 3 — Miss R. Fletcher
	,, 7 — Mr F. Betts
	,, 8 — Mr S. Stanford
	,, 14 — Capt. & Mrs J. Wright
	,, 16 — Mr & Mrs K. Booth
Luncheons	All arrivals
Arrivals p.m.	Room 4 — Rev. J. Smart
	,, 10 — Miss S. Lake
	,, 17 — Mr & Mrs Spencer
	,, 21 — Mr & Mrs F. Donaldson
	,, 22 — F/Lt. & Mrs Phipps
Afternoon teas	Room 14, 16, 4, 10, 17, 21, 22
Dinners	,, 2, 3, 7, 8, 16, 17, 21, 22
Coffees	,, 14, 16, 4, 10
Telephones	,, 2 (50p), 7 (£1.00), 21 (50p)
Chance dinners	12 @ £6.00

Write up the visitors' ledger and the monthly summary sheet and carry balance forward to the second day.

Second day

Bring forward balances from previous day.

Early morning teas	Rooms 3, 7, 16, 21, 22
Newspapers	,, 1 (£1), 7 (50p), 8 (50p), 16 (£1), 17 (50p), 21 (£1)
Breakfast	All visitors
Departures a.m.	Room 1 — Mr J. Derbyshire, account paid in cash and closed
	Room 14 — Capt. & Mrs J. Wright, account paid in cash and closed
Morning coffees	Rooms 2, 3, 7, 16, 17, 21, 22
Arrivals a.m.	Room 5 — Mr F. Sandringham

,, 6 — Mr D. Chalk
,, 13 — Mjr. & Mrs K. Jones and son
,,
,,

11 a.m. Taxi	Mrs Spencer — 4.00
Flowers	Room 7 — £7.50
Luncheons	Rooms 2, 3, 7, 8, 16, 22
Chance luncheons	18 @ £4.00
Arrivals p.m.	Room 9 — Miss Thompson
	,, 11 — Col. L. S. Ward
	,, 18 — Mr & Mrs L. Hopkins
3 p.m. Theatre tickets	Room 21 — £8.00
Afternoon teas	Rooms 8, 10, 14, 17, 18
Chance afternoon teas	12 @ £2.00
Dinners	Rooms 2, 3, 7, 10, 17, 18, 21 (1 only)
Telegrams	,, 17 (£3.50), 21 (£6.50)
Cigarettes	,, 3 (£2.00), 16 (£3.00)
Coffees	,, 8, 16, 17

Write up visitors' ledger and the monthly summary sheet and carry the balance forward to the third day.

Third day

Bring forward balances from previous day.

Early morning teas	Rooms 3, 5, 7, 13 (2 only), 16, 21, 22
Newspapers	,, 4 (50p), 7 (50p), 8 (50p), 11 (£1), 21 (£1)
Morning coffees	,, 2, 3, 13, 17, 21, 22
Departures a.m.	— Miss L. Smith, account paid in cash and closed
	— Miss Thompson, account paid in cash and closed
	— Rev. J. Smart, account closed and balance transferred to ledger
	— Mr S. Stanford, account closed and balance transferred to ledger
Arrivals a.m.	Room 15 — Mr & Mrs Jennings
Luncheons	,, 15 plus (£7.50 wine), 3 (plus £3.00 sherry), 21 (plus £8.50 cigars), 13 (2 only)
Chance luncheons	12 @ £4.00, also wines £22.50, spirits £11.00, cigarettes £5.00
Afternoon teas	Rooms 6, 17
Chance afternoon teas	18 @ £2.00
Departures p.m.	Room vacated 3, account paid in cash
Telephones	Mr Jennings 50p, Col. S, Ward £2.50
C.O.D. parcel	Mjr. Jones £2.00
Dinners	Rooms 5, 13, 18 (plus £6.00 wine)
Chance dinners	12 @ £6.00, also spirits £7.00
Private party	Mr Samuel Johnson:
	10 dinners @ £6.00, liquors £24.00, cigarettes £9.00, account transferred to ledger

Write up the visitors' ledger and the monthly summary sheet.

8 The Lowcliffe Hotel maintains personal accounts for certain non-residents frequenting its restaurant.

The following were the balances owing from non-residents on 1st January, 19...

Col. S. Merrick	£100
V. S. May & Co.	220
E. M. Browne, Esq.	130
Essex Plastics Ltd	320
Winter Sports Ltd	150

The following transactions took place with the above customers during the month of January.

January	1	Credit sales: V. C. May & Co.	£30
		Essex Plastics Ltd	40
		Col. S. Merrick	80
		Winter Sports Ltd	130
,,	8	Credit sales: E. M. Browne, Esq.	40
		Winter Sports Ltd	90
		V. S. May & Co.	50
,,	13	Cheques received from Essex Plastics Ltd	320
		Col. S. Merrick	100
		E. M. Browne, Esq.	130
,,	19	Credit sales: V. S. May & Co.	140
		Col. S. Merrick	20
		Essex Plastics Ltd	100
,,	21	Cheque from E. M. Browne, Esq. returned by bank, marked R/D	
,,	22	Credit sales: V. S. May & Co.	40
		Col. S. Merrick	50
		Essex Plastics Ltd	60
,,	28	Received cheque from V. S. May & Co.	220
,,	31	E. M. Browne, Esq. paid cash	130
,,	31	Credit sales: Winter Sports Ltd	90
		Essex Plastics Ltd	110
		V. S. May & Co.	80

You are required to: (a) write up the restaurant sales book and the cash book of the hotel; (b) post to ledger; and (c) balance all customers' accounts as at 31st January, 19...

CHAPTER 5

Accounting for other matters

The journal

An important rule of book-keeping is that all entries relating to transactions should be recorded in subsidiary books prior to being posted to the ledger. Thus purchase invoices are entered in the purchases day book and then posted to the ledger. Similarly, copies of restaurant bills signed by customers are entered in the restaurant sales book and then posted to the sales account and the accounts of the customers concerned.

There are, however, several classes of transaction which cannot be entered in any of the subsidiary books already dealt with; all such transactions are entered in what is variously described as the journal, the general journal or the journal proper.

Let us assume that a hotel buys kitchen equipment on credit for £10 000. This, not being intended for resale, does not constitute the hotel's 'purchases' and cannot, therefore, be entered in the hotel's purchases day book. Consequently, a journal entry must be made. This is shown in Figure 53.

		JOURNAL					26
19.. May	1	Kitchen Equipment A/c Dr.	L 94	10,000	00		
		X.Y.Z. Co. Ltd.	L 23			10,000	00
		Being sundry items of equipment purchased per invoice K.S. 6794					

Figure 53

Note: (1) The account to be debited is entered first. (2) Every entry in the journal is followed by a brief explanation of the transaction. This is known as the *narration* and usually starts with the word 'being'.

When the entry in the journal has been made, it is possible to post the transaction to the ledger. Following the example, double entry in the ledger would be completed as shown in Figure 54.

Kitchen Equipment A/c — 94

Date		Particulars	Fo.	£	p	Date		Particulars	Fo.	£	p
19.. May	1	X.Y.Z. Co. Ltd.	J 26	10,000	00						

X.Y.Z. Co. Ltd. — 23

Date		Particulars	Fo.	£	p	Date		Particulars	Fo.	£	p
						19.. May	1	Kitchen Equip.	J 26	10,000	00

Figure 54

As already mentioned, the journal is used for several types of transaction. Let us, therefore, now examine the main uses of the journal.

Journal opening entries

When, for one reason or another, a new set of books is being opened, the opening balances are journalized prior to being posted to the ledger.

Naturally, the occasions when journal opening entries are required are very infrequent. They are *not* necessary at the beginning of each accounting period, because the balances from the previous period are brought down.

Sometimes a business is purchased as a 'going concern' when, at the commencement of the new business, there are already in existence numerous assets and liabilities. A journal opening entry is then useful in that it enables one to calculate the capital of the new business easily and accurately before any ledger entries are made.

Example

On 1st January, 19.., V. Bright commenced in business as a guest house proprietor with the following assets and liabilities:

Freehold premises	£100 000
Furniture and equipment	20 000
China and cutlery	2 500
Food stocks	500
Cash at bank	3 000
Creditors: A.B.C. Ltd	500
D.E.F. Ltd	500

The necessary journal opening entries are made and Mr Bright's capital ascertained as follows (Figure 55).

Date	Fo.	Particulars		Dr. £		Cr. £	
19..							
Jan.	1	Freehold Premises	Dr.	100,000	00		
		Furniture and Equipment	"	20,000	00		
		China and Cutlery	"	2,500	00		
		Food Stocks	"	500	00		
		Cash at Bank	"	3,000	00		
		Creditors: A.B.C. Ltd.				500	00
		D.E.F. Ltd.				500	00
		Capital				125,000	00
				126,000	00	126,000	00
		Being assets and liabilities as at this date.					

Figure 55

Credit purchase/ sale of assets The credit purchase of an asset has already been illustrated, and a further example need not, therefore, be given. Sometimes circumstances arise which necessitate the sale of an asset e.g. when the asset is being replaced by a new one.

Example On 19th March, 19.., a hotel's restaurant furniture, standing in the books at £5 000 is sold on credit to Popular Catering Ltd. The entry necessary in the journal is shown in Figure 56.

Date	Fo.	Particulars		Dr. £		Cr. £	
19..							
Mar.	19	Popular Catering Ltd.	Dr.	5,000	00		
		Restaurant Furniture				5,000	00
		Being sale of restaurant furniture per Agreement dated.....					

Figure 56

Transfers between ledger accounts During the course of an accounting period, and particularly at the end of it, various transfers become necessary between ledger accounts. The need for such transfers may arise for a variety of reasons, but all such transfers must be journalized before any entries are made in the ledger.

Thus, during the accounting period it may be decided to write off a debt owing from a customer to a bad debts account. At the end of the accounting period it is necessary to transfer purchases, sales, etc., to the trading account, and all expenses and gains to the profit and loss account. All such transfers (known as 'closing entries') should be journalized.

Example On the 30th June, 19.., it is decided to write off the following debts due from customers:

N. O. Penny	£100
V. E. Lusiff	£50

The necessary journal entry is shown in Figure 57.

19.. June	30	Bad Debts A/c Dr.		150	00		
		N. O. Penny				100	00
		V. E. Lusiff				50	00
		Being amounts written off.					

Figure 57

Rectification of errors When errors have been made in the entering of accounts, it is wrong to correct the errors by crossing out the wrong entries and inserting new ones. The correct procedure is to insert new, additional entries offsetting and rectifying the wrong entries. Three examples are given below to make this clear.

Example 1 On 1st May, 19.., repairs to furniture of £500 were debited to furniture account.

This is obviously incorrect as the furniture account now shows a greater debit balance which would suggest that the business has more furniture. To correct this error it is necessary to credit the furniture account (thus restoring the previous balance) and debit the repairs to furniture account to show that an expense has been incurred by the business.

Example 2 On 2nd May, 19.., a cheque for £1 000, drawn in favour of and sent to W. A. Smith, was debited in error to W. Smith & Co. Ltd.

In order to correct this error it is necessary to debit the recipient of the cheque, W. A. Smith, and credit the account which was debited incorrectly, W. Smith & Co. Ltd.

Example 3 On 31st May, 19.., the monthly total of the purchases day book was posted to the purchases account as £10 500 instead of £15 000.

In this particular case only one entry is necessary to correct the error; £4 500 more must be debited in the purchases account.

The journal entries necessary to correct the above errors would appear as shown in Figure 58.

19..						
May	1	Repairs to Furniture A/c Dr.	500	00		
		Furniture A/c			500	00
		Being amount wrongly debited to Furniture A/c				
"	2	W. A. Smith Dr.	1,000	00		
		W. Smith & Co. Ltd.			1,000	00
		Being cheque wrongly debited to W. Smith and Co. Ltd.				
"	31	Purchases A/c Dr.	4,500	00		
		....			4,500	00
		Being total on page...... in Purchases Day Book £15,000 debited in Purchase A/c as £10,500				

Figure 58

Other uses of the journal

In addition to the four main uses of the journal we have already described, there are several others. The journal is used in partnerships on occasions such as the admission of a new partner and on the dissolution of the partnership. In limited companies it is used in connection with the issue of shares and debentures. In all types of business unit, the journal is used as a subsidiary book for transactions which cannot be suitably entered in any other subsidiary book.

Suspense account

Sometimes the trial balance may indicate that there is an error in the books, but it may be difficult to locate it without detailed search which may take a long time. In order to be able to proceed with the work a suspense account may be opened and debited or credited with the amount necessary to balance the trial balance. This may be necessary at the end of an accounting period when it is desired to prepare the trading and profit and loss account and the balance sheet of the business.

When the mistake is discovered, an entry is made in the journal which, when posted to the suspense account and the other accounts concerned, eliminates the balance on the suspense account and corrects the errors made.

Example

On 31st January, 19.., the trial balance of the City Hotel showed the credit side to be £800 greater than the debit. The 'difference' in the trial balance was transferred to a suspense account as shown in Figure 59.

Suspense A/c

19.. Jan.	31	Difference in Books		800	00					

Figure 59

On 17th February, 19.., it is found that::

(a) the monthly total of the restaurant sales book was posted to the sales account as £28 400 instead of £24 600, and

(b) a cheque for £3 000 received from the '64 Dining Club was debited in the cash book but was not posted to the club's account.

In order to correct the above errors and to eliminate the balance of the suspense account, it is necessary:

(1) to debit the difference between £28 400 and £24 600 (i.e. £3 800) in the sales account and credit it in the suspense account; and

(2) to debit the amount received from the '64 Dining Club in the suspense account and credit it in the club's account.

The three ledger accounts concerned are shown in Figure 60 as they would appear after the rectification of the errors.

The relevant journal entries are shown in Figure 61.

Suspense A/c

19.. Jan.	31	Difference in Books		800	00	19.. Feb.	17	Sales A/c		3,800	00
Feb.	17	The '64 Dining Club		3,000	00						
				3800	00					3,800	00

The '64 Dining Club

						19.. Feb.	17	Suspense A/c		3,000	00

Sales A/c

19.. Feb.	17	Suspense A/c		3,800	00						

Figure 60

Date		Particulars		Dr.	Cr.
19..					
Jan.	31	Suspense A/c Dr.		800 00	
		....			800 00
		Being difference in books			
Feb.	17	Sales A/c Dr.		3,800 00	
		Suspense A/c			3,800 00
		Being correction of monthly credit sales - difference between £28,400 and £24,600			
"	17	Suspense A/c Dr.		3,000 00	
		The '64 Dining Club			3,000 00
		Being cheque received, not posted to customer's account.			

Figure 61

The trial balance

The objects and methods of extracting a trial balance were explained briefly in Chapter 1. It will be convenient, at this stage, to refer to the trial balance again and consider it in more detail.

The trial balance may be defined as a list (or schedule) of balances, both debit and credit, extracted from ledger accounts including the cash book and the petty cash book.

When a system of double entry is used, the total of the debit entries must be equal to the total of the credit entries in the ledger. As a result, provided that double entry has been properly completed in respect of each transaction, the two sides of the trial balance must necessarily be equal.

It must be remembered, however, that the trial balance is proof only of the arithmetical accuracy of the ledger entries. There are certain types of error that a trial balance will not disclose.

Omission of entries

If both the debit and the credit entry of a transaction are omitted, the trial balance will not be affected and the failure to enter the transaction will not be revealed.

Compensating errors

These are two or more errors which cancel out. When one amount is, say, overdebited with £50 and another overcredited with the same amount, the agreement of the trial balance will not be affected though there are two errors in the books. In the illustration on the suspense account given above, if the cheque from the '64 Dining Club amounted to £3 800, the trial balance of the hotel at the end of January would have agreed and the existence of the two errors would not have been disclosed.

Misposting of accounts This error occurs when one of the entries is posted on the right side of the ledger but in the wrong account, e.g. when a cheque is paid to W. M. Brown & Co. and is debited in error to the account of Wm. Brown & Co. Ltd.

Errors of principle This error occurs when, though double entry is completed, the posting is not in accordance with some accounting principle, e.g. when china is purchased by a hotel and this is debited in the purchases account. China is not 'purchases' in a hotel since it is not purchased for resale to customers.

Value added tax (VAT)

Value added tax was introduced in the U.K. on 1st April, 1973. The initial rate of VAT was, apart from the zero rate, 10 per cent, but this has changed several times in recent years. VAT is payable to Customs and Excise by taxable persons, which includes individuals, partnerships and limited companies. "Taxable persons" usually means the same as "registered persons", but it also includes any person who ought to be registered but has not taken the necessary steps to secure registration.

The final burden of the tax is borne by the customer, and consequently, VAT is not an operating cost. From the tax collected from its customers (output tax) a business will deduct the tax it has paid on its own purchases (input tax) and remit the difference to Customs and Excise.

Zero rating and exemptions Both zero rating and exemption mean that no output tax is chargeable on sales. There are, however, two important differences:

(a) Zero-rated supplies are technically taxable (though the rate of tax is nil) and the VAT charged on inputs relating to them can be reclaimed like other input tax. Exempt supplies, on the other hand, are outside VAT and the input cannot be deducted or reclaimed.

(b) A person who makes zero-rated supplies will generally be registered with Customs and Excise and make VAT returns. A person who makes only exempt supplies does not have to register or make returns.

VAT: basic records Every time a business buys goods or services (other than those zero-rated or exempted) it is charged VAT. When, in turn, the business sells its goods or services to its customers, it also charges VAT.

At intervals—normally every three months—the business will add up all its input tax (i.e. tax paid to its suppliers) and all the output tax (charged to its customers). The difference is then remitted to Customs and Excise. Where the total of the output tax is less than the total of the input tax, the difference is the amount owing to the business from Customs and Excise.

It will be appreciated that the introduction of VAT must have some effect on the basic accounting records. In order to be able to calculate the totals of input and output it is necessary to design accounting records which make this information readily available. The illustrations which follow assume, for convenience, that VAT is charged at the rate of 10 per cent.

Restaurant Sales Book

Date	Customer	F	Total	Food	Bev.	VAT
May 1	Mr. J. Manning	SL 10	13.20	10.00	2.00	1.20
" 2	Mr. & Mrs B. Grace	SL 16	27.50	20.00	5.00	2.50
" 3	Capt. R. S. Elme	SL 24	11.00	8.00	2.00	1.00
	etc					
	Totals		1,430.00	1,000.00	300.00	130.00

Figure 62

Figure 62 shows an example of the type of record that may be used to record particulars of VAT output. Double entry at the end of May would be completed as follows:

(a) All food and beverages sold plus the output tax would be debited in the accounts of the guests.

(b) The totals of food sales and beverage sales would be credited in the appropriate accounts in the ledger.

(c) The monthly total of VAT collected from the customers would be credited to the Customs and Excise account.

Similar procedures would have to be applied in respect of any supplies purchased by the business which are chargeable to VAT. Any food purchased is zero-rated but alcoholic beverages are subject to VAT. The purchases day book will, therefore, have to provide for the easy recording of all the relevant VAT inputs. An example, based on VAT at 10 per cent, is shown in Figure 63.

Purchases Day Book

Date	Supplier	F	Total	Food	Bev.	VAT
May 1	Surrey Grocers Ltd	BL 44	50.00	50.00		
" 2	Spanish Wine Co	BL 76	88.00		80.00	8.00
" 3	Fine Fish Ltd.		90.00	90.00		
	etc					
			720.00	500.00	200.00	20.00

Figure 63

From the purchases day book, the totals would be posted as follows.

(a) The total of food and beverages plus the VAT input would be credited to the accounts of the suppliers.

(b) The totals of food and beverage purchases would be debited in the appropriate accounts in the ledger.

(c) The monthly total of VAT paid to the suppliers would be debited to the Customs and Excise account.

Customs & Excise A/c

May	31	Purchases Day Bk		20	00	May	31	Rest. Sales Book	130	00

Figure 64

Figure 64 shows how the monthly totals of VAT would be transferred to the Customs and Excise account. Students should remember that, in addition to any VAT paid on alcoholic beverages, input tax will be paid on other supplies such as china, cutlery, stationery, telephone, repairs to furniture and equipment, etc. All such VAT input payments should be recorded in an appropriately designed subsidiary book to enable a monthly transfer to the Customs and Excise account.

Hotels and similar establishments Hotels, boarding houses, motels, youth hostels and bed and breakfast establishments are, for VAT purposes, in the same category. VAT is chargeable at the full current rate on the full amount payable for the provision of accommodation, meals and services. For any period which follows the first four weeks of stay the value of the supply of accommodation and facilities is reduced for VAT purposes. The reduction takes the form of calculating VAT only on that part of the total charge (exclusive of VAT) which represents the provision of facilities other than the right to occupy the room; and that part is taken to be not less than 20 per cent of the amount payable for the accommodation and facilities. 'Facilities' for this purpose include cleaning, bed-making, entertainment, floral decorations, room service, television, radio and non-personal laundry.

Catering establishments VAT is chargeable at the current standard rate on the full amount payable for the food and beverages supplied in the course of catering. For this purpose 'catering' includes restaurants, cafes, industrial canteens, office canteens, etc., whether operated by the business itself or by an outside catering contractor. Also included for this purpose are catering establishments at railway stations, street stalls, beach cafés, etc. Excluded for this purpose—and hence zero-rated—are 'take-away' operations, e.g. the supply of fish and chips, Chinese food, etc.

Problems

1 Write short notes on the uses of the journal.

2 On 1st July, 19.., J. Jones started in business as a restaurateur. His assets and liabilities were:

Premises	£116 500
Kitchen plant	24 500
Restaurant furniture	12 300
Glass and china	3 200
Stock of provisions	1 100
Cash at bank	10 200
Cash in hand	200
Creditors	4 300

You are required to make the necessary journal opening entry and ascertain his capital.

3 The following balances were extracted from the books of a restaurant at 31st December, 19..:

Purchases	£39 550
Sales	110 540
Stock of provisions	4 050
Debtors	9 940
Rent and rates	6 000
Wages and salaries	26 150
Light and heat	3 050
Repairs and renewals	2 010
Furniture	12 000
Creditors	5 000
Kitchen equipment	6 000
Plate and china	4 830
Cash at bank	19 670
Cash in hand	2 290
Leasehold premises	80 000
Capital	

You are required to:
(a) arrange the above balances in trial balance form;

(b) calculate the capital of the restaurant.

4 Before extracting his trial balance, the book-keeper made the following errors:

(a) transferred monthly total of discounts received, £250, to the debit side of the discounts received account;

(b) credited two credit notes amounting to £120 to suppliers' accounts;

(c) debited the cost of repairs to furniture, £480, to the furniture account;

(d) undercast the purchases day book by £1 000;

(e) debited H. P. Smith Ltd with a payment of £360 made to H. Smith & Sons.

State by how much the trial balance was out of balance by reason of each error and calculate the total difference between the trial balance totals.

5 By means of journal entries show how you would deal with the following:

May 1st	Received letter from A. Supplier stating that he cannot allow the £7 cash discount you had deducted when paying his account.
May 2nd	Cash purchases, £24, debited in error to glass and china account.
May 31st	Monthly total of restaurant sales book overcast by £300.

6 When preparing a trial balance of a restaurant, it is found that the totals differ. On checking the books, the following errors are found:

(a) The restaurant sales book has been undercast by £200.

(b) Bank charges amounting to £15 have been entered in the cash book but not posted to the ledger.

(c) A cheque for £50 paid to H.C.I. Supplies Ltd has been posted to the account of H. & C. Supplies Co.

The difference in the trial balance drawn up previously had been placed in a suspense account. What was the balance in the suspense account?

7 George Bacon is in business as a restaurateur. On 1st January, 19.., he decided to put his books on a double entry basis. His position then was:

Leasehold premises		£32 500
Stock of provisions		1 200
Loan from A. Penny		10 000
China and cutlery		1 150
Restaurant furniture		4 150
Debtors:	A. G. Jones	200
	G. M. Browne	150
Creditors:	A.B.C. Co. Ltd	300
	Wholesalers Ltd	800
Cash at bank		6 800
Cash in hand		200

You are required to set out the journal entry required for the opening of the books.

8 Jack Parker is in business as a café proprietor. On 1st January, 19.., he decided to put his books on a double entry basis. His assets and liabilities then were:

Freehold premises		£89 400
Furniture		5 300
Kitchen equipment		8 100
Cutlery and utensils		1 900
Creditors:	X.Y.Z. Co. Ltd	500
	J. B. Brown & Co.	200
Cash at bank		4 300
Stock of provisions		900

Set out the journal entry required to open Parker's books; open the necessary accounts and enter balances.

His transactions in January were:

January	1	Purchased provisions, paid by cheque	£1 000
,,	5	Purchased additional kitchen equipment on credit from Equipment Suppliers Ltd	2 000
,,	9	Banked cash sales	1 400
,,	12	Paid wages by cheque	450
,,	16	Paid Equipment Suppliers Ltd by cheque	500
,,	18	Paid amount due to J. B. Brown & Co.	
,,	20	Purchased provisions on credit from:	
		X.Y.Z. Co. Ltd	300
		J. B. Brown & Co.	400
,,	22	Banked cash sales	1 500
,,	24	Sold old furniture worth £500 on credit to the New Catering Co.	
,,	24	Purchased new furniture on credit from Furniture Dealers Ltd	4 000
,,	27	Purchased provisions on credit from:	
		J. B. Brown & Co.	200
		X.Y.Z. Co. Ltd	500
,,	29	Paid wages by cheque	450
,,	31	Banked cash sales	1 600

You are required to write up Parker's books (including the appropriate subsidiary books) in respect of January and extract his trial balance as at the end of the month.

9 Describe the operation of value added tax and explain why it is not a business expense.

10 Give an outline of the accounting records necessary for the recording of VAT.

11 Explain how zero-rating differs from exemption.

CHAPTER 6

Organization of accounts

Having considered all the basic accounting records it is now proposed to examine what may be described as the organization of accounts. The first considerations are the component parts of a full set of books, the relationships that exist between the component parts, and some related practical problems.

Divisions of the ledger

Though we often speak of *the* ledger, in practice this important book of account is divided into a number of separate sections. The most important object of division of the ledger into sections is to enable a number of clerks to work on the books simultaneously.

The precise division of the ledger is primarily a matter of convenience, and in practice the number of the divisions will vary from two (in smaller businesses) to possibly as many as ten, fifteen, or even more (in large businesses). Most medium-sized businesses tend to divide their ledgers into three sections, as shown in Figure 65.

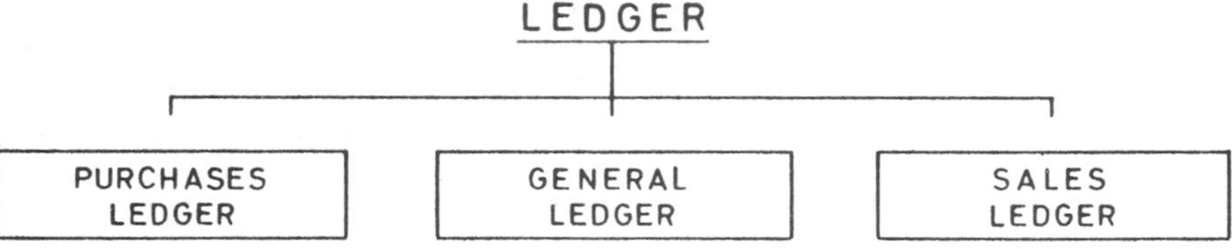

Figure 65

Purchases ledger

This ledger is also known as the bought ledger or the creditors' ledger, and contains the personal accounts of the suppliers (or creditors) of the business. It should be pointed out that the purchases account, though closely linked with this ledger, is kept in the general ledger dealt with below.

Whilst in the majority of hotel and catering establishments one purchases ledger is kept, there are some which divide it into several sub-sections. Thus a very large hotel could divide its purchases ledger into the following sub-sections: food, drink, tobaccos and sundries, and non-consumable supplies.

Each sub-section would then contain a distinct group of suppliers' accounts and might be in the charge of a separate clerk.

Sales ledger

This is also known as the sold ledger or the debtors' ledger and contains the personal accounts of the customers (or debtors) of the business. Again, it is pointed out that the sales account is not kept in this ledger but in the general ledger.

The meaning and nature of the 'sales ledger' must now be explained in relation to hotel and catering establishments. In such establishments the term sales ledger could be applied to two different sets of personal accounts.

It could be applied to the hotel visitors' ledger. This is strictly a sales ledger, in that it contains the personal accounts of the visitors. In practice, however, the visitors' ledger is not usually referred to as a sales ledger but as the visitors' ledger or the tabular ledger.

It could also be applied to the ledger containing the personal accounts of non-residents, any unpaid accounts transferred from the visitors' ledger and, possibly, advance deposits received from intending visitors. This ledger is usually referred to as the sales ledger, though there are many who describe it as the personal ledger. The latter is not an accurate description of this ledger, but is mentioned here in order to clarify the terminology in current use.

Most large hotels keep the two ledgers mentioned above. Some of the largest hotels might well sub-divide their sales ledger into two or three appropriate sections, such as non-residents, banqueting, transfers from H.V.L., etc., though it is not suggested that each such section would necessarily be looked after by a separate clerk.

Although many non-residential catering establishments maintain a sales ledger, it seems that the majority of them sell on a cash basis only and, in consequence, do not need personal accounts for their customers.

General ledger

Whilst the purchases and sales ledgers contain personal accounts, the general ledger contains impersonal accounts, i.e. accounts other than those of suppliers and customers. Impersonal accounts are of two kinds:

(1) Nominal accounts—those recording gains and losses (or income and expenditure), e.g. wages account, rent account, purchases account, discount received account.
(2) Real accounts—those may also be described as property accounts, e.g. premises account, kitchen plant account, restaurant furniture account.

In many businesses the general ledger is sub-divided into two sections:

(1) Nominal ledger—this contains all the nominal accounts of the business.
(2) Private ledger—this contains all property (real) accounts as well as accounts of a confidential nature, such as capital account, proprietor's salary account, profit and loss account.

Subsidiary books

In addition to the ledger or ledgers, a business will keep a number of subsidiary books. These are also described as day books, journals, books of prime entry, and books of original entry. The most important objects of subsidiary books are:

(1) To relieve the ledger of unnecessary detail. Thus, the periodical totals from the purchases day book are posted to the purchases account, which considerably reduces the number of entries in that account. Similarly, the periodical analysed totals from the petty cash book are posted to the respective accounts in the ledger, which, again, results in a considerable reduction of entries in the accounts concerned.
(2) To classify transactions and enable periodical totals to be posted to appropriate accounts in the ledger. To this end separate subsidiary books are kept for different kinds of transaction. There are the purchases day book for credit purchases and the purchases returns book for purchases returns. Also, there are analysis columns in the petty cash book for the different kinds of petty cash expenditure. As a result, it is possible to record different kinds of transactions in separate books. Once the subsidiary books have been written up, their totals (weekly, monthly) are available for posting to ledger accounts.

The most important subsidiary books in common use are listed below:

(1) Purchases day book
(2) Purchases returns book
(3) Sales day book
(4) Sales returns book
(5) Wages book
(6) Journal
(7) Cash book
(8) Petty cash book

Whilst the distinction between ledger accounts and subsidiary books is quite clear, there are several accounting records the nature of which needs a more detailed explanation.

The cash book, as indicated above, is a subsidiary book. Yet, at the same time, it is also part of the ledger—though usually kept as a separate book. As a result, any transaction entered in the cash book (i.e. cash transaction) must not be entered in any other subsidiary book. Thus cash purchases are not entered in the purchases day book, nor is the purchase of assets for cash journalized. All entries made in the cash book count for double entry purposes.

The petty cash book is in the same category. It is both a subsidiary book and a ledger account.

The hotel visitors' ledger is, again, a ledger and a subsidiary book. It is a ledger because it contains the personal accounts of hotel visitors; it is a subsidiary book because it collects similar transactions (apartments, breakfasts, luncheons, dinners, telephone, and other charges) together and enables a daily total of each such group of transactions to be posted, *via* the monthly summary sheet, to the appropriate nominal accounts in the ledger. In the case of the vertical type of hotel visitors' ledger, the vertical columns are the ledger accounts whilst the horizontal columns are in the nature of subsidiary books.

Finally, the monthly summary sheet is another accounting record the nature of which is rather difficult to define. It is not a subsidiary book, in that it is not a record of individual transactions but one of daily totals, nor is it a set of ledger accounts. It is a statistical summary of sales, half-way between a subsidiary book and a ledger.

Subsidiary books and double entry

At this point, it is necessary to state briefly the following important book-keeping rule. *Every transaction must be entered in a subsidiary book before being posted to the ledger.*

The above rule will have already been observed from the illustrations given in the previous chapters. Thus purchase invoices are entered in a purchases day book before being posted to the purchases account and the accounts of suppliers in the bought ledger.

Hence the book-keeping process is a two-stage process: stage one is the entries in a subsidiary book, and stage two is the ledger postings. Double entry in respect of all transactions is completed in the ledger and no entries in subsidiary books count for double entry purposes. The student's attention is, however, drawn to the exceptional position of the cash book and the petty cash book as explained above.

Sources of entries

In practice it will be found that every entry made in the books of a business is supported by a document, e.g. an invoice, credit note, or petty cash voucher. All such documents are referred to as 'sources of entries' or 'documentary evidence', and are necessary for two reasons:

(1) To provide the book-keeper with detailed information regarding the transactions of the business. Clearly, in the absence of such information it would be extremely difficult for him to maintain the books.

(2) To provide the necessary evidence that the books constitute a true record of the transactions that have taken place. As a result, it is possible to support each entry in the books by some document and, in this way, prove that the books are a true expression of the transactions of the business.

It may so happen that no actual documentary evidence is available, in which case a substitute document must be provided. For instance, when a purchase invoice is mislaid and cannot be found, it is possible to ask the supplier concerned to issue a duplicate invoice. When an amount is paid out of petty cash and no voucher can practicably be obtained for it (e.g. in respect of gratuities to delivery men, taxi fares, etc.) an internal petty cash voucher must be raised and signed by some responsible person.

The following is a list of the main source of entries used for books of account:

Purchase day book:		suppliers' invoices.
Purchases returns book:		suppliers' credit notes.
Sales day book:		copies of bills signed by customers and copies of accounts sent to banqueting debtors.
Sales returns book:		copies of credit notes sent to customers; this book is not often used in hotel and catering establishments.
Wages book:		time sheets, clock cards, and similar records.
Journal:		various documents according to the nature of transaction, e.g. invoices in respect of assets purchased on credit.
Cash book:	Dr.	in respect of cheques received, copies of receipts issued to customers; in respect of cash sales, till rolls; in respect of all amounts banked, the paying-in book; also bank statement in respect of amounts credited by the bank.
	Cr.	cheque counterfoils or copies of cheques; suppliers' accounts and statements in respect of all payments made; also the bank statement in respect of amounts debited by the bank such as bank charges, bank interest.
Petty cash book:	Dr.	cheque counterfoils in respect of any floats received by petty cashier.
	Cr.	petty cash vouchers, external and internal.
Visitors' ledger:	Dr.	departmental vouchers (see Chapter 4) 'sources of charges'.
	Cr.	copies of receipts issued in respect of accounts settled; also monthly allowances sheet or allowances book in respect of allowances to guests.

It will be appreciated that, as there is some documentary evidence in respect of each entry in the books, it is possible to trace each transaction from the ledger posting to the original documentary evidence and *vice versa*. The following illustration shows the path of a transaction in respect of a credit purchase:

Order placed to supplier	**Order form**
Goods received by hotel	**Delivery note**
Charge made by supplier	**Invoice**
Purchase recorded by hotel — stage I	**Purchases day book**
,, ,, ,, ,, — stage II	Dr. purchases account Cr. supplier's account

Ledger folios

Reference has already been made to what are known as ledger folios. A folio is a page of a ledger or subsidiary book. Folio numbers are the page numbers of the ledger or subsidiary books.

In practical book-keeping, every time an entry is made a cross-reference is provided in the folio column to the corresponding entry in some other book. This method of cross-referencing has two advantages. In respect of each entry there is an immediate cross-reference to a corresponding entry in some other book, and the insertion of ledger folios provides a proof that double entry has been completed.

Two illustrations are now given to make the foregoing clear.

Example I, cash transactions

A cash transaction is entered on one side of the cash book and on the opposite side of a ledger account (Figure 66). The page number of the ledger account concerned is shown in the folio column of the cash book; the page number of the cash book is shown in the folio column of the ledger account.

				Cash Book							46
19..						19..					
Jan.	1	Sales	GL/37	3,000	00	Jan.	2	Wages	GL/16	1,000	00
				Wages A/c							16
19..											
Jan.	2	Cash	CB/46	1,000	00						
				Sales A/c							37
						19..					
						Jan.	1	Cash	CB/46	3,000	00

Figure 66

Example 2, credit transactions

Most credit transactions occur in respect of the purchases and sales of a business. As already explained, all such credit transactions are recorded in a subsidiary book prior to being posted to the ledger (Figures 67 and 68).

		Purchases Day Book		51	
19.. Jan.	1	Supplier A	BL/24	2,000	00
"	8	" B	BL/16	1,000	00
"	23	" A	BL/24	500	00
"	29	" B	BL/16	1,500	00
"	31	Transferred to Purchases A/c	GL/61	5,000	00

Figure 67

Purchases A/c — 61

19.. Jan.	31	Sundries	PB/51	5,000	00					

Supplier A — 24

						19.. JAN.	1	Purchases	PB/51	2,000	00
						"	23	—do—	PB/51	500	00

Supplier B — 16

						19.. Jan.	8	Purchases	PB/51	1,000	00
						"	29	—do—	PB/51	1,500	00

Figure 68

The page number of the ledger accounts concerned is shown in the folio columns of the subsidiary books; the page number of the appropriate subsidiary book is shown in the ledger accounts.

The abbreviations G.L., B.L., C.B., and P.B. are in common use and refer to the general ledger, bought ledger, cash book and purchases day book respectively.

As explained in Chapter 5, there are certain transactions which are passed through the journal. All such transactions are folioed in the same manner as those shown in Example 2.

Control accounts

Another important feature of practical book-keeping is the maintenance of what are known as 'control accounts'. A control account is a device which makes a ledger 'self-balancing' by enabling a clerk to balance a section of the accounts (usually bought ledger or sales ledger) independently of the other sections.

In most businesses, including hotel and catering, it will be found that the largest group of accounts consists of personal accounts of suppliers and customers. It will be appreciated that, whilst the number of nominal and real accounts in a medium-sized business is not likely to exceed about fifty, the number of personal accounts may well run into hundreds.

When, at the end of an accounting period, a total trial balance is extracted and fails to balance, it is impossible in the absence of control accounts to determine immediately in which section of the ledger the errors have arisen. It is, therefore, often necessary to check all the accounts—real, nominal and personal: a process that may take several days.

A control account, by making a ledger self-balancing, enables the clerk concerned to determine at the end of each period whether or not his section of the ledger balances and, in this way, not only helps in the location of errors but reduces considerably the time spent by clerks on periodical checking of accounts and 'looking for errors'.

In order to understand the operation of control accounts, the following two points must be clearly appreciated.

(1) A control account is a *total account* and shows in summary from the detailed entries made in a particular ledger.

(2) A control account, though described as an account, is a *memorandum account*. Any entries made in a control account do not, therefore, count for double entry purposes. As a result, it does not really matter whether the entries are made in a control account on the same side as in the ledger controlled by it or whether such entries are reversed. In practice, when the control account is kept in the ledger concerned, the entries in the control account are usually reversed. This enables the clerk to extract what is known as a 'sectional trial balance'. When the control account is kept in another ledger (usually the general ledger), any entries made in it are usually kept on the same side as in the ledger concerned.

The following example illustrates the compilation of a control account by reference to the accounts of suppliers.

Example On 1st January, 19.., the following balances appeared in the bought ledger of a hotel:

Hotel Supplies Ltd	£1 000
B. Brown & Sons	1 500
Holland Bacon Co.	500
	£3 000

If the hotel's bought ledger control account were kept in the bought ledger then, on the above date, it would appear as shown in Figure 69.

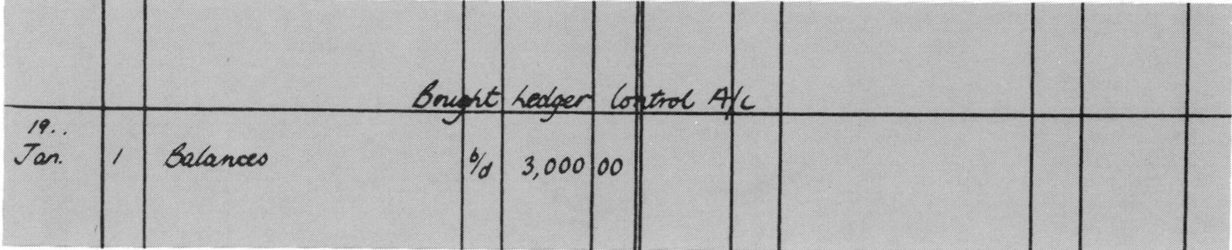

Bought Ledger Control A/c

19..					
Jan.	1	Balances	b/d	3,000	00

Figure 69

In January the hotel makes the following transactions with its suppliers:

Credit purchases

January	2	Hotel Suppliers Ltd	£250.00
,,	4	Holland Bacon Co.	300.00
,,	7	B. Brown & Sons	400.00
,,	11	Holland Bacon Co.	100.00
,,	16	Hotel Suppliers Ltd	350.00
,,	22	B. Brown & Sons	550.00
,,	25	Hotel Suppliers Ltd	600.00
,,	31	Holland Bacon Co.	250.00
		Total	£2 800.00

Purchases returns:

January	6	Hotel Suppliers Ltd	50.00
,,	18	B. Brown & Sons	100.00
,,	30	Holland Bacon Co.	50.00
		Total	£200.00

Payments to suppliers:

			Cheque	Discount	Total
January	20	Hotel Suppliers Ltd	£950.00	£50.00	£1 000.00
,,	20	B. Brown & Sons	1 430.00	70.00	1 500.00
			£2 380.00	£120.00	£2 500.00

The credit purchases and purchases returns are entered in the purchases day book and the purchases returns book and then posted to the ledger in the usual manner. In order to have the necessary information to compile the bought ledger control account, it is necessary to insert an additional bought ledger column in the cash book. Every time a payment to a supplier is made the total of cash and discount is entered in the bought ledger column. A specimen ruling of such a cash book is given in Figure 70.

Cash Book

Date		Detail	Bank	Date		Bought Ledger	Disc. Rec'd	Bank
				19..				
				Jan 20	Hotel Suppliers Ltd.	1,000 00	50 00	950 00
				" 20	B. Brown & Sons	1,500 00	70 00	1,430 00

Figure 70

Assuming that, by the end of January, all the transactions given above have been recorded in the books of the hotel, the personal accounts of the suppliers would appear as shown in Figure 71.

Hotel Suppliers Ltd.

19.. Jan	6	Returns		50 00	19.. Jan	1	Balance	b/d	1,000 00
"	20	Cash		950 00	"	2	Purchases		250 00
"	20	Disc.		50 00	"	16	-do-		350 00
					"	25	-do-		600 00

B. Brown and Sons

19.. Jan.	18	Returns		100 00	19.. Jan.	1	Balance	b/d	1,500 00
"	20	Cash		1,430 00	"	7	Purchases		400 00
"	20	Disc.		70 00	"	22	-do-		550 00

Holland Bacon Co.

19.. Jan.	30	Returns		50 00	19.. Jan.	1	Balance	b/d	500 00
					"	4	Purchases		300 00
					"	11	-do-		100 00
					"	31	-do-		250 00

Figure 71

In order to prove the accuracy of the postings to the above personal accounts, the bought ledger clerk compiles the bought ledger control account, and takes out a sectional trial balance.

He compiles the bought ledger control account by taking the totals of transactions posted to the bought ledger from the relevant subsidiary books. Thus, by referring to the purchases day book, he sees that the total of invoices credited to suppliers in January was £2 800.00. The total of credit notes, cash paid, and discounts received is ascertained by reference to the purchases returns book and the cash book. The completed bought ledger control account is shown in Figure 72.

		Bought Ledger Control A/c									
19..						19..					
Jan	1	Balances	b/d	3,000	00	Jan	31	Returns		200	00
"	31	Purchases		2,800	00	"	31	Cash + Disc.		2,500	00
						"	31	Balances	c/d	3,100	00
				5,800	00					5,800	00
Feb	1	Balances	b/d	3,100	00						

Figure 72

At this stage the clerk knows that, in the absence of any errors in the books, each and every entry in the personal accounts of suppliers is included in one of the totals he has entered in the control account. He, therefore, proceeds to extract a sectional trial balance, as shown below.

Sectional Trial balance. Bought ledger—31st January, 19..

	Dr. £	Cr. £
Hotel Suppliers Ltd		1 150.00
B. Brown & Sons		850.00
Holland Bacon Co.		1 100.00
Bought ledger control account	3 100.00	
	3 100.00	3 100.00

As the accuracy of the postings has been proved, it is safe for the clerk to balance the accounts of suppliers and bring the balances down as at the end of the month.

Some further points

The above procedure also applies to the personal accounts of the customers of a business, i.e. the sales ledger. In fact, many hotels and restaurants maintain sales ledger control accounts and prove the accuracy of the postings to such accounts before sending out monthly statements of account to the customers.

Control accounts may also be applied to accounts other than personal accounts, though in most hotel and catering establishments the scope for such applications is limited.

Finally, it is necessary to mention the treatment of certain non-routine transactions affecting control accounts, e.g. bad debts written off, legal expenses debited to customers, etc. It will be realized that any entries made in respect of such uncommon transactions will not be included in the totals of subsidiary books used to compile control accounts. It is important to ensure, therefore, that all such transactions are posted separately to the appropriate control account. The balance of the control account will not otherwise be equal to the sum total of the individual balances extracted from the ledger concerned.

Problems

1 Explain what is meant by general ledger, nominal ledger, private ledger, bought ledger, and sales ledger.

2 A large hotel keeps its ledger accounts in five separate ledgers: private, nominal, bought, sales, and visitors' ledger. You are required to indicate in which of the above ledgers you would expect to find each of the following accounts: freehold premises; rates; discount received; sales; M. W. Biscuits Ltd (supplier); Col. J. St John (customer, non-resident); repairs and renewals; capital; sales; W. R. Stillings (customer, resident); restaurant furniture; purchases returns; advertising; kitchen plant.

3 List the main subsidiary books. Enumerate their main objects. Explain the relationship between the subsidiary books and the ledger.

4 (a) What do you understand by the term 'sources of entries'?
(b) What are the sources of entries for the following:
(i) petty cash book,
(ii) purchases day book,
(iii) cash book?

5 Explain the use of ledger folios in practical book-keeping.

6 Write short notes on the objects and advantages of control accounts.

7 On 1st June, 19.., the total amount owing to the suppliers of a hotel was £3 200. During that month the hotel bought further goods from its suppliers costing £3 500. Goods found damaged, £300, were returned to suppliers. Also, the hotel paid its suppliers £2 500 and received cash discounts amounting to £150. How much did the hotel owe its suppliers on 30th June, 19..?

8 From the following information write up the sales ledger control account and the bought ledger control account of a restaurant. Assume that both accounts are kept in the general ledger.

December	1	Total bought ledger balances	£2 550
,,	1	Total sales ledger balances	5 140
,,	31	Credit purchases	3 160
,,	31	Credit sales	6 180
,,	31	Purchases returns	190
,,	31	Allowances to customers	100
,,	31	Cash paid to suppliers	2 010
,,	31	Discounts received	100
,,	31	Cash received from customers	4 140
,,	31	Bad debts written off	310

9 The Pronto Catering Co. maintains a sales ledger controlled by a control account kept in that ledger. From the information given below, you are required to write up the sales ledger control account for three months, balancing it at the end of each month.

	January	February	March
Opening sales ledger balances	£4 500		
Credit sales	5 200	5 450	5 750
Allowances to customers	100	150	200
Cash received from customers	4 300	4 800	5 200

10 From the following information you are required to:

(a) write up the purchases day book and the purchases returns book;

(b) show the necessary extracts from the cash book;

(c) post the transactions to the ledger accounts;

(d) compile a bought ledger control account;

(e) extract a sectional trial balance as at 31st January, 19. .:

Bought ledger balances on 1st January, 19. .			
		Wm. Butcher & Sons	£400
		N. O. Nicotine Ltd	300
		Catering Supplies Ltd	600
		B. N. May Ltd	700
Invoices received:			
January	1	B. N. May Ltd.	£300
,,	3	Catering Supplies Ltd	460
,,	6	Wm. Butcher & Sons	220
,,	9	N. O. Nicotine Ltd	160
,,	13	Catering Supplies Ltd	80
,,	15	Wm. Butcher & Sons	210
,,	18	B. N. May Ltd	190
,,	21	N. O. Nicotine Ltd	110
,,	24	Catering Supplies Ltd	230
,,	27	Wm. Butcher & Sons	320
,,	29	B. N. May Ltd	160
,,	31	Catering Supplies Ltd	270
Credit notes received:			
January	3	Catering Supplies Ltd	20
,,	12	Wm. Butcher & Sons	40
,,	19	B. N. May Ltd	10
,,	27	N. O. Nicotine Ltd	30
Payments to suppliers:			
January	24	Wm. Butcher & Sons	£400 less C.D. £10
,,	24	B. N. May Ltd	700 ,, ,, 20
,,	24	Catering Suppliers Ltd	600 ,, ,, 30

Having agreed your sectional trial balance, balance all personal accounts and bring balances down as at the end of January.

CHAPTER 7

Maintaining a full set of books

The purpose of the present chapter is two-fold: firstly to illustrate the operation of a full set of books; secondly to give the student adequate practice in keeping a reasonably realistic set of records.

Two suggestions are, therefore, made. First, the student is encouraged to study carefully the example given below; in particular he should study the 'explanatory notes' given in the example. Secondly, he is encouraged to tackle as many as possible of the problems following this chapter. These have been designed to give the student sufficient practice in book-keeping techniques and to equip him with ability to keep a fairly complex set of accounts.

Example On 30th November, 19. ., after eleven months' trading, the following balances were extracted from the books of the Atlantic Restaurant:

	£	£
Capital		200 000.00
Furniture	19 000.00	
Rent and rates	11 800.00	
Postage and stationery	1 350.00	
Sales		259 600.00
Repairs and renewals	9 950.00	
Petty cash	150.00	
Kitchen equipment	19 500.00	
Collector of taxes		650.00
Purchases	129 850.00	
Gas and electricity	12 100.00	
Advertising	17 300.00	
Discounts received		2 950.00
Glass, cutlery and china	3 950.00	
Miscellaneous expenses	850.00	
Wages and salaries	58 900.00	
Stock of provisions, 1st January, 19. .	5 050.00	
Creditors: A. M. Grocer & Sons		1 600.00
Wholesalers Ltd		500.00
Devon Produce Co.		2 000.00
Quick Foods Ltd		1 000.00
Debtors: The '65 Club	350.00	
Agrarian Society	600.00	
S. G. Curtis, Esq.	150.00	
Wm. Brown & Co. Ltd	250.00	
Purchase returns		800.00
Leasehold premises	150 000.00	
Cash at bank	28 000.00	
	£469 100.00	£469 100.00

Open the necessary accounts and enter the above balances. During December, the transactions of the restaurant were as follows:

			£
December	1	Withdrew from bank for petty cash	100.00
,,	1	Banked cash sales	2 650.00
,,	2	Received invoices from: Quick Foods Ltd	800.00
		Devon Produce Co.	390.00
		Wholesalers Ltd	1 220.00
,,	3	Paid out of petty cash: fruit	10.00
		duplicating paper	30.00
		floor polish	10.00
,,	4	Purchased provisions, paid by cheque	950.00
,,	5	Restaurant credit sales: Wm, Brown & Co. Ltd	100.00
		Agrarian Society	250.00
		The '65 Club	300.00
,,	6	Banked cash sales	2 050.00
,,	7	Paid wages and salaries	1 300.00
,,	7	Tax deducted on above	120.00
,,	8	Paid for new china by cheque	650.00
,,	9	Received cheques from customers: The '65 Club	350.00
		Agrarian Society	600.00
		Wm. Brown & Co. Ltd	250.00
,,	10	Received invoices from: A. M. Grocer & Sons	750.00
		Devon Produce Co.	500.00
		Quick Foods Ltd	810.00
,,	11	Banked cash sales	2 150.00
,,	12	Received credit notes from: Devon Produce Co.	50.00
		Wholesalers Ltd	30.00
,,	12	Paid out of petty cash: postage stamps	30.00
		vegetables	20.00
		gratuities	10.00
,,	13	Purchased groceries, paid by cheque	440.00
,,	14	Restaurant credit sales: S. G. Curtis Esq.	50.00
		Wm. Brown & Co. Ltd	30.00
		The '65 Club	140.00
,,	14	Paid wages and salaries	1 280.00
,,	14	Tax deducted on above	110.00
,,	15	Received invoices from: Quick Foods Ltd	190.00
		Wholesalers Ltd	640.00
		A. M. Grocer & Sons	650.00
,,	16	Banked cash sales	2 310.00
,,	17	Paid collector of taxes in respect of tax due	650.00
,,	18	Paid by cheque for stationery	370.00
,,	19	Received credit notes from: A. M. Grocer & Sons	20.00
		Devon Produce Co.	40.00
,,	20	Paid by cheque for repairs	830.00
,,	21	Restaurant credit sales: Agrarian Society	120.00
		The '65 Club	130.00
		Wm. Brown & Co. Ltd	340.00
,,	21	Paid wages and salaries	1 490.00
,,	21	Tax deducted on above	130.00
,,	22	Banked cash sales	3 950.00
,,	22	Paid for gas by cheque	540.00
	22	Paid out of petty cash: flowers	20.00
		restaurant bills	10.00
		fruit	30.00

(continued)

				£
December	23	Paid the following suppliers' accounts as at 30.11.19..:		
		A. M. Grocer & Sons—cash disc. £40.00		
		Wholesalers Ltd 4%		
		Devon Produce Co. 3%		
		Quick Foods Ltd 2%		
,,	24	Received credit notes from: Wholesalers Ltd		20.00
		Quick Foods Ltd		30.00
,,	25	Received cheque from S. G. Curtis, Esq.		150.00
,,	25	Banked cash sales		2 050.00
,,	26	Paid by cheque for advertising		300.00
,,	27	Restaurant credit sales: S. G. Curtis, Esq.		100.00
		Agrarian Society		150.00
,,	28	Paid wages and salaries		1 330.00
,,	28	Tax deducted on above		110.00
,,	29	Received invoices from: Devon Produce Co.		390.00
		A. M. Grocer & Sons		430.00
,,	30	Bank cash sales		2 990.00
,,	30	Paid out of petty cash: travelling expenses	£10	
		vegetables	£20	
,,	31	Paid by cheque for kitchen equipment		2 000.00

You are required to:

(1) write up the books of the restaurant in respect of December, 19..;
(2) compile a bought ledger control account and a sales ledger control account;
(3) prove the accuracy of the personal accounts;
(4) extract a total trial balance as at 31st December, 19...

(1) Restaurant books

		Purchases Day Book			10
19..					
Dec.	2	Quick Foods Ltd.	BL 4	800	00
"	2	Devon Produce Co.	BL 3	390	00
"	2	Wholesalers Ltd.	BL 2	1,220	00
"	10	A.M. Grocer & Sons.	BL 1	750	00
"	10	Devon Produce Co.	BL 3	500	00
"	10	Quick Foods Ltd.	BL 4	810	00
"	15	Quick Foods Ltd.	BL 4	190	00
"	15	Wholesalers Ltd.	BL 2	640	00
"	15	A.M. Grocers & Sons	BL 1	650	00
"	29	Devon Produce Co.	BL 3	390	00
"	29	A.M. Grocer & Sons	BL 1	430	00
"	31	Trans. to Purchases A/c	GL 16	6,770	00

Figure 73

		Purchases Returns Book			16
19..					
Dec.	12	Devon Produce Co.	BL/3	50	00
"	12	Wholesalers Ltd.	BL/2	30	00
"	19	A. M. Grocer & Sons	BL/1	20	00
"	19	Devon Produce Co.	BL/3	40	00
"	24	Wholesalers Ltd.	BL/2	20	00
"	24	Quick Foods Ltd.	BL/4	30	00
"	31	Trans. to Purchases Returns A/c	GL/17	190	00

Figure 74

Explanatory notes (Figures 73 and 74)

(1) The invoices and credit notes received from suppliers are entered in the subsidiary books in chronological order.

(2) In many establishments the invoices and credit notes would be numbered and after posting filed consecutively rather than alphabetically. The numbers are then shown in the subsidiary books.

(3) Against each invoice and credit note there is shown a folio of the bought ledger account to which the document has been posted.

(4) Finally, note that the totals from the subsidiary books are posted to the ledger as at the end of the period concerned.

		Restaurant Sales Book			25
19..					
Dec.	5	Wm. Brown & Co. Ltd.	SL 4	100	00
"	5	Agrarian Society	SL 2	250	00
"	5	The '65 Club	SL 1	300	00
"	14	S. G. Curtis, Esq.	SL 3	50	00
"	14	Wm. Brown & Co Ltd.	SL 4	300	00
"	14	The '65 Club	SL 1	140	00
"	21	Agrarian Society	SL 2	120	00
"	21	The '65 Club	SL 1	130	00
"	21	Wm. Brown & Co. Ltd.	SL 4	340	00
"	27	S. G. Curtis, Esq.	SL 3	100	00
"	27	Agrarian Society	SL 2	150	00
"	31	Trans. to Sales A/c	GL 18	1,980	00

Figure 75

Explanatory notes (Figure 75)

(1) As already explained, only credit sales are entered in the restaurant sales book.

(2) The sources of entries are the copies of customers' bills.

Petty Cash Book

£. p.			F.	Total	Food Purchases	Postage Stationery	Misc Expenses
150.00	19.. Nov. 30	Balance	b/d				
100.00	Dec. 1	Cash Received	CB 1				
	" 3	Fruit	1	10.00	10.00		
	" 3	Duplicating Paper	2	30.00		30.00	
	" 3	Floor Polish	3	10.00			10.00
	" 12	Postage Stamps	4	30.00		30.00	
	" 12	Vegetables	5	20.00	20.00		
	" 12	Gratuities	6	10.00			10.00
	" 22	Flowers	7	20.00			20.00
	" 22	Restaurant Bills	8	10.00		10.00	
	" 22	Fruit	9	30.00	30.00		
	" 30	Travelling Expenses	10	10.00			10.00
	" 30	Vegetables	11	20.00	20.00		
				200.00	80.00	70.00	50.00
	" 31	Balance	c/d	50.00	GL 16	GL 11	GL 15
250.00				250.00			
50.00	19.. Jan. 1	Balance	b/d				

Figure 76

Explanatory notes (Figure 76)

(1) The choice of headings for the analysis columns is primarily dependent on what expenses are actually paid out of petty cash.

(2) It is usual to enter each item of petty cash expenditure separately.

(3) It is important to remember to post the analysed totals to the ledger every time the petty cash book is balanced; also to show the folios of the ledger accounts debited.

(4) As may be seen from the folio column, all petty cash vouchers are numbered consecutively for filing purposes.

Cash Book

Date		F	Sales Ledger	Bank	Date		F	Bought Ledger	Disc Rec'd	Bank
19..					19..					
Nov. 30	Balance	b/d		28,000.00	Dec 1	Petty Cash	PC 14			100.00
Dec. 1	Sales	GL 18		2,650.00	" 4	Purchases	GL 16			950.00
" 6	-do-	GL 18		2,050.00	" 7	Wages & Salaries	GL 9			1,300.00
" 10	The '65 Club	SL 1	350.00		" 8	China	GL 4			650.00
" 10	Agrarian Society	SL 2	600.00		" 13	Purchases	GL 16			440.00
" 10	William Brown & Co	SL 4	250.00	1,200.00	" 14	Wages & Salaries	GL 9			1,280.00
" 11	Sales	GL 18		2,150.00	" 17	Collector of Taxes	GL 8			650.00
" 16	-do-	GL 18		2,310.00	" 18	Stationery	GL 11			370.00
" 22	-do-	GL 18		3,950.00	" 20	Repairs	GL 12			830.00
" 25	S. G. Curtis, Esq.	SL 3	150.00	150.00	" 21	Wages & Salaries	GL 9			1,490.00
" 25	Sales	GL 18		2,050.00	" 22	Gas	GL 13			540.00
" 30	-do-	GL 18		2,990.00	" 23	A.M. Grocer & Sons	BL 1	1,600.00	40.00	1,560.00
					" 23	Wholesalers Ltd.	BL 2	500.00	20.00	480.00
					" 23	Devon Produce Co.	BL 3	2,000.00	60.00	1,940.00
					" 23	Quick Foods Ltd.	BL 4	1,000.00	20.00	980.00
					" 26	Advertising	GL 14			300.00
					" 28	Wages & Salaries	GL 9			1,330.00
					" 31	Kitchen Equip.	GL 3			2,000.00
					" 31	Balance	c/d			30,310.00
			1,350.00	47,500.00				5,100.00	140.00	47,500.00
19..										
Jan 1	Balance	b/d		30,310.00					GL 7	

Figure 77

Explanatory notes (Figure 77)

(1) The object of the sales ledger and bought ledger columns is to accumulate totals for control accounts. Thus, by reference to the bought ledger column, it may be seen that the total of cash and discounts debited in suppliers' accounts in December was £5 100.00.

(2) The discount received column is in the nature of a subsidiary book; any amount entered in it does not count for double entry purposes. Whenever the cash book is balanced, the total of discounts received should be posted to the credit of the discount received account.

GENERAL LEDGER

Capital A/c — 1

Date		Particulars	Fo.	Amount		Date		Particulars	Fo.	Amount	
						19.. Nov.	30	Balance	b/d	200,000	00

Furniture A/c — 2

Date		Particulars	Fo.	Amount		Date		Particulars	Fo.	Amount	
19.. Nov.	30	Balance	b/d	19,000	00						

Kitchen Equipment A/c — 3

Date		Particulars	Fo.	Amount		Date		Particulars	Fo.	Amount	
19.. Nov.	30	Balance	b/d	19,500	00						
Dec.	31	Cash	CB/1	2,000	00						

Glass, Cutlery & China A/c — 4

Date		Particulars	Fo.	Amount		Date		Particulars	Fo.	Amount	
19.. Nov.	30	Balance	b/d	3,950	00						
Dec.	8	Cash	CB/1	650	00						

Leasehold Premises A/c — 5

Date		Particulars	Fo.	Amount		Date		Particulars	Fo.	Amount	
19.. Nov.	30	Balance	b/d	150,000	00						

Stock A/c — 6

Date		Particulars	Fo.	Amount		Date		Particulars	Fo.	Amount	
19.. Nov.	30	Balance		5,050	00						

Discount Received A/c — 7

Date		Particulars	Fo.	Amount		Date		Particulars	Fo.	Amount	
						19.. Nov.	30	Balance	b/d	2,950	00
						Dec.	31	Cash	CB/1	140	00

Collector of Taxes A/c — 8

Date		Particulars	Fo.	Amount		Date		Particulars	Fo.	Amount	
19.. Dec.	17	Cash	CB/1	650	00	19.. Nov.	30	Balance	b/d	650	00
						Dec.	7	Wages & Salaries	GL/9	120	00
						"	14	-do-	GL/9	110	00
						"	21	-do-	GL/9	130	00
						"	28	-do-	GL/9	110	00

Figure 78 Ledger pages 1—8. See note to Fig. 77.

Wages & Salaries A/c — 9

19..					
Nov.	30	Balance	b/d	58,900	00
Dec.	7	Cash	CB/1	1,300	00
"	7	Coll. of Taxes	GL/8	120	00
"	14	Cash	CB/1	1,280	00
"	14	Coll. of Taxes	GL/8	110	00
"	21	Cash	CB/1	1,490	00
"	21	Coll. of Taxes	GL/8	130	00
"	28	Cash	CB/1	1,330	00
"	28	Coll. of Taxes	GL/8	110	00

Rent and Rates A/c — 10

19..					
Nov.	30	Balance	b/d	11,800	00

Postage and Stationery A/c — 11

19..					
Nov.	30	Balance	b/d	1,350	00
Dec.	18	Cash	CB/1	370	00
"	31	Petty Cash	PC/14	70	00

Repairs and Renewals A/c — 12

19..					
Nov.	30	Balance	b/d	9,950	00
Dec.	20	Cash	CB/1	830	00

Gas and Electricity A/c — 13

19..					
Nov.	30	Balance	b/d	12,100	00
Dec.	22	Cash	CB/1	540	00

Figure 78 Ledger pages 9—13

Explanatory notes (Figure 78)

(1) The pages of the ledger are numbered, and it will be seen that similar accounts are grouped together: accounts 2—6 are those for assets, accounts 9—15 are those for recording expenses, and accounts 16—18 record the buying and selling of goods. In practice, one, two, or more pages of the ledger would be allotted to each account.

(2) Note how certain accounts collect totals from various subsidiary books.

(3) The balance of the purchases returns account is usually transferred to the purchases account before the preparation of the trading account.

(4) The accounts are not balanced, as some would be transferred to the trading and profit and loss accounts. Others would require certain adjustments.

Advertising A/c 14

Date		Particulars	Fo.	Amount		Date		Particulars	Fo.	Amount	
19.. Nov.	30	Balance	b/d	17,300	00						
Dec.	26	Cash	CB/1	300	00						

Miscellaneous Expenses A/c 15

Date		Particulars	Fo.	Amount		Date		Particulars	Fo.	Amount	
19.. Nov.	30	Balance	b/d	850	00						
Dec.	31	Petty Cash	PC/14	50	00						

Purchases A/c 16

Date		Particulars	Fo.	Amount		Date		Particulars	Fo.	Amount	
19.. Nov.	30	Balance	b/d	129,850	00						
Dec.	4	Cash	CB/1	950	00						
"	13	-do-	CB/1	440	00						
"	31	Sundries	PB/10	6,770	00						
"	31	Petty Cash	PC/14	80	00						

Purchases Returns A/c 17

Date		Particulars	Fo.	Amount		Date		Particulars	Fo.	Amount	
						19.. Nov.	30	Balance	b/d	800	00
						Dec.	31	Sundries	PR/16	190	00

Sales A/c 18

Date		Particulars	Fo.	Amount		Date		Particulars	Fo.	Amount	
						19.. Nov.	30	Balance	b/d	259,600	00
						Dec.	1	Cash	CB/1	2,650	00
						"	6	-do-	CB/1	2,050	00
						"	11	-do-	CB/1	2,150	00
						"	16	-do-	CB/1	2,310	00
						"	22	-do-	CB/1	3,950	00
						"	25	-do-	CB/1	2,050	00
						"	30	-do-	CB/1	2,990	00
						"	31	Sundries	SB/25	1,980	00

Figure 78 Ledger pages 14—18

BOUGHT LEDGER

A.M. Grocer & Sons A/c — 1

Date		Particulars	Fo.	£	p	Date		Particulars	Fo.	£	p
19.. Dec.	19	Returns	PR/16	20	00	19.. Nov.	30	Balance	b/d	1,600	00
"	23	Cash	CB/1	1,560	00	Dec.	10	Purchases	PB/10	750	00
"	23	Discount	CB/1	40	00	"	15	-do-	PB/10	650	00
"	31	Balance	c/d	1,810	00	"	29	-do-	PB/10	430	00
				3,430	00					3,430	00
						19.. Jan.	1	Balance	b/d	1,810	00

Wholesalers Ltd. A/c — 2

Date		Particulars	Fo.	£	p	Date		Particulars	Fo.	£	p
19.. Dec.	12	Returns	PR/16	30	00	19.. Nov.	30	Balance	b/d	500	00
"	23	Cash	CB/1	480	00	Dec.	2	Purchases	PB/10	1,220	00
"	23	Discount	CB/1	20	00	"	15	-do-	PB/10	640	00
"	24	Returns	PR/16	20	00						
"	31	Balance	c/d	1,810	00						
				2,360	00					2,360	00
						19.. Jan.	1	Balance	b/d	1,810	00

Devon Produce Co. A/c — 3

Date		Particulars	Fo.	£	p	Date		Particulars	Fo.	£	p
19.. Dec.	12	Returns	PR/16	50	00	19.. Nov.	30	Balance	b/d	2,000	00
"	19	-do-	PR/16	40	00	Dec.	2	Purchases	PB/10	390	00
"	23	Cash	CB/1	1,940	00	"	10	-do-	PB/10	500	00
"	23	Discount	CB/1	60	00	"	29	-do-	PB/10	390	00
"	31	Balance	c/d	1,190	00						
				3,280	00					3,280	00
						19.. Jan.	1	Balance	b/d	1,190	00

Quick Foods Ltd A/c — 4

Date		Particulars	Fo.	£	p	Date		Particulars	Fo.	£	p
19.. Dec.	23	Cash	CB/1	980	00	19.. Nov.	30	Balance	b/d	1,000	00
"	23	Discount	CB/1	20	00	Dec.	2	Purchases	PB/10	800	00
"	24	Returns	PR/16	30	00	"	10	-do-	PB/10	810	00
"	31	Balance	c/d	1,770	00	"	15	-do-	PB/10	190	00
				2,800	00					2,800	00
						19.. Jan.	1	Balance	b/d	1,770	00

Figure 79 Bought ledger

Explanatory notes (Figure 79)

(1) Personal accounts are not balanced before being agreed with the bought ledger or sales ledger control account.

(2) In practice, one or more pages would be allotted to each personal account.

SALES LEDGER

The '65 Club A/c — 1

Date		Particulars	Fo.	£	p	Date		Particulars	Fo.	£	p
19.. Nov.	30	Balance	b/d	350	00	19.. Dec.	10	Cash	CB 1	350	00
Dec.	5	Sales	SB 25	300	00	"	31	Balance	c/d	570	00
"	14	-do-	SB 25	140	00						
"	21	-do-	SB 25	130	00						
				920	00					920	00
19.. Jan.	1	Balance	b/d	570	00						

Agrarian Society A/c — 2

Date		Particulars	Fo.	£	p	Date		Particulars	Fo.	£	p
19.. Nov.	30	Balance	b/d	600	00	19.. Dec.	10	Cash	CB 1	600	00
Dec.	5	Sales	SB 25	250	00	"	31	Balance	c/d	520	00
"	21	-do-	SB 25	120	00						
"	27	-do-	SB 25	150	00						
				1,120	00					1,120	00
19.. Jan.	1	Balance	b/d	520	00						

S.G. Curtis Esq. A/c — 3

Date		Particulars	Fo.	£	p	Date		Particulars	Fo.	£	p
19.. Nov.	30	Balance	b/d	150	00	19.. Dec.	25	Cash	CB 1	150	00
Dec.	14	Sales	SB 25	50	00	"	31	Balance	c/d	150	00
"	27	-do-	SB 25	100	00						
				300	00					300	00
19.. Jan.	1	Balance	b/d	150	00						

Wm. Brown & Co. Ltd. A/c — 4

Date		Particulars	Fo.	£	p	Date		Particulars	Fo.	£	p
19.. Nov.	30	Balance	b/d	250	00	19.. Dec.	10	Cash	CB 1	250	00
Dec.	5	Sales	SB 25	100	00	"	31	Balance	c/d	740	00
"	14	-do-	SB 25	300	00						
"	21	-do-	SB 25	340	00						
				990	00					990	00
19.. Jan.	1	Balance	b/d	740	00						

Figure 80 Sales Ledger

Explanatory notes (Figure 80)

(1) See notes following bought ledger accounts.

(2) It is important to ensure that no statements are sent to the customers before sales ledger accounts are proved. This is achieved by means of a sectional or total trial balance.

(2) Bought and sales ledger control accounts

Bought Ledger Control A/c

				£	p					£	p
19.. Dec.	31	Returns		190	00	19.. Nov.	30	Balances	b/d	5,100	00
"	31	Cash & Disc.		5,100	00	Dec.	31	Purchases	PB 10	6,770	00
"	31	Balances	c/d	6,580	00						
				11,870	00					11,870	00
						19.. Jan.	1	Balances	b/d	6,580	00

Sales Ledger Control A/c

				£	p					£	p
19.. Nov.	30	Balances	b/d	1,350	00	19.. Dec.	31	Cash	CB 1	1,350	00
Dec.	31	Sales	SB 25	1,980	00	"	31	Balances	c/d	1,980	00
				3,330	00					3,330	00
19.. Jan.	1	Balances	b/d	1,980	00						

Figure 81

Explanatory notes (Figure 81)

(1) In this case the control accounts are kept in the general ledger and, as explained previously, show in summary form the detailed transactions posted to the bought ledger and the sales ledger. Thus, by reference to the bought ledger control account, the total amount owing to the suppliers of the restaurant is, at the end of December, £6 580.00.

(2) The control accounts are compiled at the end of each period (week, month, quarter) by extracting the necessary totals from the relevant subsidiary books.

(3) As the balance of a control account is equal to the sum total of the individual balances in the ledger it controls, when extracting a total trial balance it is not necessary to list the individual personal accounts. Instead, the balance of the control account may be shown in the total trial balance.

(3) Proving personal accounts

The method of extracting a sectional trial balance has already been explained. In this case the control accounts are kept in the general ledger and the extraction of a sectional trial balance is not, therefore, possible.

The accuracy of the personal accounts may still be proved by listing all the personal accounts and their balances and agreeing the total of such balances with the balance of the appropriate control account as at that date. This method of controlling personal accounts is illustrated below.

Bought ledger control as at 31st December, 19..

A. M. Grocer & Sons	£1 810.00
Wholesalers Ltd	1 810.00
Devon Produce Co.	1 190.00
Quick Foods Ltd	1 770.00
Control account balance	£6 580.00

Sales ledger control as at 31st December, 19..

The '65 Club	£570.00
Agrarian Society	520.00
S. G. Curtis, Esq.	150.00
Wm. Brown & Co. Ltd	740.00
Control account balance	£1 980.00

It will be realized that whether one extracts a sectional trial balance or proves the personal accounts as shown above does not really matter. In both cases one is, in fact, agreeing a number of individual balances with the balance of a control account, which does not form a part of the system of double entry.

(4) Trial balance

Trial balance as at 31st December, 19..

			£	£
Capital account	1			200 000.00
Furniture account	2		19 000.00	
Kitchen equipment account	3		21 500.00	
Glass, cutlery and china account	4		4 600.00	
Leasehold premises account	5		150 000.00	
Stock account	6		5 050.00	
Discount received account	7			3 090.00
Collector of taxes account	8			470.00
Wages and salaries account	9		64 770.00	
Rents and rates account	10		11 800.00	
Postage and stationery account	11		1 790.00	
Repairs and renewals account	12		10 780.00	
Gas and electricity account	13		12 640.00	
Advertising account	14		17 600.00	
Miscellaneous expenses account	15		900.00	
Purchases account	16		138 090.00	
Purchases returns account	17			990.00
		c/f	458 520.00	204 550.00

		b/f	458 520.00	204 550.00
Sales account	18			279 730.00
Cash book	1		30 310.00	
Petty cash book	14		50.00	
Bought ledger control account				6 580.00
Sales ledger control account			1 980.00	
			£490 860.00	£490 860.00

Explanatory notes

(1) It is useful to show the folios of the accounts listed in the trial balance in case any of them have to be referred to or checked.

(2) Should the trial balance fail to balance, only the general ledger accounts (including the cash book and the petty cash book) would have to be checked as the accuracy of the personal accounts has already been proved by means of the control accounts.

Problems

1 The following trial balance was extracted from the books of a restaurant as at 1st January, 19...

	£	£
Capital		100 000
Premises	74 500	
China and cutlery	4 350	
Stock	2 150	
Rent and rates		250
Cash at bank	19 150	
Petty cash	100	
Gas and electricity		350
Creditors: A. Allen		500
B. Bailey		150
C. Cooper		450
Debtors: M. Maynard	350	
B.I.C. Ltd	600	
Midland Motors Ltd	500	
	£101 700	£101 700

The following were the transactions of the restaurant in January:

January	1	Paid gas by cheque	£1 250
,,	1	Cash sales	650
,,	2	Petty cash payments: fruit	20
		manager's fares	10
,,	2	Cash sales	550
,,	2	Credit sales: B.I.C. Ltd	50
		M. Maynard	30
,,	5	Paid A. Allen's account less 4% cash discount	
,,	5	Credit purchases: A. Allen	750
		C. Cooper	1 210
		D. Dawson	180

(continued)

,,	5	Cash sales	810
,,	6	Purchased new china, paid by cheque	200
,,	6	Petty cash payments: stationery	10
		postage stamps	20
,,	7	Midland Motors Ltd paid their account as at 1.1.19..	
,,	7	Cash sales	870
,,	7	Credit sales: B.I.C. Ltd	80
		M. Maynard	20
		B.S.A. Society	110
,,	8	Cash sales	530
,,	8	Paid wages and salaries by cheque	1 660
,,	11	Purchased stationery, paid by cheque	140
,,	11	Cash sales	650
,,	11	Credit sales: B.S.A. Society	90
		B.I.C. Ltd	30
,,	12	Credit purchases: A. Allen	370
		B. Bailey	830
,,	12	Cash sales	550
,,	13	Purchased provisions, paid by cheque	910
,,	13	Cash sales	880
,,	14	Paid C. Cooper's account as at 1st January less £20 cash discount	
,,	14	Cash sales	620
,,	16	Credit purchases: D. Dawson	410
		C. Cooper	190
		B. Bailey	1 190
,,	18	Cash sales	710
,,	19	Credit sales: Midland Motors Ltd	80
		B.S.A. Society	70
,,	19	Cash sales	810
,,	20	Paid B. Bailey's account as at 1st January	
,,	20	Cash sales	490
,,	21	Balanced petty cash—drew cheque to make up imprest to £200	
,,	21	Cash sales	1 010
,,	22	Credit purchases: D. Dawson	550
		A. Allen	470
,,	22	Cash sales	760
,,	25	Paid wages and salaries by cheque	1 490
,,	26	Credit sales: B.S.A. Society	80
,,	26	Cash sales	810
,,	27	Petty cash payments: gratuities	10
		vegetables	20
		flowers	10
,,	27	Cash sales	640
,,	28	B.I.C. Ltd paid their account as at 1st January	
,,	28	Cash sales	740
,,	29	Credit purchase: B. Bailey	230
,,	29	Cash sales	690
,,	30	Paid out of petty cash: manager's fares	10
,,	30	Cash sales	880
,,	30	Purchased provisions from D. Dawson, paid by cheque	170
,,	31	Credit sales: Midland Motors Ltd	40
		B.S.A. Society	10
,,	31	Cash sales	880

You are required to pass the above transactions through the books of the business, extract a trial balance as at 31st January, 19.., close the cash book and the petty cash book and all personal accounts. Use separate sheets of paper for the main divisions of the ledger.

2 The following were the balances in the book of a restaurant after eleven months' trading at 30th November, 19 . . .

Trial Balance

	£	£
Capital		100 000
Stock of provisions, 1st January 19 . .	3 100	
Sales		130 200
Purchases	65 300	
Wages and salaries	29 450	
Collector of taxes		350
Advertising	8 550	
Fuel and light	7 400	
Cash at bank	13 900	
Petty cash	100	
Repairs and replacements	4 850	
Restaurant furniture	9 000	
China, glass and cutlery	2 150	
Miscellaneous expenses	750	
Rates	6 300	
Discounts received		1 450
Leasehold premises	74 000	
Kitchen plant	9 500	
Purchases returns		500
Creditors: Food Sellers Ltd		250
Dutch Dairy Co.		1 000
Catering Supplies Ltd		500
Oriental Foods Ltd		800
Postage and stationery	700	
	£235 050	£235 050

Open the necessary accounts and enter the above balances.

During December the transactions of the restaurant were as shown below:

December			
	1	Withdrew from bank for petty cash	£150
,,	2	Banked cash sales	350
,,	2	Received invoices from: Oriental Foods Ltd	150
		Catering Supplies Ltd	250
		Dutch Dairy Co.	200
		Food Sellers Ltd	180
,,	3	Petty cash payments: provisions	20
		stationery	30
		cleaning materials	10
,,	4	Banked cash sales	1 150
,,	5	Purchased cutlery on credit from Sheffield Cutlery Co.	1 750
,,	6	Banked cash sales	850
,,	6	Paid wages and salaries	760
,,	6	Tax deducted on above	80
,,	7	Received invoices from: Dutch Dairy Co.	350
		Food Sellers Ltd	300
		Catering Suppliers Ltd	250
,,	8	Banked cash sales	800
,,	8	Paid by cheque for provisions	720

(continued)

,,	8	Petty cash payments: postage	40
		provisions	30
		cleaning materials	20
,,	9	Paid for electricity by cheque	900
,,	9	Received credit notes from: Food Sellers Ltd	50
		Dutch Dairy Co	60
		Oriental Foods Ltd	40
,,	10	Banked cash sales	850
,,	10	Paid by cheque for stationery	370
,,	11	Purchased groceries, paid by cheque	740
,,	11	Received credit note from Dutch Dairy Co.	20
,,	12	Banked cash sales	830
,,	12	Paid wages and salaries by cheque	690
,,	12	Tax deducted on above	70
,,	13	Received invoices from: Dutch Dairy Co.	200
		Catering Supplies Ltd	300
		Oriental Foods Ltd	400
		Food Sellers Ltd	100
,,	13	Paid by cheque for repairs	430
,,	14	Banked cash sales	790
,,	14	Paid the following suppliers' accounts as at the end of the previous month, and deducted discounts as indicated:	
		Food Sellers Ltd CD 4%	
		Dutch Dairy Co. ,, 3%	
		Catering Suppliers Ltd ,, 4%	
		Oriental Foods Ltd ,, 5%	
,,	15	Petty cash payments: stationery	10
		provisions	40
,,	16	Banked cash sales	830
,,	16	Drew cheque for tax deducted in respect of previous month	350
,,	17	Received invoices from: Food Sellers Ltd	230
		Oriental Foods Ltd	130
		Dutch Dairy Co.	150
,,	19	Banked cash sales	880
,,	19	Paid for advertising by cheque	370
,,	20	Banked cash sales	610
,,	20	Paid wages and salaries by cheque	800
,,	20	Tax deducted on above	80
,,	21	Received credit note from Catering Suppliers Ltd	30
,,	22	Banked cash sales	830
,,	23	Paid out of petty cash for stationery	10
,,	24	Banked cash sales	890
,,	24	Received invoices from: Dutch Dairy Co.	470
		Oriental Foods Ltd	410
,,	25	Purchased provisions, paid by cheque	160
,,	26	Received credit note from Dutch Dairy Co.	20
,,	26	Banked cash sales	390
,,	27	Paid by cheque for kitchen plant	750
,,	28	Banked cash sales	370
,,	28	Paid wages and salaries by cheque	760
,,	28	Tax deducted on above	60
,,	29	Invoices received from: Catering Supplies Ltd	160
		Food Sellers Ltd	390
,,	30	Banked cash sales	830
,,	30	Paid by cheque for kitchen fuel	450
,,	30	Sold for cash old cutlery	50
,,	31	Banked cash sales	820
,,	31	Paid by cheque for stationery	110

You are required to write up the books of the restaurant in respect of December, 19.., extract a trial balance and balance all personal accounts, the cash book and the petty cash book.

3 J. Robinson started in business on 1st January, 19.., with a capital in cash of £10 000, which he paid into his business bank account.

His transactions in January were:

January	1	Paid three months' rent by cheque	£1 550
,,	2	Purchased kitchen equipment by cheque	2 550
,,	3	Paid by cheque for cutlery and utensils	530
,,	4	Bought provisions by cheque	830
,,	9	Paid wages by cheque	310
,,	13	Banked sales	770
,,	16	Bought provisions on credit from XYZ Supplies Ltd	740
,,	19	Bought provisions on credit from A. K. Jones & Co.	460
,,	22	Banked sales	690
,,	25	Paid wages by cheque	370
,,	27	Bought provisions on credit from XYZ Supplies Ltd	380
,,	28	Withdrew from bank for private use	300
,,	29	Banked sales	1 070
,,	31	Bought provisions on credit from A. K. Jones & Co.	330
,,	31	Bought cutlery on credit from Catering Supplies Ltd	600

You are required to enter the above transactions in appropriate subsidiary books, post to ledger and extract Robinson's trial balance as at 31st January, 19...

(H.C.I. Inter. Modified)

CHAPTER 8

Preparation of final accounts

Introduction The most important purpose of any business is to earn a profit. It is, therefore, necessary from time to time—and in practice at least once a year—to prepare an account showing how much profit (or loss) has in fact been made. Similarly, it is essential from time to time to review the financial position of the business to ascertain what assets (property) it owns, and what liabilities (debts) it owes to outsiders.

In order to achieve the foregoing it is necessary to prepare what is known as the 'final accounts' of the business. These consist of:

(1) the trading, profit and loss account—this shows the income and expenditure of a particular accounting period and the resulting gross profit (or gross loss) and the net profit (or net loss).

(2) the balance sheet—this, strictly speaking, is not an 'account' but a financial statement showing the assets of the business on one side and the liabilities on the other.

It is usual to prepare the final accounts from a trial balance extracted from the ledger at a particular date. It will be recalled that a debit balance may be one of two things: an asset or an expense. A credit balance, on the other hand, represents either a liability or a gain (income).

Balances which represent expenses and income are used to construct the trading, profit and loss account; balances which represent assets and liabilities are used to construct the balance sheet. Students will find it useful to remember, therefore, that the balances from the trial balance are, so to speak, channelled in two directions—some to the trading, profit and loss account, others to the balance sheet.

Example The following trial balance was extracted from the books of A. Caterer at 31st December, 19.., after a year's trading.

Trial balance as at 31st December, 19..

Account	Dr.	Cr.	Nature of balance	Destination of item
Sales		200 000	Income	Trading account
Premises	100 000		Asset	Balance sheet
Rent and rates	17 000		Expense	Profit and loss account
Kitchen plant	41 000		Asset	Balance sheet
Creditors		6 000	Liability	Balance sheet
Repairs & renewals	8 500		Expense	Profit and loss account
Furniture	27 000		Asset	Balance sheet
Purchases	80 000		Expense	Trading account
Cash at bank	14 000		Asset	Balance sheet
Wages & salaries	55 000		Expense	Profit and loss account
Debtors	4 000		Asset	Balance sheet
Capital		150 000	Liability	Balance sheet
Light & heat	9 500		Expense	Profit and loss account
	£356 000	£356 000		

When we have determined the nature of each balance in the trial balance, and its destination, we may proceed to construct the final accounts. This is done by:
(1) debiting all expenses (losses) and crediting all income (gains) in the trading, profit & loss account,
(2) listing all assets on the right-hand side and all the liabilities on the left-hand side of the balance sheet. A. Caterer's final accounts would then appear as shown in Figure 82.

Trading, profit and loss account for year ended 31st December, 19..

	£		£
Purchases	80,000	Sales	200,000
Gross profit c/d	120,000		
	£ 200,000		£ 200,000
Wages and Salaries	55,000	Gross Profit b/d	120,000
Repairs, Renewals	8,500		
Rent and Rates	17,000		
Light and heat	9,500		
Net profit	30,000		
	£ 120,000		£ 120,000

Balance sheet as at 31st December, 19..

Liabilities	£		Assets	£
Capital at 1st January, 19..	150,000		Premises	100,000
Add Net Profit	30,000		Kitchen plant	41,000
			Furniture	27,000
		180,000	Debtors	4,000
Creditors		6,000	Cash at Bank	14,000
		186,000		186,000

Figure 82

Note: (1) It will be observed that there is no opening or closing stock in this illustration. The stocks have been left out for the sake of clarity and will be dealt with later in this chapter.
(2) The net profit of £30 000 is, in the balance sheet, added to the capital as at the

beginning of the year. As a result, the capital at the end of the year is £180 000. The capital of a business is a debt from the business to the proprietor and is, therefore, listed under the heading of 'liabilities'.

Trading account

The object of the trading account is to show how much gross profit (or gross loss) has been earned during the period under consideration. Gross profit may be defined as the excess of sales over the 'cost of sales' (also referred to as the 'cost of goods sold').

The gross profit on food sales (also known as the 'kitchen profit') is food sales less the cost of food consumed. Expenses such as kitchen and restaurant wages, kitchen fuel, breakages and replacements are not normally deducted in arriving at the figure of kitchen profit. Similarly, the gross profit on bar sales (also known as 'bar profit') is the excess of bar sales over the cost of wines, spirits, beers, minerals, etc. consumed.

The gross profit on other sales—cigars, cigarettes, tobaccos, and any shops or kiosks operated by the establishment—is calculated in a similar manner.

It will be realized that the preparation of a trading account for a residential establishment (hotel, motel, hostel, residential club, etc.) presents a certain difficulty, arising from the fact that a proportion of the income is derived from the sale of a service. Thus, the treatment of a hotel's room sales in final accounts is difficult in that it is not easy to establish what constitutes the 'cost of sales', and therefore 'gross profit', in that department.

The actual treatment of room sales in the trading, profit & loss account of a hotel will depend on the number of revenue-producing departments as well as the method of presentation chosen. For the time being we may assume that it is not incorrect to credit room sales in a hotel's trading account without debiting therein a corresponding figure of cost of sales, and consider possible improvements in the treatment of this and other items in Chapter 16.

Treatment of stocks

In order to arrive at the cost of sales, it is necessary to add to the opening stock the purchases for the period and to deduct the closing stock. The basic formula for arriving at the cost of sales is, therefore:

OPENING STOCK + PURCHASES – CLOSING STOCK = COST OF SALES.

A typical trading account of a non-residential catering establishment will therefore take the form shown in Figure 83.

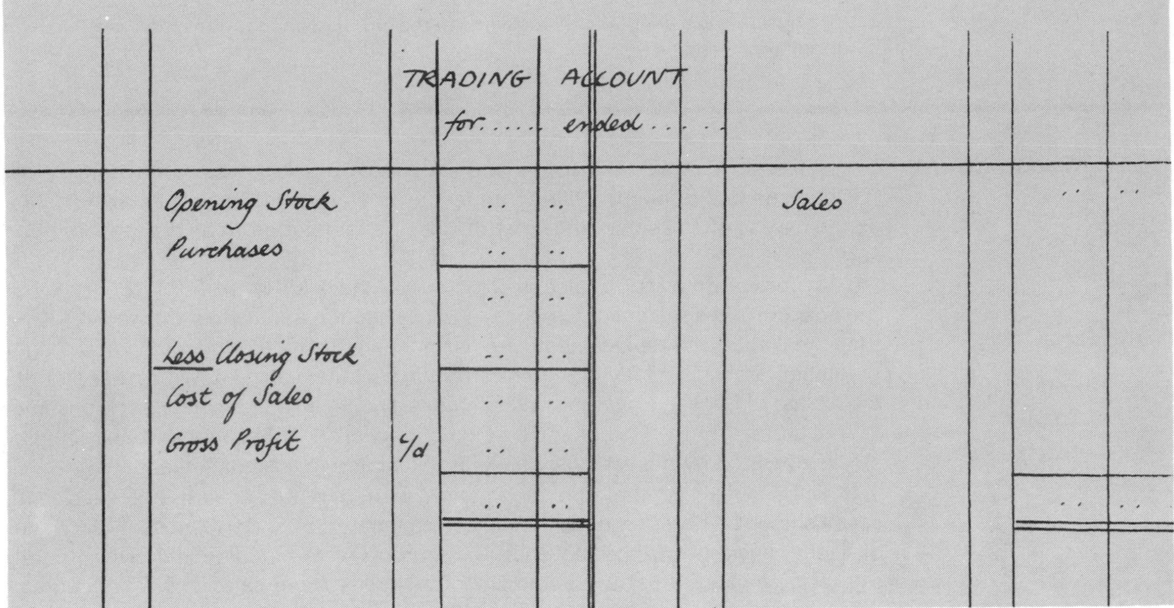

TRADING ACCOUNT for.... ended....

				£	p					£	p
		Opening Stock		..	..			Sales		..	..
		Purchases		..	..						
				..	..						
		Less Closing Stock		..	..						
		Cost of Sales		..	..						
		Gross Profit	c/d	..	..						
				..	..					..	..

Figure 83

The trading, profit & loss account forms a part of the system of double entry. As a result, for every one entry made in that account there must be a corresponding entry made in some account in the ledger. Double entry in respect of the opening and closing stocks in the trading account is completed in the stock account.

Let us assume that on 1st January, 1981, a restaurant had a stock of food valued at £2 000. During the year ended 31st December, 1981, the purchases of the restaurant amounted to £80 000 and the sales £200 000. At 31st December, 1981, the stock of the restaurant was valued at £2 500.

On 1st January, 1981, the stock account appeared as in Figure 84.

Stock A/c

				£	p					£	p
1981											
Jan.	1	Balance	b/d	2,000	00						

Figure 84

At 31st December, 1981, the stock available at the beginning of the year would be debited in the trading account, and credited in the stock account.

The stock account would then appear as in Figure 85.

				Stock A/c							
1981						1981					
Jan.	1	Balance	b/d	2,000	00	Dec.	31	Trading A/c		2,000	00

Figure 85

Also at 31st December, 1981, it would be necessary to enter the closing stock in the trading account (to arrive at the cost of sales) as well as in the stock account (to show the value of the stock in existence at that date). This would be done by debiting the stock account, and crediting the trading account.

The entry in the stock account would be dated 1st January, 1982, as the closing stock for 1981 immediately becomes the opening stock for 1982.

In the trading account, the closing stock may be credited under the figure of sales, but it is usual to show it as a deduction on the debit side. Whether we do one or the other does not affect the amount of gross profit.

When the above entry has been made the stock account will appear as in Figure 86.

				Stock A/c							
1981						1981					
Jan.	1	Balance	b/d	2000	00	Dec.	31	Trading A/c		2,000	00
1982											
Jan.	1	Balance	b/d	2,500	00						

Figure 86

As may be seen from Figure 86, the same procedure is adopted from one year to another and the same stock account is used over a period of years.

Finally, the trading account of the restaurant would be prepared as shown in Figure 87.

TRADING ACCOUNT
for year ended 31st Dec., 19..

Opening Stock		2,000 00	Sales		200,000 00
Purchases		80,000 00			
		82,000 00			
Less Closing Stock		2,500 00			
Cost of Sales		79,500 00			
Gross Profit	c/d	120,500 00			
		200,000 00			200,000 00

Figure 87

Staff meals Many hotel and catering establishments properly regard the cost of staff meals as a labour cost. Where that is so an adjustment should be made in respect of the actual or estimated cost of such meals for the purpose of final accounts. As that portion of food purchases which is consumed by the staff is not available for sale to customers the necessary adjustment is: Dr. staff meals account, and Cr. purchases account.

In the trading account the amount of purchases debited will then be net, after deduction of staff meals. The latter will be debited, together with other labour costs, in the profit and loss account. As a proportion of total purchases, the cost of staff meals will vary from one section of the industry to another, being generally more in hotels than in restaurants and less in industrial canteens than in restaurants. Where there is a separate staff kitchen requisitioning its own food from the stores, the cost of employee meals may be calculated quite easily. In most hotel and catering establishments, however, that is not so and, in such circumstances, an estimate of the cost must be made. This is usually expressed as so much per employee per day, due allowance being made for part-time employees.

Where an adjustment in respect of staff meals is made the formula for arriving at the cost of sales is:

OPENING STOCK + (PURCHASES − STAFF MEALS) − CLOSING STOCK
= COST OF SALES

Other items affecting trading account The book-keeping treatment of *purchases returns* was considered in Chapter 3. When the final accounts are prepared from a trial balance showing an item of purchases returns, it is usual to show the latter as a deduction from the purchases in the trading account.

The item *carriage inwards* does not often appear in the accounts of hotel and catering establishments. This is the charge made by a supplier for conveyance of goods to the buyer's premises. It is usual for the majority of suppliers to supply goods free of charge in this industry. Where, however, a charge is made, it is clear that the effect of it is to increase the cost of the goods to the buyer. Carriage inwards, if any, should therefore be debited in the trading account.

Finally, the item *allowances to customers* is sometimes shown as a separate balance in the trial balance—particularly in the case of hotels. This, as explained in Chapter 4, is a reduction of sales and should, therefore, be shown as such in the trading account.

The specimen trading account shown in Figure 88 is the correct layout for the various items discussed above.

TRADING ACCOUNT
for ..... ended .....

Opening Stock		2,000	Sales	251,000	
Purchases	100 000		Less Allowances	1,000	250,000
Add Carriage in	1,000				
	101,000				
Less Returns	500				
	100,500				
Less Staff meals	8,500	92,000			
		94,000			
Less Closing Stock		3,000			
Cost of Sales		91,000			
Gross Profit	c/o	159,000			
		250,000			250,000

Figure 88

Note: Where there are several items affecting the purchases, as in the above trading account, the formula for calculating the cost of sales must be adjusted accordingly.

Profit and loss account

The object of the profit and loss account is to show how much net profit (or net loss) has been earned by the business. Net profit may be defined as the difference between total income and total expenditure in respect of the period concerned. It may also be defined as the excess of gross profit, plus any other income, over the expenditure for the period covered by the accounts. Hence:

TOTAL INCOME − TOTAL EXPENDITURE = NET PROFIT,
OR
GROSS PROFIT + OTHER INCOME − EXPENDITURE = NET PROFIT

It is emphasized that in arriving at the net profit for any one accounting period, it is essential to take into account only items of income and expenditure in respect of that period. This is further explained in the next two chapters.

A fuller specimen profit and loss account is shown in Figure 89.

PROFIT AND LOSS ACCOUNT
for........ ended........

		£	p				£	p
	Wages & Salaries	86,000	00		Gross Profit	b/d	190,000	00
	National Insurance etc.	6,500	00		Rent Received		8,000	00
	Staff Meals	8,500	00		Discount Rec'd		2,000	00
	Repairs, Renewals	16,500	00					
	Depreciation	30,000	00					
	Rent and Rates	18,500	00					
	Light and Heat	9,500	00					
	Postage, Telephone	2,000	00					
	Bank Interest	1,000	00					
	Accountancy Fees	250	00					
	Legal Expenses	500	00					
	Miscellaneous Exp.	750	00					
	Net Profit	20,000	00					
		200,000	00				200,000	00

Figure 89

Note: (1) The gross profit together with the other income of the establishment amounts to £200 000; the expenses for the current year are £180 000 and the resulting net profit is thus £20 000.

(2) When constructing profit and loss account care must be taken to ensure that similar items are placed together.

(3) The net profit is transferred from the profit and loss account to the credit side of the proprietor's capital account.

Items peculiar to hotel and catering establishments

An examination of profit and loss accounts of hotel and catering establishments would disclose certain items which are not usually found in the final accounts of other businesses. Some of the important items are listed below.

Hire of equipment

This is a charge paid in respect of various items of equipment (e.g. cutlery, china, furniture) hired by an establishment, usually in connection with outdoor catering activities. Any amounts so paid out must be debited in the profit and loss account.

Rentals This is similar to the hire of equipment, explained above. Rentals paid by hotel and catering establishments are usually in respect of hire of television, though it is not unusual for hotel-keepers and caterers to pay such rentals in respect of kitchen equipment and furniture.

Commissions payable This item is often found in the profit and loss account of hotels rather than non-residential establishments. Commissions are payable usually to travel agents in respect of hotel bookings secured by them.

Staff meals As already explained, this is the cost of food consumed by the staff of an establishment and is regarded as a labour cost.

Plants and flowers This is the cost of floral decorations in guests' bedrooms as well as the public rooms of a hotel.

Professional charges This usually consists of fees, etc. paid to solicitors and/or auditors. Many licensed establishments employ professional stocktakers for the stocktaking of alcoholic beverages. Where that is so the fees of the stocktakers are often debited in the same account as those of the solicitors and/or auditors, and subsequently written off to the profit and loss account.

Household supplies These are mainly cleaning materials and other non-consumable supplies (brooms, dusters, detergents, etc.) used in the housekeeping department.

Rents received This constitutes additional income of a hotel sub-letting (usually) ground floor accommodation to banks, shops and other businesses. Any such rents received may form a substantial source of income, especially in the case of hotels.

Sundry receipts The nature of this item will vary from one business to another. In many hotel and catering establishments sundry may include amounts received in respect of the sale of swill, used linen and similar items.

Closing entries

As mentioned in connection with the trading account above, the trading, profit and loss account constitutes a part of the system of double entry, and therefore no entry should be made in that account without there being a corresponding entry made in some other account. Hence, every entry made in the trading, profit and loss account requires a corresponding entry in the ledger. Thus, when we debit the purchases in the trading account we must credit the purchases account. The credit entry in the trading account in respect of sales must be represented by a corresponding debit in the sales account. The debit in the profit and loss account for wages and salaries must have a corresponding credit entry in the wages and salaries account.

All such entries, made at the end of an accounting period, are known as closing entries and have to be journalized. When the closing entries have been completed, the only balances remaining in the ledger are those in respect of assets and liabilities—balances used in the construction of the balance sheet. In other words, the effect of the closing entries is to transfer all balance in respect of gains and losses (income and expenditure) to the trading, profit and loss account and to leave in the ledger balances representing assets and liabilities only. A few specimen closing entries are shown overleaf.

Example At 31st December, 19.., the following were some of the balances in the ledger of a restaurant:

Purchases	£200 000
Sales	450 000
Wages and salaries	120 000
Rent and rates	20 000
Light and heat	10 000

The first step is to set out the necessary journal entries as in Figure 90. Double entry is then completed in the appropriate nominal account in the ledger (Figure 91) and in the trading, profit and loss account (Figure 92).

		Journal				
19..						
Dec.	31	Trading A/c Dr.	200,000	00		
		Purchases A/c			200,000	00
		Being transfer at above date				
"	31	Sales A/c Dr.	450,000	00		
		Trading A/c			450,000	00
		Being transfer at above date				
"	31	Profit and Loss A/c Dr.	150,000	00		
		Wages and Salaries			120,000	00
		Rent and Rates			20,000	00
		Light and Heat			10,000	00
		Being transfer at above date				

Figure 90

Ledger

Purchases A/c

Date		Particulars	Folio	£	p	Date		Particulars	Folio	£	p
19..						19..					
various				....		Dec.	31	Trading A/c		200,000	00
dates		Balance		200,000	00						
				200,000	00					200,000	00

Sales A/c

Date		Particulars	Folio	£	p	Date		Particulars	Folio	£	p
19..						19..					
Dec.	31	Trading A/c		450,000	00	various				....	
						dates		Balance		450,000	00
				450,000	00					450,000	00

Figure 91

Wages and Salaries A/c

Date		Particulars	Folio	£	p	Date		Particulars	Folio	£	p
19..						19..					
various				....		Dec.	31	P/L A/c		120,000	00
dates		Balance		120,000	00						
				120,000	00					120,000	00

Rent and Rates A/c

Date		Particulars	Folio	£	p	Date		Particulars	Folio	£	p
19..						19..					
various				....		Dec.	31	P/L A/c		20,000	00
dates		Balance		20,000	00						
				20,000	00					20,000	00

Light and Heat A/c

Date		Particulars	Folio	£	p	Date		Particulars	Folio	£	p
19..						19..					
various				....		Dec.	31	P/L A/c		10,000	00
dates		Balance		10,000	00						
				10,000	00					10,000	00

Figure 91 (continued)

(Extract from)

TRADING, PROFIT AND LOSS A/C

Purchases	200,000	00	Sales	450,000	00
Wages & Salaries	120,000	00			
Rent & Rates	20,000	00			
Light & Heat	10,000	00			

Figure 92

Balance sheet The object of the balance sheet is to show, at a particular point in time, the financial position of a business. That means, to show what assets the business owns, what liabilities it has, and how much capital there is in the business. The balance sheet is *not* an account but a list of balances remaining in the ledger (i.e. assets and liabilities), after the preparation of the trading, profit and loss account.

The right-hand side of the balance sheet is known as the 'assets side'. Here we list all the assets (debit balances in the ledger) in what is known as the 'order of liquidity', i.e. according to how easy or how difficult it is to turn the asset concerned into cash. Whether one starts with the most liquid or with the least liquid asset does not really matter, though in businesses with a substantial proportion of fixed assets (see below) it is usual to start with the least liquid assets (premises, kitchen plant, restaurant furniture) and to end with the most liquid (cash). As most hotel and catering establishments have a large proportion of non-liquid (fixed) assets these are usually shown at the top of the balance sheet.

The left-hand side of the balance sheet is known as the 'liabilities side', and here, of course, we list all the liabilities of the business, represented by credit balances in the ledger. These are set out in the same manner as the assets. The more permanent liabilities—the capital account and long-term liabilities—are usually shown at the top, and creditors and other short-term liabilities at the bottom of the balance sheet.

Kinds of assets and liabilities In order to make the balance sheet more intelligible and meaningful, it is usual to provide suitable sub-headings, and to show the different kinds of assets and liabilities separately. The sub-headings commonly provided are:

Fixed assets These are the assets of a permanent nature, intended for use in the business as distinct from resale to customers, e.g. premises, kitchen equipment, restaurant furniture, glass, china and cutlery.

Current assets These are cash balances and other assets intended for conversion into cash, e.g. stocks of provisions, beverages, tobaccos, as well as debtors.

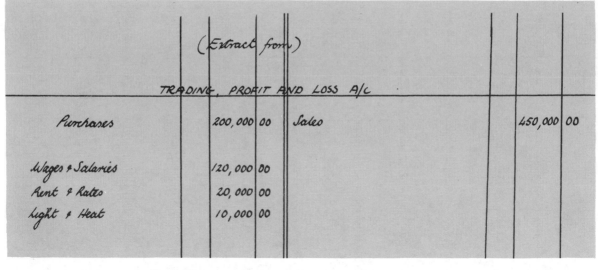

It will be appreciated that the distinction between fixed and current assets also depends on the nature of the business. Thus, furniture in a hotel is a fixed asset, whilst in the case of a dealer in furniture it is a current asset. What, then, matters is the intention of the owner of the asset—i.e. whether he has acquired it for the purpose of increasing the income-earning capacity of the business (retention of asset), or for resale to customers (conversion of asset into cash).

Capital The capital account of a business represents a liability from the business to its proprietor. On the liabilities side of the balance sheet particulars relating to the capital account are shown separately from any other liabilities.

Long-term liabilities These are liabilities of a more permanent nature, such as mortgages, bank loans extending over more than six months, and similar items.

Current liabilities These are liabilities of a temporary nature, usually payable within weeks or months of the date of the balance sheet. Examples of current liabilities are creditors expenses due but unpaid, and bank overdrafts, though the latter are sometimes permanent rather than temporary.

Example The following balances remained in the ledger of the Grand Hotel *after* the preparation of the trading, profit and loss account for the year ended 31st December, 19...

	£	£
Capital		390 000
Stock	5 000	
Kitchen plant	60 000	
Debtors	5 000	
City Finance Co.—loan account		100 000
Cash at bank	10 000	
Furniture	30 000	
Creditors		10 000
Drawings	10 000	
Freehold hotel	400 000	
Profit and loss account		30 000
China and cutlery	10 000	
	£530 000	£530 000

From the above balances the balance sheet of the hotel would be drawn up as shown in Figure 93.

GRAND HOTEL
BALANCE SHEET
as at 31st., Dec., 19..

Capital	£	£	Fixed Assets	£	£
Capital at 1st Jan., 19..	390,000		Freehold Hotel	400,000	
Add Net Profit	30,000		Kitchen Plant	60,000	
	420,000		Furniture	30,000	
Less Drawings	10,000	410,000	China and Cutlery	10,000	500,000
Long-Term Liabilities			**Current Assets**		
City Finance Co. – Loan A/c		100,000	Stocks	5,000	
Current Liabilities			Debtors	5,000	
Creditors		10,000	Cash in Bank	10,000	20,000
		£520,000			£520,000

Figure 93

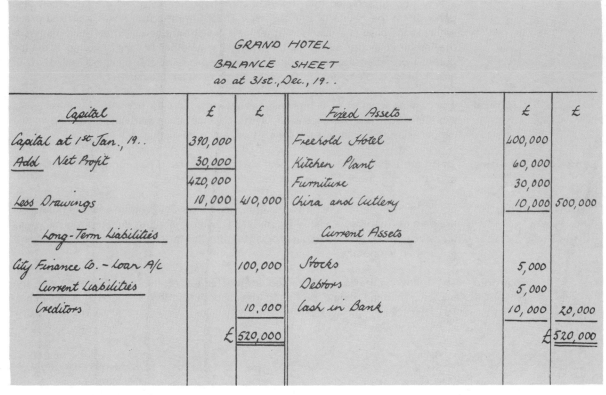

Capital account From the balance sheet given above it may be seen that the balance of the capital account increased from £390 000 to £410 000. The capital of a business is not static but is, in fact, changing continually, being increased by any profits made as well as by any fresh capital introduced by the proprietor, and decreased by any losses incurred as well as amounts, if any, withdrawn by the proprietor.

At the end of each accounting year it is necessary, therefore, to transfer all additions, as well as all withdrawals of capital, to the capital account in order that the correct amount of capital may be shown in the balance sheet. As already mentioned above, the net profit for the year is debited in the profit and loss account and credited in the capital account. If a net loss were made, the opposite entries would be required.

Any drawings (amounts of cash withdrawn by the proprietor for private use) are credited in the cash book and debited in the drawings account. At the end of each year the balance of the drawings account is transferred to the debit side of the capital account. Drawings in goods (food, wines, spirits and tobaccos consumed by the proprietor) should be credited in the purchases account and debited in the drawings account; these, too, are then debited in the capital account.

The capital account given in the balance sheet above would appear in the ledger as shown in Figure 94.

Problems 1 Explain the object of each of the following: trading account; profit and loss account; balance sheet.

		Capital A/c											
19..						19..					
Dec.	31	Drawings		10,000	00	Jan.	1	Balance	b/d	390,000	00
"	31	Balance	c/d	410,000	00	Dec.	31	Net Profit		30,000	00
				420,000	00					420,000	00
						19..					
						Jan.	1	Balance	b/d	410,000	00

Figure 94

2 Write short, explanatory notes on the treatment of: staff meals; drawings; carriage inwards.

3 Set out the necessary journal closing entries in respect of the balances below, transferred to the trading account of a restaurant at 31st December, 19...

Purchases	£150 000
Sales	350 000
Opening stock	2 000
Closing stock	3 000

4 Explain what is meant by: fixed asset; current asset; long-term liability; current liability.

5 Arrange the following assets in the order of liquidity, starting with the least liquid asset: debtors; restaurant furniture; china and cutlery; premises; kitchen plant; cash at bank.

6 Distinguish clearly between 'fixed assets' and 'current assets'. State which of the following are fixed and which current: leasehold premises; cash at bank; glass, china and linen; restaurant furniture; banqueting debtors; liquor stock.

7 The following balances were extracted from the ledger of Nix Restaurant at 31st December, 19..:

		£	£
Capital			10 000
Stocks, 1st January, 19..		750	
Wages and salaries		5 000	
Rent		1 000	
Sales			20 000
Purchases		10 000	
Insurance		200	
Gas and electricity		500	
	c/f	17 450	30 000

		£	£
	b/f	17 450	30 000
Kitchen utensils		1 500	
Restaurant furniture		4 000	
Creditors			2 000
Postage and telephone		300	
China and cutlery		1 000	
Kitchen equipment		5 000	
Cash at bank		2 750	
		£32 000	£32 000

You are required to prepare the restaurant's trading, profit and loss account for the year ended 31st December, 19.., and a balance sheet as at that date. Stocks at 31st December, 19.. were valued at £500.

8 From the following trial balance prepare a trading, profit and loss account for the year ended 31st December, 19.., and a balance sheet as at that date:

	£	£
Capital		150 000
Gas and electricity	8 900	
Rent and rates	9 500	
Stock, 1st January, 19..	3 100	
Discounts received		800
Sundry receipts		250
China and cutlery	6 100	
Purchases	92 300	
Freehold premises	110 000	
Purchases returns		500
Printing and stationery	3 150	
Furniture	12 500	
Cash in hand	100	
Creditors		5 950
Wages and salaries	50 200	
Staff meals	6 000	
Postage and telephone	2 100	
Drawings	8 500	
Sales		216 100
Kitchen equipment	24 000	
Miscellaneous expenses	3 500	
Professional charges	3 000	
Cash at bank	30 650	
	£373 600	£373 600

Note: Stock at 31st December, 19.. was valued at £3 300.

9 On 1st December, 19.., after eleven months' trading, Jack Mason had the following balances in his books:

	£
Capital	22 000
Sales	17 500
Purchases	6 200
Cash at bank	8 400

(continued)

Premises	17 250
Wages	3 700
China and cutlery	800
Furniture	1 250
Insurance	150
Drawings	2 500
Gas and electricity	750
Creditors: V. A. Rigby	500
O. Kay	1 000

Arrange these in the form of a trial balance and enter balances in accounts.

Mason's transactions in December were:

			£
December	2	Purchased provisions by cheque	1 500
,,	6	Drew cheque for private expenses	500
,,	10	Paid amount due to O. Kay	
,,	14	Banked sales to date	850
,,	16	Paid wages by cheque	600
,,	19	Paid rates by cheque	770
,,	23	Bought groceries on credit:	
		V. A. Rigby	1 200
		A. M. Williams	600
,,	27	Paid by cheque for insurance	150
,,	31	Banked sales to date	1 410

(a) Enter these transactions in Mason's books and extract a trial balance as at 31st December, 19...

(b) Prepare Mason's trading, profit and loss account for the year ended 31st December, 19.., and a balance sheet as at that date. The stock of provisions at 31st December, 19.. was valued at £600.

CHAPTER 9

Adjustments in nominal and personal accounts

Capital and revenue expenditure

We said in the previous chapter that the balances in the trial balance fell into two categories. The debit balances were either assets or expenses, and the credit balances liabilities or income. This was, in fact, an over-simplification as in practice what is an expense and what is an asset depends on what the accountant describes as the distinction between capital and revenue. A particular debit balance may be an asset, or an expense or partly one and partly the other.

The distinction between capital and revenue expenditure is of fundamental importance in the construction of final accounts, and may be summarized as follows.

(1) When, during an accounting period, an expenditure has taken place and at the end of that period there is *something to show for it* the expenditure is regarded as capital expenditure. Examples would be expenditure on premises, kitchen plant and furniture.

(2) When, on the other hand, an expenditure takes place and at the end of the current accounting period there is *nothing to show for it* the expenditure is regarded as revenue expenditure. Examples of revenue expenditure would be rent, rates, wages, salaries, insurance, etc.

It will be appreciated, on reflection, that the distinction between capital and revenue expenditure depends on the time factor: over a sufficiently long period all expenditure is of a revenue nature as (with the exception of land) nothing will last indefinitely.

All expenditure of a business results in the accrual of benefits. Whilst some of the benefits accrue over a long period (use of furniture, kitchen equipment, premises), others are short-lived (services of employees—resulting from wages paid, insurance against risks—resulting from premiums paid). When, therefore, we consider expenditure in relation to the time factor, we may distinguish between capital and revenue expenditure as follows.

(1) Where the benefits of expenditure are completely exhausted within the accounting period the expenditure is of a revenue nature. It must, therefore, be debited in the profit and loss account (sometimes also referred to as the revenue account).

(2) Where the benefits of expenditure are prolonged beyond the end of the accounting period, the expenditure is, to that extent, capital expenditure and must be carried to the balance sheet.

Finally, it may be added that, in general, capital expenditure consists of expenditure incurred in acquiring assets for the purpose of earning income or increasing the earning capacity of the business, whereas revenue expenditure consists of expenditure in replacing and repairing fixed assets as well as of the current expenses of the business.

Cases sometimes arise when it is rather difficult to decide whether a particular item of expenditure is of a capital or a revenue nature. Thus legal expenses are usually a revenue expense. When, however, these are incurred in connection with the purchase of premises they must be regarded as capital expenditure and debited in the premises account. Repairs are usually a revenue item. When, however, the effect of the repairs is to improve the asset in some way (rather than maintain it in its usual condition), the cost of such repairs should be capitalized, i.e. debited in the asset account rather than written off to the profit and loss account. For instance, when a new restaurant front is put in, it is quite legitimate to capitalize a part of the cost as, invariably, a new restaurant front is an improvement on an old one.

Finally, advertising is usually regarded as revenue expenditure. When, however, a newly-established hotel undertakes an advertising campaign in order to create a market for the accommodation, food and services offered, the whole cost of advertising should not be charged against the profits of the first accounting period but spread over several years.

From what has been said it will be realized that before the final accounts are prepared it is necessary to examine all items of expenditure and ensure that only revenue expenses are charged against the income of the period concerned. Otherwise the profit and loss account will not show the correct profit or loss; similarly items other than those of a capital nature might be carried to the balance sheet.

Capital and revenue receipts

Our consideration of the distinction between capital and revenue has, so far, been in connection with the expenditure side of the business. It will be appreciated, however, that the same considerations apply on the income side. Thus, whilst most of the receipts of a business are of a revenue nature, constituting proper income for the current accounting period, certain kinds of receipts (such as deposits on advance bookings, or any amounts received on the sale of fixed assets) may at the end of a period, be regarded as capital items.

As a result, it is also necessary to examine all items of income to ensure that the fundamental distinction between capital and revenue is observed in the preparation of final accounts. This is further explained under the heading 'Adjustment of Income' later in this chapter.

Adjustments in nominal accounts

Pre-paid expenses

Several expenses (e.g. insurance) are payable in advance and, at the end of an accounting period, it is necessary to ensure that only that part of the expense which applies to the current period (i.e. revenue portion) is debited to the profit and loss account.

Example 1

A hotel's accounting year ends on 31st December. On 31st March, 1981, the hotel takes out an insurance policy and pays the full annual insurance premium of £200.

Clearly, at the end of 1981, of the £200 that has been paid only £150 (the revenue portion) applies to the current accounting period. The balance of £50 (the capital portion) has been paid in respect of the following accounting period. At the end of 1981, the balance of £50 represents a benefit which is still to come and must, therefore, be shown in the hotel's balance sheet.

The hotel's insurance account for 1981 and 1982 as well as the relevant extracts from the corresponding profit and loss accounts and balance sheet are shown in Figures 95 and 96.

Insurance A/c

1981						1981					
March	31	Cash		200	00	Dec.	31	P/L A/c		150	00
						"	31	Balance	c/d	50	00
				200	00					200	00
1982						1982					
Jan.	1	Balance	b/d	50	00	Dec.	31	P/L A/c	c/d	200	00
March	31	Cash		200	00	"	31	Balance		50	00
				250	00					250	00
1983											
Jan.	1	Balance	b/d	50	00						

Figure 95

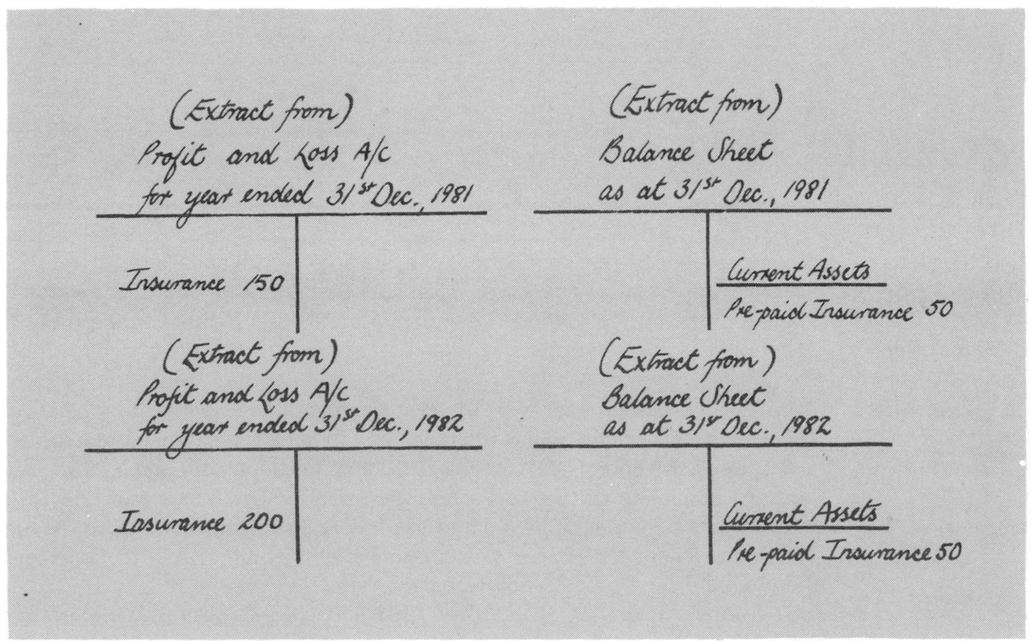

(Extract from)
Profit and Loss A/c
for year ended 31st Dec., 1981

Insurance 150

(Extract from)
Balance Sheet
as at 31st Dec., 1981

Current Assets
Pre-paid Insurance 50

(Extract from)
Profit and Loss A/c
for year ended 31st Dec., 1982

Insurance 200

(Extract from)
Balance Sheet
as at 31st Dec., 1982

Current Assets
Pre-paid Insurance 50

Figure 96

Example 2 At 31st December, 19.., before the preparation of the final accounts the stationery account of a restaurant appears as in Figure 97.

Stationery A/c

19..								
Jan.	17	Cash		300 00				
May	4	-do-		100 00				
Oct.	31	Petty cash		50 00				
Dec.	14	Cash		250 00				

Figure 97

You then ascertain that there is a stock of unused stationery valued at £100.

Clearly then, although £700 has been paid in respect of stationery, the amount consumed during the current accounting period (the revenue portion) is £600. The balance of £100 represents benefits still to come (capital expenditure) and must be shown in the balance sheet.

The stationery account would be adjusted as shown in Figure 98.

Stationery A/c

19..						19..						
Jan.	17	Cash		300	00	Dec.	31	P/L A/c		600	00
May	4	-do-		100	00	"	31	Balance	c/d	100	00
Oct.	31	Petty Cash		50	00						
Dec.	14	Cash		250	00						
				700	00					700	00
19..											
Jan.	1	Balance	b/d	100	00						

Figure 98

As a result of the above adjustment, £600 will be debited in the restaurant's profit and loss account, and the unused stationery of £100 will be shown as a current asset in the balance sheet.

Accrued expenses Some expenses are payable in advance and others are payable in arrear. Often there are, at the end of an accounting period, expenses which have been incurred but which have not been paid. Such expenses are called accrued expenses.

In order to arrive at the true net profit (or net loss) for a given period, it is necessary to show in the profit and loss account all income and all expenditure in respect of that period. Actual payment does not matter; what matters is when an expense is incurred. Consequently all expenses in respect of a particular period must be charged against the income of that period.

Example 1 A restaurateur pays £500 rent quarterly *after* occupation of the premises. When he prepares his final accounts on 31st December, 1981, he finds that he has not paid last quarter's rent due.

Show the entries necessary in the rent account, and the relevant extracts from the profit and loss account and the balance sheet. The entries required are given in Figure 99 (a) and the extracts in Figure 99 (b).

Rent A/c

Date		Particulars	Fo.	£	p	Date		Particulars	Fo.	£	p
1981						1981					
March	31	Cash		500	00	Dec.	31	P/L A/c		2,000	00
June	30	-do-		500	00						
Sept.	30	-do-		500	00						
Dec.	31	Balance	c/d	500	00						
				2,000	00					2,000	00
						1982					
						Jan.	1	Balance	b/d	500	00

Figure 99 (a)

Notes:

(1) As the rent incurred in 1981 is £2 000 this must be debited in the profit and loss account, even though the full amount of the rent has not been paid.

(2) At the end of 1981, £500 is owing to the landlord, and this is shown as a current liability in the balance sheet.

(3) When the accrued rent is actually paid the £500 will be credited in the cash book and debited in the rent account, thus closing the latter.

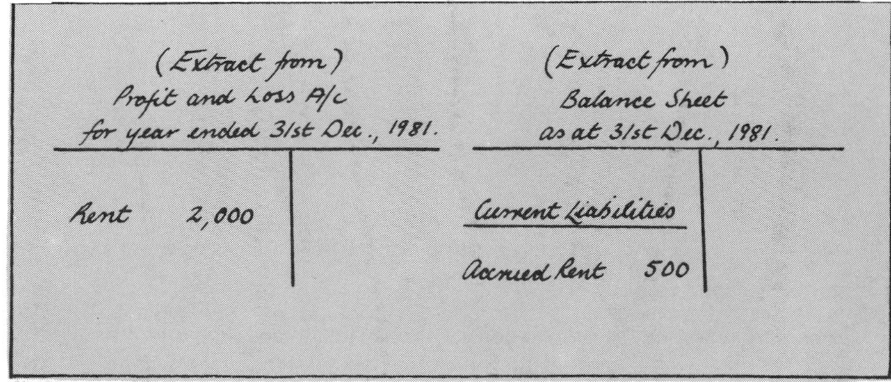

(Extract from)
Profit and Loss A/c
for year ended 31st Dec., 1981.

Rent 2,000	

(Extract from)
Balance Sheet
as at 31st Dec., 1981.

Current Liabilities	
Accrued Rent 500	

Figure 99 (b)

Example 2 A hotel prepares its annual profit and loss account at 30th September each year. At 30th September, 19.., before the preparation of the profit and loss account, the electricity account of the hotel shows a debit balance of £5 600, and you are informed that electricity consumed but not yet paid amounts to £400.

You are required to make the necessary adjustment in the electricity account (see Figure 100).

				Electricity A/c							
19..						19..					
Sept.	30	Sundries		5,600	00	Sept.	30	P/L A/c		6,000	00
"	30	Balance	c/d	400	00						
				6,000	00					6,000	00
						19..					
						Oct.	1	Balance	b/d	400	00

Figure 100

As a result of the adjustment in the above electricity account the full cost of electricity consumed (£6 000) is debited in the hotel's profit and loss account. The amount of electricity accrued is shown as a current liability in the balance sheet.

Adjustment of income Sometimes income due in respect of a particular period is not received until the following period. Similarly, certain items of income may be received before they are due. Hence, as in the case of various items of expenditure, adjustment of income items is often necessary.

Example 1 On 31st March, 19.., a hotel sub-lets ground floor accommodation to a travel agency. The full annual rent of £6 000 is payable in advance. The hotel prepares its annual accounts on 31st December each year.

You are required to show the adjustment necessary in the hotel's rent receivable account as well as the relevant extracts from the profit and loss account and the balance sheet. Proceed as shown in Figures 101 and 102 overleaf.

				Rent Receivable A/c							
19..						19..					
Dec.	31	P/L A/c		4,500	00	March	31	Cash		6,000	00
"	31	Balance	c/d	1,500	00						
				6,000	00					6,000	00
						19..					
						Jan.	1	Balance	b/d	1,500	00

Figure 101

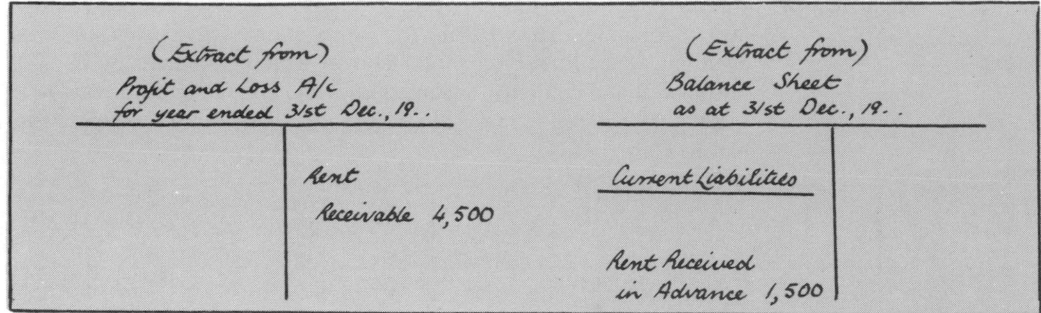

(Extract from)
Profit and Loss A/c
for year ended 31st Dec., 19..

	Rent Receivable 4,500

(Extract from)
Balance Sheet
as at 31st Dec., 19..

Current Liabilities	
Rent Received in Advance 1,500	

Figure 102

Notes: (1) As during 19.. the premises were sub-let for 9 months only 9/12ths of the rent is transferred to the profit and loss account. (2) The above credit balance of £1 500 represents a liability from the hotel to the travel agency, and must be shown as such in the balance sheet.

Example 2 A hotel company has certain investments, the income from which is receivable twice a year at 30th June and 31st December, the latter being the end of the company's accounting year.

Before the company's profit and loss account is prepared, it is ascertained that whilst the investment income in respect of the first half year, £600, has been duly received, the income due for the second half year has not. Show how you would deal with the above in the investment income account, profit and loss account and balance sheet.

Investment Income A/c

19..						19..					
Dec.	31	P/L A/c		1,200	00	June	30	Cash		600	00
						Dec.	31	Balance	c/d	600	00
				1,200	00					1,200	00
19..											
Jan.	1	Balance	b/d	600	00						

Figure 103

The debit balance of £600 shown in Figure 103 represents a debt owing to the hotel company and must, therefore, be shown as an asset in the balance sheet (see Figure 104).

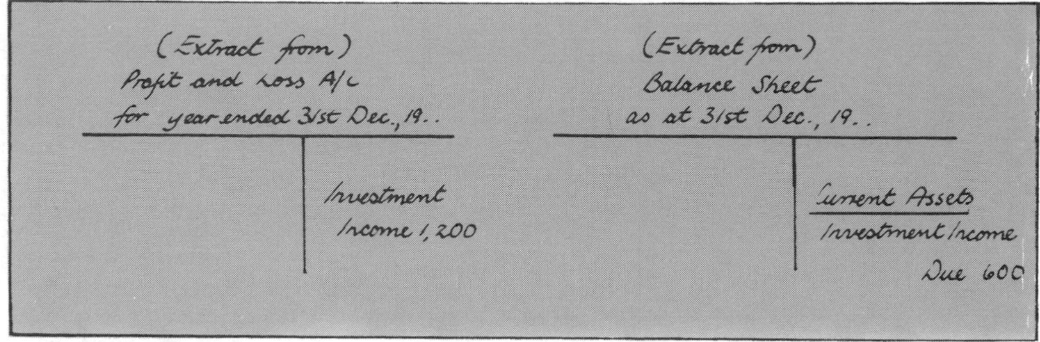

Figure 104

Adjustments in personal accounts*

Quite apart from any adjustments that may have to be made in nominal accounts, there are several kinds of adjustments that often become necessary in personal accounts, i.e. adjustments in respect of debtors and creditors.

Bad debts

A debt is regarded as bad, or irrecoverable, when all reasonable efforts to secure payment have failed. Then, quite obviously, there is no point in keeping the customer's account with a debit balance; and the only solution is to close it by transfer to the bad debts account. Double entry in respect of any bad debts written off is, therefore: Dr. bad debts account; Cr. debtor's personal account. At the end of the accounting period, the total of any bad debts written off is transferred from the bad debts account to the debit of the profit and loss account.

Example

The following balances appeared in the sales ledger of a hotel:

V. Brite Enterprises Ltd	£100
N. O. Cash	50
S. O. Pennyless	25

You are informed that V. Brite Enterprises Ltd are not able to pay the full amount due and that a dividend of only 25p in the £ will be received. Similarly you are informed that no payment is to be expected from either N. O. Cash or S. O. Pennyless.

Show the entries necessary in the accounts of the above customers, the bad debts account and the relevant extract from the profit and loss account.

Proceed as shown in Figures 105 (a) and (b), 106 and 107.

---

* Some of the adjustments dealt with in this section concern accounts other than personal accounts. It is, however, convenient to deal with them in this section rather than elsewhere.

V. Brite Enterprises Ltd.

19..						19..					
Dec.	31	Balance	b/d	100	00	Dec.	31	Bad Debts		75	00
						"	31	Balance	c/d	25	00
				100	00					100	00
19..											
Jan.	1	Balance	b/d	25	00						

Figure 105 (a)

N.O. Cash

19..						19..					
Dec.	31	Balance	b/d	50	00	Dec.	31	Bad Debts		50	00

S.O. Pennyless

19..						19..					
Dec.	31	Balance	b/d	25	00	Dec.	31	Bad Debts		25	00

Figure 105 (b)

Bad Debts A/c

19..											
Dec.	31	V. Brite Enterprises Ltd.		75	00	Dec.	31	P/L A/c		150	00
"	31	N.O. Cash		50	00						
"	31	S.O. Pennyless		25	00						
				150	00					150	00

Figure 106

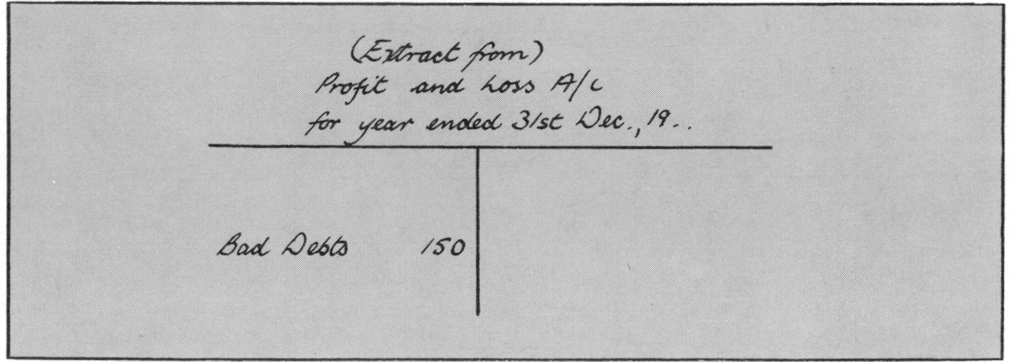

(Extract from)
Profit and Loss A/c
for year ended 31st Dec., 19..
Bad Debts 150

Figure 107

Note: When the dividend of 25p in the £ is actually received from the customer it will be debited in the cash book and credited in the personal account, thus closing the latter.

Bad debts recovered Sometimes it so happens that a debt previously written off is eventually recovered from the debtor. In such circumstances it is impossible to re-open and adjust the accounts for the past accounting period and the amount recovered must, therefore, be treated as a current receipt.

There are two methods of dealing with bad debts recovered. The simpler and more usual method is to debit such amounts in the cash book and credit the bad debts account. The effect of this method is to reduce the amount of bad debts debited in the profit and loss account. The alternative method is to open a bad debts recovered account and credit it with all amounts recovered. When this second procedure is adopted the balance from the bad debts recovered account is transferred to the credit side of the profit and loss account as a gain for the current accounting period.

Example On 31st December, 1981, the bad debts account of a restaurant shows a balance of £1 000. Before the final accounts are prepared you are informed that two further debts are to be treated as irrecoverable, viz:

A. Smith	£200
B. Brown	£300

You also find that an amount of £250 has been recovered in respect of a debt written off as bad three years previously. Show how you would deal with the above in the bad debts account of the restaurant, assuming that a bad debts recovered account is not kept.

Proceed as shown in Figure 108.

Bad Debts A/c

1981						1981					
Dec.	31	Balance	b/d	1,000	00	Dec.	31	Cash (Bad Debt Recovered)		250	00
"	31	A. Smith		200	00	"	31	P/L A/c		1,250	00
"	31	B. Brown		300	00						
				1,500	00					1,500	00

Figure 108

If, on the other hand, the restaurant did maintain a bad debts recovered account the entries would be recorded as in Figure 109.

Bad Debts A/c

				£	p					£	p
1981						1981					
Dec.	31	Balance	b/d	1,000	00	Dec.	31	P/L A/c		1,500	00
"	31	A. Smith		200	00						
"	31	B. Brown		300	00						
				1,500	00					1,500	00

Bad Debts Recovered A/c

				£	p					£	p
1981						1981					
Dec.	31	P/L A/c		250	00	Dec.	31	Cash		250	00

Figure 109

Provision for bad debts

At the end of each accounting period it is usually found that whilst certain debts are definitely bad others are doubtful, in that it is difficult to foresee whether or not they will, in fact, be paid.

As already explained, all debts which are regarded as definitely bad are treated as a loss and, therefore, written off to the profit and loss account. Clearly, however, it is prudent to make some provision for debts which may prove bad, especially if it is known from experience that a certain more or less fixed percentage of debtors fail to pay the amounts due from them in each accounting period. As a result, many businesses create a provision for bad debts; this is also known as a provision for doubtful debts or provision for bad and doubtful debts. The actual amount of the provision to be created may be arrived at in three different ways:

(1) It may, from past experience, be expressed as a percentage of total debtors.

(2) It may be based on amounts provided for specific doubtful debts, e.g. £50 in respect of the amount due from A, £20 in respect of the sum owing from B, etc.

(3) Finally, the amount of the provision may be based partly on method (1) and partly on method (2).

Example

On 31st December, 1981, the debtors of a hotel amounted to £1 000. On the basis of past experience it was expected that 5 per cent of the debts due would prove bad.

Show how you would deal with the above in the appropriate ledger accounts, the profit and loss account and the balance sheet.

Figure 110 shows the necessary entry in the profit and loss account.

(Extract from) Profit and Loss A/c
for year ended 31st Dec., 1981.

			£	p				£	p
		Provision for Bad Debts	50	00					

Figure 110

The provision for bad debts is an anticipated loss and must, therefore, be debited in the profit and loss account. Double entry is completed by crediting the provision for bad debts account, as is shown in Figure 111.

Provision for Bad Debts A/c

		£	p					£	p
				1981					
				Dec.	31	P/L A/c		50	00

Figure 111

In the balance sheet the provision is shown as a deduction from the debtors, as in Figure 112.

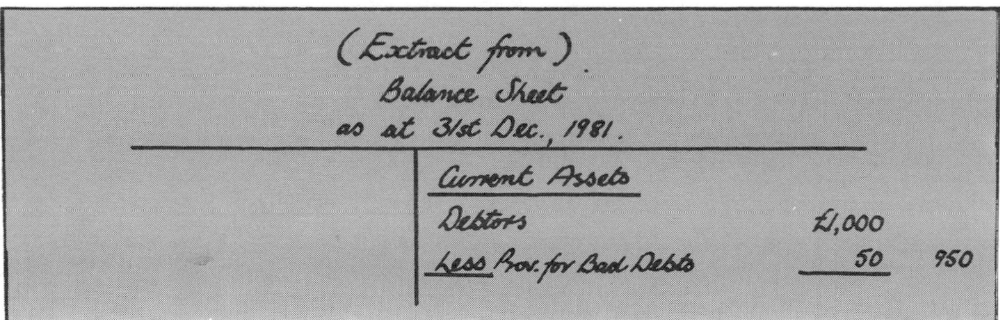

Figure 112

It will have been noticed that the creation of the provision does not involve any adjustments in the personal accounts of the debtors. That, in any case, would be difficult as it is not known which of them will prove bad nor how far any particular debt is to be regarded as bad. An important result of the provision is that the figure of debtors in the balance sheet is stated more realistically. Surely, it would have been wrong to show the debtors as £1 000 if it is known that £1 000 is not likely to be collected from them. In the balance sheet above we say, in effect: 'Our customers owe us £1 000, but we expect that £50 will not be paid by them and, therefore, the value of this asset is £950.'

Changes in provision for bad debts

The balance of the provision for bad debts account in Figure 111 will appear as an opening balance for the following year, when the amount of debtors need not necessarily be as at the end of 1981. Let us assume that at 31st December, 1982, the debtors of the hotel amount to £1 400, and that it is desired to maintain the provision for bad debts at 5 per cent of the debtors. Clearly, the provision created at the end of 1981 is now inadequate and has to be increased. This would be done as follows:

Provision for bad debts required at 31st December, 1982	
(5 per cent of £1 400)	£70
Less existing provision (from previous year)	50
Increase in provision necessary	£20

Now, in order to increase the balance of the provision for bad debts account, we must credit that account with £20. Double entry is then completed by debiting the profit and loss account with this increase of £20, as shown in Figure 113.

Provision for Bad Debts A/c

		1982				
		Jan.	1	Balance	b/d	50 00
		Dec.	31	P/L A/c		20 00

(Extract from) Profit and Loss A/c for year ended 31st Dec., 1982.

Prov. for Bad Debts	20 00		

Figure 113

In the balance sheet, the *already adjusted* provision of £70 is then deducted from the debtors, as shown in Figure 114.

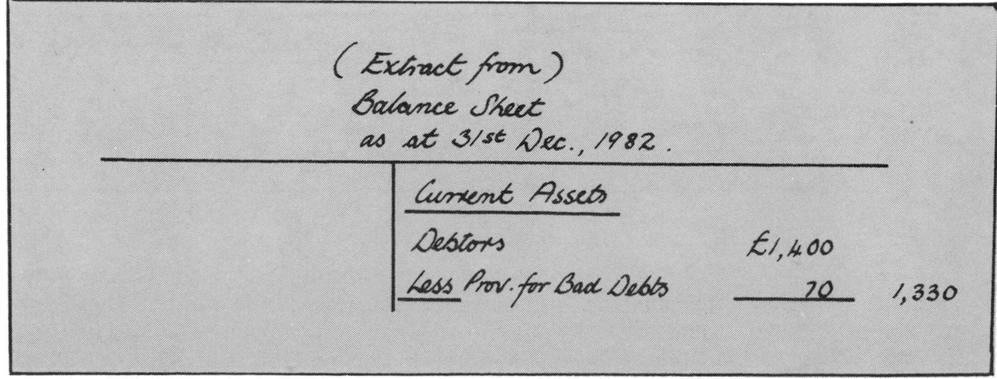

(Extract from)
Balance Sheet
as at 31st Dec., 1982.

Current Assets		
Debtors	£1,400	
Less Prov. for Bad Debts	70	1,330

Figure 114

When it is necessary to decrease the provision for bad debts the reverse procedure is adopted. Thus, to continue with the above hotel, if at the end of 1983 the debtors amounted to £800, a provision of only £40 would be necessary, and the balance of the provision for bad debts account would have to be decreased by £30. This would be achieved by crediting the difference of £30 in the profit and loss account and debiting the provision for bad debts account. In the balance sheet of the hotel we would show the debtors as (£800– £40) = £760.

Students should note that, once the provision has been created, only the difference (increase or decrease) is shown in the profit and loss account. In the balance sheet, the already adjusted provision is deducted from the debtors.

Combining bad debts account with provision for bad debts account

In some businesses, the bad debts account is combined with the provision for bad debts account. The combined account is written up as shown in the following example.

Example

At 31st December, 1981, a hotel has an existing provision for bad debts of £40. You are informed that during the year ended 31st December, 1981, bad debts amounting to £60 were written off, and that at the above date it is desired to maintain the provision at 5 per cent of the debtors, which then were £1 000.

Provision for Bad Debts A/c

1981						1981					
Dec.	31	Bad Debts		60	00	Jan.	1	Balance	b/d	40	00
"	31	Balance (5% of Debtors £1000)		50	00	Dec.	31	P/L A/c		70	00
				110	00					110	00
						1982					
						Jan.	1	Balance		50	00

Figure 115

As may be seen from Figure 115 when this method is adopted all bad debts are written off to the provision for bad debts account. The provision required at the end of the year (£50) is shown as the balance carried down. The balance of the account (£70) is then transferred to the profit and loss account. It should be added that whether one uses separate accounts or one account for the bad debts and the provision does not affect the net profit. If we used separate accounts, the profit and loss would still be debited with £70 as follows:

Bad debts written-off	£60
Increase in provision for bad debts	10
Total Dr. in profit and loss account	£70

Provision for discount allowed

In addition to the provision for bad debts, many businesses create a provision for discounts allowed, i.e. for the loss of income resulting from cash discounts being allowed to customers.

Few hotel and catering establishments allow cash discounts to their customers. When it is desired to give more favourable terms to particular customers (e.g. airline companies who book blocks of rooms over long periods or customers booking accommodation in the off-season) this is usually achieved by quoting them lower rates rather than offering cash discounts.

Where, however, it is necessary to create a provision for discounts allowed this is done exactly in the same manner as in respect of the provision for bad debts. Also any changes in the provision for discounts allowed are effected in the same way as those in the provision for bad debts.

Provision for discount received

In addition to any provision that may be created on the debtors side, it is quite common to create a provision in respect of the creditors of a business. This is known as the provision for discounts received, and its object is to include in the final accounts any income that will accrue to the business from cash discounts receivable from the creditors. Although the discounts will not be received until the following period, it is argued that they are the result of credit purchases in the current period and should, therefore, be regarded as current profit.

Any amount provided for discounts received (an anticipated gain) should be credited in the profit and loss account. Double entry is then completed by debiting the provision for discounts received account. In the balance sheet, the provision for discounts received should be shown as a deduction from the creditors.

Example

At 31st December, 1981, the creditors of a hotel amount to £1 000. On the basis of past experience it is expected that cash discount received from the creditors will average 3 per cent.

You are required to create a provision for discount received, showing the entries necessary in the ledger as well as the relevant extracts from the profit and loss account and the balance sheet.

Proceed as indicated in Figures 116 and 117.

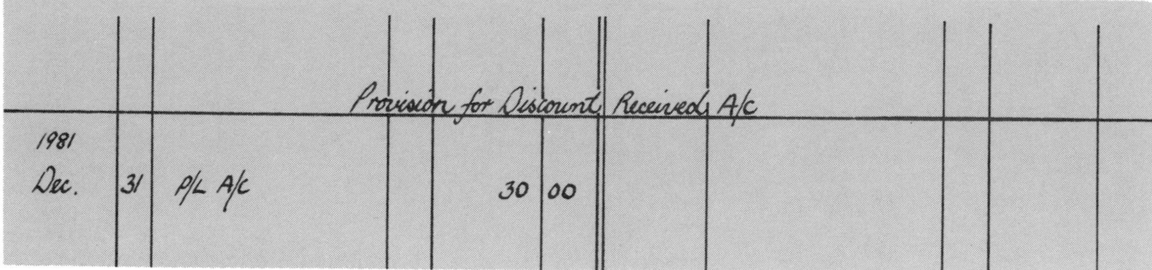

Figure 116

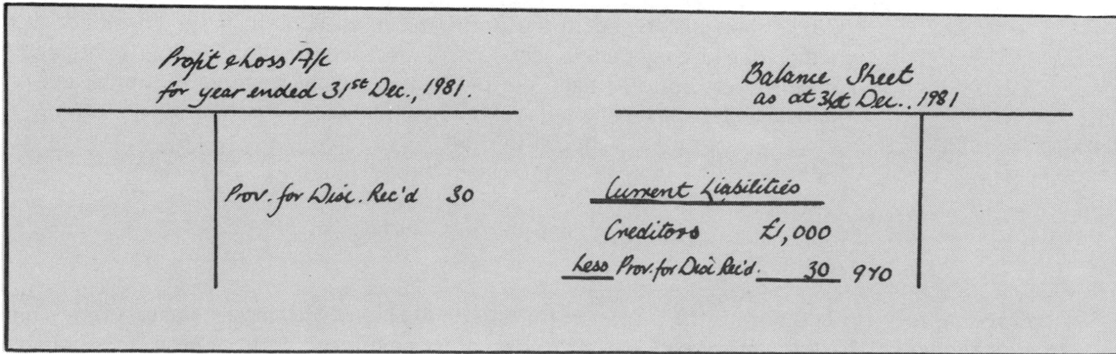

Figure 117

It will be observed that as a result of the creation of the provision for discount received, we are able to show in the balance sheet a more realistic figure of creditors. We show, in effect, that although a total of £1 000 is owing to the suppliers, because we expect to receive cash discounts from them the net liability is in fact £970.

Any changes in the provision for discount received, resulting from changes in the level of the creditors from one year to another, are effected in a similar manner to the changes in the provision for bad debts.

Thus, if at the end of the following year the creditors of the hotel were £1 200, and if it were desired to maintain the provision for discount received at 3 per cent, the balance of the provision for discount account would obviously have to be increased to (3 per cent of £1 200) £36. The increase in the provision (i.e. £6) would have to be credited in the profit and loss account and debited in the provision for discount received account. In the balance sheet we would show the creditors as (£1 200 less £36) £1 164. A decrease in the provision for discount received would, of course, necessitate the reverse entries—a debit in the profit and loss account and a credit in the provision for discount received account.

In some businesses the provision for discount received account is combined with the discount received account. When this procedure is adopted the combined account is written up as shown in the illustration below.

Example At 31st December, 1981, you find that a restaurant has already received cash discounts of £400. You also find that the restaurant has an existing provision for discount received of £200 and that, at the above date, it is desired to maintain the provision at 4 per cent of the creditors, which then amounted to £4 000. Show how you would deal with the above in the provision for discount received account.

Proceed as shown in Figure 118.

Provision for Discount Received A/c

				£	p					£	p
1981						1981					
Jan.	1	Balance	b/d	200	00	Dec.	31	Cash		400	00
Dec.	31	P/L A/c		360	00	"	31	Balance	c/d	160	00
				560	00					560	00
1982											
Jan.	1	Balance	b/d	160	00						

Figure 118

Journalizing adjustments

It was explained in Chapter 5 that all transactions are in the first instance recorded in subsidiary books and then posted to the ledger. It will be appreciated that the same principle must be applied to the adjustments dealt with in the present chapter. Thus, it would be incorrect, when writing off bad debts, to make the necessary entries in the ledger without first recording them in the journal. Equally, it would be incorrect to create or adjust a provision on debtors or creditors without first recording this in the journal.

The method of journalizing the adjustments we have now dealt with is illustrated below.

Example 1 The following balances appeared in the sales ledger of the City Hotel at 31st December, 19..:

A. C. Brown	£500
M. G. Blake	300
B. W. Gray	250

You are informed that only 50p in the £ can be recovered from Brown and that Blake's and Gray's debts should now be regarded as bad.

Show the journal entries necessary to deal with the above matters, by proceeding as shown in Figure 119.

JOURNAL

19.. Dec.	31	Bad Debts A/c Dr.	800	00		
		A.C. Brown			250	00
		M.G. Blake			300	00
		B.W. Gray			250	00
		Being bad debts written off.				

Figure 119

Example 2 At 31st December, 19.., a hotel has brought forward from the previous year a provision for bad debts of £100, and a provision for discount received of £50.

You are required, at the above date, to adjust the provision for bad debts to 5 per cent of the debtors, amounting to £2 600; also to adjust the provision for discount received to 3 per cent of the creditors, which then amounted to £2 000.

To show the journal entries necessary to adjust the above provisions, the provisions required are:

Provision for bad debts—5 per cent of £2 600	= £130
Provision for discount received—3 per cent of £2 000	= £60

Therefore they have to be increased by £30 and £10 respectively. The journal entries will appear as in Figure 120.

		JOURNAL				
19.. Dec.	31	Profit and Loss A/c Dr.	30	00		
		Provision for Bad Debts			30	00
		Being adjustment of above provision to 5 per cent of debtors				
"	31	Provision for Discount Received A/c Dr.	10	00		
		Profit and Loss A/c			10	00
		Being adjustment of above provision to 3 per cent of creditors				

Figure 120

Problems

1 Distinguish clearly between capital and revenue expenditure. Explain why this distinction is important in the compilation of final accounts.

2 Explain what information is conveyed to you by the following balances standing in the ledger of a restaurant at 31st December, 19.., after balancing the accounts and preparing the final accounts for the year ended at that date: a debit balance on rent account; a credit balance on rent receivable account; a debit balance on stationery account; a credit balance on electricity account.

3 A hotel maintains a provision for bad debts account, which is also used to record the actual bad debts. From the information given below you are required to reconstruct the hotel's provision for bad debts account for four years.

Accounting period	Bad debts written off	Debtors at year-end	Provision required
			%
Year 1	—	£800	5
Year 2	£35	900	5
Year 3	50	700	5
Year 4	25	860	5

You are also required to show the relevant extracts from each year's profit and loss account, and balance sheet.

4 From the information given below, you are required to reconstruct certain nominal accounts of a restaurant, and to show clearly in each case the amount of expenditure transferred to the profit and loss account.

Account	Opening balance at 1st January, 19..	Cash paid during 19..	Closing balance at 31st December, 19..
Wages account	Cr. £2 000	£180 000	Cr. £3 000
Insurance account	Dr. 500	550	Dr. 700
Repairs account	Cr. 3 000	12 350	Dr. 500
Stationery account	Dr. 300	6 200	Dr. 100
Electricity account	Cr. 800	14 700	Cr. 600
Telephone account	Cr. 400	3 600	Cr. 300

5 (a) At 31st December, 1981, a hotel has debtors amounting to £600. You are required to create a provision for bad debts equal to 5 per cent of the debtors. Show the necessary ledger entries and the relevant extracts from the hotel's profit and loss account and the balance sheet.

(b) At 31st December, 1982, the debtors of the same hotel amount to £400. You are required to adjust the provision for bad debts to 5 per cent of the debtors. Show the necessary ledger entries and the relevant extracts from the profit and loss account and the balance sheet.

6 At 31st December, 1981, the bad debts provision of a caterer amounted to £210. During the ensuing year debts amounting to £176 were written off as irrecoverable and a payment of £21 was received in respect of a debt which had been treated as bad four years previously. It was estimated that at 31st December, 1982, a provision of £240 would be sufficient to cover any loss in respect of the debts then outstanding.

7 (a) On 30th June, 1982, the balance of the provision for bad and doubtful debts account was £875. During the financial year ending 30th June, 1983, accounts to the value of £54 were written off as bad. On 30th June, 1983, the total of the sundry debtors was £18 200 and it was decided to maintain the provision at 5 per cent of the debtors.

Prepare the provision for bad and doubtful debts account for the year ended 30th June, 1983 (all items are posted to this account).

(b) What other methods (other than a percentage on sundry debtors as used in section (a) of this question) could be used to arrive at the amount of the provision for bad and doubtful debts at the end of a financial year?

M.H.C.I.

8 The following trial balance was extracted from the books of a restaurant at 31st December, 1981.

	£	£
Capital		100 000
China and cutlery	4 000	
Restaurant furniture	2 000	
Sales		52 500
Purchases	24 600	
Legal and professional charges	1 250	
Purchases returns		900
Wages and salaries	13 100	
Bank charges	200	
Cash in hand	750	
Creditors		4 500
Debtors	1 000	
Provision for bad debts		100
Stock at 1st January 1981	1 200	
Postage and stationery	1 600	
Rent and rates	3 200	
Leasehold premises	90 000	
Discounts received		150
Drawings	5 000	
Cash at bank	6 150	
Cleaning materials	600	
Repairs and replacements	1 300	
Telephone	550	
Miscellaneous expenses	1 650	
	£158 150	£158 150

You are required to prepare the restaurant's trading, profit and loss account for the year ended 31st December 1981, and a balance sheet as at that date.

The following are to be taken into account:

(i) Final stock was valued at £1 400;

(ii) Provision for bad debts to be decreased to £50; create a provision for discounts received equal to 2 per cent of the creditors;

(iii) Accrued salaries £200.

9 A. Caterer presents the following trial balance of the books of his restaurant at 31st December, 19. .

		£	£
Capital			100 000
Bad debts recovered			100
Banqueting debtors		4 000	
Repairs and replacements		1 000	
Sales			120 000
Provision for discounts received		200	
Furniture		6 000	
Purchases returns			500
Postage and telephone		800	
Purchases		60 000	
Wages and salaries		29 500	
Provision for bad debts			300
Drawings		2 500	
Creditors			6 000
Stock		2 000	
	c/f	106 000	226 900

		£	£
	b/f	106 000	226 900
Cash at bank		21 600	
Premises		90 000	
Gas and electricity		6 800	
Bad debts		500	
China, cutlery and linen		2 000	
		£226 900	£226 900

You are asked to prepare the trading, profit and loss account for the year ended 31st December, 19.., and a balance sheeet as at that date, taking the following into consideration:

(i) Stock at 31st December, 19.. was valued at £2 200;

(ii) An invoice for advertising for £350 was due for payment but had not been included in the accounts;

(iii) The estimated cost of staff meals is £500 per month;

(iv) Two purchase invoices amounting to £1 000 had not been entered in the books;

(v) Provision for bad debts should be made equal to 5 per cent of the debtors;

(vi) It is estimated that cash discounts on creditors will amount to 3 per cent of total creditors;

(vii) Caterer estimates that £3 000 included in the purchases represents private consumption by himself and his family.

CHAPTER 10

Adjustments in real accounts

Nature and causes of depreciation

Depreciation may be defined as the loss in the value of an asset. The term *depreciation* has, however, more than one meaning. To most people depreciation denotes a physical deterioration of an asset. To the accountant, however, it means an amount of expense, arising out of the physical deterioration and other causes, that has to be charged against profits. It is with the latter meaning of depreciation that we shall be mainly concerned in this chapter.

There are several distinct factors causing assets to lose value, and these may be summarized as follows:

Wear and tear

This is the most common cause of depreciation and arises out of the actual usage of the asset in the normal course of business. Assets which lose in value as a result of this cause are: kitchen plant, furniture, bedding, linen, glass, china and similar assets. Also under the heading of wear and tear we have exceptional damage or deterioration, due to accidental happenings taking place in the course of business, resulting in breakage and destruction.

Time factor

There are several assets that lose in value simply as a result of the passage of time, e.g. leasehold premises. Thus, when a lease of premises is purchased for £100 000, and the lease has ten years to run, the cost of the lease (loss in value) is £10 000 p.a. and, quite irrespective of the actual use made of the premises, depends on the passage of time.

Obsolescence

An asset is said to be obsolete when it has to be scrapped before the end of its effective life because, owing to an improved version of the asset being available on the market, its continued use in the business would be uneconomical. In other words, obsolescence takes place when an asset, still in a good working condition, has to be replaced because it no longer pays to use it in the business. An example would be the replacement of an old-fashioned type of charcoal grill by an under-fired gas grill.

Other causes

There are one or two other causes of depreciation. A change in consumer demand may necessitate a different type of service (e.g. self-service rather than waitress service) and result in some of the existing equipment being scrapped. Similarly, an asset may become inadequate for the purpose for which it was initially intended. For instance, as a result of an extension of the premises assets of larger capacity (central heating boilers) may be required.

From what has been said it will be appreciated that different assets may depreciate for different reasons. Whilst leasehold premises depreciate because of the time factor, china, cutlery and kitchen utensils lose in value as a result of wear and tear. Finally, furniture, in common with other assets, depreciates as a result of both. It is mainly for this reason that different methods of depreciation have been evolved to deal with different kinds of assets.

Method of dealing with depreciation

There are three main methods of dealing with depreciation used in hotel and catering establishments: the straight-line method; the reducing balance method; the revaluation method.

Straight-line method Under this method the amount of depreciation to be charged against profits in any one year is calculated by deducting from the initial cost of the asset its scrap value (if any), and dividing the result by the estimated life of the asset in terms of years. The formula for calculating depreciation under this method is, therefore:

$$\frac{\text{INITIAL COST} - \text{SCRAP VALUE}}{\text{ESTIMATED LIFE}} = \text{ANNUAL DEPRECIATION.}$$

Example A hotel buys heavy kitchen equipment for £103 000. It is estimated that the equipment will have an effective working life of ten years, and that it will fetch (scrap value) £3 000 at the end of that period. Calculate the annual depreciation that should be debited to the hotel's profit and loss account in respect of the above equipment.

Thus from the equation above: $\frac{£103\,000 - £3\,000}{10} = £10\,000$

Two main advantages may be claimed for this method of depreciation: first, it is easy to calculate; secondly, it is possible to depreciate an asset completely within a definite period. Its disadvantage is that a separate calculation is necessary for every asset and that, consequently, more detailed records of assets have to be kept. The straight-line method is, however, widely used in hotel and catering establishments in respect of assets such as furniture, heavy kitchen equipment and leaseholds.

Reducing balance method Under this method the annual depreciation is expressed as a given percentage of the book value of the asset at the beginning of each year. As the book value of the asset diminishes, so does the annual depreciation.

Example A hotel buys two billing machines costing £20 000 and it is decided to write off depreciation at the rate of 20 per cent per annum. Calculate the amount of depreciation to be debited to the profit and loss account of the hotel for the first three years, following the acquisition of the billing machines.

	Cost of billing machines	£20 000
less:	Depreciation, year 1, (20 per cent of £20 000)	4 000
	book value—end of first year	16 000
less:	Depreciation, year 2, (20 per cent of £16 000)	3 200
	book value—end of second year	12 800
less:	Depreciation, year 3, (20 per cent of £12 800)	2 560
	book value—end of third year	£10 240

The reducing balance method is easy to apply as all assets of a particular type (furniture, office equipment, kitchen plant) may be lumped together and depreciated at the same rate (percentage). Further, it is often said that the cost of an asset consists of two things: (a) the actual depreciation and (b) the cost of repairing and maintaining the asset. Whilst, under this method, the depreciation charge becomes less and less, the cost of repairs and maintenance tends to rise towards the end of the life of the asset. As a result, it is claimed, the total charge to the profit and loss account tends to be spread evenly over the entire life of the asset. A disadvantage of this method is that it is impossible to write off an asset completely. Even at the end of the nth year, when the book value might be 4p, a depreciation of 20 per cent will only reduce the book value to 3½p!

Revaluation method Assets such as glass, china, cutlery and light kitchen equipment consist of a large number of individual items which require to be replaced at fairly frequent intervals. The simplest method of writing off any losses of such equipment is to revalue it at the end of each accounting period. The decrease in the value of such equipment, as disclosed by the annual inventories, between the beginning and the end of a year is regarded as the depreciation for that year.

Example On 31st December, 19.., a restaurant has a stock of china and cutlery valued at £4 000. At 31st December, 19.., an inventory of the china and cutlery shows that it then has a value of £3 200. The difference of £800 represents losses of china and cutlery in respect of the period and must, therefore, be debited to the restaurant's profit and loss account as depreciation.

Entries in the ledger

The entries in the ledger in respect of depreciation follow the same lines whichever of the three methods is used. This will become evident from the illustrations given below.

Example 1 On 1st January, 1981, a hotel buys furniture costing £15 000 and having an estimated life of fifteen years. Show the furniture account of the hotel for three years to 31st December, 1983, and give the relevant extracts from the hotel's profit and loss account for the year ended 31st December, 1981, and the balance sheet as at the latter date.

Proceed as shown in Figures 121 and 122.

Furniture A/c

				£	p					£	p
1981						1981					
Jan.	1	Cash		15,000	00	Dec.	31	P/L A/c		1,000	00
						"	31	Balance	c/d	14,000	00
				15,000	00					15,000	00
1982						1982					
Jan.	1	Balance	b/d	14,000	00	Dec.	31	P/L A/c		1,000	00
						"	31	Balance	c/d	13,000	00
				14,000	00					14,000	00
1983						1983					
Jan.	1	Balance	b/d	13,000	00	Dec.	31	P/L A/c		1,000	00
						"	31	Balance	c/d	12,000	00
				13,000	00					13,000	00
1984											
Jan.	1	Balance	b/d	12,000	00						

Figure 121

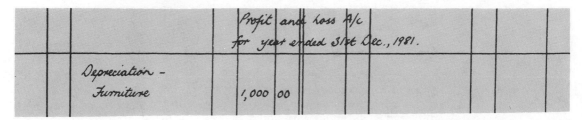

Profit and Loss A/c for year ended 31st Dec., 1981.				
Depreciation – Furniture	1,000	00		

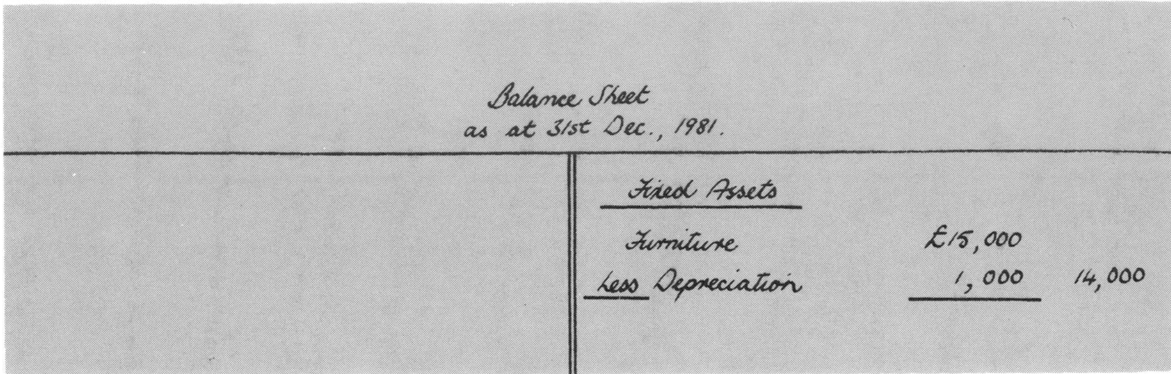

Balance Sheet
as at 31st Dec., 1981.

	Fixed Assets		
	Furniture	£15,000	
	Less Depreciation	1,000	14,000

Figure 122

Notes: (1) If the straight-line method is used, the depreciation debited in the profit and loss account will be constant throughout the life of the asset. (2) In the balance sheet, we show the book value of the asset at the beginning of the current period; deduct the annual depreciation and extend the book value at the end of the current period. The following year's balance sheet (i.e. as at 31st December, 1982) will, therefore, show the furniture as (£14 000 less £1 000) £13 000.

Example 2 On 1st January, 1981, a catering company operating self-service restaurants buys five cash registers costing £4 000 each. The cash registers are to be depreciated at the rate of 20 per cent per annum. Show the cash registers account for the three years ending 31st December, 1983, the relevant extracts from the company's profit and loss account for the year ended 31st December, 1981, and the balance sheet as at that date.

Proceed as shown in Figures 123, 124 and 125.

Cash Registers A/c

Date		Particulars	Fo.	£	p	Date		Particulars	Fo.	£	p
1981						1981					
Jan.	1	Cash		20,000	00	Dec.	31	P/L A/c		4,000	00
						"	31	Balance	c/d	16,000	00
				20,000	00					20,000	00
1982						1982					
Jan.	1	Balance	b/d	16,000	00	Dec.	31	P/L A/c		3,200	00
						"	31	Balance		12,800	00
				16,000	00					16,000	00
1983						1983					
Jan.	1	Balance	b/d	12,800	00	Dec.	31	P/L A/c		2,560	00
						"	31	Balance	c/d	10,240	00
				12,800	00					12,800	00
1984											
Jan.	1	Balance	b/d	10,240	00						

Figure 123

Profit and Loss A/c
for year ended 31st. Dec, 1981.

		Particulars		£	p			Particulars		£	p
		Depreciation - Cash Registers		4,000	00						

Figure 124

Balance Sheet
as at 31st Dec., 1981.

	Fixed Assets		
	Cash Registers	£ 20,000	
	Less Depreciation	4,000	16,000

Figure 125

As may be seen the ledger entries are the same whether the straight line or the reducing balance method is used.

Example 3 On 1st January, 1981, a restaurant has glass and china valued at £3 000. During the year ended 31st December, 1981, further glass and china are purchased for £500. The inventory at 31st December, 1981 shows that the stock of glass and china is then worth £2 800. Show the glass and china account for the period concerned and the relevant extracts from the restaurant's profit and loss account and balance sheet.

Proceed as shown in Figures 126, 127 and 128.

Glass and China A/c

				£	p					£	p
1981						1981					
Jan.	1	Balance	b/d	3,000	00	Dec.	31	P/L A/c		700	00
...	..	Cash		500	00	"	31	Balance	c/d	2,800	00
				3,500	00					3,500	00
1982											
Jan.	1	Balance	b/d	2,800	00						

Figure 126

Profit and Loss A/c for year ended 31st. Dec., 1981.

				£	p					£	p
		Depreciation - Glass and China		700	00						

Figure 127

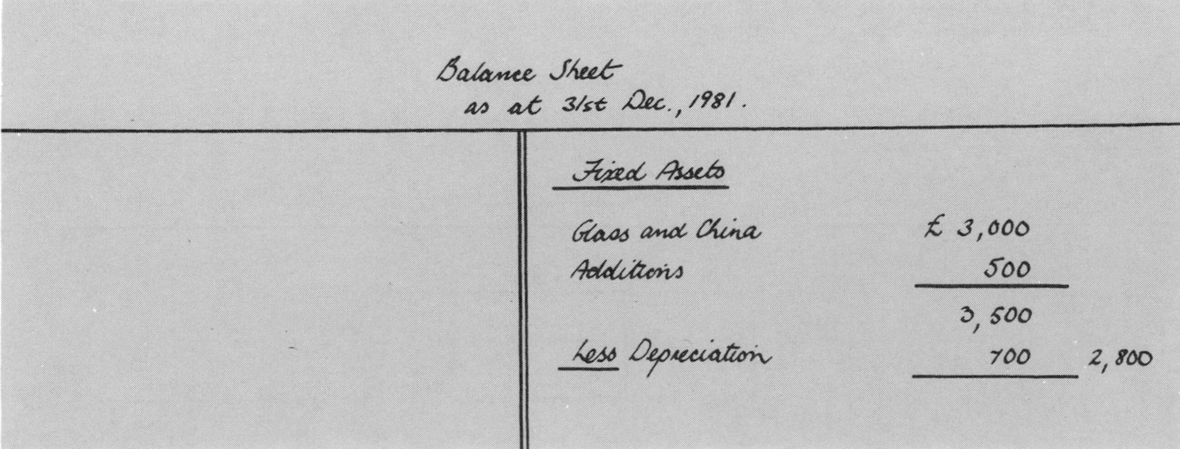

Balance Sheet as at 31st Dec., 1981.

	Fixed Assets		
	Glass and China	£ 3,000	
	Additions	500	
		3,500	
	Less Depreciation	700	2,800

Figure 128

Other methods of depreciation In addition to the three principal methods of depreciation outlined above there are one or two other methods used in some businesses.

Sinking fund method Under this method a fixed amount of depreciation is debited in the profit and loss account each year, and a corresponding amount of cash is invested in gilt-edged securities each year. As a result, provision is made for the replacement of the asset at the end of its life, when the proceeds from the sale of the securities become available for the purchase of a new asset.

Endowment insurance policy method Under this method, instead of investing amounts of cash in gilt-edged securities, the cash is used in payment of the premium on what is known as a capital redemption policy, which will mature at the end of the existing asset's life.

Annuity method Under this method it is assumed that the capital sunk in the purchase of the asset might, if used in some other direction, have earned a certain rate of interest each year. Consequently, interest on the diminishing balance is debited to the account of the asset and a fixed annual depreciation is written off. The balance of the account is completely eliminated at the end of the life of the asset.

Provision for depreciation account The ledger entries in respect of depreciation illustrated follow the traditional practice of debiting the profit and loss account and crediting each asset with the annual charge for depreciation

There is, however, another method of dealing with depreciation in the accounts which has become popular in recent years. Under this alternative method we leave the asset in the ledger at cost and, each year, debit the depreciation charge in the profit and loss account and credit it in the provision for depreciation account. The balance of the latter account will thus increase from one year to another and represent the aggregate amount of depreciation written off to-date.

In the balance sheet we show the asset at cost less aggregate depreciation written off, which, no doubt, results in a clearer picture of the assets owned by the business being given. When the asset concerned has been completely depreciated the balance of the provision for depreciation account is transferred to the asset account: both balances are thus eliminated. The method of dealing with depreciation may be applied whether we use the straight line or the reducing-balance method.

Example On 1st January, 1981, a hotel buys an asset for £3 000 which has an estimated life of three years. It is decided to depreciate it by the straight line method. Show the necessary ledger entries and the appropriate extracts from the final accounts of the hotel.

Proceed as shown in Figures 129, 130 and 131.

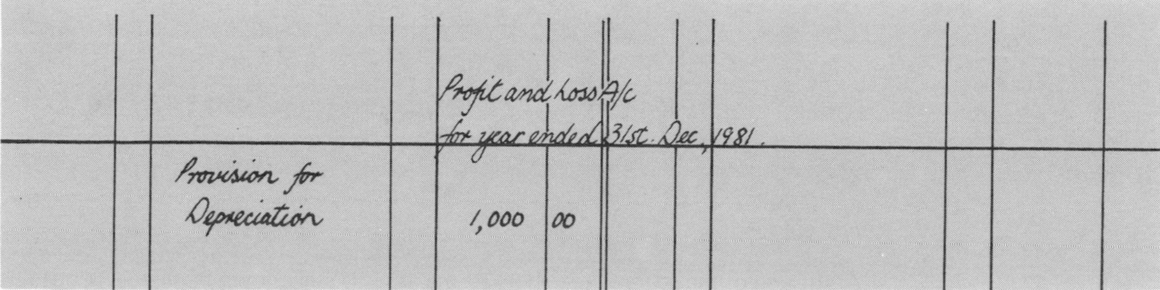

Figure 129

Provision for Depreciation A/c

				£	p					£	p
1981 Dec.	31	Balance	c/d	1,000	00	1981 Dec.	31	P/L A/c		1,000	00
1982 Dec.	31	Balance	c/d	2,000	00	1982 Jan.	1	Balance	b/d	1,000	00
						Dec.	31	P/L A/c		1,000	00
				2,000	00					2,000	00
1983 Dec.	31	Asset		3,000	00	1983 Jan.	1	Balance	b/d	2,000	00
						Dec.	31	P/L A/c		1,000	00
				3,000	00					3,000	00

Figure 130

Asset A/c

				£	p					£	p
1981 Jan.	1	Cash		3 000	00	1983 Dec.	31	Prov. for Depreciation		3,000	00

Figure 131

At the end of the first year the asset would be shown as in Figure 132.

Balance Sheet
as at 31st Dec., 1981.

	Fixed Assets		
	Assets at cost	£3,000	
	Less Depreciation	1,000	2,000

Figure 132

At the end of the second year (1982), the asset is still shown at cost (£3 000) less the aggregate depreciation to date (£2 000), i.e. at £1 000. See Figure 133.

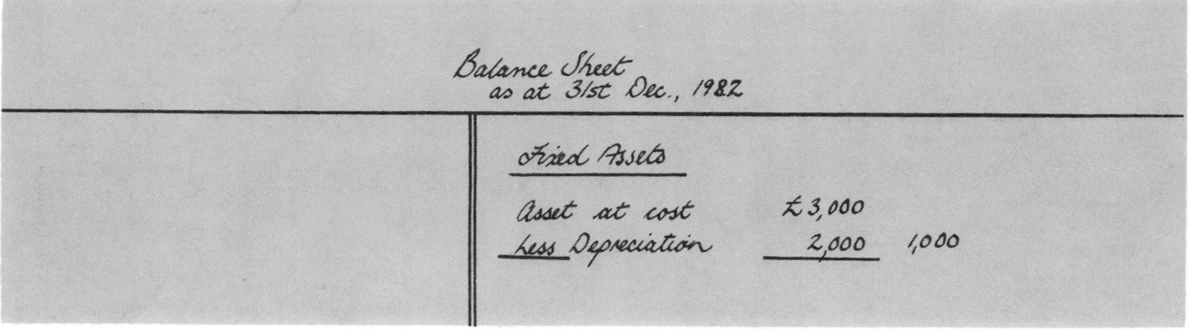

Balance Sheet
as at 31st Dec., 1982

	Fixed Assets		
	Asset at cost	£3,000	
	Less Depreciation	2,000	1,000

Figure 133

Repairs equalization account

As mentioned already the cost of an asset consists of two parts: the depreciation and any repairs or renewals necessary. Whilst the depreciation charge is predetermined well in advance, the cost of repairs may fluctuate quite considerably from one year to another. Extensive repairs to an asset may be carried out in one year and scarcely anything may, therefore, have to be spent the following year.

In order to avoid the effect of fluctuating repair costs on profits it is sometimes the practice to create a repairs equalization account. Each year a fixed amount is debited in the profit and loss account and credited in the repairs equalization account. The actual expenditure on repairs is then debited in the repairs equalization account. As a result, the cost of repairs is spread evenly over a period of years.

Example A restaurant's actual expenditure on repairs over a period of four years was:

Year 1	£2 950
,, 2	6 530
,, 3	2 320
,, 4	7 660

At the end of the first year it was decided to open a repairs equalization account and to credit it, each year, with a fixed amount of £5 000. Show the repairs equalization account for the four years concerned as well as the relevant extracts from the cash book and the profit and loss account for year 1.

Proceed as shown in Figures 134, 135, 136 and 137.

Repairs Equalisation A/c

Year 1						Year 1					
Dec.	31	Cash		2,950	00	Dec.	31	P/L A/c		5,000	00
"	31	Balance	c/d	2,050	00						
				5,000	00					5,000	00
Year 2						Year 2					
Dec.	31	Cash		6,530	00	Jan.	1	Balance	b/d	2,050	00
"	31	Balance	c/d	520	00	Dec.	31	P/L A/c		5,000	00
				7,050	00					7,050	00

Figure 134 First and second years

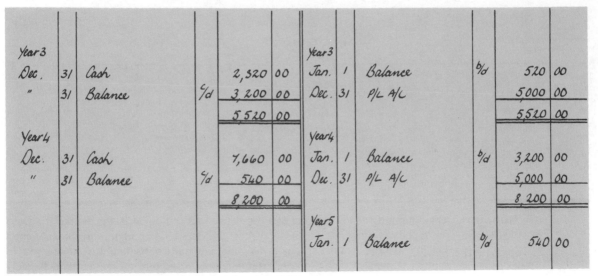

Year 3						Year 3					
Dec.	31	Cash		2,320	00	Jan.	1	Balance	b/d	520	00
"	31	Balance	c/d	3,200	00	Dec.	31	P/L A/c		5,000	00
				5,520	00					5,520	00
Year 4						Year 4					
Dec.	31	Cash		7,660	00	Jan.	1	Balance	b/d	3,200	00
"	31	Balance	c/d	540	00	Dec.	31	P/L A/c		5,000	00
				8,200	00					8,200	00
						Year 5					
						Jan.	1	Balance	b/d	540	00

Figure 135 Third, fourth and fifth years

Cash Book
Year 1

								Repairs Equal A/c		2,950	00

Figure 136

Profit and Loss A/c
end of year 1

		Repairs Equal. A/c		5,000	00						

Figure 137

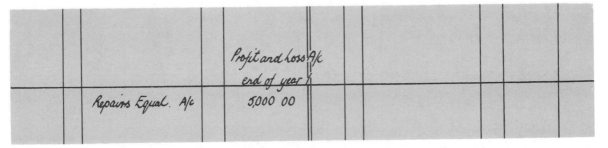

As may be seen, the charge for repairs in each year's profit and loss account is constant. At the end of each year the repairs equalization account will show a debit or a credit balance. A debit balance would indicate that the cost of actual repairs has exceeded the repairs (fixed amounts) so far debited in the profit and loss account; a credit balance would, on the other hand, indicate that more has been debited in the profit and loss account than has actually been spent on repairs.

Journal entries In accordance with the principle that every transaction must be entered in a subsidiary book before being posted to the ledger, all ledger entries in respect of depreciation should be journalized.

Specimen journal entries in respect of depreciation are illustrated in Figure 138.

Example On 1st January, 1981, a hotel had the following balances in its ledger:

Leasehold premises	£160 000
Furniture	60 000
Kitchen equipment	40 000

At 31st December, 1981, you are required to provide for depreciation as follows: leasehold premises, £5 000; furniture 10 per cent; kitchen equipment $12\frac{1}{2}$ per cent. Set out the necessary journal entries. Proceed as shown in Figure 138.

		JOURNAL				
1981						
Dec.	31	Profit and Loss A/c Dr.		16,000	00	
		Leasehold Premises				5,000
		Furniture				6,000
		Kitchen Equipment				5,000
		Being depreciation written off.				

Figure 138

Funds flow statements Funds flow statements have become very common in recent years throughout the hotel and catering industry. It is essential, therefore, that students should understand what they mean and how they are compiled.

A funds flow statement has one important purpose, which is to explain the change in total working capital from one balance sheet to another. It does not examine the factors affecting working capital in any minute detail but, simply, lists the principal factors which have operated to increase or decrease the working capital.

The balance sheet: current and non-current items It is possible to think of the balance sheet as consisting of current and non-current items. If we draw a horizontal line, we will have, below the line, current assets and current liabilities and, above this horizontal line, items of a non-current nature.

Balance Sheet	
Capital Long-term Liabilities	Fixed Assets
Current Liabilities	Current Assets

Now that we have separated the current and non-current elements of the balance sheet, we can trace the effect of any one transaction on the working capital. From the point of view of the impact on the working capital, transactions may be divided into three groups.

Transactions which increase working capital

If the owners of a business introduce more capital then the effect is as follows. Capital (above the horizontal line) is increased and cash (below the line) is also increased. As current liabilities are unchanged and current assets have increased, we have an increase in working capital, or 'funds' for this purpose. The same effect is obtained if we raise a long-term loan: just an increase in current assets (cash) below the line and an increase in working capital. Any withdrawal/reduction of capital will have the opposite effect. Thus any drawings will decrease the current assets and, as current liabilities are not affected, the effect will be to decrease the working capital.

All profitable transactions have the effect of increasing working capital. If we sell for cash beverages costing £100 for £200, the effect is this. Current assets will increase by £100 (stock decreased by £100, but cash increased by £200). Net profit (above the line) will increase by £100. As current liabilities are not affected by the transaction, the working capital is increased by £100.

Transactions which decrease working capital

The purchase of fixed assets for cash will decrease current assets (cash) and increase fixed assets (above the line). As current liabilities are unchanged the effect will be to decrease working capital. Any withdrawal of owners' capital will, as already explained reduce working capital.

The effect of unprofitable transactions is to decrease working capital. If we sell food, costing £50, for £25 on credit, the effect is as follows. Current assets are decreased by £25 (food stocks having decreased by £50 and debtors increased by £25). Net profit (profit & loss account—above the line) will be decreased by £25. The working capital of the business will be decreased by £25.

Transactions which have no effect on working capital

There are several transactions which have no effect on working capital. Thus if we purchase fixed assets and finance the transaction by a long-term loan, both effects are above the line, and neither current assets nor current liabilities are in any way affected. When we pay suppliers, there is a decrease in current assets (cash) and a corresponding decrease in current liabilities (creditors) and the amount of working capital remains unaffected. If we purchase goods on credit, we have an increase in current assets (stocks) and an increase in current liabilities (creditors) and hence no change in working capital. Finally, when we write off depreciation we reduce both the fixed assets and the net profit. Both these items are non-current, above the line, and the effect on the working capital is nil.

Example 1 Given below is the balance sheet of a restaurant drawn up on 1st May, 19...

Balance Sheet as at 1st May, 19..

Capital	£	£	Fixed Assets	£	£
Capital A/c	100,000		Sundry Assets		115,000
Add N. Profit	20,000	120,000			
Current Liabilities			Current Assets		
Creditors	8,000		Food + Bev. Stocks	11,000	
Accruals	2,000	10,000	Debtors	1,000	
			Cash	3,000	15,000
		£130,000			£130,000

Figure 139

On 2nd May, 19.., the following transactions took place:

(a) Beverage stocks, costing £200, were sold for £400 cash
(b) The proprietor withdrew cash, £500, for private use
(c) Cutlery was purchased for cash, £1 000
(d) Food was purchased on credit, £2 000
(e) Cash, £500, was received from debtors
(f) Unwanted kitchen equipment was sold for cash, £400.

You are required:

(1) to show the effect of each of the above transactions on the working capital;
(2) to prepare a funds flow statement, explaining the change in the total working capital between 1st and 2nd May, 19..;
(3) to prepare the balance sheet of the restaurant as at 2nd May, 19...

Solutions
Part 1—Effect of transactions on working capital

(a) Current assets increased by £200; no change in current liabilities; working capital increased by £200.
(b) Current assets decreased by £500; no change in current liabilities; working capital decreased by £500.
(c) Current assets decreased by £1 000; no change in current liabilities; working capital decreased by £1 000.
(d) Both current assets and current liabilities increased by £2 000; no change in working capital.
(e) Current assets unchanged as decrease in debtors of £500 offset by corresponding increase in cash; hence no change in working capital.
(f) Current assets increased by £400; no change in current liabilities; increase in working capital of £400.

Part 2—Funds flow statement

From the analysis of the impact of the six transactions on working capital we may prepare a simple statement explaining the change in the overall working capital position between 1st and 2nd May, 19.. as follows.

Funds Flow Statement

		£
Working capital at 1st May, 19.. (£15 000–£10 000)		5 000
Add Sources of funds:		
Net profit	200	
Sale of equipment	400	600
		5 600
Less Applications of funds:		
Drawings	500	
Purchase of cutlery	1 000	1 500
Working capital at 2nd May, 19.. (£16 100–£12 000)		£4 100

Students should note that of the six transactions in Example 1, two increased the working capital, two decreased it and, finally, two had no effect at all on the working capital of the restaurant. Transactions (d) and (e) operated wholly under the horizontal line and were thus neutral. Each of the other four transactions operated across the horizontal line and had some effect on the working capital.

Part 3—Balance sheet We may now show the balance sheet of the restaurant on 2nd May, 19.. as follows.

Balance Sheet as at 2 May, 19..

Capital	£	£	Fixed Assets	£	£
Capital A/c	100,000		Sundry Assets		115,600
Add N. Profit	20,200				
	120,200		Current Assets		
Less Drawings	500	119,700	Food & Bev. Stocks	12,800	
Current Liabilities			Debtors	500	
Creditors	10,000		Cash	2,800	16,100
Accruals	2,000	12,000			
		£131,700			£131,700

Figure 140

Example 2 Given below are the balance sheets of the Acton Restaurant as at 31st December, 1981 and 1982 as well as the capital account written up to 31st December, 1982.

Balance Sheet as at 31st Dec, 1981.

	£	£		Cost £	Dep'n £	Net £
Capital			**Fixed Assets**			
Capital A/c		120,000	Premises	100,000	-	100,000
Long-term Liabilities			Plant	40 000	15,000	25,000
Loan A/c		30,000	Furniture	30,000	10,000	20,000
			China, etc.	5,000	2,000	3,000
Current Liabilities				175,000	27,000	148,000
Creditors	15,000		**Current Assets**			
Accruals	5,000	20,000	Stocks		10,000	
			Debtors		4,000	
			Cash		8,000	22,000
		£170,000				£170,000

Figure 141

Balance Sheet as at 31 Dec., 1982.

	£	£		Cost £	Dep'n £	Net £
Capital			**Fixed Assets**			
Capital A/c		139,000	Premises	100,000	-	100,000
Long-term Liabilities			Plant	40,000	20,000	20,000
Loan A/c		20,000	Furniture	30,000	15,000	15,000
			China, etc.	5,000	3,000	2,000
Current Liabilities				175,000	38,000	137,000
Creditors	10,000		**Current Assets**			
Accruals	3,000	13,000	Stock		15,000	
			Debtors		6,000	
			Cash		14,000	35,000
		£172,000				£172,000

Figure 142

Capital A/c

				£	p					£	p
1982						1982					
Dec	31	Drawings		2,000	00	Jan	1	Balance	b/f	120,000	00
"	31	Balance	c/f	139,000	00	Apr	16	Cash		10,000	00
						Dec	31	Net Profit		11,000	00
				141,000	00					141,000	00
						1983					
						Jan	1	Balance	b/f	139,000	00

Figure 143

From the information given above prepare the funds flow statement of the Acton Restaurant.

Solution From the balance sheets given above we can see that the amounts of working capital are as follows:

(a) 31st December 1981 – £22 000 less £20 000 = £2 000
(b) 31st December 1982 – £35 000 less £13 000 = £22 000

Funds Flow Statement

Working Capital at 31st Dec., 1981.		£2,000
Add Sources of Funds:		
Net Profit	£11,000	
Depreciation	11,000	
Fresh Capital	10,000	32,000
		34,000
Less Applications of Funds:		
Loan Repayment	£10,000	
Drawings	2,000	12,000
Working Capital at 31st Dec., 1982.		£22,000

Figure 144

Cash flow statements Quite apart from funds flow statements, many businesses prepare cash flow statements at least once a year. Whilst the aim of the funds flow statement is to explain the change in the working capital from one balance sheet to another, the aim of the cash flow statement is to explain the change in the cash balance from one balance sheet to another.

A funds flow statement may be converted into a cash flow statement by taking into account changes which have occurred within the working capital, i.e. changes in the items below the line. Let us look at a few examples.

Given the total working capital, a decrease in debtors represents an increase in cash, as cash must have been received in settlement of the debts owing to the business. An increase in stock means a decrease in cash. A decrease in creditors means that cash must have been applied in the payment of the amounts owing to the creditors. Finally, an increase in accrued expenses represents a saving of cash resources, etc. To make this clearer let us now convert the funds flow statement given in Figure 144 into a cash flow statement.

Cash Flow Statement

Opening Cash Balance at 1st Jan., 1982.		£8,000
Add Sources of Cash:		
Net Profit	£11,000	
Depreciation	11,000	
Fresh Capital	10,000	32,000
		40,000
Less Applications of Cash:		
Loan Repayment	£10,000	
Drawings	2,000	
Increase in Stock	5,000	
Increase in Debtors	2,000	
Decrease in Creditors	5,000	
Decrease in Accrual	2,000	26,000
Closing Cash Balance at 31st Dec., 1982		£14,000

Figure 145

Problems 1 (a) What are the main causes of depreciation?

(b) What are the main methods of dealing with depreciation?

2 List the main advantages and disadvantages of each of the following methods of dealing with depreciation: straight-line method; reducing-balance method; revaluation method.

3 The A-n-B Restaurant purchased heavy kitchen equipment on 1st January 1981 for £10 000. Show by means of ledger accounts how the equipment would be depreciated between this date and 31st December, 1983, using the straight-line method, and the reducing-balance method.

Provide in each case depreciation at the rate of 20 per cent.

4 (a) Explain what is meant by 'repairs equalization account'.

(b) A hotel's actual expenditure on repairs over four years was:

Year 1	£2 370
,, 2	6 720
,, 3	2 530
,, 4	7 870

At the end of the first year it was decided to open a repairs equalization account and to credit it each year with £5 000. Show the ledger entries in the accounts concerned for the above period as well as the relevant extracts from the cash book and the profit and loss account.

5 The following trial balance was extracted from the books of the Acropolis Restaurant on 30th June, 19...

	£	£
Capital		200 000
Purchases and sales	90 000	235 500
Stock on 1st July, 19..	6 500	
Trade creditors		7 500
Banqueting debtors	8 500	
Rent and rates	4 500	
Wages and salaries	49 750	
Light and heat	7 750	
Repairs and renewals	3 900	
Furniture	19 000	
Kitchen equipment	22 000	
China and cutlery	8 300	
Drawings	550	
Cash at bank	2 750	
Leasehold premises	220 000	
Provision for bad debts		500
	£443 500	£443 500

You are required to prepare the restaurant's trading, profit and loss account for the year ended 30th June, and a balance sheet as at that date. Take the following into account:

(a) The final stock of provisions was valued at £7 000;
(b) Adjust the provision for bad debts to 5 per cent of the debtors;
(c) Provide the depreciation as follows:

Furniture	10 per cent;
Kitchen equipment	£2 000;
Leasehold premises	£10 000;
China and cutlery were revalued at	£7 100.

(d) The cost of staff meals is estimated at £8 000;
(e) Unrecorded invoices in respect of purchases amounted to £500;
(f) You are informed that the Society for the Promotion of Neat Book-Keeping owes the restaurant £1 000 in respect of a banquet; this has not been recorded in the books;
(g) The item 'repairs and renewals' includes an amount of £700 in respect of repairs to the proprietor's house.

6 After a firm had completed its profit and loss account for the year ended 31st December, 1981, showing a net profit of £5 000, the following errors were discovered:
(1) An invoice for the purchase of goods value £500 had not been entered in the Purchases Day Book;
(2) Depreciation at the rate of 5 per cent p.a. on office furniture value £5 000, had not been allowed for;
(3) Rent for the quarter ended 31st December, 1981 (£1 000 p.a.) was not paid until 3rd January, 1982.
(4) Insurance of £480 p.a. was paid up to 31st March, 1982 and no adjustment had been made.
(5) A cheque, value £300, received from a customer had not been entered in the Cash Book.

Calculate the adjusted net profit in the form of a statement.

7 From the following trial balance prepare a trading, profit and loss account for the year ended 31st December, 19.., and a balance sheet as at that date.

	£	£
Stock at 1st January, 19..	12 500	
Receipts from visitors		352 460
Fuel and light	9 640	
Rent and rates	12 330	
Advertising	7 200	
Purchases	112 760	
China, linen and cutlery	14 270	
Wages and salaries	104 110	
Carriage inwards	3 400	
Furniture and fittings	74 300	
Bad debts	2 150	
Drawings	15 300	
Capital		249 000
Visitors' ledger balances	13 150	
Creditors		12 500
A. Penny—loan account	80 000	
Leasehold premises	105 000	
Cash at bank	43 750	
Provision for bad debts		400
Repairs to furniture	4 500	
	£614 360	£614 360

Notes: (a) Stocks on hand at 31st December, 19.. amounted to £9 450; (b) Provide for depreciation as follows:

(i) Furniture and fittings — 10 per cent;
(ii) Leasehold premises — £3 000;
(iii) China, linen and cutlery were revalued at £12 500;

(c) Increase the provision for bad debts to £500 and create a provision for discount received equal to 2 per cent of the creditors;
(d) Provide for the outstanding loan interest (£4 000) on the loan to A. Penny;
(e) Treat £1 700 of the advertising as paid in advance.

8 A. Gallop is proprietor of the Old Colonial Restaurant and the following trial balance was extracted from his books at 31st December, 19...

	£	£
Capital		60 000
Freehold	41 000	
Debtors and creditors	500	9 500
Drawings	10 600	
Cash at bank	12 530	
Purchases and sales	30 560	73 020
Restaurant change float	100	
Repairs and renewals	2 710	
Motor van expenses	1 830	
Motor van	4 000	
Purchases returns		260
Wages	8 000	
Salaries	6 340	
Stock 1st January, 19..	3 850	
Lighting and heating	3 960	
Restaurant furniture	12 500	
Printing and stationery	570	
Postage and telephone	640	
China, utensils and cutlery	2 600	
Insurance	330	
Bad debts	160	
	£142 780	£142 780

You are required to prepare Gallop's trading, profit and loss account for the year ended 31st December, 19.. and a balance sheet as at that date. The following are to be taken into account:

(1) Stock at 31st December, 19.. was valued at £4 980;
(2) Outstanding lighting and heating £190;
(3) Prepaid insurance £80;
(4) Create a provision for discount received equal to 2 per cent of the creditors;
(5) Depreciation is to be provided as follows:
 (a) Motor van 20 per cent;
 (b) Restaurant furniture 10 per cent;
 (c) China, utensils and cutlery were revalued at £2 200.

9 The following trial balance was extracted from the books of the White Eagle Restaurant at 31st March, 19... You are required to prepare the restaurant's trading, profit and loss account for the year ended 31st March, 19.., and a balance sheet as at that date.

	£	£
Capital		197 000
Purchases	92 340	
Kitchen equipment	19 200	
Printing and stationery	4 340	
Creditors		10 000
Postage and telephone	3 240	
Stock of provisions, 1st April, 19..	4 220	
Wages and salaries	47 940	
Sales		218 620
National Insurance	3 520	
Fuel and light	9 960	
Leasehold premises	153 500	
Discounts received		380
Cash in hand	300	
Repairs and renewals	6 320	
Bad debts	1 280	
Carriage inwards	1 520	
Rates	7 480	
Restaurant furniture	9 200	
Advertising	9 940	
Cash at bank	32 300	
China and utensils	7 000	
Debtors	2 400	
Drawings	10 000	
	£426 000	£426 000

Notes: (a) The stock of provisions at 31st March, 19.. was valued at £3 960;
(b) £9 800 of the cost of provisions consumed is to be treated as the cost of staff meals;
(c) Accrued wages and salaries amounted to £560;
(d) Create a provision for bad debts of £100;
(e) Provide for depreciation as follows:

(i) Leasehold premises £10 300;
(ii) Kitchen equipment 10 per cent;
(iii) Restaurant furniture £1 200;
(iv) China and utensils were revalued at £5 800;

10 The following trial balance was extracted from the books of a restaurant after the compilation of the trading account for the year ended 31st December, 19...

		£	£
Trading account			99 500
Stock		3 150	
Kitchen equipment		14 600	
Drawings		7 500	
Postage and telephone		2 450	
Cash at bank		16 980	
Wages and salaries		36 010	
National Insurance		2 650	
Creditors			8 000
Restaurant furniture		8 000	
Printing and stationery		3 210	
China and cutlery		5 200	
Debtors		2 100	
	c/f	101 850	107 500

		£	£
	b/f	101 850	107 500
Advertising		7 430	
Discount received			290
Fuel and light		7 420	
Repairs and renewals		4 850	
Bad debts		990	
Rates		5 900	
Leasehold premises		120 000	
Cash in hand		1 200	
Capital			142 000
Provision for discounts received		150	
		£249 790	£249 790

You are required to prepare the profit and loss account of the restaurant for the year ended 31st December, 19. ., and a balance sheet as at that date. You are to take into account the information given below.

(a) Provide for depreciation as follows:

(i) Leasehold premises £6 000;
(ii) Kitchen equipment 10 per cent;
(iii) Restaurant furniture 12 per cent;
(iv) China and cutlery were revalued at £4 400.

(b) Make provision for the following accrued expenses:

(i) Advertising £250;
(ii) Audit fee £350;
(iii) Stationery £120.

(c) Increase the provision for discounts received to 3 per cent of the creditors.
(d) Treat £100 of the debtors as bad.
(e) Rates paid in advance amounted to £200.

11 The following errors have been made by the book-keeper of an hotel:
(a) Provisions purchased from a supplier for £113.00 have been posted to the credit of his account as £131.00.
(b) An amount of £75.00, being insurance paid in advance in the previous year, has not been brought forward as an opening balance in the insurance account.
(c) Discount amounting to £35.50 received from a supplier has been entered in his account but not posted to the discount account.
(d) Replacement of linen purchased for £175.00 has been entered in the purchases day book, the total of which has been posted to the purchases account.

(1) Explain what effect each of the above errors would have on the net profit of the hotel.

(2) Calculate the total difference in the trial balance resulting from the above errors.

12 The following trial balance was extracted from the books of Allan May at 31st December, 19. . .

		£	£
Capital			100 000
Purchases and sales		39 550	110 540
Stock of provision, 1st January, 19. .		4 050	
Bought ledger control account			5 000
	c/f	43 600	215 540

		£	£
	b/f	43 600	215 540
Banqueting debtors		9 940	
Rent and rates		6 000	
Wages and salaries		26 150	
Lighting and heating		3 050	
Repairs and renewals		2 010	
Furniture		12 000	
Kitchen equipment		6 000	
Plate, china and cutlery		4 830	
Cash at bank		19 670	
Cash in hand		2 290	
Leasehold premises		80 000	
		£215 540	£215 540

Notes: (1) Stock of provisions at 31st December, 19. . was valued at £3 800.
(2) Depreciation is to be provided as follows:

(a) Furniture	10 per cent;
(b) Leasehold	15 per cent;
(c) Kitchen equipment	15 per cent;
(d) Plate china and cutlery were revalued at £4 500	

(3) Of the banqueting debtors £440 is considered irrecoverable.
(4) Create the following:

(a) Provision for bad debts	2 per cent
(b) Provision for discount received	3 per cent

You are required to prepare May's trading profit and loss account for the year ended 31st December, 19. ., and a balance sheet as at that date.

13 (a) At 31st December, 1981, a restaurant has debtors amounting to £900. You are required to create a provision for bad debts equal to 4 per cent of the debtors. Show the relevant ledger entries and extracts from the restaurant's profit and loss account and the balance sheet.
(b) At 31st December, 1982, the debtors of the same restaurant amount to £500. and it is desired to maintain the provision for bad debts at 4 per cent. Show the ledger entries required at this date and the relevant extracts from the profit and loss account and the balance sheet.

14 Explain what you understand by:
(a) funds flow statement;
(b) cash flow statement.

15 Describe the effect of transactions on working capital. Give examples of transactions which: (a) increase; (b) decrease; and (c) have no effect on working capital.

16 Given below is the balance sheet of a catering business as at 1st January, 1982.

Balance Sheet

Capital			*Fixed Assets*		
		£			£
Capital a/c		210 000	Sundry Assets		200 000
Current Liabilities			*Current Assets*		
Creditors	15 000		F. & B. Stocks	15 000	
Accruals	5 000		Debtors	5 000	
		20 000	Cash	10 000	
					30 000
		£230 000			£230 000

During January the transactions of the business were as follows:
(a) Sold food and beverages, costing £12 000, for £25 000 cash.
(b) Purchased food and beverage stocks on credit for £10 000.
(c) Sold food and beverages, costing £5 000, on credit for £10 000.
(d) Paid accrued expenses, £2 000.
(e) Withdrew for private use £1 000.
(f) Collected debts from customers, £10 000.
(g) Purchased light kitchen equipment for cash, £3 000.
(h) Paid creditors £16 000.

You are required to:
(1) explain the effect of each transaction on
  (a) the working capital, and
  (b) the cash position of the business;
(2) prepare a funds flow and a cash flow statement as at 31st January 1982;
(3) draw up the balance sheet of the business as at 31st January 1982.

CHAPTER 11

Single entry

Nature of single entry

It is sometimes said that there are two systems of book-keeping: double entry and single entry. Double entry book-keeping—which we have assumed so far in this book—is a system under which we record the *double aspect of each transaction* in the books of a business. Thus for each transaction we have a debit and a credit entry in the ledger. As a result, at the end of each accounting period, we are able to extract a trial balance and then proceed to the preparation of the final accounts.

Single entry book-keeping, though sometimes described as a 'system', is not really a system of book-keeping. Indeed, it is the absence of systematic recording of transactions that characterizes single entry.

The term single entry (also referred to as 'incomplete records') is usually applied to a set of books which do not amount to a complete double entry system. It will be appreciated, therefore, that—in terms of the books kept—single entry covers many possibilities. Thus a snack-bar proprietor may keep a cash book only and no other records at all. A guest-house proprietor may keep a cash book, a petty cash book and a simple form of visitors' ledger. A medium-sized restaurant may keep a cash book, a petty cash book and a wages book and some record of purchases and sales. In all these cases some accounting records are kept, but these do not constitute a complete record of all the transactions of the business; accounts of suppliers are not kept; there are no real or nominal accounts. At the end of an accounting period, a trial balance cannot be extracted and, therefore, the preparation of final accounts is difficult.

Preparation of final accounts from incomplete records

From what has been said it will be appreciated that the compiliation of final accounts from incomplete records is a more complicated matter than when this is done from an agreed trial balance. The main reason for this is that it is necessary to extract information from several different sources and, sometimes, reconstruct accounts from whatever data are actually available. As the nature and scope of the accounting records kept varies from one establishment to another, it is impossible to suggest a method that can be applied to every set of incomplete records. Provided, however, that the student understands double entry book-keeping he should not find single entry too difficult.

There are several sources of information that usually have to be consulted when compiling final accounts from incomplete records.

Cash book

Even where there are few accounting records kept there is, more often than not, some form of cash book being maintained. Where a cash book is not kept, particulars of cash transactions may be obtained by reference to the bank statements of the business. An analysis of the cash transactions for the period concerned will provide information relating to cash sales, cash purchases, and the payment of suppliers, as well as payments in respect of business expenses.

Previous final accounts

As ledger accounts for assets, liabilities and, often, business expenses are not kept it is usually necessary to refer to the final accounts for the previous accounting period. For instance, when preparing the balance sheet, particulars of the assets at the end of the current period may have to be obtained partly from the last balance sheet (to ascertain what was owned at the beginning of the current period) and partly from the cash book (to ascertain what was purchased during the current period). Similarly, particulars of the capital will be compiled by taking from the last balance sheet the opening capital, adding the current net profit and deducting the proprietor's drawings. The latter would be obtained by analysing the cash payments for the period concerned.

Other sources In addition to the cash book and the previous final accounts there are usually some other records being kept. Thus there are many smaller establishments which keep an analysed record of purchases and sales under headings such as food, beverages, cigarettes and sundries. Any such records are helpful in the preparation of the trading account. Particulars of the creditors at the end of the current period may be obtained by listing all suppliers' invoices remaining unpaid at the date of the balance sheet. It is often found that many smaller establishments, which do not maintain ledger accounts, keep a reasonably accurate record of any wages paid which, again, is helpful when preparing the profit and loss account.

To sum up, as the nature and extent of the books kept vary from one case to another so must the method used in the compilation of the final accounts. Not infrequently, in the process of preparing final accounts from incomplete records, it is necessary to rely on the proprietor's memory as well as on any records he may have chosen to keep.

Example 1 On 1st January, 19. ., A. M. Field started in business as a snack-bar proprietor with a capital of £50 000 made up as follows:

Cutlery and utensils	£5 000
Furniture	£10 000
Cash	£35 000

Figure 146 is a summary of his cash book for the year ended 31st December, 19. . . You are informed that he pays all expenses by cheque and banks all amounts received.

CASH BOOK SUMMARY

Balance		35,000	00	Wages		16,000	00
Sales		70,000	00	Furniture		5,000	00
				Rent and Rates		6,000	00
				Light and Heat		4,000	00
				Kitchen Equip.		19,000	00
				Private Expenses		5,000	00
				Purchases		32,000	00
				Balance	c/d	18,000	00
		105,000	00			105,000	00
Balance	b/d	18,000	00				

Figure 146

At 31st December, 19 . ., Field owed £500 in respect of electricity used and £2 000 for the last quarter's rent. His stock of provisions was valued at £2 000.

You are required to prepare Field's trading, profit and loss account for the year ended 31st December, 19 . . and the balance sheet as at that date. Depreciate the kitchen equipment and the furniture by 10 per cent and the cutlery and utensils by £1 000.

Proceed as shown in Figures 147, 148 and 149.

Trading Account for year ended 31st Dec, 19. .

		£				£
Purchases		32,000 00		Sales		70,000 00
Less Closing Stock		2,000 00				
Cost of Sales		30,000 00				
Gross Profit	c/d	40,000 00				
		70,000 00				70,000 00

Figure 147

Notes: (1) It will be observed that the information necessary to compile the above trading account is obtained from the cash book summary and other sources, rather than the trial balance.

(2) It is assumed in this illustration that all purchases and sales were on a cash basis.

Profit and Loss Account for year ended 31st Dec, 19. .

		£			£
Wages		16,000 00	Gross Profit	b/d	40,000 00
Rent and Rates		8,000 00			
Light and Heat		4,500 00			
Depreciation:					
Furniture	1,500				
Kitchen Equip.	1,900				
Cutlery and Utensils	1,000	4,400 00			
Net Profit		7,100 00			
		40,000 00			40,000 00

Figure 148

Notes: (1) The debit in the profit and loss account in respect of the rent and rates (£8 000) and the light and heat (£4 500) are arrived at by extracting from the cash book summary the amounts actually paid out and adding the amounts due but unpaid.

(2) It is assumed that the additional furniture purchased for £5 000 was acquired at the commencement of the current year. Depreciation is, therefore, based on £15 000.

Balance Sheet
as at 31st Dec., 19..

Capital	£	£	Fixed Assets	Cost £	Dep'n £	Net £
Capital at 1st Jan., 19..	50,000		Furniture	15,000	1,500	13,500
Add Net Profit	7,100		Kitchen Equipment	19,000	1,900	17,100
	57,100		Cutlery and Utensils	5,000	1,000	4,000
Less Drawings	5,000	52,100		39,000	4,400	34,600
Current Liabilities			Current Assets			
Accrued Electricity	500		Stock Provisions		2,000	
Accrued Rent	2,000	2,500	Cash at Bank		18,000	20,000
		£54,600				£54,600

Figure 149

Notes: (1) Particulars of the assets of the business are obtained by reference to the state of affairs at the beginning of the period and to the cash book summary.
(2) The 'capital' section of the balance sheet is written up by ascertaining the opening capital, adding the net profit for the year and deducting the drawings, as shown in the cash book summary.

Example 2 M. Price, a restaurant proprietor, does not keep a full set of books. His assets and liabilities on 1st January 1981 and 31st December 1981 were:

	1st January 1981	*31st January 1981*
Cash at bank	£5 500	£11 850
Debtors	600	700
Stocks	3 000	2 500
Furniture	2 750	2 750
Glass and china	1 750	1 750
Premises	30 000	30 000
Creditors	1 300	1 600
Accrued expenses	300	500

Figure 150 shows his bank summary for 1981.

BANK SUMMARY

Balance		5,500	00	Private Expenses		5,500	00
Cash Sales		80,000	00	Business "		20,500	00
Receipts from Debtors		19,950	00	Wages		27,750	00
				Payments to Suppliers		39,750	00
				Bank Charges		100	00
				Balance	c/d	11,850	00
		105,450	00			105,450	00
Balance	b/d	11,850	00				

Figure 150

You are asked to prepare the restaurant's trading profit and loss account for the year ended 31st December 1981, and a balance sheet as at that date. Depreciate the furniture by £250, and the glass and china by £150.

Proceed as shown in Figure 151.

Trading Account for year ended 31st Dec., 1981.

Opening Stock		3,000	00	Cash Sales		80,000	00
Purchases		40,050	00	Credit "		20,050	00
		43,050	00				
Less Closing Stock		2,500	00				
Cost of Sales		40,550	00				
Gross Profit	c/d	59,500	00				
		100,050	00			100,050	00

Figure 151

What presents some difficulty about the above trading account is that, whilst the opening and the closing stocks are given, the purchases and sales for the year have to be calculated from the information available.

From the particulars given it is clear that all the purchases were on credit. We know how much he owed the suppliers at the beginning and at the end of the period as well as the amount of cash paid to them. From these data we calculate the credit purchases for the year as follows:

Cash paid to suppliers during 1981	£39 750
Less Amount owing to suppliers at 1st January 1981	1 300
Cash paid to suppliers for 1981 credit purchases	38 450
Add Purchases not yet paid for (i.e. creditors at 31st December, 1981)	1 600
Total credit purchases in 1981	£40 050

An alternative method of arriving at the amount of credit purchases is to construct a total creditors account, i.e. one personal account for all the suppliers from whom goods were purchased (see Figure 152).

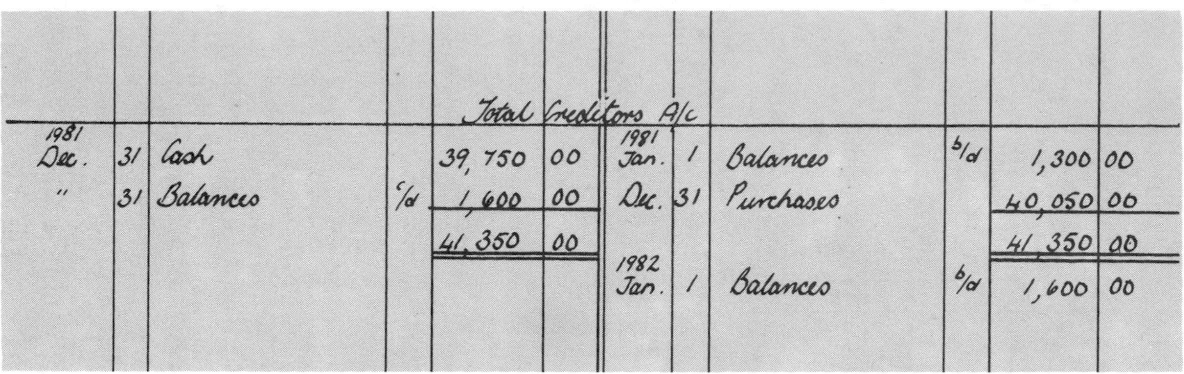

Total Creditors A/c

Date		Particulars	Fo.	£	p	Date		Particulars	Fo.	£	p
1981 Dec.	31	Cash		39,750	00	1981 Jan.	1	Balances	b/d	1,300	00
"	31	Balances	c/d	1,600	00	Dec.	31	Purchases		40,050	00
				41,350	00					41,350	00
						1982 Jan.	1	Balances	b/d	1,600	00

Figure 152

The amount of £40 050 (i.e. the purchases) is simply a balancing figure and, had the restaurateur kept a full set of books, would be equal to the total of invoices that would have been credited in the personal accounts of his suppliers.

By reference to the bank summary it may be seen that the restaurant had credit as well as cash sales. The cash sales, assuming that all the cash taken has been banked, may be obtained from the bank summary; here they amount to £80 000.

The credit sales of the restaurant may be calculated in the same way as we calculated the credit purchases above.

Cash received from customers in 1981	£19 950
Less Amount owing from customers at 1st January 1981	600
Cash received from customers for 1981 credit sales	19 350
Add Sales not yet settled by customers (debtors at 31st December, 1981)	700
Total credit sales in 1981	£20 050

The total debtors account in respect of the year ended 31st December, 1981, would be constructed as in Figure 153.

			Total Debtors A/c								
1981 Jan.	1	Balances	b/d	600	00	1982 Dec.	31	Cash		19,950	00
Dec.	31	SALES		20,050	00	"	31	Balances	c/d	700	00
				20,650	00					20,650	00
1982 Jan.	1	Balances	b/d	700	00						

Figure 153

The profit and loss account of the restaurant would be drawn up as in Figure 154.

			Profit and Loss A/c for year ended 31st Dec., 1981.								
		Business Exp.		20,700	00			Gross Profit	b/d	59,500	00
		Wages		27,750	00						
		Bank Charges		100	00						
		Depreciation:									
		Furniture	250								
		Glass & China	150	400	00						
		Net Profit		10,550	00						
				59,500	00					59,500	00

Figure 154

When a profit and loss account is compiled from incomplete records most of the debits in that account will be based on details obtained from the cash book. It must, however, be remembered that in most cases the *cash paid out* during a period does not usually correspond with the *expense* for the period.

In the above illustration the cash paid out in 1981 in respect of business expenses is £20 500 and the amount debited in the profit and loss account, £20 700. This is because accrued business expenses at the end of the year were £200 more than they were at the beginning of the year. It is helpful to construct a (total) business expenses account as shown in Figure 155 to decide exactly how much should be charged to the profit and loss account.

Total Business Expenses A/c

1981 Dec.	31	Cash		20,500 00	1981 Jan.	1	Balance	b/d	300 00
"	31	Balance	c/d	500 00	Dec.	31	EXPENSES		20,700 00
				21,000 00					21,000 00
					1982 Jan.	1	Balance	b/d	500 00

Figure 155

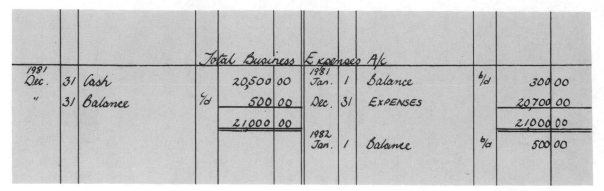

Balance Sheet
as at 31st Dec., 1981.

Capital			Fixed Assets			
Capital as at 1st Jan., 1981.	42,000		Premises		30,000	
Add Net Profit	10,550		Furniture	2,750		
	52,550		Less Depreciation	250	2,500	
Less Drawings	5,500	47,050	Glass and China	1,750		
			Less Depreciation	150	1,600	34,100
Current Liabilities			Current Assets			
Creditors	1,600		Stocks		2,500	
Accrued Expenses	500	2,100	Debtors		700	
			Cash at Bank		11,850	15,050
		£49,150				£49,150

Figure 156

The capital of the restaurant at 1st January, 1981 was not given and had to be ascertained. Capital has already been defined as the total of assets less any external liabilities. Hence:

Assets at 1st January 1981:	Premises	£30 000
	Furniture	2 750
	Glass and china	1 750
	c/f	34 500

			£
	b/f		34 500
Stocks			3 000
Debtors			600
Cash at bank			5 500
			43 600
Less Liabilities at above date: Creditors		1 300	
Accrued expenses		300	1 600
	Capital at 1st January 1981		£42 000

Alternative solution to Example 2

Sometimes the ascertainment of profit from incomplete records is difficult because the information available is insufficient to construct a profit and loss account. When that is so the net profit for the year has to be calculated by comparing the capital at the beginning and the capital at the end of the period concerned.

In the absence of any drawings, the opening capital increased by the net profit for the year will give the closing capital.

Hence:

CAPITAL AT END−CAPITAL AT BEGINNING = NET PROFIT.

Where the proprietor has withdrawn some cash (or goods) it is obvious that this has the effect of decreasing his capital as at the end of the period. Therefore, to arrive at his net profit any drawings must be added to the closing capital and, therefore:

(CAPITAL AT END+DRAWINGS)−CAPITAL AT BEGINNING = NET PROFIT.

Applying the above line of approach, we may produce an alternative solution to Example 2, as shown below.

		£	£
Capital at 31st December 1981			
	Assets	49 150	
	Liabilities	2 100	47 050
Add Drawings in 1981			5 500
			52 550
Less Capital at 1st January 1981			
	Assets	43 600	
	Liabilities	1 600	42 000
		Net Profit	£10 550

Simplified treatment of purchases

In practice it is often difficult to draw a line of division between double entry and single entry. In fact, there are numerous hotel and catering establishments with systems of book-keeping which fall somewhere in between the two. Where, however, an otherwise sound system of book-keeping falls short of the traditional concept of double entry, the reason is, usually, the necessity to keep the cost of book-keeping within reasonable limits in relation to the size of the business. Numerous methods of 'simplifying' and thus reducing the book-keeping work are consequently found in various sections of the hotel and catering industry.

In smaller establishments the maintenance of a full bought ledger may not necessarily be justified having regard to either the clerical labour or the number of suppliers dealt with. Consequently many smaller establishments do away with the bought ledger and keep what is known as a purchases book instead.

The following procedure is usually adopted:

(a) All invoices and credit notes received from suppliers during the course of each month are checked and filed away alphabetically under suppliers' names.

(b) When, usually at the beginning of the following month, a supplier's statement of account arrives, the relevant invoices and credit notes are withdrawn from the file and checked against the statement of account.

(c) When the accuracy of a supplier's statement has been proved, the cash discount, if any, is deducted and a cheque in favour of the supplier is drawn.

(d) All cheques, so drawn, are then entered in an analysed purchases book and credited in the cash book. The analysed totals from the purchases book are then debited in the appropriate accounts in the nominal ledger.

Example Let us assume that a hotel receives the following documents from its supplier, Surrey Food Co. Ltd, during January, 19...

January	3	invoice	£60
,,	11	,,	130
,,	24	,,	70
,,	28	C/note	10

At the beginning of February the hotel receives a statement of account, subject to a cash discount of 4 per cent.

As under this simplified system a personal account is not kept for the supplier, the procedure outlined above in (a), (b) and (c) will be adopted. The amount of the cheque in favour of Surrey Food Co. Ltd will then be:

Invoices	£60
	130
	70
	260
Less C/note	10
	250
Less 4 per cent cash discount	10
Amount of cheque	£240

When the cheque has been drawn and signed by the authorised person(s), it will be entered in an analysed purchases book together with the cheques drawn in favour of other suppliers. A specimen purchases book is shown in Figure 157.

PURCHASES BOOK — January 19..

SUPPLIER	Chq No.	TOTAL		FOOD		BEV.		CIGARETTES		SUNDRIES	
Surrey Food Co. Ltd.	016	240	00	240	00						
etc.											
Totals		5,000	00	3,000	00	1,500	00	400	00	100	00

Figure 157

When all the cheques in respect of the January statements have been entered in the purchases book, the latter is totalled and double entry, is then completed as shown in the ledger accounts and cash book in Figure 158.

				Purchases A/c - Food							
19.. Jan	31	Purchases Book		3,000	00						
				Purchases A/c - Drink							
19.. Jan	31	Purchases Book		1,500	00						
				Purchases A/c - Cigarettes							
19.. Jan	31	Purchases Book		400	00						
				Purchases A/c - Sundries							
19.. Jan	31	Purchases Book		100	00						
				Cash Book							
						19.. Jan	31	Surrey Food Co. Ltd.		240	00
						"	31	etc			
								Cheques credited here total		(5,000	00)

Figure 158

The number of the analysed columns in the purchases book may vary considerably depending on the nature of the establishment's purchases. Many establishments use the purchases book not only for recording payments in respect of their purchases but also for other payments such as rent and rates, gas and electricity, repairs and renewals and similar items. The procedure in respect of such non-purchase payments is the same as illustrated above.

Advantages and disadvantages

The purchases book method has some obvious advantages but it also suffers from certain disadvantages.

The following are the main advantages:

(a) Suppliers' personal accounts are not kept. Similarly, no purchases day book or purchases return book is necessary.

(b) Less clerical labour is required.

(c) As a result of (b) above, this method tends to be less costly.

The following are the main disadvantages:

(a) Invoices and credit notes are not entered in the books of the business. This is objectionable in so far as the books kept do not truly reflect current transactions.

(b) As some suppliers render statements at intervals other than monthly, the amounts posted from the purchases books do not represent monthly purchases.

(c) All credit transactions are treated as if they were cash transactions.

(d) The maintenance of the purchases book requires an efficient system of filing; otherwise invoices and credit notes tend to get mislaid, which makes the checking of suppliers' statements difficult.

M.. ROOM NO:..............

WEEK ENDING 19 TOTAL

Brought Forward
En Pension
Apartments
Early Morning Tea
Breakfast
Luncheon
Afternoon Tea
Dinner

KEY AT THE OFFICE

M.. ROOM NO:..............

	WEEK ENDING						19		TOTAL	
Brought Forward										
En Pension										
Apartments										
Early Morning Tea										
Breakfast										
Luncheon										
Afternoon Tea										
Dinner										
Supper										
Tea, Coffee, Milk										
Beers										
Wines, Spirits										
Minerals										
Cigars, Cigarettes										
Telephone										
Newspapers										
Laundry										
Garage										
Sundries										
Paid Outs										
Service Charge										
Total										
Deductions										
Carried Forward										

PLEASE LEAVE KEY AT THE OFFICE

Figure 159

Simplified treatment of visitors' accounts

Another example of a method designed to reduce the volume of book-keeping work is the maintenance of duplicate bills, replacing the visitors' ledger.

The procedure adopted is this:
(1) In respect of each guest there is a duplicate bill kept in a specially designed binder.
(b) A sheet of carbon paper is inserted between the two copies of each bill.
(c) At the end of each day a summary of business done (charges to visitors) is extracted from the bills and the necessary statistical records are then produced.
(d) On a guest's departure the top copy of the appropriate bill is handed over to the guest and the carbon copy is retained by the hotel.
A specimen duplicate bill is shown in Figure 159.

An advantage of this method of keeping the accounts of visitors is that a full visitors' ledger is not kept. Similarly, at the end of each day's business it is not necessary to write out guests' bills. A disadvantage is the cumbersome method of extracting particulars of business done. An adding machine is, no doubt, then helpful.

Whilst this is not an adequate substitute for a proper visitors' ledger, there is no reason why the ledgerless system of visitors' accounts should not prove satisfactory in smaller hotels, guest houses and other small residential establishments.

Problems

1 Distinguish between double entry and single entry book-keeping.

2 George Bacon is in business as a restaurateur. His postion on 1st January, 19 was:

Debtors	£350
Creditors	3 460
Leasehold premises	34 600
Food stocks	1 300
Loan from Wm. Penny	5 000
Cash at bank	6 130
Glass and china	1 200
Kitchen equipment	4 000
Restaurant furniture	3 800

On 30th June, 19.., you ascertain that his total assets less liabilities amount to £60 000, and that during the half year he withdrew for private purposes £5 200.
Calculate Bacon's net profit for the six months to 30th June, 19...

3 A. Sloecoach failed to keep proper records from the date of purchasing his snack-bar on 1st January, 1981. The following details are, however, ascertained:

	1st January 1981	*31st December 1983*
Food stocks	£400	£600
Kitchen equipment	2 000	2 500
Cutlery and utensils	500	700
Creditors	1 000	1 200
Accrued expenses		300
Cash at bank	3 000	4 200

During the years 1981 and 1982, Sloecoach had drawn £100 per week from the snack-bar for his private use, and in 1983 this was increased to £150 per week.

It is estimated that the profits for the year 1983 were twice as much as those for 1982 and for the last mentioned year twice as much as for 1981.

Prepare a statement setting out your calculations of the estimated profit for each of the three years concerned.

4 A. Winter is proprietor of the 'Four Seasons' guest house. His balance sheet on 1st January, 19.., was:

Balance sheet

Capital		88 000	Premises	49 000	
Creditors	2 500		Furniture	12 000	
Advance bookings	800		Equipment	11 000	
Accrued expenses	1 750		Glass and china	4 000	
		5 050			76 000
			Stock of provisions	1 000	
			Debtors	500	
			Prepaid expenses	750	
			Cash at bank	14 800	
					17 050
		93 050			93 050

The following is a summary of Winter's cash book for the year ended 31st December, 19..

Cash book summary

Balance b/d	14 800	Private expenses	12 000
Receipts from:		Business expenses	78 550
Visitors	250 700	Creditors	90 350
Other customers	50 300	Wages and salaries	93 500
Sale of furniture	4 000	Bank charges	200
		Furniture	7 250
		Balance c/d	37 950
	£319 800		£319 800
Balance b/d	£37 950		

You are required to prepare Winter's trading, profit and loss account for the year ended 31st December, 19.., and a balance sheet as at that date.

Notes: (1) At 31st December, 19.., stock of provisions amounted to £1 700; debtors were £600; advance bookings £400; prepaid expenses were £900 and accrued expenses £1 950.
(2) Depreciate furniture by £3 000; equipment by £2 500 and glass and china by £750.
(3) The furniture sold during the year stood in the books of the guest house at £6 000.

(4) You are informed that the new furniture purchased during the year includes a wardrobe, costing £500, for the proprietor's private flat.

5 A hotel uses the purchases book method of recording its purchases and pays its suppliers at the end of each month. The following invoices and credit notes were received by the hotel during the month of March, 19...

Suppliers	A	B	C	D	E	F
Invoices	£200	£450	£300	£600	£700	£350
	450	350	150	250	200	300
	850	300	50	550	300	450
	350	150		650	350	
	250	200		350	450	
Credit notes	£100	£ 50		£150	£100	

Assume that all the suppliers' statements were received, checked and paid at the end of March, 19.., and that the following cash discounts were deducted:

Suppliers A, B and C	4 per cent;
Suppliers D, E and F	5 per cent.

Write up the purchases book of the hotel in respect of March, 19.., and show the relevant extracts from the cash book and the ledger accounts concerned.

The following analysis columns are required: food (suppliers A and E); drink (suppliers B and D); tobaccos (suppliers C and F).

6 G. H. Gupta is a restaurant proprietor. His assets and liabilities on 31st January and 31st December, 19.., were:

	1st January, 19..	*31st December, 19..*
Cash at bank	£5 000	£10 000
Food stocks	1 100	1 000
Furniture	3 000	3 000
China and cutlery	1 000	1 000
Premises	40 000	40 000
Pre-paid expenses	200	300
Creditors	1 200	1 400
Banqueting debtors	500	400
Accrued wages		200

The following is his bank summary for the year:

Balance on 1st January, 19..		£5 000
Add Cash sales	£150 000	
Banqueting receipts	50 000	200 000
		205 000
Less Wages	55 000	
Suppliers	92 000	
Expenses	30 000	
Drawings	18 000	195 000
Balance on 31st December, 19..		£10 000

You are required to prepare Gupta's trading, profit and loss account for the year ended 31st December, 19.., and a balance sheet as at that date. Depreciate his furniture by 10 per cent, his china and cutlery by £200 and the premises by 3 per cent.

7 O. Yesser is a café proprietor. His assets and liabilities on 1st January, 19.., and 31st December, 19.., were as below:

	1st January, 19..	*31st December, 19..*
Premises	£30 000	£30 000
Creditors	900	1 900
China and utensils	1 100	1 100
Furniture	3 250	3 250
Stock of provisions	1 500	1 600
Accrued expenses	3 200	4 400
Pre-paid expenses	400	200
Cash at bank	5 500	6 850

The following is a summary of his bank account in respect of the year ended 31st December, 19...

Bank account summary

Balance b/d	5 500	Private expenses	5 500
Total receipts	99 950	Business expenses	25 500
		Wages	27 750
		Suppliers	39 750
		Bank charges	100
		Balance c/d	6 850
	£105 450		£105 450
Balance b/d	£6 850		

Prepare Yesser's trading, profit and loss account for the year ended 31st December, 19.., and his balance sheet as at that date, taking the following into account: depreciate his furniture by £350, and china and utensils by £300.

8 The balance sheet of A. Bee, a café proprietor, on 1st January, 19.., was as follows:

Balance sheet

Capital	£20 000	Premises	£15 000
Creditors	1 900	Furniture	3 000
Accrued expenses	600	Cutlery	1 500
		Food stocks	1 000
		Bank balance	2 000
	£22 500		£22 500

You are informed that Bee pays all receipts into his bank account and pays all expenses by cheque.

His transactions for the year ended 31st December, 19. ., were:

Receipts from customers	£49 950
Payments to creditors	6 200
Cash purchases	14 950
Payments for expenses	6 150
Drawings	2 150

On 31st December, 19. ., his creditors amounted to £1 500 and the food stocks were valued at £1 300. You are required to prepare:

(a) a summary of his bank account and
(b) his trading, profit and loss account for the year ended 31st December, 19. ., and a balance sheet as at that date.

Depreciate Bee's premises by 4 per cent, the furniture by 1·0 per cent and the cutlery by £300.

CHAPTER 12

Accounts of non-profit making bodies

We have so far considered the preparation of final accounts by reference to a type of business (the sole trade), where the business is carried on with a view to profit.

There are, however, many organizations which do not seek to make a profit but, primarily, exist to promote their objects. Examples of such non-profit making bodies are: sports clubs, charitable, political, religious and social institutions, professional bodies and several forms of welfare catering. The final accounts of such bodies are prepared according to the principles explained in the previous chapters, i.e. in the same manner as those of a sole trader. What is rather different about these accounts is, however, mainly the terminology used.

Income and expenditure account

This is the equivalent of the profit and loss account of a trading organization. It is credited (as with the profit and loss account) with all income earned, whether actually received or not, and debited with all expenses incurred, whether actually paid or not.

A credit balance arising in the income and expenditure account is not described as net profit but as 'net surplus' or the 'excess of income over expenditure'. A debit balance arising in the income and expenditure account (the equivalent of the net loss in a trading organization) is described as the 'net deficit' or the 'excess of expenditure over income'.

Balance sheet

The balance sheet of a non-profit making organization is prepared in the same manner as the balance sheet of a trading concern. What is usually described as 'capital' is, sometimes, in a non-profit making organization referred to as 'capital fund' or 'accumulated fund'.

Example The following trial balance was extracted from the books of the Old Chiswick Club at 31st December, 19...

		£	£
Refreshment creditors			1 500
Stock of refreshments on 1st January, 19..		500	
Refreshment takings			14 250
Purchases of refreshments		9 000	
Postage and telephones		250	
Furniture		1 000	
Leasehold		25 000	
Cleaning		300	
Wages—general		2 500	
Wages—catering		1 600	
Secretary's honorarium		500	
Cash at bank		5 150	
Games equipment		2 000	
Additions to equipment (28 December, 19..)		200	
	c/f	48 000	15 750

		£	£
	b/f	48 000	15 750
Printing and stationery		350	
Donations			250
Repairs		100	
Prizes		500	
Sundry receipts			700
Rent		2 000	
Accumulated fund			27 000
Subscriptions			7 250
		£50 950	£50 950

You are required to prepare the club's catering account, and income and expenditure account for the year ended 31st December, 19.., and a balance sheet as at that date. Take the following notes into account:

(a) The club's stock of refreshments at 31st December, 19.. was valued at £1 000.
(b) Subscriptions due but unpaid amounted to £250;
(c) Depreciation is to be provided for as follows: furniture 10 per cent, equipment 10 per cent, leasehold 2 per cent.

Figures 160, 161 and 162 show the catering account, the income and expenditure account and the balance sheet respectively.

Catering A/c
for year ended 31st Dec, 1981.

Opening Stock		500	00	Sales		14,250	00
Purchases		9,000	00				
		9,500	00				
Less Closing Stock		1,000	00				
Cost of Sales		8,500	00				
Catering Wages		1,600	00				
Catering Profit	c/d	4,150	00				
		14,250	00			14,250	00

Figure 160

Note: The catering wages are debited in order that the catering account may show the true trading results of the catering facilities provided by the club.

Income and Expenditure A/c
for year ended 31st Dec. 19..

Rent		2,000	00	Catering Profit	b/d	4,150	00
Printing and Stationery		350	00	Subscriptions		7,500	00
Postage and Telephone		250	00	Donations		250	00
Sec. Honorarium		500	00	Sundry Receipts		700	00
Wages		2,500	00				
Cleaning		300	00				
Repairs		100	00				
Depreciation:							
Furniture	100						
Equipment	200						
Leasehold	500	800	00				
Prizes		500	00				
Net Surplus		5,300	00				
		12,600	00			12,600	00

Figure 161

Students should observe that the above income and expenditure account is prepared in the same manner as the profit and loss account of a profit-making organization. As has been explained above the construction of an income and expenditure account follows the same lines as that of a profit and loss account; any differences between the two are apparent rather than real and are, in the main, a matter of terminology.

Subscriptions owing but not yet received have been added to those already paid by members because they are due in respect of the period covered by the accounts.

Balance Sheet
as at 31st Dec., 19..

Accumulated Fund			Fixed Assets			
Balance on 1st Jan., 19..	27,000		Leasehold	25,000		
Add Net Surplus	5,300	32,300	Less Depreciation	500	24,500	
			Furniture	1,000		
			Less Depreciation	100	900	
			Games Equipment	2,000		
			Additions	200		
				2,200		
			Less Depreciation	200	2,000	27,400
Current Liabilities			Current Assets			
Refreshment Creditors		1,500	Stock of Refreshments		1,000	
			Subscriptions Due		250	
			Cash at Bank		5,150	6,400
		£ 33,800				£ 33,800

Figure 162

Note: Here again, it will be observed that except for the occasional differences in terminology and one or two items peculiar to clubs the construction of a balance sheet of non-profit making bodies follows the usual lines.

Receipts and payments account

In addition to an income and expenditure account, and a balance sheet, some non-profit making bodies prepare what is known as a 'receipts and payments account'. Some smaller organizations, and these are fortunately few, prepare a receipts and payments account instead of a proper set of final accounts.

A receipts and payments account is simply a summary of all cash received and all cash paid during an accounting period. It does not take into account any accruals or pre-payments of expenditure; similarly it ignores adjustments in respect of income accrued due or received in advance. Often a receipts and payments account includes capital receipts and payments. The balance of this account represents the cash balance available at the end of the period concerned. A specimen receipts and payments account is shown in Figure 163.

			Receipts and Payments A/c for year ended 31st Dec, 19..						
Balance	b/d	1,000	00	Rent		2,200	00
Subscription		3,000	00	Furniture		1,800	00
Donations		500	00	Postage & Stationery		600	00
Profit on Dances		1,200	00	Sec. Honorarium		500	00
Refreshment takings		2,000	00	Refreshments		1,200	00
Sundry Receipts		300	00	Prizes		200	00
				Balance	c/d	1,500	00
		8,000	00			8,000	00
Balance	b/d	1,500	00				

Figure 163

The receipts and payments account is a useful financial statement when it is presented in addition to a set of final accounts (income and expenditure account and balance sheet). On its own it is quite inadequate and a poor substitute for proper final accounts.

Items peculiar to non-profit making bodies

Subscriptions

This is usually one of the most important sources of revenue in most clubs and other non-profit making bodies. Ideally, each year should be credited with the subscriptions received in respect of that year. In practice, however, it is often found that a proportion of subscription income is not paid until after the end of the period in respect of which it is due.

The actual treatment of accrued subscriptions depends on the nature of the membership. Where this is stable, it is reasonable to assume that outstanding subscriptions will eventually be recovered. In such circumstances accrued subscriptions are credited in the income and expenditure account. Where, however, the membership of a club is not stable and its composition changes constantly, it is doubtful whether many of the outstanding subscriptions will be paid. Where that is so no credit is usually taken for accrued subscriptions and any subscriptions received in arrear are credited in the income and expenditure account as and when actually received.

Subscriptions received in advance, i.e. before they are due, must, of course, be carried forward to the future years in respect of which they have been paid.

Example

On 1st January, 1981, the '66 Club' had subscriptions paid by members in advance (i.e. for the year 1981) amounting to £200. At the same time subscriptions due but unpaid amounted to £400.

During 1981 the club received subscriptions amounting to £5 050 of which £150 was paid in advance (for 1982) and £400 was paid in respect of the year ended 31st

December, 1980. At 31st December, 1981, it is ascertained that current subscriptions due but not paid amounted to £300.

The club's subscriptions account would be adjusted as shown in Figure 164.

		Subscriptions A/c									
1981						1981					
Jan.	1	Balance	b/d	400	00	Jan.	1	Balance	b/d	200	00
Dec.	31	Balance	c/d	150	00	Dec.	31	Cash		5,050	00
"	31	Inc. & Exp. A/c		5,000	00	"	31	Balance	c/d	300	00
				5,550	00					5,550	00
1982						1982					
Jan.	1	Balance	b/d	300	00	Jan.	1	Balance	b/d	150	00

Figure 164

Entrance fees These are payable in some clubs and other bodies on admission to membership. Where the amount of entrance fees received is stable from one year to another they are usually credited in the income and expenditure account.

It is often argued, however, that as such fees are paid by members for benefits extending over a long period of years they should be regarded as capital receipts. Where this view prevails, entrance fees are excluded from the income and expenditure account, and are credited direct to the capital fund account.

Donations These may be donations received or donations paid. Where there are both kinds, each should be recorded in a separate account and then transferred to the income and expenditure account.

Club catering Most clubs provide some kind of catering service. Whilst in the smallest clubs the catering facilities usually take the form of refreshments, many of the large clubs operate good-class restaurants and bars for their members. Whatever the nature of the catering facilities it is desirable periodically to prepare a catering account, showing separate trading results of the catering department.

The catering account will be debited not only with the cost of provisions used but also other catering costs, i.e. costs directly attributable to the catering department. Such costs will include catering wages, stock-taker's fees (if any), losses of light equipment, depreciation of heavy kitchen equipment, kitchen fuel, etc. At the end of the period the balance of the catering account is transferred to the income and expenditure account.

Problems

1 Prepare from the following trial balance: (a) refreshment trading account, (b) income and expenditure account of the City Club for the year ended 31st December, 19.., and (c) balance sheet as at that date.

	£	£
Cash register	300	
Refreshment stock at 1st January, 19..	650	
Stocktaker's fee	60	
Purchases of refreshment	13 150	
Gas and electricity	810	
Telephone	230	
Games accessories	90	
Papers and periodicals	100	
Printing and stationery	260	
Refreshment creditors		2 950
Bank loan		17 300
Refreshment takings		18 010
Subscriptions		770
Playing fees		310
Rents received		140
Cash at bank	3 210	
Kitchen utensils	900	
Secretary's honorarium	500	
Furniture	950	
Catering wages	2 000	
General wages	760	
Freehold premises	24 200	
Glass, china and cutlery	1 020	
Sundry receipts		30
Sundry expenses	210	
Accumulated fund		9 890
	£49 400	£49 400

You are required to take the following into account:

(a) At 31st December, 19.., subscriptions receivable but unpaid amounted to £150.
(b) The stock of refreshments was valued at £2 180.
(c) Accrued gas and electricity amounted to £190.
(d) The stock of unused stationery was valued at £80.
(e) Provide for depreciation as follows:
  (1) Cash register, £70;
  (2) Furniture, £150;
  (3) Kitchen utensils, £100;
  (4) Glass, china and cutlery were valued at £800.

2 The following is the summary of the cash book of the Mayfair Club for the year to 31st December, 1982.

Receipts and payments account

		£		£
Balance at bank 1st January, 1982		3 600	Restaurant and bar supplies	60 000
Members' subscriptions:			Wages	21 200
For year 1981	850		Printing, stationery & postage	1 400
,, ,, 1982	25 750		New furniture	6 500
,, ,, 1983	1 000		General expenses	18 300
		27 600	Balance at bank 31 December,	
Restaurant and bar takings		80 000	1982	3 800
		£111 200		£111 200

Additional information is obtained as follows:

	31st December, 1981	*31st December, 1982*
Freehold premises	£50 000	£50 000
Stock of restaurant and bar supplies	6 180	5 480
Creditors for restaurant and bar supplies	4 500	4 900
Wages accrued	250	300

The club furniture was valued at £36 200 on 31st December, 1981. During 1981, £800 was received in respect of members' subscriptions for 1982.

You are required to prepare:

(a) trading account for the restaurant and bar for the year 1982;
(b) income and expenditure account for the year 1982, and
(c) balance sheet as on 31st December, 1982.

The gross profit of the restaurant and bar trading account is to be transferred to the income and expenditure account.

It is the practice to take no credit in the annual income and expenditure account for subscriptions in arrear at the end of the accounting period.

3 The following is a summary of the cash book of the Beefeaters' Club for the year 1982.

Cash book summary

		£		£
Balance at bank and cash in			Payments for restaurant and	
hand 1st January, 1982		3 400	bar supplies	52 100
Subscriptions:			Rent, lighting & heating	4 900
for 1981	£250		New furniture	4 500
for 1982	7 200		General expenses	4 000
for 1983	100		Wages	10 000
		7 550	Balance at bank and cash in	
Restaurant and bar sales		73 950	hand, 31st December, 1982	9 400
		£84 900		£84 900

You are given the following information:

(a)	31st December, 1981	31st December, 1982
	£	£
Restaurant and bar stocks	5 500	5 000
Creditors for restaurant and bar supplies	6 200	7 000

(b) The club's furniture was valued at £10 000 on 31st December, 1981;
(c) Subscriptions for 1982 received during 1981 amounted to £150.

You are required to prepare a restaurant and bar trading account, and a general income and expenditure account for the year 1982, and a balance sheet as at 31st December, 1982. No credit is to be taken for any subscriptions in arrear at 31st December, 1982, and you may assume that this principle was followed in the preparation of the accounts for 1981. Ignore depreciation.

4 The Gourmets' Club prepares its accounts annually to 31st December. The restaurant and bar of the club are managed by a firm of outside caterers, Outdoor Catering Ltd, who pay the club by way of rent a percentage of their gross takings. On 1st January, 1981 the club's position was as follows:

	£
War loan at cost	7 500
Furniture	13 400
Kitchen plant and utensils	8 400
Stamps and stationery	150
Rent due from Outdoor Catering Ltd	250

At the same time £1 200 was owing for one quarter's rent and £200 for the telephone. Subscriptions received in advance in respect of 1981 amounted to £500. Given below is the summary of the cash book of the club for the year ended 31st December, 1981.

Cash book summary

	£		£
Balance	6 000	Rent (12 months)	4 800
Donations	1 000	Rates	1 300
Green fees	2 100	Sec. Honorarium	2 000
Entrance fees	250	Light and heat	1 500
Sale of furniture	3 400	Cleaning	350
Rent—Outdoor Catering Ltd	2 750	Prizes	300
War loan interest	200	Postage, stationery and telephone	1 100
Subscriptions 1981	4 000	Furniture	6 000
,, 1982	300	Bank charges	100
		Balance	2 550
	20 000		20 000
Balance	2 550		

You are required to prepare the club's income and expenditure account for the year ended 31st December, 1981 and a balance sheet as at that date. Take the following into account:

(a) Provide for accrued audit fee of £200;

(b) At the date of the balance sheet £350 was owing from Outdoor Catering Ltd; the stock of stamps and stationery unused was valued at £250 and £150 was owing for the telephone.

(c) Provide for depreciation as follows: furniture £800; kitchen plant and utensils, £2 000.

5 The following is the receipts and payments account of the Welcome Club for the year ended 31st December, 1980:

Receipts and payments account

	£		£
Opening balance	2 350	Rent and rates	5 600
Bar takings	40 580	Printing and stationery	1 200
Outside catering receipts		Repairs	870
(credit bar account)	2 500	Fuel and lighting	2 600
Subscriptions	4 530	Equipment	2 000
Garden fête net receipts	1 300	Cleaning and sundries	650
Investment income	500	Barman's wages	7 500
Donations	1 000	Caretaker's wages	2 500
		Additional bar help	1 200
		Bar purchases	24 680
		Closing balance	3 960
	£52 760		£52 760

You are required to prepare an income and expenditure account, and a balance sheet as at 31st December, 1980, for presentation to the club members at the general meeting, taking into consideration the following:

(a) A separate bar account should be shown and the net profit on the bar transferred to income and expenditure account.

(b) At 1st January, 1980, the club furniture and equipment stood at £8 000; charge depreciation at 10 per cent p.a. on this figure.

(c) At 1st January, 1980, the value of the furnishings was £2 500; depreciate these by £500.

(d) At 1st January, 1980, the accumulated capital fund stood at £25 000.

(e) At 1st January, 1980, the renovations fund stood at £5 350.

(f) The club has investments of £10 000.

(g) The bar stocks were: 1st January, 1980, £7 500; 31st December, 1980, £8 300.

(h) At 31st December, 1980, the following accounts were owing: rent £750; printing and stationery £200; repairs £130; fuel £450.

(i) At 31st December, rates paid in advance were £350.

(j) Of the subscriptions £100 referred to 1981, and £170 was owing at the end of the year.

(k) One-half of the surplus for the year is to be added to the accumulated fund, and one-half added to the renovations fund.

(M.H.C.I.)

CHAPTER 13

Accounting for partnerships

Nature of partnership

A partnership is defined by the Partnership Act, 1890, as 'the relation which subsists between persons carrying on a business in common with a view to profit'. It is possible to form a partnership with only two partners. The maximum number of partners is twenty, except in the case of solicitors, accountants and members of a recognized stock exchange where partnerships of more than twenty persons are allowed.

Two main advantages may be claimed for the partnership over the sole trader type of business unit.

(a) It has access to more capital. Other things being equal, two or more people can raise a larger amount of capital than one person.

(b) As the partnership is managed by more than one person, it has at its disposal a wider range of ability and experience than a business owned and managed by one person. Thus, in a hotel owned by two partners, the reception, control and accounts may be managed by one partner and the kitchen, restaurant and the bars by the other.

All partners have unlimited liability for the debts of the firm. If the firm ceases business and the assets, when sold, do not realize enough cash to pay the creditors, the partners will be called upon to contribute to the debts of the firm from their private resources. In other words the liability of each partner extends to the whole of the firm's debts irrespective of what he or his partners have invested as capital.

Partners who take an active part in the running of the business are known as *active partners*. Those who have contributed some capital but do not take an active part in the management are known as *sleeping partners* or *dormant partners.* The distinction between active and sleeping partners is not one made in law. From the legal point of view both kinds of partners are regarded as general partners.

The Limited Partnerships Act, 1907, allows what is known as *limited partners*. A limited partner is one who invests money in a firm, shares in the profits but does not take an active part in the management. His liability for the debts of the partnership is limited to the amount of capital contributed by him. A limited partnership must, in addition to the limited partners, have at least one general partner whose liability is unlimited. As it is relatively easy to form a private limited company (see next chapter) limited partnerships are at present extremely uncommon. We will, therefore, be concerned with ordinary partnerships only.

The partnership agreement

It is obvious that the partners must from the outset reach agreement on certain specific points, such as their contributions to the capital, the sharing of profits and losses, etc. In order to avoid possible misunderstanding on such points, it is usual for them to have drawn up what is known as the partnership agreement (also referred to as the Articles of partnership and the Deed of partnership). This will be concerned with matters such as:

(a) The duration of the partnership;

(b) The capital contributions of the partners and the rate of interest, if any, to be allowed on their capitals;

(c) The sharing of profits and losses;

(d) The salaries, if any, to be paid to the partners;
(e) The amounts which the partners may draw out of the business;
(f) Arrangements for the preparation of final accounts;
(g) The admission of a new partner and the retirement or death of an existing partner.

Partners may in general make whatever arrangements they please with regard to the above matters. Where, however, there is no satisfactory evidence of the nature of their arrangements and a dispute occurs, it will be settled in accordance with section 24 of the Partnership Act, 1890, which provides, amongst others, that:
(a) Partners share profits and losses equally;
(b) They are not entitled to interest on their capitals or to remuneration for acting in the partnership business;
(c) They are allowed interest at 5 per cent per annum on any loans over and above their capital contributions.

Students should note that where an examination question is silent on the sharing of profits and losses, the provisions of section 24 should be applied.

Accounts of partners

In general it may be said that the accounts of a partnership do not differ from those of any other type of business. We still keep the same subsidiary books and ledger accounts, and transactions are recorded as explained in the previous chapters.

The only changes that are introduced arise from the fact that there is more than one proprietor and that, in consequence, the profits of the business have to be shared between them. As a result, whilst in the sole trader type of business there is one capital account, in a partnership a separate capital account must be opened for each partner. Similarly, each partner will have to have a separate drawings account and, where partnership salaries are paid, a separate salary account.

In the case of a sole trader, the net profit is transferred from the profit and loss account direct to the capital account. In a partnership the net profit is divided in what is known as the appropriation account before being transferred to the capital accounts of the partners. The appropriation account is a continuation of the profit and loss account and, as its name indicates, is used for the purpose of appropriating, or dividing, the profits or losses of the business.

Example A and B are proprietors of the Metropolitan Hotel. Their capitals at 1st January, 19.., were: A—£40 000; B—£30 000. During the year ended 31st December 19.., their drawings amounted to £1 000 and £4 000 respectively, and the net profit for the year was £20 500.

Prepare the hotel's appropriation account for the year ended 31st December, 19.., and the partners' capital accounts as at that date, taking the following provisions of the partnership agreement into account:
(a) Partners are entitled to interest on their capitals at the rate of 5 per cent per annum;
(b) Partners are allowed salaries as follows: A—£6 000; B—£7 000;
(c) The balance of profit or loss is to be shared by the partners equally.

The appropriation account of the hotel would be drawn up as in Figure 165.

Appropriation A/c
for year ended 31st Dec., 19..

Interest on Capitals:			Net Profit b/d	20,500
A	2,000			
B.	1,500	3,500		
Salaries:				
A	6,000			
B	7,000	13,000		
Net Profit:				
A	2,000			
B	2,000	4,000		
		20,500		20,500

Figure 165

It should be noted that interest on the partners' capital and partnership salaries are debited in the appropriation account and not in the profit and loss account. This is because these items are not regarded as expenses (charges against profits) but as a convenient means of appropriating or distributing the net profit.

The capital accounts of the partners would be written up as in Figure 166.

Capital A/c - A

19.. Dec.	31	Drawings		1,000	00	19.. Jan.	1	Balance	b/d	40,000	00
"	31	Balance	c/d	49,000	00	Dec.	31	Int. on Capital		2,000	00
						"	31	Salary		6,000	00
						"	31	Net Profit		2,000	00
				50,000	00					50,000	00
						19.. Jan.	1	Balance	b/d	49,000	

Capital A/c - B

19.. Dec.	31	Drawings		4,000	00	19.. Jan.	1	Balance	b/d	30,000	00
"	31	Balance	c/d	36,500	00	Dec.	31	Int. on Capital		1,500	00
						"	31	Salary		7,000	00
						"	31	Net Profit		2,000	00
				40,500	00					40,500	00
						19.. Jan.	1	Balance	b/d	36,500	00

Figure 166

It will be observed that the capital accounts of partners are written up in the same way as the capital account of a sole trader, except that the net profit is credited to them in the form of several separate elements rather than in total.

In the balance sheet of a partnership, it is usual to show all the details affecting the partners' capital accounts rather than the net capitals as at the end of the current period. This is illustrated in Figure 167.

(Extract from) Balance Sheet
as at 31st Dec., 19..

Capital Accounts	£	£	Fixed Assets
A: Balance on 1st Jan., 19..	40,000		
Add Int. on Capital	2,000		
Salary	6,000		
Net Profit	2,000		
	50,000		
Less Drawings	1,000	49,000	
B: Balance on 1st Jan., 19..	30,000		
Add Int. on Capital	1,500		
Salary	7,000		
Net Profit	2,000		
	40,500		
Less Drawings	4,000	36,500	
Proprietors' Interest		85,500	
Current Liabilities			Current Assets

Figure 167

'Proprietors' interest' is the total of the capitals of the partners. Alternatively, it may be defined as the total of assets less any external liabilities.

Fixed capital method

When additions to capital (interest, salary and share of net profit) and deductions from it (drawings) are transferred direct to the capital accounts the balances of those accounts vary from one year to another. Many partners, however, prefer to have a fixed amount of capital invested in their business. Further, it is not uncommon for partnership agreements to provide that the capital contributions of the partners shall be fixed and not varied except by agreement.

In order to keep the capitals of partners fixed it is possible to use the fixed capital method, which has become very popular in recent years. Under the fixed capital method, the capitals of the partners remain constant and no postings to the capital accounts are made.

Any additions to capital and deductions from it are transferred to each partner's current account.

A credit balance on a partner's current account represents a debt from the business to the partner and, conversely, a debit balance on a partner's current account represents a debt from the partner concerned to the business. The capital accounts and current accounts of partners A and B in Figure 167 above would, under the fixed capital method, appear as in Figure 168.

Capital A/c – A

				£	p					£	p
19.. Dec.	31	Balance	c/d	40,000	00	19.. Jan.	1	Balance	b/d	40,000	00
						19.. Jan.	1	Balance	b/d	40,000	00

Capital A/c – B

				£	p					£	p
19.. Dec.	31	Balance	c/d	30,000	00	19.. Jan.	1	Balance	b/d	30,000	00
						19.. Jan.	1	Balance	b/d	30,000	00

Current A/c – A

				£	p					£	p
19.. Dec.	31	Drawings		1,000	00	19.. Dec.	31	Int. on Capital		2,000	00
"	31	Balance	c/d	9,000	00	"	31	Salary		6,000	00
						"	31	Net Profit		2,000	00
				10,000	00					10,000	00
						19.. Jan.	1	Balance	b/d	9,000	00

Current A/c – B

				£	p					£	p
19.. Dec.	31	Drawings		4,000	00	19.. Dec.	31	Int. on Capital		1,500	00
"	31	Balance	c/d	6,500	00	"	31	Salary		7,000	00
						"	31	Net Profit		2,000	00
				10,500	00					10,500	00
						19.. Jan.	1	Balance	b/d	6,500	00

Figure 168

In the balance sheet, the capitals of the partners and their current accounts are shown as in Figure 169.

(Extract from) Balance Sheet
as at 31st Dec., 19. .

	£	£	
Capital Accounts			**Fixed Assets**
A –	40,000		
B –	30,000	70,000	
Current Accounts			
A: Interest on Capital	2,000		
Salary	6,000		
Net Profit	2,000		
	10,000		
Less Drawings	1,000	9,000	
B: Interest on Capital	1,500		
Salary	7,000		
Net Profit	2,000		
	10,500		
Less Drawings	4,000	6,500	
Proprietors' Interest		85,500	
Current Liabilities			**Current Assets**

Figure 169

Interest on drawings Sometimes the partnership agreement of a firm provides that interest shall be charged against the partners on any amounts withdrawn by them on account of profits. In such circumstances the interest is debited in the partners' current accounts, and credited in the appropriation account.

Where the dates of withdrawal are given it is possible to calculate the amount of such interest accurately. Where, on the other hand, the dates of withdrawal are not given it is usual to assume that the drawings were spread equally throughout the accounting period, and charge the interest at half rate.

Example A.B. and C.D. are proprietors of the Esplanade Hotel. Their capitals at 1st January, 19 . ., were £70 000 and £40 000 respectively. Their partnership agreement provided that:

(a) Partners' capitals remain constant;

(b) Partners are entitled to interest on their capitals at the rate of 4 per cent per annum;

(c) Partners are to be charged with interest on drawings at the rate of 5 per cent per annum;

(d) A.B. and C.D. share profits and losses in the proportion 2:1.

During the year ended 31st December, 19.., A.B. withdrew £8 000 and C.D. withdrew £2 000. The hotel's net profit for the year amounted to £20 050. Prepare the hotel's appropriation account and the partners' current accounts. Proceed as in Figures 170 and 171.

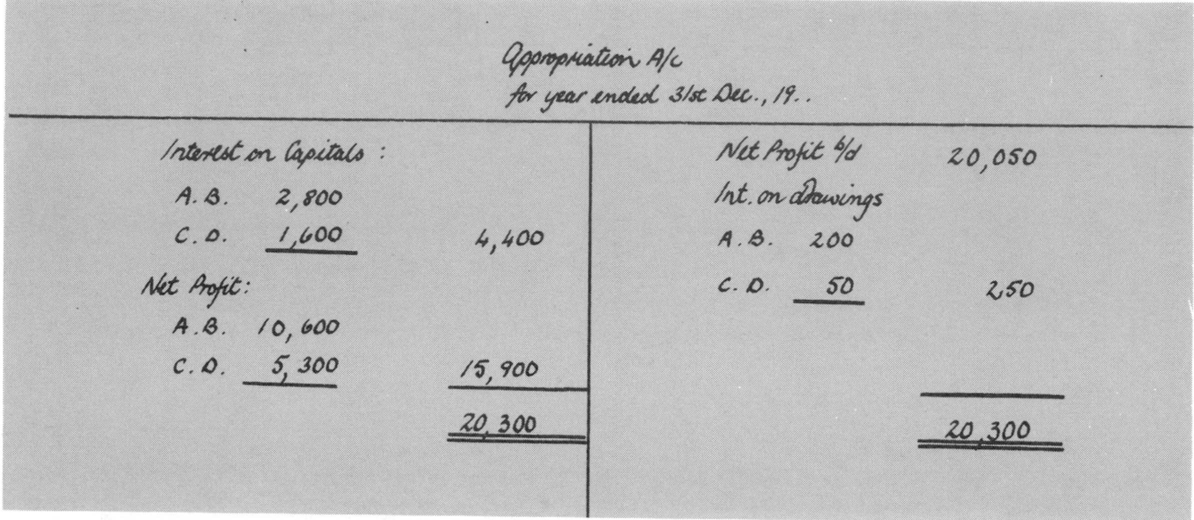

Appropriation A/c
for year ended 31st Dec., 19..

Interest on Capitals:			Net Profit b/d		20,050
A.B.	2,800		Int. on drawings		
C.D.	1,600	4,400	A.B.	200	
Net Profit:			C.D.	50	250
A.B.	10,600				
C.D.	5,300	15,900			
		20,300			20,300

Figure 170

Current A/c – A.B.

				£	p					£	p
19.. Dec.	31	Int. on Drawings		200	00	19.. Dec.	31	Int. on Capital		2,800	00
"	31	Drawings		8,000	00	"	31	Net Profit		10,600	00
"	31	Balance		5,200	00						
				13,400	00					13,400	00
						19.. Jan.	1	Balance	b/d	5,200	00

Current A/c – C.D.

				£	p					£	p
19.. Dec.	31	Int. on Drawings		50	00	19.. Dec.	31	Int. on Capital		1,600	00
"	31	Drawings		2,000	00	"	31	Net Profit		5,300	00
"	31	Balance	c/d	4,850	00						
				6,900	00					6,900	00
						19.. Jan.	1	Balance	b/d	4,850	00

Figure 171

Debit balance on current accounts

When a partner's current account shows a debit balance, all particulars relating to it are still shown on the liabilities side of the balance sheet. The net debit balance is then transferred, as a contra entry, to the assets side of the balance sheet. This is illustrated in Figure 172.

(Extract from) Balance Sheet
as at 31st Dec., 19..

Capital Accounts	£	£	Fixed Assets	£	£
Current Accounts					
A: Interest on Capital	2,000				
Salary	4,000				
Net Profit	1,000				
	7,000				
Less Drawings	8,000				
Dr Balance. see ¢	1,000				
Current Liabilities			Current Assets		
			Current A/c – A ¢	1,000	

Figure 172

Partners' loans

A partner may advance a loan to the business over and above his contribution to the capital. Any sum so received by the partnership will be debited in the cash book, and credited in a loan account.

Any interest paid on the loan would be credited in the cash book, and debited in the loan interest account. At the end of each year the total of loan interest payable should be transferred to the profit and loss account.

End-of-year adjustments

At the end of an accounting period, it is sometimes found that certain adjustments are necessary in respect of items such as partnership salaries and loan interest due.

When it is found that a partner has not drawn the full salary to which he is entitled, the balance still owing to him must be credited to his current account. Similarly any loan interest due to a partner, but remaining unpaid at the end of the year, must be credited to his current account.

From the information given overleaf prepare the appropriation account for the year ended 31st December, 19.., and the partners' current accounts as at that date.

Net profit for the year	£10 970
Capital account—A	20 000
,, ,, —B	30 000
Drawings—A	2 000
,, —B	4 000
Salaries actually paid—A	5 500
,, ,, ,, —B	3 750
Salaries, accrued due—A	500
,, ,, ,, —B	250
Current accounts as 1st January, 19..—A Dr.	1 000
,, ,, ,, ,, ,, ,, —B Cr.	2 000

Provide for interest on the partners' capital at 5 per cent per annum, and for interest on drawings at the rate of 6 per cent per annum. Profits and losses are shared in the ratio: A$\frac{2}{3}$: B$\frac{1}{3}$.

Note: interest on B's loan was debited in the profit and loss account as follows:

To Interest	£750	
Add Accrued	250	
		£1 000

Figure 173 shows the appropriation account and Figure 174 Partner B's current account.

Appropriation A/c
for year ended 31st Dec., 19..

Interest on Capital:			Net Profit b/d		10,970
A	1,000		Int. on Drawings:		
B	1,500	2,500	A	60	
Salaries:			B	120	180
A	6,000		Net Loss:		
B	4,000	10,000	A	900	
			B	450	1,350
		12,500			12,500

Figure 173

Current A/c – B

19.. Dec.	31	Drawings		4,000	00	19.. Jan.	1	Balance	b/d	2,000	00
,,	31	Int. on Drawings		120	00	Dec.	31	Int. on Capital		1,500	00
,,	31	Net Loss		450	00	,,	31	Salary due		250	00
						,,	31	Loan Int. due		250	00
						,,	31	Balance	c/d	570	00
				4,570	00					4,570	00
19.. Jan.	1	Balance	b/d	570	00						

Figure 174

Problems

1 Write short explanatory notes on each of the following: partnership; partnership agreement; active partner; sleeping partner; limited partner.

2 What are the main provisions of section 24 of the Partnership Act, 1890?

3 (a) X, Y and Z are in partnership as catering contractors. Their capitals are: £40 000, £20 000 and £20 000 respectively. How much should each receive out of the first year's profits of £18 200 if they divide the profits in proportion to capital?
(b) A. Day and B. Knight are proprietors of the Battersea Catering Company. Their capitals are: Day £25 000, Knight £45 000. They agreed to allow 5 per cent interest on capital and divide the remaining profits in the proportion 3:5.

How much should each receive at the end of a year in which profits are £30 940?
(c) The proprietors of the Black Rose Hotel are A. B. Black and C. D. Rose. Their capitals are £60 000 and £25 000 respectively. They have agreed to divide the firm's profits as follows:

(i) Black is to receive a salary of £6 000 per annum;
(ii) Rose is to receive a salary of £5 000 per annum;
(iii) Each partner is to receive 4 per cent interest on capital;
(iv) The remaining profits are to be divided in the proportion 6:4.

Calculate the total amount due to each partner at the end of 19.., when the hotel's profit amounted to £35 500.

4 Whiting and Herring are partners in a catering business. Their partnership agreement provides that:
(a) Partners' capital accounts remain constant;
(b) Partners are entitled to 5 per cent interest on their capitals;
(c) Herring is entitled to a salary of £5 000 per annum;
(d) Whiting and Herring share profits and losses in the proportion 3:1;
On 1st January, 19.., their capitals were: Whiting, £60 000, Herring £20 000. During the year ended 31st December, 19.., they withdrew £3 000 and £2 000 respectively.

The firm's net profit in 19.. amounted to £21 200. Prepare the partners' current accounts for the year ended 31st December, 19...

5 The following trial balance was extracted from the books of a firm on 30th June, 19...

		£	£
Capital: A. B. Brown			60 000
C. D. Brown			30 000
E. F. Brown			20 000
Drawings: A. B. Brown		4 000	
C. D. Brown		3 000	
E. F. Brown		2 000	
Purchases		80 000	
Sales			195 000
Stocks on 1st July, 19..		3 500	
Freehold premises		75 000	
Wages and salaries		49 200	
Rate		8 300	
Postage and telephone		3 050	
Kitchen utensils and equipment		8 500	
Cash at bank		44 000	
Printing and stationery		1 650	
	c/f	282 000	305 000

		£	£
	b/f	282 000	305 000
Cash in hand		450	
Insurances		1 700	
Trade creditors			8 000
Gas and electricity		9 350	
Furniture		8 800	
China and linen		3 050	
Office equipment		2 150	
Discount received			1 000
Debtors		1 300	
Repairs and renewals		5 000	
		£314 000	£314 000

Prepare the firm's trading account, profit and loss account and appropriation account for the year ended 30th June, 19.., and a balance sheet as at that date.

The following notes are to be taken into account:
(1) Final stock was valued at £4 000;
(2) Accrued salaries amounted to £700;
(3) Accrued electricity amounted to £550;
(4) Prepaid insurance amounted to £450;
(5) Provide depreciation as follows: furniture $12\frac{1}{2}$ per cent; kitchen utensils and equipment £1 500; china and linen were revalued at £2 500.
(6) Profits are to be distributed as follows: interest on capital 4 per cent; C. D. and E. F. Brown are entitled to salaries of £4 000 and £5 000 respectively; divide remaining profits in the proportion 5:3:2.

6 Fox and Hunt are proprietors of the Excelsior Hotel. The following trial balance was extracted from their books on 30th June, 19.., after the compilation of the annual trading account.

		£	£
Capitals: Fox			35 000
Hunt			30 000
Drawings: Fox		2 000	
Hunt		4 000	
Current accounts: Fox		250	
Hunt			100
Trading account			60 790
Wages and salaries		22 760	
Deposits—advance bookings			750
Trade creditors			4 330
Fuel and light		4 840	
Leasehold premises		50 000	
Cash at bank		22 710	
Cash in hand		330	
Repairs and replacements		1 870	
China, cutlery and linen		4 500	
Discounts received			780
Debtors		2 270	
Furniture and fittings		6 800	
Advertising		2 510	
	c/f	124 840	131 750

		£	£
	b/f	124 840	131 750
Bad debts		390	
Loan account—Hunt			5 000
Rates		3 350	
Laundry		2 220	
Postage and telephone		1 840	
Insurance		610	
Stock		3 500	
		£136 750	£136 750

Prepare the hotel's profit and loss account, and appropriation account for the year ended 30th June, 19.., and a balance sheet as at that date.

Notes: (1) Accrued salaries amounted to £190.
(2) Treat £510 of the advertising as paid in advance.
(3) You are informed that £170 of the debtors are definitely bad.
(4) Provide for the depreciation as follows: china, cutlery and linen were revalued at £4 000; furniture and fittings—10 per cent; leasehold premises—£8 000.
(5) Provide for interest on Hunt's loan at 5 per cent.
(6) The following provisions of the partnership deed must also be taken into account: partners are entitled to 4 per cent interest on capital; Fox is entitled to a salary equal to 10 per cent of the net profit; Fox and Hunt share profits and losses in the proportion 5:4.

N.B. All calculations to the nearest £.

7 You are required to prepare a balance sheet as at 31st December, 19.., in good style. The trading, and profit and loss accounts have been completed and show a net profit of £9 693.

The following balances appear on 31st December, 19.., in the ledger of the Excellent Hotel Co., which is owned by Mr Robson and Mr Carr. They share profits and losses in proportion to their capitals.

	£
Capital accounts: Robson	60 000
Carr	30 000
Current accounts:	
Balance, 1st January, 19..	
Robson	3 250 (cr)
Carr	1 055 (cr)
Freehold premises, 1st January, 19..	60 000
Equipment, 1st January, 19..	15 500
Motor vans	4 480
Furniture, etc.	20 014
Trade creditors	5 946
Cash in hand	556
Bank overdraft	10 000
Investment in 4% War loan	5 000
Drawings accounts: Robson	6 000
Carr	4 000
Sundry debtors	2 460

The following adjustments have been made in the revenue accounts and are required to be included in your balance sheet:

	£
(a) The stocks at 31st December, 19 . . were	
Food and provisions	4122
Cigarettes and tobacco	901

(b) The following are the rates of depreciation:

Equipment	10 per cent per annum
Motor vans	12 per cent per annum
Furniture, etc.	15 per cent per annum

(c) One-half of the advertising account, which totals £5 000, has been charged forward to 19 . . .

(d) The provision for bad debts is 5 per cent on the sundry debtors.

(e) Mr Carr has had goods value £129, which are charged to his account;

(f) A personal telephone bill of Mr Robson, amount £61, has been paid through the business accounts;

(g) Outstanding expenses are:

Audit and accountancy	£250
Printing and stationery	161

(h) £45 water rates have been paid in advance;

(i) One-quarter interest on the War loan has accrued;

(j) £250 has been charged in respect of bank overdraft interest accrued.

A.M.H.C.I.

8 Black and White are partners in the Black and White Catering Co. The following trial balance was extracted from their books on 30th June, 19 . . .

		£	£
Capital accounts: Black			60 000
White			30 000
Drawings accounts: Black		4 000	
White		3 500	
Current accounts: Black			1 000
White		1 000	
Purchases		81 500	
Sales			198 200
Carriage inwards		500	
Stock of provision on 1st July, 19 . .		3 750	
Repairs and renewals		5 150	
Debtors		1 450	
Creditors			8 500
Freehold premises		90 000	
Discount received			2 300
	c/f	190 850	300 000

		£	£
	b/f	190 850	300 000
Cash in hand		200	
Cash at bank		33 400	
Kitchen equipment		9 600	
Rates		5 750	
China and cutlery		3 350	
Furniture		6 500	
Gas and electricity		7 700	
Wages and salaries		48 000	
Printing and stationery		3 050	
Postage and telephone		1 600	
Loan account: White			10 000
		£310 000	£310 000

You are asked to prepare the firm's trading account, profit and loss account and appropriation account for the year ended 30th June, 19. ., and a balance sheet as at that date.

Take into account the following notes:
(1) The final stock of provisions was valued at £4 950.
(2) Accrued gas and electricity amounted to £800; unused stationery was valued at £250.
(3) Provide depreciation as: furniture 10 per cent; kitchen equipment $12\frac{1}{2}$ per cent china and cutlery was revalued at £2 850.
(4) Create a provision for discounts received equal to 4 per cent of the creditors.
(5) Provide for interest on White's loan at 5 per cent per annum.
(6) Partners are entitled to interest on their fixed capitals at the rate of 4 per cent per annum.
(7) Black and White share profits and losses in proportion to their capitals.

9 Anley and Burns are proprietors of the Seaside Hotel. The following trial balance was extracted from their books on 31st December, 19. ., after the compilation of the trading, and profit and loss account.

	£	£
Capital account: Anley		100 000
Capital account: Burns		100 000
Freehold premises	200 000	
Furniture	75 000	
Glass and china	5 000	
Profit and loss account		32 000
City Finance Co.: loan account		100 000
Plant and equipment	40 000	
Stocks	12 000	
Debtors	4 500	
Current account: Anley	1 000	
Current account: Burns		4 000
Trade creditors		6 400
Cash at bank	6 500	
Light and heat		1 600
	£344 000	£344 000

(a) You are asked by the partners to verify the figure of net profit above and, in the course of your investigations, you find the following:

(1) Depreciation on plant and equipment was under-provided for to the extent of £2 200.

(2) Two invoices, in respect of advertising, amounting to £1 900, have not been entered in the books.

(3) A customer's cheque for £300, banked on 30th December, 19.., was returned by the bank marked R/D.

(4) You find that the total of debtors shown in the above trial balance includes a bad debt of £400.

(5) No provision has been made for the annual interest due to the City Finance Co. which amounts to £5 000.

(b) You are also required to prepare the partners' appropriation account for the year ended 31st December, 19.., and their balance sheet as at that date, taking the notes below into account:

(1) Allow interest on partners' capital at 5 per cent.

(2) Provide for partnership salaries as follows:
Anley—£4 500; Burns—£3 500.

(3) The balance of profit is to be shared by the partners equally.

10 Ashley, Brown and Cooper are trading under the name of A.B.C. Catering Co. and share profits and losses in the ratio 1/2, 1/3 and 1/6 respectively. The net profit of their business for the year ended 31st December, 19.., amounted to £32 000. From the following information you are required to prepare the appropriation account and the partners' current accounts for the year ended 31st December, 19...

	Ashley	*Brown*	*Cooper*
Capital accounts	£40 000	£30 000	£20 000
Current accounts on 1st January, 19...	Cr. 2 050	Cr. 150	Dr. 650
Drawings	6 000	3 000	4 000
Partnership salaries: due	6 000	4 000	3 000
paid	5 000	4 000	2 500

On 1st July, 19.., Brown advances a loan of £20 000 to the business at 5 per cent interest per annum. No interest has been paid to him in respect of the loan.

Provide for interest on partners' capital at 5 per cent and for interest on drawings at 4 per cent per annum.

11 Ashton and Benson are proprietors of the Florida Restaurant. Their balance sheet on 1st January, 19.., was:

Balance Sheet

Capital accounts:			*Fixed assets:*		
Ashton	135 000		Leasehold premises	200 000	
Benson	100 000		*Less* depreciation	60 000	
		235 000			140 000
Current liabilities:			Restaurant furniture	80 000	
Benson: current account	2 500		*Less* depreciation	25 000	
Trade creditors	12 000				55 000
Accrued expenses:			Kitchen plant	55 000	
Gas	500		*Less* depreciation	20 000	
Advertising	800				35 000
Repairs	1 200		*Current assets:*		
		17 000	Stocks	6 500	
			Banqueting debtors	1 500	
			Ashton: current account	1 000	
			Prepaid rates	200	
			Cash at bank	12 800	
					22 000
		£252 000			£252 000

You are also given a summary of their cash book for the year ended 31st December, 19.., as follows:

Cash Book Summary

Balance b/d	12 800	Cash purchases		52 500
Banqueting debtors	22 000	Trade creditors		100 500
Cash sales	283 000	Wages and salaries		94 500
Ashton, current account	1 000	Repairs and renewals		5 700
		Gas and electricity		6 300
		Rates		4 200
		Advertising		3 100
		Partners' salaries		
		Ashton	15 000	
		Benson	10 000	
				25 000
		Balance c/d		27 000
	£318 800			£318 800
Balance b/d	£27 000			

Prepare the partners' trading, and profit and loss account for the year ended 31st December, 19.., and their balance sheets as at that date, taking the following into account:

(a) Stocks at 31st December, 19.., were valued at £5 500;
(b) Trade creditors amounted to £11 000;
(c) Banqueting debtors amounted to £2 000;
(d) Accrued gas was estimated at £600;
(e) Rates paid in advance were £250;

(continued)

(f) Regard £1 000 of the repairs and renewals as paid in advance;
(g) Provide for depreciation as follows:
 (i) Leasehold premises £7 500
 (ii) Restaurant furniture 10 per cent of cost;
 (iii) Kitchen plant, etc. 10 per cent of cost.
(h) The partnership agreement provides as follows:
 (i) Partners are entitled to an annual salary of £15 000 each,
 (ii) Profits and losses are shared equally.

N.B. All calculations to the nearest £.

12 A and B are equal partners carrying on business as the proprietors of the Beachside Hotel. At 31st December, 19.., the following balances appeared in their books after the compilation of the trading and profit and loss account for the year which ended on that date.

			£
Hotel premises at cost			200 000
Furnishings at cost			100 000
Kitchen equipment at cost, less depreciation			50 000
Plate, cutlery, linen etc., at cost			80 000
Station van at cost, less depreciation			11 000
Sundry debtors			2 800
Rates paid in advance			1 200
Cash in hand			800
Stocks at 31st December 19..			
	Provisions	3 800	
	Liquors	20 200	
	Cigarettes	5 200	
			29 200
Sundry creditors			24 000
Bank overdraft			4 000
Provision for outstanding items:			
	Wages	1 700	
	National Insurance	100	
	Fire and other insurances	700	
			2 500
Reserves for renewals:			
	Furnishings	20 000	
	Plate, cutlery & linen	7 000	
			27 000
Deposits received for advance bookings			2 500
Partners' current accounts:			
	A. (cr. balance)	10 000	
	B. (cr. balance)	5 000	
			15 000

You are required:
(a) to compile the balance sheet of Messrs. A and B as at 31st December, 19... The amount necessary to complete the balance sheet is that of the capital, which is owned by the partners in equal shares;
(b) to state the total value of the fixed assets;
(c) to state the net value of the floating (or current) assets.

A.M.H.C.I.

CHAPTER 14

Accounting for limited companies

The last few decades have witnessed a rapid growth of limited companies. This is, no doubt, mainly due to the privilege of limited liability enjoyed by the shareholders and the ability of limited companies to raise more capital than is usually possible in the sole trader or partnership type of business. As in other industries, a large proportion of hotel and catering establishments are limited companies.

The conduct of limited companies is regulated by the Companies Acts. The legal provisions which currently govern limited companies are: the Companies Act, 1948, the Company Law Amendment Act, 1967 and the Companies Act, 1980, which came into force on 23 June of that year.

Kinds of companies

Under the 1948 Companies Act a company was a public company unless it complied with the criteria for being private. This has now been changed: a company is now a private company unless it is registered as a public company and, in this way, becomes subject to the more stringent requirements relating to its capital, the payment of dividends and other matters that apply to private companies.

Public companies

Under the Companies Act, 1980, a public company must:
(a) have at least two members;
(b) be limited by shares and have a share capital;
(c) state in its memorandum that it is a public company;
(d) have a name which ends with "public limited company" or p.l.c.
A public limited company must have an authorised and allotted capital of at least £50 000. It is also subject to new regulations with regard to the payment for its shares, as explained later in this chapter.

Private companies

Under the 1980 Act private companies will continue as limited companies. A private company must have at least two members and is subject to the following principal restrictions. It is not allowed, directly or indirectly, to offer its shares to the general public. The restriction on the number of members of a private company to fifty, imposed by the 1948 Act, has now been abolished.

Companies limited by guarantee

After 23 June 1980 no company may be formed as a company limited by guarantee with a share capital. Those then in existence were to be re-registered under the 1980 Act as public companies and were expected to comply with the provisions of the new Act.

Unlimited companies

In recent years there was a small number of so-called "unlimited companies". The position of the members of these companies was similar to that of general partners in a partnership, i.e. their liability was unlimited. The Companies Act, 1967, specified a procedure by means of which an unlimited company might re-register as a limited company. Under the 1980 Act new rules have been introduced to enable an unlimited company to register as a public company.

Re-registration of limited companies

Following the introduction of the new concepts of public and private companies, it will be essential for all limited companies to consider their new status under the Companies Act, 1980. Thus an existing public company may decide to re-register as a private company under the new Act or seek the public limited company status as now defined. Similarly, a private company formed under the 1948 Act may decide to re-register as a public company or remain private.

Memorandum and Articles of Association

When forming a limited company various documents must be sent to the Registrar of Companies. The two main documents that must be sent by both public and private companies are the Memorandum of Association, and the Articles of Association.

The Memorandum of Association defines the relationship between the company and the outside world and contains five clauses, stating:

(1) the name of the proposed company, this must end with the word 'limited';

(2) the situation of the registered office of the company, i.e. whether the company is to be situated in England or Scotland;

(3) the objects of the company;

(4) that the liability of the members is limited;

(5) the nominal capital of the company and its division into shares.

The new public limited companies, as defined by the Companies Act, 1980, must have names which end with 'public limited company' (p.l.c.) or the permitted Welsh equivalent. Also they must state in their memorandum that they are public companies.

The Articles of Association are the internal regulations of the company. They contain clauses dealing with matters such as the issue of shares and debentures, the meeting of shareholders and directors, the rights of shareholders, the powers and duties of directors, etc. A company may have prepared a set of articles of its own, but it is quite usual for companies to adopt a model set of articles (an appendix to the Companies Act, 1948) known as table A.

Kinds of capital

In the context of the accounts of limited companies the term 'capital' may be used in several different senses. We may distinguish the following main kinds of capital:

Nominal, authorized or registered capital

This is the amount of capital, stated in the Memorandum of Association, which the company is authorized to issue.

Subscribed or issued capital

This is the amount of capital actually issued to the members of the company. A company may have a nominal capital of 10 000 shares of £1 each but, for one reason or another, issue only 8 000 shares. Its subscribed (issued) capital is then £8 000.

Called-up capital

This is the amount of capital, payment for which has actually been demanded by the company. This applies only where shares are issued and are payable by instalments rather than in full on application. Thus where 8 000 shares of £1 each have been issued by a company and in the meantime only 75p per share called, the called-up capital is £6 000.

Paid-up capital

This is the amount of the called-up capital that has actually been paid by the members. To continue with the above example, if a member holding 100 shares failed to pay a call of 25p per share, the paid-up capital of the company would have been (£6 000 less 25p on 100 shares) £5 975. Any such unpaid calls are referred to as calls in arrear.

Uncalled capital This is the amount of capital which, for the time being, has not been called up by the company. In the above example this amounts to (£8 000 less £6 000) £2 000.

Unissued capital This is the amount of capital which has not been offered to members or has not been subscribed by them. Unissued capital in the above example amounts to (£10 000 less £8 000) £2 000.

Loan capital This term is sometimes used to describe any capital raised by a company by means of debentures or other long-term loans, rather than by means of shares. Loan capital is quite distinct from the share capital of a company.

Shares and debentures A share is a portion of the capital of a limited company owned by a shareholder. The shares of a company may be divided into several different classes. The main ones are described below.

Preference shares Holders of these shares have a right to a fixed dividend before any dividend is paid to holders of other shares. Preference shares are of different kinds.

Cumulative preference shares Holders of these shares are entitled to any arrears of dividend unpaid in previous years. Preference shares are assumed to be cumulative unless stated otherwise in the Memorandum of Association or the Articles of Association.

Non-cumulative preference shares Holders of these shares have a prior claim to a fixed dividend out of the profits of each year. Where in any one year no profits are available, any amount unpaid on such shares cannot be recovered by the shareholders in subsequent years.

Participating preference shares These give the holders a prior right to a fixed dividend and, additionally, a right to participate in any surplus profit after other classes of shares have been paid at a given rate.

Redeemable preference shares These are rather uncommon: they may be issued by a company which is authorized to issue such shares by its Articles of Association. Redeemable preference shares may be redeemed (repaid) out of profits or out of the proceeds of a fresh issue of shares and only when fully paid.

Ordinary shares The holders of these shares have no special rights. Dividends on these shares are paid after those on preference shares and vary with the fortunes of the company. In a lean year there may be no ordinary dividend paid at all; when profits are high, the ordinary dividend is usually much more than any preference dividends paid.

Deferred or founders' shares These shares are usually taken up by the vendors of a business in part payment of the purchase price. Deferred shareholders do not receive any dividend until the other shareholders have been paid an agreed amount of dividend. They are, however, often entitled to a considerable proportion of surplus profits.

Debentures In addition to any shares a company may issue debentures. There are some important differences between the two. First of all debentures are loans to the company, and do not constitute part of its share capital. As a result, a debenture holder is a creditor and not a part proprietor (shareholder) of the company. The payment of a dividend is dependent on the availability of profits; if there is no profit no dividend may be paid. Debenture interest must, however, be paid even when losses are incurred.

Issue of shares and debentures*

The shares and debentures of a company may be issued in several different ways. With regard to the method of payment, they may be: (a) payable in full on application, or (b) payable by instalments.

With regard to the price, they may be issued at par or at a premium. The issue of shares at a discount, allowed by the Companies Act, 1948, is now prohibited.

Issue of shares and debentures payable in full on application

In this case prospective members and debenture holders of the company send, when applying for any shares or debentures, the full price thereof. When the shares or debentures have been formally allotted to the applicants, the net effect of the transaction is an increase of the cash balance of the company, and a corresponding increase in the share capital or debentures.

Let us assume that X Hotel Ltd offers for subscription 10 000 ordinary shares of £1 each and 500 6% debentures of £10 each both payable in full on application. If all the shares and debentures are taken up the net effect of this transaction is shown in Figure 175.

Cash Book

Ord. Shares	10,000	00					
6% Debentures	5,000	00					

Ordinary Shares A/c

				Cash		10,000	00

6% Debentures A/c

				Cash		5,000	00

Figure 175

Note: Where the company issues several different classes of shares, a separate account is opened for each class.

Issue of shares and debentures payable by instalments

In this case the full amount due in respect of any shares or debentures issued by a company is received over a period of time. Applicants are required to pay so much on application, so much when the shares or debentures have been allotted to them and the balance then due from them is collected by means of periodical calls. A typical arrangement in respect of £1 shares payable by instalments might be:

30 p per share on application;
20p ,, ,, ,, allotment;
25p ,, ,, ,, first call;
25p ,, ,, ,, second and final call.

Let us assume that the above arrangement has been made by a company offering 20 000 10% preference shares of £1 each. If all shares were subscribed, and all the allotment money paid by the members then, before the first call were made, the position would be as in Figure 176.

---

* The treatment of the issue of shares and debentures which follows is rather simplified and designed to explain the effect of an issue on the structure of a company's capital rather than to explain the detailed book-keeping entries involved.

Cash Book

	10% Pref. Shares	10,000	00				

10% Preference Shares A/c

					Cash	10,000	00

Figure 176

If, a few months later, the first call of 25p per share were made and all the money called by the company received, the cash balance would be increased by £5 000 and so would the called-up (and paid-up) capital (see Figure 177).

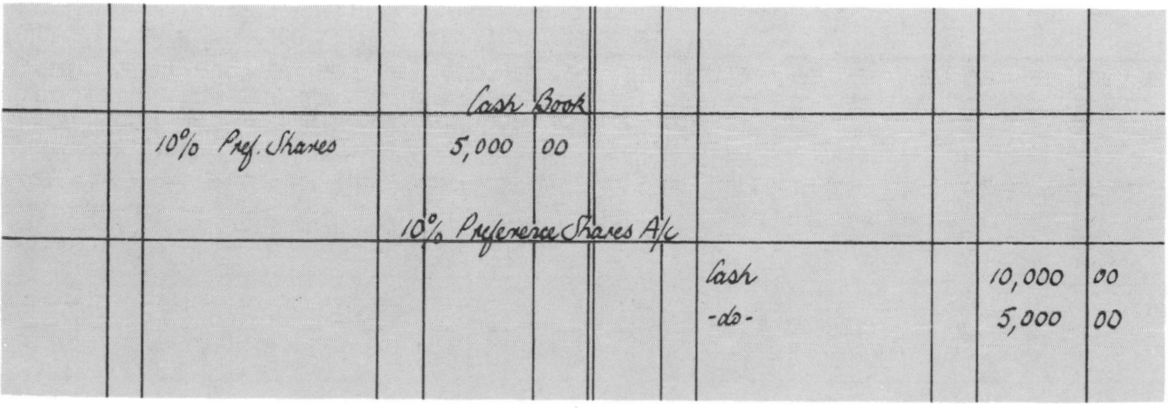

Cash Book

	10% Pref. Shares	5,000	00				

10% Preference Shares A/c

					Cash	10,000	00
					-do-	5,000	00

Figure 177

After the second and final call the 10% preference shares account would show a balance of £20 000, representing the full nominal value of the preference capital issued by the company.

Calls in arrear and calls in advance

When shares are payable by instalments members sometimes fail to pay the calls due from them. The amounts due but unpaid by members are transferred to the debit of a calls in arrear account.

Let us assume that a company has issued 10 000 ordinary shares of £1 each, payable 25p per share on application, 25p per share on allotment and that all the allotment money has been received. The company then makes a call of 25p per share, and all members pay the calls due with the exception of one holding 100 shares. The calls in arrear are therefore (100 × 25p) £25. In the ledger of the company this would be reflected as in Figure 178.

Cash Book

Particulars	£	p	Particulars	£	p
Ord. Shares A/c	2,475	00			

Ordinary Shares A/c

Particulars	£	p	Particulars	£	p
			Cash	5,000	00
			-do-	2,500	00

Calls in Arrear A/c

Particulars	£	p	Particulars	£	p
Ord. Shares A/c	25	00			

Figure 178

It will be observed that the ordinary shares account is credited with the full amount of the calls due. The calls in arrears account represents a debt from the members to the company. In the balance sheet of the company, the calls in arrear should be deducted from the issued capital.

Some shareholders do not wish to be troubled with repeated calls, and pay for their shares in advance of any calls actually made by the company. Any such calls paid before they fall due are transferred to a calls in advance account.

Let us revert to the previous example and assume that when the call of 25p per share was made all members paid the amounts due and that, in addition, one member holding 200 shares paid for them in full. The amount of calls paid in advance is therefore (200 × 25p) £50. This would be reflected in the books of the company as in Figure 179.

Cash Book

Particulars	£	p	Particulars	£	p
Ord. Shares A/c	2,500	00			
Calls in Advance	50	00			

Ordinary Shares A/c

Particulars	£	p	Particulars	£	p
			Cash	5,000	00
			-do-	2,500	00

Calls in Advance A/c

Particulars	£	p	Particulars	£	p
			Cash	50	00

Figure 179

Any calls paid in advance do not form part of the share capital of the company and are, for the time being, a liability from the company to the members concerned. In the balance sheet they must, therefore, be shown as a current liability.

Issue of shares and debentures at a premium

We have assumed so far that when shares or debentures are issued the company receives cash equal to their nominal value. This is not always the case. A company which has been successful and paid substantial dividends may issue shares at a premium, i.e. at a price higher than their nominal value. This is often so in the case of companies whose shares are quoted at a price above nominal value.

Let us assume that a company issues 10 000 ordinary shares of £1 each at a premium of 10p per share. The amount received from the members will therefore be (10 000 × £1.10) £11 000, the share premium being £1 000. The effect of this issue is shown in Figure 180.

Cash Book

	Ord. Shares and Premium		11,000	00					

Ordinary Shares A/c

						Cash		10,000	00

Share Premium A/c

						Cash		1,000	00

Figure 180

In the balance sheet the share premium account will be shown under the heading 'Reserves'.

Payment for share capital

The Companies Act, 1980 has introduced several changes relating to the payment for any shares allotted by a limited company. The main points which are relevant in this connection are summarized below.

As a general principle any shares allotted by a company may be paid for either in money or money's worth. The latter may include goodwill and what is described as 'know-how'.

A public company is subject to an additional restriction in this context. It is not allowed to accept payment for its shares (including any premium) in the form of an undertaking given by a person that he, or some other person, should either do work or offer services to the company.

A public company may not allot shares unless they are paid up to the extent of one-quarter of the nominal value together with the whole of any premium, whether in cash or otherwise. However, these provisions do not apply to any shares allotted in connection with an employee share scheme. Where a public company allots shares fully or partly paid by an undertaking to transfer to the company a non cash asset at a future date, the Act insists that any such transfer must be actually effected within five years.

Finally, a public company is not allowed to allot shares as partly or fully paid up otherwise than for cash, unless the non-cash consideration has been independently valued and an appropriate report submitted to the company and the allottee.

Final accounts of limited companies

The final accounts of a limited company may be prepared for two main purposes. All companies prepare internal (unpublished) accounts; these are prepared for the same purposes as the final accounts of partners and sole traders. Such internal accounts are, of course, prepared in accordance with current accounting practice. Their form, layout and method of presentation are within the discretion of the company concerned.

In addition to internal accounts, limited companies (both public companies and private companies) have to prepare what is known as *published accounts.* These are the final accounts which are sent to the Registrar of Companies, the shareholders and the auditors of the company. The contents, as well as the method of presentation of such accounts, are regulated by the Companies Acts of 1948, 1967 and 1980.

Unpublished or internal accounts

The trading account of a limited company is prepared in exactly the same way as that of a partnership or sole trader.

The unpublished profit and loss account would, again, be prepared in the same manner as in other types of business unit, except that it would contain certain items of expenditure peculiar to limited companies, e.g. directors' fees, debenture interest, and auditors' fees and expenses. The net profit from the profit and loss account is, as in the case of the partnership, transferred to the appropriation account.

Appropriation account

Students often find it difficult to decide which items should be debited in the profit and loss account, and which in the appropriation account of a company. The division of items is based on the following principles:

(a) All *charges against profits*, i.e. all current expenditure, as well as expenses which must be paid whether or not there is any profit available (directors' fees, debenture interest, audit fees) must be debited in the profit and loss account. These, it will be appreciated, are items of expenditure which must be taken into account to arrive at the net profit for the period concerned.

(b) All *appropriations of profits*, i.e. items affecting the application or distribution of the profits available are debited in the appropriation account. Examples of such items are dividends, taxation and amounts written out of profits which do not apply to any particular year, e.g. preliminary expenses, goodwill. A specimen appropriation account is shown in Figure 181.

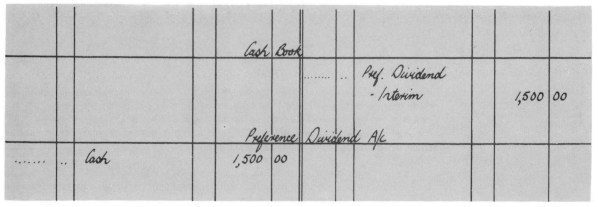

Appropriation A/c for year ended ......

			£	p				£	p
	Pref. Dividend				(1)	Net Profit 1·1·19..	b/f	1,000	00
(3)	- Interim		1,500	00	(2)	Net Profit	b/d	19,000	00
(4)	- Final		1,500	00					
(5)	Ord. Dividend		4,000	00					
(6)	Taxation		6,000	00					
(7)	General Reserve		3,500	00					
(8)	Prelim. Expenses		500	00					
(9)	Balance	c/f	3,000	00					
			20,000	00				20,000	00
						Balance	b/f	3,000	00

Figure 181

Notes: (1) The net profit of £1 000 is the balance of net profit brought forward from the previous accounting period;
(2) The net profit of £19 000 is the current year's net profit from the profit and loss account. The total of profits available in the current year is, therefore, £20 000;
(3) An interim dividend is a dividend which is declared by the directors and paid before the end of the company's accounting year. When the interim dividend of £1 500 was paid the entries shown in Figure 182 were made in the books of the company.

Cash Book

			£	p				£	p
					....	.. Pref. Dividend - Interim		1,500	00

Preference Dividend A/c

			£	p				£	p
....	..	Cash	1,500	00					

Figure 182

At the end of the accounting year the balance of the preference dividend account is transferred to the appropriation account as in Figure 183. The entries then required are a credit in the preference dividend account and a debit in the appropriation account.

Preference Dividend A/c

			£	p	19..			£	p
....	..	Cash	1,500	00	Dec.	31	Appropriation A/c	1,500	00

Appropriation A/c

			£	p				£	p
		Pref. Dividend Interim	1,500	00					

Figure 183

(4) It should be noted that whilst the directors usually have power to declare an interim dividend, any final dividend is recommended by the directors, and requires the approval of the annual general meeting of the company. Students will appreciate, therefore, that at the date of the balance sheet final dividend is only a recommendation or proposal of the directors in respect of which no cash has yet been paid out. The entries required in respect of the final preference dividend in the above example are shown in Figure 184.

Preference Dividend A/c

			£	p	19..			£	p
		Cash	1,500	00	Dec.	31	Appropriation A/c	1,500	00
					Dec.	31	Appropriation A/c	1,500	00

Appropriation A/c

			£	p				£	p
		Pref. Div: Final	1,500	00					

Figure 184

When the annual general meeting approves the final dividend (as it invariably does), the credit balance in the preference dividend account becomes a debt from the company to the members. In the balance sheet the final dividend would be shown as a 'proposed dividend' under the heading of current liabilities. It should be added that the company pays tax on the whole of its profit and any dividends paid are regarded as being paid out of profits already taxed.

(5) The ordinary dividend of £4 000 is also a proposed dividend, and requires the following entries: dr. appropriation account, and cr. ordinary dividend account. The amount provided for this proposed dividend would also be shown in the balance sheet as a current liability.

(6) The full treatment of taxation is outside the scope of this volume, but students should note that companies are subject to 'corporation tax' which will normally appear as an item in the appropriation account.

(7) The corresponding credit entry for the £3 500 in the appropriation account would be made in the general reserve account. In the balance sheet this would be shown under the heading 'Reserves'.

(8) Preliminary expenses are the expenses of forming a limited company and include items such as legal expenses, registration fees, stamp duties and similar costs. It is usual to write off the preliminary expenses over a period of several years. The entries required are a debit in the appropriation account and a credit entry in the preliminary expenses account. The amount not yet written off is shown in the balance sheet as a fictitious asset.
(9) The balance of net profit of £3 000 is carried forward to the next accounting period. In the balance sheet it is shown under the heading 'Reserves'.

Example At 1st January, 19..., a hotel company had a credit balance on its appropriation account of £20 000 and its net profit for the year amounted to £180 000. During the year a half-year's dividend of £25 000 was paid on its preference shares and the directors propose the following distribution of the remaining profits:

(a) to pay a final preference dividend of £25 000;
(b) to pay an ordinary dividend of £60 000;
(c) to transfer £30 000 to General Reserve;
(d) to write £15 000 off the goodwill;
(e) to write £5 000 off the preliminary expenses;
(f) to transfer £20 000 to staff welfare fund;
(g) to carry the balance of profits to the following year.

Prepare the hotel's appropriation account. Proceed as in Figure 185.

Appropriation A/c
for year ended 31st. Dec., 19..

Pref. Div. Interim	25,000	Net Profit 1-1-19..	20,000
- do - Final	25,000	Net Profit b/d.	180,000
Ordinary Dividend	60,000		
General Reserve	30,000		
Goodwill	15,000		
Preliminary Expenses	5,000		
Staff Welfare Fund	20,000		
Balance	c/f 20,000		
	200,000		200,000

Figure 185

Balance sheet

The unpublished balance sheet of a limited company may be prepared in several different ways. The layout and method of presentation shown below follow the conventional lines; other methods of presentation will be considered in Chapter 16.

A typical balance sheet of a limited company will be drawn up as indicated in Figure 186 (overleaf).

X.Y.Z. Co. Ltd.
Balance Sheet
as at......

Authorised Capital			Fixed Assets		
Issued Capital			Investments		
Reserves			Current Assets		
Long-Term Liabilities					
Current Liabilities					

Figure 186

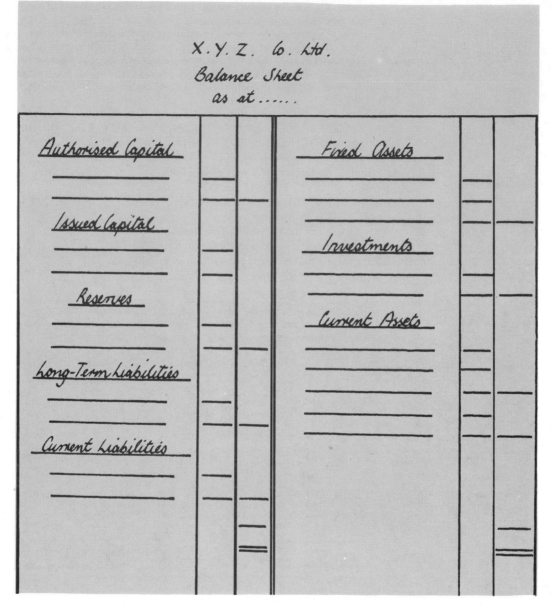

Fixed assets These are usually shown at cost less aggregate depreciation to date. This method of writing off the depreciation was explained in Chapter 10.

Investments Where a company holds shares, debentures or other securities these are shown under this heading.

Current assets These are listed in the same manner as in other types of business unit. Any fictitious assets, e.g. share discount account or preliminary expenses account, are entered in the balance sheet under the current assets and extended separately to the effective column.

Authorized capital This is a memorandum note only and shows what shares the company is authorized to issue by its Memorandum of Association.

Issued capital This shows particulars of any shares actually issued. Any calls in arrear should be deducted from the issued capital.

Reserves Students should be familiar with the main items which are likely to appear under this heading. Reserves may be of a capital nature such as the share premium account or of a revenue nature such as the general reserve which consists of profits set aside in past years. Any credit balance on the profit and loss account will also be shown under this heading.

Long-term liabilities This comprises any debentures and other long-term liabilities of the company.

Current liabilities Under this heading are all the usual items such as trade creditors and accrued expenses, as well as any proposed dividends.

Example Grand Hotel Ltd. has an authorized capital of £500 000, consisting of 200 000 ordinary shares of £1 each and 300 000 10% preference shares of £1 each. The following balances were extracted from the books of the hotel after the preparation of the profit and loss appropriation account for the year ended 31st December, 19...

	£	£
200 000 ordinary shares, 75p paid		150 000
300 000 preference shares, fully paid		300 000
Stocks	5 000	
Banqueting debtors	10 000	
Trade creditors		16 000
Cash at bank	15 000	
Accrued expenses		15 000
Proposed dividend—ordinary		12 000
,, ,, —preference		10 000
Share discount account	12 000	
Deposits—advance bookings		3 000
Preliminary expenses	3 000	
Shares in A.B.C. Ltd	20 000	
Shares in D.E.F. Ltd	30 000	
Reserve for future taxation		50 000
China and furnishings, at valuation	20 000	
Profit and loss account		60 000
General reserve		50 000
10 000 9% debentures of £10 each		100 000
Furniture (cost £200 000)	150 000	
Leasehold hotel (cost £450 000)	400 000	
Kitchen plant (cost £130 000)	100 000	
Calls in arrear	1 000	
	£766 000	£766 000

The balance sheet as at 31st December, 19.., is shown in Figure 187 (overleaf).

GRAND HOTEL LTD.
Balance Sheet
as at 31st Dec., 19..

Authorised Capital	£	£	Fixed Assets	£	£	£
200,000 Ord. Shares of £1 ea.	200,000		Leasehold Hotel	450,000		
300,000 10% Pref. Shares of £1 ea.	300,000	500,000	Less Depreciation	50,000	400,000	
Issued Capital			Kitchen Plant	130,000		
200,000 Ord. Shares 75p paid	150,000		Less Depreciation	30,000	100,000	
Less Calls in Arrear	1,000		Furniture	200,000		
	149,000		Less Depreciation	50,000	150,000	
300,000 10% Pref. Shares fully paid	300,000	449,000	China & Furnishings		20,000	670,000
Reserves			Investments			
			Shares in A.B.C. Ltd.		20,000	
General Reserves	50,000		Shares in D.E.F. Ltd.		30,000	50,000
Reserve for future tax	50,000		Current Assets			
Profit & Loss A/c	60,000	160,000	Stocks		5,000	
Long-term Liabilities			Banqueting Debtors		10,000	
10,000 9% Debentures of £10 ea.		100,000	Cash at Bank		15,000	30,000
Current Liabilities			Share Discount A/c		12,000	
Trade Creditors	16,000		Preliminary Expenses		3,000	15,000
Accrued Expenses	15,000					
Deposits - Ad Bankings	3,000					
Proposed Dividends:						
Ordinary	12,000					
Preference	10,000	56,000				
		765,000				765,000

Figure 187

Published accounts

As already mentioned, the contents and method of presentation of published accounts are regulated by the Companies Acts, 1948, 1967 and 1980.

Published accounts are, generally, less informative than internal accounts; this applies particularly to the published profit and loss account. The Companies Acts require limited companies to disclose particular items of income and expenditure and, usually, items which are not expressly required to be disclosed are not shown in the accounts. The effect of this non-disclosure of information is that items such as purchases, sales, wages, salaries, rent and insurance are not disclosed in the published profit and loss account.

The main provisions of the Acts relating to published accounts are given below in summary form.

The profit and loss account must show the following information:

(a) Loan interest: the amount of interest on loans advanced to the company on bank loans, overdrafts and debentures.

(b) Taxation: the amount of the charge to revenue for United Kingdom corporation tax.

(c) Investment income: the separate amounts of income from quoted and unquoted investments.

(d) Rents: if a substantial part of the company's revenue for the financial year consists in rents from land, the amount, after deducting ground-rents and other outgoings.

(e) Plant hire: if it is material, the amount charged to revenue in respect of the hire of plant and machinery.

(f) Dividends: the aggregate of dividends paid and proposed must be shown.

(g) Depreciation: all amounts charged to revenue by way of depreciation or diminution in the value of any assets.

(h) Auditors' remuneration: this must be shown under a separate heading, whether fixed by the company in general meeting or not.

(i) Turnover: the turnover of the company must normally be disclosed, but there are certain relaxations in the case of small companies.

(j) Comparative figures: these must be shown, except in relation to the first account laid before the company in general meeting.

(k) Directors' emoluments: these must be disclosed in the accounts or in a statement annexed to the accounts.

The balance sheet must show the following information:

(a) Capital: the authorized, issued and paid-up capital.

(b) Reserves and provisions: particulars of all reserves and provisions must be shown. It is no longer necessary to show separately capital reserves and revenue reserves.

(c) Loans: particulars of all loans and overdrafts must be given.

(d) Investments: the distinction between trade investments and other investments has now been abolished. Companies must now show separately the aggregate of their quoted investments and unquoted investments.

(e) U.K. taxation: the company's tax liabilities and the basis on which any amount set aside for U.K. corporation tax has been computed must be stated.

(f) Loans to directors: particulars of these must be given.

(g) Proposed dividends: the aggregate of any proposed dividends must be shown.

(h) Assets: particulars of all fixed and current assets must be shown; the basis of valuation of fixed assets must be disclosed. The amount attributable to freehold land and the amount attributable to leaseholds must be shown separately. With regard to the latter particulars of short leases and long leases must also be given.

Reserves and provisions

The terms 'reserve' and 'provision' have been used several times, and it is convenient at this stage to define more accurately what is meant by these terms as well as to explain the main kinds of provisions.

Before the Companies Act, 1948, came into force the terms 'reserve' and 'provision' were used loosely and no clear distinction between them was made.

The Act defines a 'provision' as:

'any amount written-off or retained by way of providing for depreciation, renewals or diminution in the value of assets or retained by way of providing for any known liability of which the amount cannot be determined with substantial accuracy.'

The Act defines a 'reserve' as:
'an amount set aside out of divisible profits or other surpluses which is not designed to meet any liability, contingency or diminution in the value of assets known to exist at the date of the balance sheet.'

From the quotations given above it will be appreciated that whilst a provision is a charge against profits (e.g. provision for bad debts, provision for depreciation) a reserve is an appropriation of profits (e.g. general reserve, dividend equalization reserve).

Reserves are of two main kinds: capital reserves and revenue reserves.

A reserve is a capital reserve if it is regarded as not being available for distribution (payment of dividend). Examples of capital reserves are share premium account and capital redemption reserve fund. The latter is a reserve created in connection with the redemption (repayment) of redeemable preference shares.

All reserves other than capital reserves are revenue reserves, i.e. available for distribution in dividend, e.g. general reserve, dividend equalization reserve, balance of profit and loss account.

Problems

1 Explain what is meant by: unlimited company; company limited by guarantee; company limited by shares.

2 Distinguish between public companies and private companies.

3 Write short notes on: articles of association; memorandum of association.

4 What are the main changes introduced by the Companies Act 1980 relating to the payment for shares allotted by public companies?

5 Explain what you understand by the following: nominal capital; subscribed capital; called-up capital; paid-up capital; unissued capital; loan capital.

6 Distinguish between each of the following: shares and debentures; ordinary shares and preference shares; cumulative preference shares and non-cumulative preference shares.

7 A hotel company issued the following:
(a) 100 000 ordinary shares of £1 each at a premium of 10p per share, and
(b) 200 000 10% debentures of £1 each at par.

Show by means of appropriate extracts how the above would be shown in the balance sheet of the company.

8 Explain the difference between the published and unpublished (internal) accounts of a company.

9 Distinguish between each of the following: a charge against profits and an appropriation of profits; an interim dividend and a final dividend; capital reserve and revenue reserve.

10 The following balances appeared on the books of Cakes-n-Ale Ltd, after closing the profit and loss account for the year ending 31st January, 19...

	£
Share capital—authorized, 200 000 shares of £1 each; issued 180 000 shares	180 000
Premises at cost	100 000
Kitchen equipment, at cost less depreciation to date £35 000	115 000
Creditors	25 880
Preliminary expenses	2 200
Stock as valued by the directors	57 960
Debtors	83 290
Share premium account	10 000
Profit and loss account—accumulated profit at 31st January	22 730
Debentures	40 000
General reserve	50 000
Furniture, etc. at cost less depreciation to date of £6 500	4 500
Balance at bank	53 640
Provision for bad debts	1 380
Profit for year to 31st January 19...	86 600

It was resolved that:

(a) preliminary expenses be written off;
(b) general reserve be increased to £75 000
(c) a dividend to 15 per cent on the issued share capital be declared.

Prepare the company's appropriation account for the year to 31st January, 19..., and a balance sheet at that date.

11 The A.B.C. Catering Co. Ltd. has authorized capital of £1 000 000 divided into 500 000 10% preference shares of £1 and 500 000 ordinary shares of £1 each.

From the following trial balance prepare the company's trading, and profit and loss and appropriation account for the year ended 31st December, 19.., and a balance sheet as at that date.

	£	£
Issued capital:		
400 000 ordinary shares £1.00 called		400 000
500 000 10% preference shares 80p called		400 000
Cash at bank	452 750	
Sales		1 200 000
Preliminary expenses	15 000	
Discounts received		9 500
Glass, china and cutlery	22 750	
Gas and electricity	67 500	
Stock on 1st January, 19..	12 500	
Furniture	22 000	
Bank interest		1 500
Debtors and creditors	17 500	43 500
Directors' fees	25 000	
Purchases returns		15 000
Repairs and renewals	43 500	
Profit and loss account, 1st January, 19..		10 500
Purchases	550 500	
Bad debts	6 000	
9% mortgage debentures		100 000
Kitchen equipment	85 000	
c/f	1 320 000	2 180 000

		£	£
	b/f	1 320 000	2 180 000
Wages and salaries		244 000	
General reserve			50 000
Rent and rates		72 000	
Leasehold premises		570 000	
Calls in advance—preference shares			1 000
Travelling expenses		3 500	
Cleaning materials		1 500	
Preference dividend (half year)		20 000	
		£2 231 000	£2 231 000

Take the following notes into account:

(1) the stock at 31st December, 19.. was valued at £15 000;
(2) accrued gas and electricity amounted to £500;
(3) invoices received from suppliers but not entered in the books amounted to £5 000:
(4) create a provision for bad debts equal to 2 per cent of the debtors;
(5) provide for depreciation as follows:
 (a) kitchen equipment, 10 per cent;
 (b) furniture, 10 per cent;
 (c) leasehold, 2 per cent;
 (d) glass, china and cutlery £2 000.
(6) provide for one year's debenture interest due;
(7) write £5 000 off the preliminary expenses;
(8) provide for the balance due to preference shareholders and for a proposed ordinary dividend of 10 per cent;
(9) transfer £50 000 to general reserve.

12 X Hotel Ltd. has an authorized capital of £700 000 divided into 200 000 ordinary shares of £1 each and 500 000 preference shares of £1 each.

After closing the trading, profit and loss account for the year ended 31st December 19.., the balances in the books are:

	£	£
Ordinary share capital		100 000
5% preference share capital		400 000
Leasehold premises (cost £115 000)	75 000	
Kitchen equipment (cost £263 000)	200 000	
Stocks	210 240	
Creditors and accrued expenses		31 980
Debtors and prepayments	149 870	
Balance at bank	89 270	
Cash in hand	500	
Restaurant furniture (cost £9 500)	6 500	
General reserve		100 000
Profit and loss account 1st January, 19..		20 360
Net profit for the year		79 040
	£731 380	£731 380

The directors of the hotel recommend that:
(a) the dividend on preference shares be paid;
(b) a dividend of 20 per cent be paid on the ordinary shares;

(c) £10 000 be transferred to a general reserve.
Prepare the hotel's appropriation account for the year ended 31st December 19.., and a balance sheet as at that date.

13 The Welcome Hotel Ltd has an authorized capital of £1 000 000 divided into 500 000 ordinary shares of £1 each and 250 000 10 per cent preference shares of £2 each. On 1st March, 1981, the following balances appeared in the ledger of the hotel after the preparation of the profit and loss and appropriation account for the year ended on that date:

	£
500 000 ordinary shares, 50p paid	250 000
250 000 10% preference shares, £1.50 paid	375 000
Cash at bank	59 000
Cash in advance—preference shares	2 000
Leasehold hotel, at cost less depreciation	630 000
Preliminary expenses	2 500
Cash in hand	500
Plate, cutlery and linen at valuation	13 400
Provision for bad debts	100
10% mortgage debentures	50 000
Trade creditors	10 400
Profit and loss account cr.	30 600
Reserve of future taxation	55 000
Insurance dr.	200
Shares in X.Y.Z. Catering Ltd (unquoted)	22 500
General reserve	85 000
Provision for discounts received	500
Gas and electricity cr.	1 050
Banqueting debtors	2 550
Rates cr.	550
Furniture and equipment, at cost less depreciation	160 000
Proposed dividends—ordinary	12 500
" " —preference	37 500
Stocks	18 550

You are required to prepare the balance sheet of the hotel as at 31st March, 1981, taking the following into account:
(a) in your answer ignore comparative figures for the year ended 31st March, 1980;
(b) depreciation is written off the leasehold hotel at the rate of $2\frac{1}{2}$ per cent, and furniture and equipment at the rate of 5 per cent p.a. (both on the straight-line method). All these assets were purchased on 1st April, 1977.

14 The Magnificent Catering Co. Ltd was incorporated on 1st January, 1981 with a nominal capital of £800 000, divided into 400 000 ordinary shares of £1 each and 400 000 10 per cent preference shares of £1 each. Early in that year the company issued all its ordinary shares and 200 000 of the preference shares.

The following is a summary of the cash transactions of the company in respect of the year ended 31st December, 1981.

Cash received

	£
Sum received for ordinary shares	400 000
Sum received for preference shares	198 000
Cash sales and receipts from debtors	484 950
	£1 082 950

Cash paid

Leasehold premises	400 000
Plant and equipment	148 000
Furniture	51 500
Light and heat	15 200
Postage, stationery and telephone	7 900
Advertising	18 400
Preliminary expenses	5 500
Cash purchases and payments to suppliers	261 150
Wages and salaries	130 050
Directors' salaries	30 000
Balance	15 250
	£1 082 950

You are required to prepare the trading, and profit and loss account of the company for the year ended 31st December, 1981, and a balance sheet as at that date. Take the following additional information into account:

(1) the stock of provisions at 31st December, 1981 was valued at £4 500;

(2) at 31st December, 1981 debtors amounted to £2 250 and creditors were owed £5 150;

(3) provide for depreciation as follows:

(a) premises, 2 per cent, (b) plant and equipment 10 per cent, (c) furniture 10 per cent.

(4) accrued lighting and heating amounted to £800; an invoice for £950 in respect of stationery had not been entered in the books and remained unpaid; postage stamps unused amounted to £100;

(5) carry forward to 1982 £4 000 of the advertising;

(6) write £1 000 off the preliminary expenses;

(7) directors' salaries due but unpaid at 31st December, 1981 amounted to £5 000; unremitted PAYE and insurance contributions amounted to £700;

(8) You are informed that the £2 000 remaining unpaid on the preference shares represents an unpaid call of 25p per share on 8 000 shares.

CHAPTER 15

Goodwill

Nature of goodwill

The term 'goodwill' is frequently used and its general meaning is usually understood quite well. It is a term, however, which is very difficult to define.

Goodwill has been defined as 'the benefit arising from connection and reputation'; also as 'the probability that the old customers will resort to the old place'. Clearly, however, a restaurant or any other business for that matter may have certain connections, some reputation and so many customers, and still be neither prosperous nor a profitable business.

From the accounting point of view we may define goodwill as that factor which enables a business to earn higher than average profits. What constitutes average profits for an industry or a section of an industry is, clearly, a matter of fact.

Goodwill may be due to any one or a combination of the following:

(a) the location of the business (proximity to seaside resorts, railway stations, motorways, theatres, cinemas and other places of entertainment);

(b) the quality of food and service provided (this, obviously, is of particular importance in all hotel and catering establishments);

(c) the personal reputation of the proprietors;

(d) other factors such as advertising campaigns, satisfied and loyal employees, ability to maintain the quality of food, service and the general standard of comfort provided.

Valuation of goodwill

Goodwill is as difficult to value as it is to define. There are, however, three main methods of valuing goodwill.

Average profits method

Under this method the average profits of past years are multiplied by an agreed number. Thus, if a snack bar has earned an average net profit of £10 000, then at 'three years' purchase' of average profits the value of its goodwill would be £30 000.

This, it will be appreciated, is not an accurate method of valuing goodwill. Let us assume that the capital of a guest house is £200 000, and that its average net profit for the past six years has been £7 500. On the basis of 'four years' purchase' the goodwill should be worth £30 000. Yet it is clear that few people would be willing to pay (£200 000+ £30 000) £230 000 for a business earning £7 500 a year.

In most methods of valuing goodwill some quantity (e.g. average profits) is multiplied by an 'agreed number', the latter being usually between 1 and 5. The reasoning behind this mysterious number is this. As soon as a business is sold the old goodwill begins to decline and, usually, the new owners of the business begin to create a new goodwill of their own. It is often said that the old goodwill cannot last more than about five years. Hence, the argument runs, the vendors should not be entitled to any benefit arising out of the goodwill after that period has elapsed.

Gross income method

Under this method, used mainly in respect of professional businesses such as solicitors, accountants and consultants, the value of goodwill is arrived at by multiplying the average gross income (receipts or fees) by an agreed number.

Thus, if a catering consultant's average gross income for the past five years was £20 000, and he wished to sell his practice, he might ask for a payment for his goodwill. This might be valued on the basis of 'two years' purchase' in which event the goodwill of the business would be worth £40 000.

This method is, again, very unsatisfactory, and it probably does no more than provide some basis for further negotiations.

Super-profits method

We said earlier on that, from the accounting point of view, goodwill is that factor which enables a business to earn more than average profits. It is clear, therefore, that in valuing goodwill we should relate it to the expected or future profits which are in excess of average profits for that type of business, i.e. super-profits. In arriving at the expected amount of super-profits adequate provision must be made for a fair remuneration in respect of the proprietors' services and the degree of risk involved in the business.

Under the super-profits method, we multiply super-profits by an agreed number to arrive at the value of goodwill.

Example

The expected future profits of the Seaside Guest House are £30 000. The capital of the guest house is £100 000. The usual return on capital invested in this type of business is 10 per cent, and it is considered that the value of the proprietors' services is £14 000.

According to the super-profits method the goodwill of the guest house would be valued as follows:

Expected future profits		£30 000
Less return on capital	£10 000	
Proprietors' services	14 000	
		24 000
Super-profits		£6 000

On the basis of 'three years' purchase' the goodwill would be valued at £18 000.

Vendors' accounts

When considering the purchase of a business it is not unusual to ask the vendors to produce their accounts relating to past years. An examination of such accounts often discloses items of income and expenditure which require some adjustment which, in turn, affects the profits disclosed by such accounts.

The following are some of the main points that should be examined:

(a) have depreciation charges been adequate?

(b) have the charges for proprietors' remuneration been correct?

(c) does the trading account contain any exceptional items which are not likely to recur, e.g. a profit on a function of a non-recurring nature?

(d) do the accounts contain charges for exceptional non-recurring losses made in the past?

When the examination of the accounts has been completed and the necessary adjustments made, the trend of profits should be considered. This, together with other information (e.g. local circumstances, competition, etc.) will enable the purchaser to predict what profits may be expected in the future.

Treatment of goodwill in accounts

Goodwill is an intangible asset, one whose value in an existing business is difficult to assess. Whatever the actual value of it may be, it will change over a period of time. For these reasons it may be taken that goodwill does not normally appear in the books of a business unless it has been paid for or actually valued on the admission, death or retirement of a partner.

Purchase of business A goodwill account is often raised on the purchase of a business as a going concern. This would be necessary if the purchase price were in excess of the assets (or assets less liabilities) taken over.

Example The Grand Catering Co. has agreed to purchase for £110 000 the restaurant of V. Small, whose assets and liabilities on 1st January, 19 . . were:

Premises	£50 000
Kitchen plant	25 000
Furniture	15 000
China and cutlery	5 000
Stocks	5 000
Creditors	2 000

The payment made in respect of goodwill would be calculated as follows:

Assets: premises		50 000
kitchen plant		25 000
furniture		15 000
china and cutlery		5 000
stocks		5 000
		100 000
Less: liabilities—creditors		2 000
Net assets taken over		£98 000
Purchase price	£110 000	
Less: Net assets	98 000	
Goodwill	£12 000	

In the books of Grand Catering Co., the above transaction would be journalized as shown in Figure 188.

		JOURNAL					
19. .							
Jan.	1	Goodwill	Dr.	12,000	00		
"	1	Premises	"	50,000	00		
"	1	Kitchen Plant	"	25,000	00		
"	1	Furniture	"	15,000	00		
"	1	China and Cutlery	"	5,000	00		
"	1	Stocks		5,000	00		
"	1	Vendor - V. Small				110,000	00
		Creditors				2,000	00
		Being assets and liabilities taken over per Agreement dated....					

Figure 188

After journalizing the above transaction all the items would be posted to the ledger as explained in Chapter 5. If the company had no existing goodwill account one would, of course, have to be opened and debited with the £12 000.

Goodwill in partnership accounts

When a new partner is admitted into a partnership he acquires the right to participate in the profits of the business. On the other hand the existing partners, who have built up the business, give up a proportion of any subsequent profits. As a result, it is usual, in such circumstances, for the existing partners to be compensated by the incoming partner. This may be done in one of the three main ways:

(a) The new partner may pay the old partners personally a premium. This being a personal arrangement, it might or might not be recorded in the books of the business.

(b) The new partner may pay a premium of so much, the latter to be retained in the business. The necessary entries would be a debit in the cash book and credit entries in the capital accounts of the old partners.

(c) Finally, it is possible to compensate the existing partners by crediting their capital accounts and debiting the goodwill account. When this arrangement takes place, the old partners benefit from additional interest on their capitals—if this is payable under the terms of the partnership agreement. Similarly, in the event of dissolution of the partnership, they would benefit through larger repayments of their respective capitals.

A goodwill account may also have to be raised on the death or retirement of a partner, when it is usual to ascertain his share of the goodwill and credit it in his capital account.

Goodwill in company accounts

Goodwill does not usually arise in company accounts, except in connection with the purchase of a business. The only difference between the purchase of a business by a limited company and by some other type of business unit is that, in the former case, the purchase price might be settled partly or wholly in shares.

The Companies Act, 1948, provides that goodwill, patents and trade-marks may be shown as one composite total. An attempt should, however, be made to show goodwill as a separate item in the balance sheet.

Goodwill account

When a goodwill account has, for some reason or another, been raised two courses of action are possible: (a) to keep the goodwill in the books or (b) to write it off. Many businesses prefer to write it off, usually over a period of years.

In the case of sole traders and partnerships the entries then required are: dr. profit and loss account; cr. goodwill account.

In the case of limited companies the entries would be: dr. appropriation account; cr. goodwill account.

The balance of the goodwill account not yet written off should be shown in the balance sheet as a fixed asset.

Problems

1 (a) Give a brief description of the three main methods of valuing goodwill.

(b) V. Young is interested in taking over A. Tick's practice as adviser on hotel systems; Tick's average gross fees for the past five years have been £17 000 and his office expenses £5 000. They have agreed that Tick's office machinery and furniture should be valued at £4 000.

The vendor insists that the goodwill of his practice should be valued at three years' purchase of his average gross fees.

Would you advise Young to accept Tick's terms? Give reasons for your answer.

2 On 1st January, 1981, the Expanding Catering Co. agreed to purchase the business of Wm. Bacon, whose balance sheet then was:

Balance sheet

	£		£
Creditors	1 800	Cash at bank	4 550
Accrued expenses	100	Debtors	430
Capital	60 000	Stocks	2 170
		Cutlery and utensils	3 150
		Restaurant furniture	4 100
		Freehold premises	47 500
	£61 900		£61 900

The Expanding Catering Co. was to take over all the assets and liabilities with the exception of the cash at bank and the accrued expenses. They agreed that the following assets should be revalued:

Stocks	at £1 800
Cutlery and utensils	„ 3 000
Premises	„ 50 000

In addition, the company agreed to make a payment to Bacon in respect of goodwill; this was to be calculated on the basis of two years' purchase of his average net profits in the past five years. Bacon's accounts showed that his past profits were: 1976—£9 670; 1977—£6 890; 1978—£8 920; 1979—£10 500; 1980—£8 620.

(a) Calculate the purchase price;

(b) Journalize the purchase of Bacon's business in the books of Expanding Catering Co.

3 The capital employed in the Punjab Restaurant is £100 000, and the profits in the past six years have been as follows:

1975—£14 670
1976— 15 900
1977— 17 780
1978— 19 930
1979— 21 560
1980— 20 160

The restaurant is a non-seasonal personally managed business. The figures of profits given above were arrived at before taking into account the value of the proprietor's services (estimated at £8 000 p.a.) and the interest on the capital invested.

An investigation of the accounts of the restaurant shows that the net profit for 1979 includes an amount of profit on a function of a non-recurring nature; this profit is estimated at £2 000. You also find that the depreciation debited to the restaurant's profit and loss account for 1980 was understated by £1 000.

The proprietor wishes to dispose of the business and claims that the goodwill of the business should be valued on the basis of 'three years' purchase of the average net profits for the past six years' as disclosed by his accounts.

You are asked to make an independent valuation of the goodwill assuming that a reasonable return on capital invested in this type of business is 10 per cent.

4 At 31st December, 19. ., the goodwill account of a hotel shows a debit balance of £7 500. The proprietors have decided that £2 500 should be written off, and that the balance of £5 000 be carried to the following year. Show the relevant entries in the goodwill account, profit and loss account and balance sheet.

5 On 1st May, 19. ., the Express Hotel Co. purchased the County Hotel, whose balance sheet then was as shown below:

Balance sheet

	£		£
Capital	190 000	Premises	100 000
Creditors	10 000	Furniture	50 000
		Kitchen plant	30 000
		Stocks	5 000
		Debtors	5 000
		Cash at bank	10 000
	200 000		200 000

The Express Hotel Co. took over all the assets and liabilities with the exception of the cash at bank and the creditors, and agreed to pay the proprietor of County Hotel an amount in respect of goodwill. This was to be calculated on the basis of one year's purchase of the average net profits of County Hotel for the last four years, which were; £25 000; £27 000; £21 000; £26 000.

You are required to calculate the purchase price paid by the Express Hotel Co. and to journalize the above transaction in its books.

CHAPTER 16

Presentation of accounting information

More and more attention has recently been paid to the presentation and layout of accounts. It seems that there have been two main reasons for this trend. First, it has been felt that inadequate use was being made of the large amount of accounting information available in most businesses. Secondly, managements have come to realise that whatever accounting information was given to them was not presented in the best possible manner.

Deficiencies of conventional accounts

In particular, conventional accounts suffer from the following deficiencies:

(1) The period covered by conventional accounts is usually one calendar year. When such accounts are actually presented to management (which could well be three months after the end of the accounting period) it is too late for any corrective action to be taken. A set of annual accounts is very much in the nature of an historical document. It may contain interesting information relating to the past but it provides little guidance as to the future.

(2) Conventional accounts tend to be over-loaded with unnecessary detail. Their superficial accuracy (agreement of the balance sheet to the last penny) may impress the layman—and confuse him at the same time. When the turnover of a hotel is half a million pounds then, it is suggested, it is quite permissible to omit the pence and show all the figures to the nearest pound.

(3) Little attention has been paid to the classification of income and expenditure. Suitable sub-headings for different classes of expenditure, assets, liabilities, etc. are not used often enough.

(4) Whilst there is usually too much unimportant detail, significant information is not always shown. Thus in hotel accounts, there is often no information on departmental gross profit margins, departmental expenditure, distinction between controllable and uncontrollable expenditure, etc.

(5) Comparative figures are not usually given except in published accounts. Even less frequently are the current results shown in relation to the budgeted results.

Main principles of presentation and layout

It will be appreciated that there are many different parties interested in the accounts of any one business: the proprietors, the management, bankers, suppliers and the employees. Each of these will look at the accounts from a different point of view; the presentation and layout of the accounts should therefore be in conformity with the particular recipient in mind.

It is impossible to suggest a particular layout or method of presentation that will be appropriate on all occasions. Indeed, every set of accounts should be designed to meet the particular requirements of the recipient concerned. It is, however, possible to suggest some main principles which should always be borne in mind when preparing any set of accounts.

Principle of simplicity

The layout of accounts should be such as to make them simple, unambiguous and intelligible. No set of accounts is well designed unless it can be understood by a reasonably intelligent person with no special knowledge of accounting.

Principle of frequency

Accounts should be presented to management at sufficiently frequent intervals to be of value as a means of control. It is now almost generally accepted that accounts must be prepared more often than once a year. Most hotel and catering establishments have some accounts drawn up at least once a quarter. This is discussed in Chapter 19.

Principle of disclosure

This simply means that the layout of accounts must be such as to disclose what is important. Thus, in every hotel and catering establishment having several revenue-producing departments, separate trading results should be ascertained and shown for each department. Similarly, a well drawn-up balance sheet will show not only separate totals of current assets and current liabilities, but also the working capital.

Principle of comparison

In order to give the recipient of a set of accounts some indication of the progress of the business it is not enough to show the relevant figures for a particular accounting period. The fact that a hotel had a turnover of £2 000 000 is, in itself, rather meaningless. When we show the corresponding figure of turnover for the previous year, say £1 700 000, the information given begins to have some meaning. In businesses operating a system of budgetary control, all current (actual) figures should be shown in relation to the budgeted figures.

Principle of relevance

Most hotel and catering establishments are market oriented* which, amongst others, means that their profitability is greatly influenced by factors which operate on the revenue side of the business. Thus changes in sales mix, room occupancy, restaurant occupancy, average spending power, gross profit margins, etc. will have a powerful impact on profitability. It is essential, therefore, to give adequate prominence to all those factors when compiling accounts, reports and periodical accounting statements.

Methods of presentation and layout

Conventional accounts

Conventional final accounts may be made easier to follow and thus more intelligible in various ways. One possibility is to show the corresponding figures for the previous accounting period. All relatively unimportant detail (purchases, returns, allowances to customers, opening and closing stocks, etc.) may be omitted or shown in separate supporting schedules. Charges debited in the profit and loss account as well as balance sheet items, can be shown under suitable headings. Percentages may be shown in the accounts to show the relationships between various items (e.g. cost of sales and expenses to sales; fixed and current assets to total assets). Care must, however, be taken to ensure that the accounts are not over-loaded and to decide what, if any, information should be shown in a supporting schedule rather than in the main body of the accounts.

Vertical accounts

Though, as suggested above, various improvements in the conventional accounts are possible, to the layman the debit-and-credit type of account is always rather puzzling. An alternative layout of accounts, known as the vertical layout, has therefore become very popular in recent years.

Because of the debit-and-credit arrangement of conventional accounts, these tend to be read horizontally, from left to right. When the vertical method is used the accounts are read vertically, from the top downwards: hence the *vertical* method. A specimen set of vertical accounts is shown in Figure 189.

---

* The significance of market orientation is discussed fully in Kotas, R. (Ed.), *Market Orientation in the Hotel and Catering Industry*, Surrey University Press, 1975.

THE SILVER DOLLAR RESTAURANT

Trading, profit and loss account for year ended 31st December, 19..

	Sales	%	Cost of Sales	%	Gross profit	%
Food	£240,000	100·0	£94,000	39·2	£146,000	60·8
Beverages	140,000	100·0	64,000	45·7	76,000	54·3
Tobaccos	20,000	100·0	18,200	91·0	1,800	9·0
Total	£400,000	100·0	£176,200	44·1	£223,800	55·9
Less: Labour costs:						
Wages		£89,500				
Salaries		24,200				
Staff welfare		2,500	116,200	29·1		
Overheads:						
Rent and Rates		£22,500				
Light and Heat		14,200				
Depreciation		18,700				
Repairs		5,250				
Printing and stationery		2,450				
Advertising		2,600				
Miscellaneous expenses		2,900	68,600	17·1	184,800	46·2
Net Profit					£39,000	9·7

Figure 189

Notes: (1) Corresponding figures are not shown but, if required, they could appear in a previous year column on the left-hand side of the account.

(2) If particulars of the stock levels were required these could be given in a separate schedule.

(3) The percentages of the total line, 44·1% and 55·9% relate to the total sales of £400 000.

The balance sheet of the restaurant would appear as in Figure 190 (overleaf).

THE SILVER DOLLAR RESTAURANT

Balance Sheet as at 31st December, 19..

Fixed assets		Cost	Dep'n	Net
Leasehold premises		£200,000	£40,000	£160,000
Restaurant furniture		20,000	5,000	15,000
Kitchen equipment		24,000	6,000	18,000
China and cutlery		6,000	2,000	4,000
Total		£250 000	£53 000	£197 000
Add: Working capital				
Current assets				
Stocks		£17,800		
Debtors		5,000		
Cash at Bank		13,700		
		36,500		
Less: Current liabilities				
Trade creditors	£19,000			
Accrued expenses	3,000	22,000		14,500
Capital (net total assets)				£211,500
Capital at 1st January, 19..				£190,000
Add: Net Profit				39,000
				229,000
Less: Drawings				17,500
Capital at 31st December, 19..				£211,500

Figure 190

Notes: (1) the total of depreciation, £53 000 is the aggregate depreciation to date and therefore, is in excess of the amount debited in the profit and loss account.
(2) working capital, dealt with in the following chapter, is the difference between current assets and current liabilities.

Supporting schedules These are often added to the actual final accounts to give further information which it is not convenient to show in the accounts themselves. Quite obviously the contents of such schedules will vary, depending on what important supplementary information there is and the needs of the recipient concerned. The example which follows (Figure 191) relates to the vertical accounts shown in Figure 190.

THE SILVER DOLLAR RESTAURANT

SUPPLEMENTARY INFORMATION ON ACCOUNTS

for year ended 31st December, 19. .

Sales Statistics

	THIS YEAR		LAST YEAR	
Food	£240,000	60.0%	£225,000	59.2%
Beverages	140,000	35.0%	137,000	36.1%
Tobaccos	20,000	5.0%	18,000	4.7%
Total	£400,000	100.0%	£380,000	100.0%

Gross Profit Statistics

	THIS YEAR		LAST YEAR	
Food	£146,000	60.8%	£136,100	60.5%
Beverages	76,000	54.3%	81,250	59.3%
Tobacco	1,800	9.0%	1,620	9.0%
Total	£223,800	55.9%	£218,870	57.6%

Cost and Profit Statistics

	THIS YEAR		LAST YEAR	
Cost of Sales	£176,200	44.1%	£161,030	42.4%
Labour Costs	116,200	29.1%	110,200	29.0%
Overheads	68,600	17.1%	65,350	17.2%
Net Profit	39,000	9.7%	43,420	11.4%
Total	£400,000	100.0%	£380,000	100.0%

Disposal of Net Profit

	19..	19..
Net Profit Earned	£39,000	£43,420
Less Proprietor's Drawings	17,500	15,400
Profits Ploughed Back	£21,500	£28,020

Figure 191

Application of vertical layout to residential establishments

The preparation of the trading account of a residential establishment (hotel, motel, hostel, club, etc.) was discussed in Chapter 8. We then noted the difficulties arising out of the fact that, in such establishments, a proportion of the income is received from the sale of a service, in respect of which the cost of sales cannot be calculated.

The application of a vertical layout avoids the difficulty. As may be seen from the specimen trading, profit and loss account in Figure 192, we show the departmental gross profits, and all other income of the residential establishment, and then deduct the expenses to arrive at the net profit.

GEORGE HOTEL

Trading, Profit & Loss Account

for year ended . . .

Department	Sales	Cost of Sales	Dept'l Payroll	Dept'l Expenses	TOTAL	Dept'l Profit
	£	£	£	£	£	£
Rooms	268,350	–	57,600	27,800	85,400	182,950
Food and Beverages	281,850	93,050	111,900	28,950	233,900	47,950
Minor Operated Depts.	34,150	15,300	12,250	2,300	29,850	4,300
Total	584,350	108,350	181,750	59,050	349,150	235,200
Add Store Rentals					7,350	
Other Receipts					11,150	18,500
						253,700
Less Undistributed Operating Expenses:						
Administrative and General					£ 49,300	
Advertising and Sales Promotion					17,800	
Heat, Light and Power					23,700	
Repairs and Maintenance					33,900	
Depreciation					18,400	143,100
Net Profit						£110,600

Figure 192

Statistical methods of presentation

In addition to any accounting information that may be presented by means of accounts (whether conventional or horizontal), a great deal of useful information may be presented to management by means of simple statistical methods.

A full description of such methods would be outside the scope of this text book and, therefore, only some of the main methods can be dealt with.

Tabular statements

One of the most useful statistical methods of presentation is the tabular statement. This may be usefully employed to show a large amount of data which it would be difficult to incorporate in an account.

The tabular statement is particularly useful in multiple businesses and businesses having several revenue-producing departments, when it is important to show the trading results of each unit or each department. The tabular statement is also useful when it is desired to show the progress of a business over a period of several years. An example is shown in Figure 193.

THE FULL MOON CAFÉ
Trading Results : 1975-81

Year Ended	SALES		GROSS	NET PROFIT	
31st December	£	% Increase on Previous Yr.	PROFIT %	£	% on Sales
1975	252,000	12·6	57·9	33,950	12·5
1976	285,000	13·1	56·2	35,200	12·3
1977	316,000	10·9	56·3	37,920	12·0
1978	343,500	8·7	58·1	35,550	10·3
1979	363,000	5·7	57·1	36,500	10·1
1980	380,000	4·7	57·6	43,420	11·4
1981	400,000	5·2	55·9	39,000	9·7

Figure 193

It will be observed that the above tabular statement gives much more information than is usually possible to incorporate into a set of accounts. One is thus able to show not only the turnover, net profit and other figures over a long period of time but also indicate significant trends, both absolutely and in terms of percentages. From the tabular statement given above we may see, for example, that although the turnover is increasing all the time, the rate of increase from one year to another is less and less. Also the figures shown in the statement are not adjusted for inflation. The increase in the sales volume of about 5 per cent during the last three years is far from being impressive.

Bar charts

There are several kinds of bar charts; the one shown in Figure 194 is known as a 'component bar chart'. Bar charts may be used to present different kinds of information, e.g. sales, costs, profits, as well as comparative figures. When prepared and presented in the appropriate manner, a bar chart may create a greater impression on the recipient of the information than a set of tabulated figures.

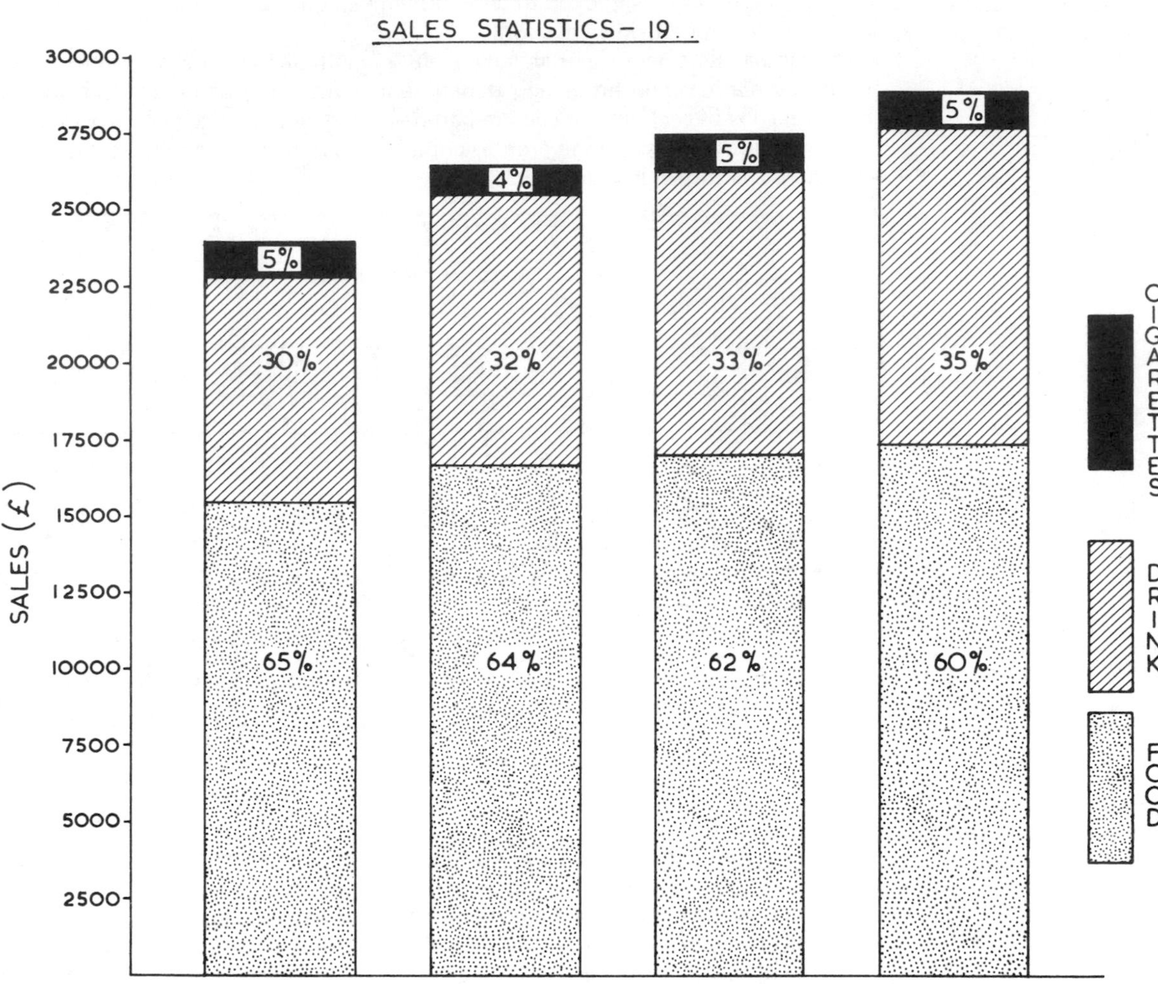

Figure 194

Graphs The graph is becoming a very popular method of presentation in all kinds of hotel and catering establishments. It is especially useful when it is desired to bring out the relationships between various quantities, e.g. sales and gross profit, sales and the various kinds of costs.

Quite often figures presented in an account or in tabular form are difficult to absorb. When the same information is presented in graph form, it immediately becomes more intelligible and meaningful. A simple example is shown in Figure 195.

Notes: (1) The aim of the diagram is to show, month by month, actual gross profit performance.
(2) The graph would be up-dated at the end of each month. Separate lines could be drawn for the gross profit percentage on food and on beverage sales.

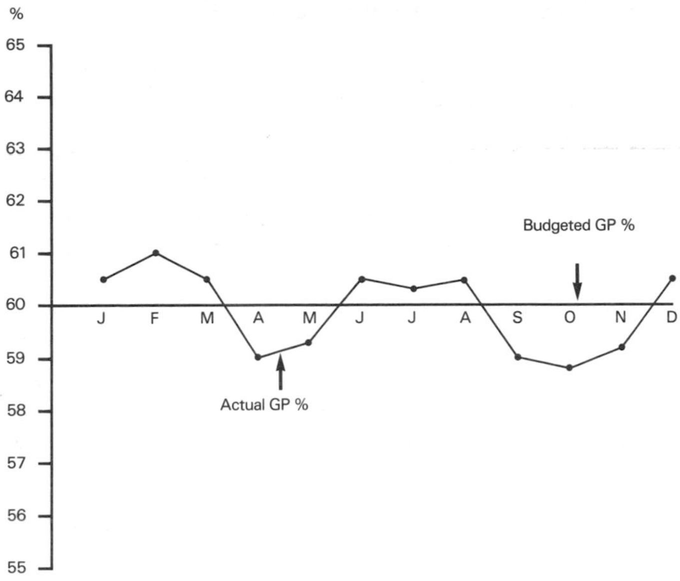

Figure 195

Pie charts Finally the pie chart is a convenient statistical method of showing the component parts of a total quantity, e.g. the composition of sales, costs, individual meals, banquet costs, as well as the break-down of profits. The pie chart is especially useful when it is important to present some information in the simplest possible form. An example is shown in Figure 196.

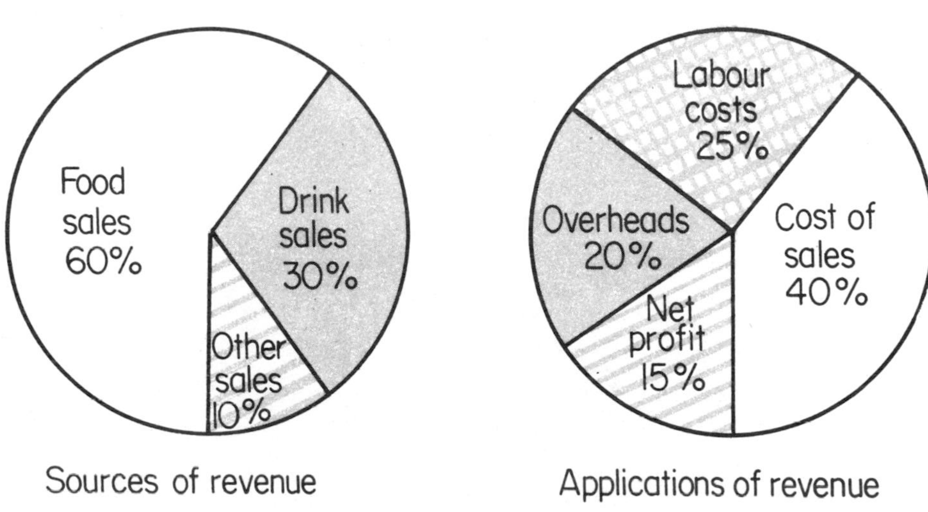

Figure 196

Problems

1 Comment on the deficiencies of conventional double-sided accounts.

2 What are the main points to be borne in mind when designing a set of final accounts?

3 What are the main advantages of the vertical layout of accounts?

4 The following balance sheet was prepared by the book-keeper of a hotel. You are required to re-draft it and present it in vertical form.

CHIC HOTEL LIMITED
Balance sheet as at 31st December, 19..

Authorized and issued capital			*Fixed assets*		
100 000 ordinary shares			Leasehold hotel	120 000	
at £1 each	100 000		*Less* depreciation	8 000	
30 000 6% preference shares					112 000
at £1 each	30 000		Furniture and equipment	25 000	
		130 000	*Less* depreciation	5 000	
Revenue reserves					20 000
General reserve	20 000		China and utensils	7 000	
Profit and loss account	5 000		*Less* depreciation	1 000	
		25 000			6 000
Current liabilities			*Current assets*		
Trade creditors	5 000		Stock	12 000	
Accrued expenses	2 000		Banqueting debtors	8 000	
Proposed dividend	8 000		Cash at bank	12 000	
		15 000			32 000
		£170 000			£170 000

5 The information given below was extracted from the books of the Sorrento Restaurant in respect of the year ended 31st December, 19.... You are required to prepare the Restaurant's trading, profit and loss account for the year ended as at the above date, using the vertical method of presentation. Show appropriate percentages in your account.

	£
Stocks, 1st January, 19.. food	6 000
beverages	21 000
cigarettes	2 500
Purchases: food	235 000
beverages	135 000
cigarettes	26 000
Sales: food	500 000
beverages	250 000
cigarettes	30 000
Stock, 31st December, 19.. food	4 000
beverages	19 000
cigarettes	1 500
Rates and rent	48 600
Postage and stationery	5 200
Wages	185 000
Advertising	5 500

(continued)

Depreciation	14 000
Salaries	39 300
Repairs and renewals	12 100
Employers N.I.C.	5 000
Light and heat	26 300
Staff welfare	7 500
Miscellaneous expenses	1 000

6 The A-n-B Catering Co., operates two restaurants, A and B. The following were the sales of the two restaurants in 19...

	£	£
Food sales	400 000	650 000
Beverage sales	250 000	100 000
Other	50 000	50 000

Show the above information by means of a simple pie chart.

7 The information give below was extracted from the records of a seasonal hotel:

Month	*Sales*	*F & B Cost*	*Labour*	*Overheads*
January	£25 000	£5 000	£10 000	£11 000
February	30 000	6 000	12 000	12 000
March	40 000	8 000	13 000	12 000
April	50 000	10 000	16 000	13 000
May	65 000	13 000	17 000	13 000
June	75 000	15 000	18 000	14 000
July	80 000	16 000	21 000	14 000
August	65 000	13 000	20 000	13 000
September	55 000	11 000	18 000	13 000
October	40 000	8 000	16 000	12 000
November	35 000	7 000	13 000	12 000
December	25 000	5 000	11 000	11 000

You are required to present this in graph form.

8 The following balance sheet was prepared by the book-keeper of the Black Rose Hotel.

Balance sheet

Liabilities		*Assets*		
Capitals: Black	120 000	Cash balances		2 000
Rose	100 000	Debtors		8 500
Current accounts: Black	1 250	Stocks		12 500
Rose	1 750	Glass and china	8 000	
Trade creditors	8 000	Depreciation	3 000	
Expenses due	4 500			5 000
Advance bookings	500	Furniture	60 000	
		Depreciation	12 000	
				48 000
		Hotel premises	200 000	
		Depreciation	40 000	
				160 000
	£236 000			£236 000

You are required to re-draft the above balance sheet, and present it in vertical form.

CHAPTER 17

Interpretation of accounts

The process of reviewing, appraising and criticising accounts is known as the *interpretation* of accounts.

We said in the previous chapter that there are different parties interested in the accounts and that, consequently, they all look at the accounts from different points of view. The creditors, before they grant credit, want to be satisfied with the liquidity of the business. The proprietors are primarily interested in the profits earned and the dividends paid.

The management of a business have, obviously, a much greater and comprehensive interest in the accounts than any other party. It is, therefore, primarily from the point of view of the management that we shall deal with the interpretation of accounts.

In order to be able to interpret a set of accounts, it is necessary to examine not only many individual figures in the accounts but also several important relationships between such figures.

Trading account

There are three main things that should be considered when reviewing the trading account: the volume of sales, sales mix and gross profit margins.

Volume of sales

The level of sales is important for several reasons. First, a business which does not sell enough cannot make a profit. Secondly, the higher the volume of sales the lower the incidence of fixed costs per unit sold (meal, banquet, room) and the higher, therefore, the profit per unit. Similarly, because most hotel and catering establishments have a high proportion of fixed costs, any given increase in sales invariably results in a more than proportional increase in total net profit. Finally, it is important to compare the current volume of sales with the corresponding figure of sales for the previous accounting period.

Sales mix

The term 'sales mix' refers to the composition of total sales, and is usually expressed in percentage terms, e.g.

Food sales	55 per cent
Beverage sales	35 per cent
Other sales	10 per cent
Total =	100 per cent

It will be appreciated that, because there is a different margin of profit on each section of the sales, the sales mix of a business must be watched very closely. An increase in the sales of cigarettes of £100 will usually result in an increase in gross profit of about £8. The same increase in beverage sales may well bring an additional gross profit of over £65.

Gross profit margins Finally, attention should be paid to the gross profit margins of the various revenue-producing departments. Past experience will indicate whether or not the current percentages of gross profit are what they should be.

Gross profit margins vary from one type of establishment to another. In general, it is true to say that the better the type of business the higher the percentage of gross profit, and vice versa. This is necessary in order to cover the relatively higher cost of labour and overheads entailed by the provision of a better type of service.

As between the various components of the sales mix the position is this. Beverage sales will usually produce a percentage of gross profit which is very similar to that on food sales. The gross profit on cigarettes is normally very modest and invariably under 10 per cent.

Needless to say gross profit margins are one of the important determinants of the profitability of a business and should, therefore, be reviewed carefully and frequently.

Profit and loss account

However satisfactory the total amount of gross profit of a business, its net profit will not be adequate if the labour costs and overheads are too high. When examining the profit and loss account it is, therefore, important to relate each of the following to total sales:

Labour costs These are usually in the region of 25 per cent of sales in restaurants, about 30 per cent in most hotels and between 30 and 35 per cent in industrial canteens.

Overheads These tend to be about 5 per cent less than the labour costs in most hotel and catering establishments. They may appear to be very low in industrial canteens, where many fixed charges are sometimes not debited but borne by the company.

Net profit The percentage of net profit on sales varies considerably and may be anything from a very small percentage to over 20 per cent. Past experience will, however, indicate what this percentage should be in each particular case.

Balance sheet

A review of the balance sheet of a business tends to centre around two main problems: the profitability of the business, and the adequacy or otherwise of its liquid resources.

Profitability This is usually measured by expressing the net profit as a percentage of the capital of the business.

It is pointed out that whilst the percentage of net profit on sales is an appropriate measure of the operating efficiency of a business from one trading period to another, it is not an adequate index of its profitability. A restaurant which has a capital of £100 000, a turnover of £10 000 and a net profit equal to 20 per cent of its sales is not a profitable business by any means. What matters, from the point of view of the proprietors, and what is important in the long run, is the percentage return on the capital.

What the percentage return on capital should be can only be determined by reference to the particular circumstances of each individual business. As a general rule it may, however, be taken that a business will aim at a return which:

(a) is in excess of the return obtainable on government securities and other more or less riskless investments such as debentures and preference shares of well-established companies;
(b) compensates for the risks inherent in the nature of the business concerned; generally, the more risky the business the higher the expected return on capital;
(c) is not so high as to be prejudicial to the quality of service and standard of comfort expected by the customers. It is, surely, bad policy to earn a high return in the short run at the expense of loss of customers due to inadequate portions, badly presented food, inefficient service, etc.

When calculating the return on capital, it should be remembered that, more often than not, the fixed assets are shown in the accounts as historical costs, which do not correspond with current economic values. A freehold hotel purchased before the last war for £10 000 may now be worth twenty times as much, and yet be shown in the balance sheet at cost. Similarly, equipment purchased five years before a balance sheet date may have a replacement cost well above its book value. It is, therefore, often necessary to adjust the values of the fixed assets to arrive at the *true* return on capital.

Liquidity The liquidity of a business is usually measured by relating its current assets to its current liabilities. The excess of current assets over current liabilities is known as 'working capital'.

Whilst the current assets represent a source of liquid funds, current liabilities represent a claim on such funds. Clearly, therefore, the former should stand in some relationship to the latter. What this exact relationship should be depends on the circumstances of each business. In general, however, we may say that:
(a) each business requires an excess of current assets over current liabilities, i.e. some working capital;
(b) the amount of working capital depends on factors such as the period of credit obtained from suppliers and granted to customers; the degree to which the business is seasonal; the level of stocks it has to carry, and the way heavy fixed expenses are spread over the calendar year.

A business which allows a long period of credit to its customers needs a relatively larger working capital; it takes it longer to convert the debts into cash, which may be urgently required. The opposite applies to the length of credit received from the suppliers. In seasonal hotel and catering establishments, the pattern of sales (and the consequent cash inflow) tends to differ quite considerably from the pattern of expenditure. Often heavy expenses are payable when the volume of sales is low. This calls for a larger excess of current assets over current liabilities. A licensed business has a higher proportion of its total capital invested in (liquor) stock and, therefore, will tend to have a relatively larger working capital. Finally, a business whose heavy expenses are spread reasonably evenly over the year needs rather less working capital than one whose expenses are not.

In addition to the examination of the overall amount of working capital, it is essential to review the components of working capital. The cash position should be considered in relation to the immediate commitments of the business. The debtors should be related to credit sales to ensure that the period of credit allowed to them is reasonable. Stock levels should be reviewed to see if they are reasonable in relation to the volume of business. Finally, creditors should be related to credit purchases to ensure that the amount owing to them is reasonable. Where it is not, it is quite likely that cash discounts are being lost through dilatory payment of suppliers.

Other matters There are one or two other points that should be considered when interpreting a balance sheet. Thus, it is important to examine the basis of the valuation of fixed assets and ensure that depreciation charges have been adequate. Where there are any long-term loans, it is essential to ascertain the date of repayment and its effect on the liquidity of the business. In the case of a limited company, it is important to review the reserves available and the profits earned in relation to the dividends payable.

Accounting ratios

Reference has already been made to the desirability of ascertaining the relationships between various figures in the accounts, e.g. sales and gross profit, and current assets and current liabilities. A convenient way of achieving this is to apply what is known as 'accounting ratios'. A ratio is, simply, one figure expressed in terms of another.

Though it is possible to calculate dozens of different ratios from a set of final accounts, only some of them are of practical value. From the point of view of the management of a business two sets of ratios are especially valuable in the interpretation of accounts. These are the ratios showing the profitability and the ratios showing the liquidity of the business.

Ratios measuring profitability

Gross profit ratio

This measures the relationship between gross profit and net sales, e.g.

$$\frac{\text{GROSS PROFIT}}{\text{NET SALES}} = \frac{£6\,000}{£10\,000} = 6{:}10 \text{ (or 60\%)}.$$

In most hotel and catering establishments, it is more usual to speak of the 'gross profit percentage' rather than the 'gross profit ratio'. In fact whether we speak of the ratio or the percentage does not matter at all.

Net profit ratio

This measures the relationship between net profit and net sales, e.g.

$$\frac{\text{NET PROFIT}}{\text{NET SALES}} = \frac{£10\,000}{£100\,000} = 1{:}10 \text{ (or 10\%)}.$$

Return on net worth

The net worth of a business is equal to the total of its assets less the external liabilities. Return on net worth, therefore, means return (before or after tax) on the capital of a business. The formula for this ratio is illustrated below:

$$\frac{\text{NET PROFIT (AFTER TAX)}}{\text{NET WORTH}} = \frac{£5\,000}{£50\,000} = 1{:}10 \text{ (or 10\%)}.$$

Ratios measuring liquidity

The current ratio

This measures the relationship between current assets and current liabilities, and is therefore an indication of the short-run solvency of the business. The ratio is calculated as follows:

$$\frac{\text{CURRENT ASSETS}}{\text{CURRENT LIABILITIES}} = \frac{£15\,000}{£10\,000} = 3{:}2.$$

The acid test ratio

This measures the relationship between the liquid assets (cash, debtors, temporary investments) and current liabilities. A business may have an adequate current ratio but, if too high a proportion of its current assets is represented by stocks rather than cash balances and debtors, insufficient liquid funds remain for current operations. In the acid test ratio, only liquid assets are related to the current liabilities. The formula is:

$$\frac{\text{LIQUID ASSETS}}{\text{CURRENT LIABILITIES}} = \frac{£12\,500}{£10\,000} = 5{:}4.$$

The average collection period

This, strictly speaking, is not a ratio but a measure of how quickly or otherwise debts are collected by the business. The formula is:

$$\frac{\text{DEBTORS}}{\text{AVERAGE DAILY SALES}} = \frac{£1\,000}{£50} = 20 \text{ days.}$$

The rate of stock turnover

This measures the speed with which stocks move through the business. A high rate of stock turnover indicates that stocks are low in relation to the turnover and, usually, means efficient buying. A low rate of stock turnover indicates that high stocks are kept in relation to the volume of turnover and, usually, points to over-buying. The formula is:

$$\frac{\text{COST OF SALES}}{\text{AVERAGE STOCK AT COST}} = \frac{£4\,000}{£100} = 40.$$

The rate of stock turnover varies from one section of sales to another, as indeed from one business to another. In respect of food sales the rate varies from about 25 to 50. In other words the average stock held represents from two to about one week's consumption. The amount of wines, spirits, minerals, etc. held depends, amongst others, on the type of business. Usually, the better the type of business the larger the relative size of the liquor stocks. Cigarettes and tobaccos are usually purchased monthly; this would indicate a rate of stock turnover of about twelve.

Concepts of profitability

We said earlier in this chapter that the usual and most appropriate method of measuring profitability is to relate the net profit to the capital (net worth) of the business. There are, however, one or two other possible measures of profitability and the purpose of the present section is to list and explain them in some detail.

Profit in relation to net worth

This, as already indicated, is the most common and appropriate method. There are few profit-making hotel and catering establishments to which this method could not be applied.

Profit in relation to turnover

In most establishments this is simply a method of assessing the operating efficiency over a period of time. There are, however, some businesses which have a substantial turnover but, at the same time, relatively little capital. This applies to a number of catering contractors who organize and manage the catering departments of their clients without supplying any of the fixed equipment. In such businesses the return on net worth is rather meaningless, and it is more appropriate to measure profitability in relation to turnover.

Profit per unit sold

This is a useful additional measure of profitability. The 'unit' may be a meal, banquet or room sold.

Profit in relation to time factor

This is also a useful additional method of assessing profitability. It would be applied in cases where the time factor is of paramount importance, e.g. in particular forms of outdoor catering for functions of limited duration such as exhibitions, flower shows, etc. and, possibly, in highly seasonal establishments, where it is known that so much profit must be made during the season to provide a reasonable annual return on capital.

Operating ratios

In addition to selecting the correct measure(s) of profitability, a business will adopt several operating ratios, i.e. ratios which measure the current operating efficiency of a business. An advantage of operating ratios is that they can be applied at frequent intervals (daily, weekly) to check the progress of the business.

Rate of room occupancy

This shows the number of rooms occupied in relation to the number of rooms available, and it is usually expressed as a percentage. Thus a hotel which has 200 rooms and, on a particular day, lets 150 rooms, has a room occupancy of:

$$\frac{\text{ROOMS OCCUPIED}}{\text{ROOMS AVAILABLE}} = \frac{150}{200} \times 100 = 75\%.$$

Room occupancy is somewhat misleading when there is a high proportion of double or twin-bedded rooms let as singles.

Rate of guest occupancy

This is also referred to as the rate of 'bed occupancy'. It shows the number of guests staying in the hotel in relation to the guest capacity. The formula for calculating guest occupancy is:

$$\frac{\text{ACTUAL NUMBER OF GUESTS}}{\text{GUEST CAPACITY}} = \frac{120}{200} \times 100 = 60\%.$$

Guest occupancy is a more accurate indication than room occupancy of the extent to which the capacity of the hotel is used.

Average room rate

This measures the relationship between room sales and rooms occupied, e.g.

$$\frac{\text{ROOM SALES £4 000}}{\text{ROOMS OCCUPIED 200}} = £20.$$

Gross profit percentage

This is, traditionally, one of the most important indications of the efficiency of food and beverage operations.

Net margin

This is also referred to as 'after-wage profit'. This ratio is important in establishments employing a high proportion of part-time and casual labour.

Rate of restaurant occupancy

This shows the number of meals sold in relation to the normal seating capacity of a restaurant. Thus if a restaurant, which serves luncheons and dinners, has a seating capacity of 100, it has a total daily capacity of 200. If, on a particular day, it serves 300 meals its rate of restaurant occupancy is:

$$\frac{\text{MEALS SERVED}}{\text{SEATING CAPACITY}} = \frac{300}{200} = 1{\cdot}5.$$

The rate of 1·5 shows that on that particular day the average seat available was re-laid 1·5 times. Quite obviously the higher this rate, the more economical the utilization of the fixed equipment and other facilities of the restaurant.

Average spending power The total turnover of a business depends on two factors: the number of customers, and the average amount spent by them. Many hotel and catering establishments review the average spending at regular intervals to ensure that it is adequate and that menus are planned in accordance with what customers want to spend. Average spending power is calculated by dividing sales by the number of meals served, e.g.:

$$\frac{\text{SALES}}{\text{NUMBER OF COVERS}} = \frac{£3000}{200} = £15.$$

Spending power may be calculated on total sales or separately in relation to food sales, beverage sales and other sales.

Example 1 Figure 197 shows a balance sheet as prepared by the book-keeper of a small hotel.

Balance Sheet
as at 31st Dec., 19..

Capital				Fixed Assets			
		£	£		£	£	£
Capital at 1.1.19..		65,000		Leasehold Premises	60,000		
Add Net Profit		15,220		Less Depreciation	5,000	55,000	
		80,220		Restaurant Furniture	6,000		
Less Drawings		7,750	72,470	Less Depreciation	500	5,500	
				China and Cutlery	4,500		
				Less Depreciation	250	4,250	64,750
Current Liabilities				**Current Assets**			
Trade Creditors	14,500			Food Stocks		7,550	
Less {Provision for Disc. Recd.}	1,000	13,500		Debtors		9,140	
Expense Creditors		1,500	15,000	Cash at Bank		5,780	
				Cash in Hand		250	22,720
			£ 87,470				£ 87,470

Figure 197

You are required to comment on the financial position of the hotel, taking the following additional information into account:

The sales of the hotel for the year ended as at the date of the balance sheet were:

Cash sales	£100 000
Credit	60 000
Total	£160 000

The purchases for the same period were:

Cash purchases	£20 000
Credit	60 000
Total	£80 000

Comments—Working capital

The overall working capital position is thus:

Current assets	£22 720
Less current liabilities	15 000
Working capital	£7 720

The current ratio of the hotel is about 3:2, which seems reasonably adequate. The acid test ratio is:

$$\frac{\text{LIQUID ASSETS}}{\text{CURRENT LIABILITIES}} = \frac{£15\,170}{£15\,000} \approx 1{\cdot}1.$$

From the above acid test ratio it appears that the liquid resources of the hotel only just about cover its immediate commitments.

Components of working capital

Food stocks The total purchases of the hotel for the year under review were £80 000. Assuming that the hotel is non-seasonal, this indicates a monthly cost of sales of about £6 660. The food stocks of £7 550 are, therefore, equal to about five weeks' consumption, which appears quite excessive. This would indicate a rate of stock turnover of about 10, which again is very much less than is normally the case in the majority of hotels.

Debtors The credit sales of the hotel were £60 000 and, assuming that the hotel is non-seasonal, this would indicate monthly credit sales of £5 000. The £9 140 owing from the debtors amounts, therefore, to almost two months' credit sales. As the figure of debtors certainly includes a proportion of visitors' ledger balances, it is still possible that the hotel does not collect its debts quickly enough. It is quite likely that some of the debts have been owing for more than two or three months.

Cash position The total of cash available is £6 030. This is quite inadequate in relation to the current liabilities of £15 000. It is imperative for the hotel to run down its stocks and collect its debts more speedily in order to improve its cash position.

Trade creditors As the hotel buys on credit at the rate of about £5 000 per month, the debts owing to the suppliers represent about three months' credit purchases. This is bad as it is quite likely that cash discounts are being lost. Secondly, in view of the usual level of cash discounts, it seems that it is too optimistic to hope for £1 000 cash discounts on £14 500, a proportion of which has been outstanding for three months.

Expense creditors The nature of this debt is not known and no comment is therefore possible.

Profitability

Assuming that the fixed assets are shown in the balance sheet at realistic values and that adequate proprietor's renumeration has been debited in the hotel profit and loss account, the return on net worth is:

$$\frac{\text{NET PROFIT}}{\text{NET WORTH}} = \frac{£15\,220}{£72\,470} = 21\% \text{ (before tax)}.$$

This ratio is very satisfactory, but it would have to be considered in conjunction with the corresponding ratios for past years. If, as already assumed, the profit and loss account of the hotel contains a debit in respect of the proprietor's salary, the drawings of £7 750 are probably excessive in view of the unsatisfactory cash position of the hotel.

Fixed assets No information is available on how the fixed assets have been valued and, therefore, it is difficult to comment on them. It appears, however, that the depreciation of china and cutlery is inadequate, having regard to the normal expected life of this asset.

Example 2 The following information was extracted from the records of a large unlicensed restaurant:

	May	June	July
	£	£	£
Food sales	100 000	110 000	120 000
Cost of sales	40 000	46 200	52 800
Labour costs	25 000	28 600	32 400
Overheads	20 000	20 900	21 600
Number of covers served	200 000	244 440	300 000

From the information given above it is possible to construct a comparative table of trading results as shown below.

Comparative trading results for quarter ended 31st July, 19..

	May		June		July	
	£	%	£	%	£	%
Food sales	100 000	100	110 000	100	120 000	100
Less cost of sales	40 000	40	46 200	42	52 800	44
Gross profit	60 000	60	63 800	58	67 200	56
Less labour costs	25 000	25	28 600	26	32 400	27
After-wage results	35 000	35	35 200	32	34 800	29
Less overheads	20 000	20	20 900	19	21 600	18
Net profit	15 000	15	14 300	13	13 200	11
Number of covers	200 000		244 440		300 000	
Average spending power	£5.00		£4.50		£4.00	

Having analysed the trading results we may offer the following comments:

Food sales These show a substantial upward trend, which would have to be compared with the trend for the same quarter of the previous year. Though the volume of sales seems satisfactory, it is clear that the rise over the three months is due to an increasing number of covers rather than any increase in the customers' spending power.

Cost of sales The percentage of cost of sales in relation to the turnover is rising and this could be due to higher prices being paid to suppliers, inefficient kitchen operations or other reasons. Immediate action is now required to keep this percentage in line with the volume of sales.

Gross profit Although this is increasing in absolute terms, as a percentage of sales it is becoming less and less. As a result the restaurant does not obtain much benefit out of the increasing turnover.

Labour costs These are rising both absolutely and in relation to sales. This is bad as, normally, when sales are rising labour costs tend to lag behind. Reasons for this must be sought and the appropriate action taken.

After-wage percentage This has declined from 35 per cent to 29 per cent due to increased labour and commodity costs.

Overheads These show a moderate rise, which is to be expected in conditions of rising turnover.

Net profit This, in spite of the increase in sales, shows a downward trend. Quite obviously, what the restaurant gains in a lower incidence of fixed overheads due to a larger turnover is more than offset by higher food costs and labour costs.

Average spending power This has declined more than seems reasonable over a period of three months. It is important that reasons for this unfavourable trend are found and some corrective action taken as soon as possible.

Problems

1 Enumerate the main points that you would examine when interpreting a set of final accounts.

2 Explain what is meant by the 'liquidity' and 'profitability' of a business.

3 Comment on the usefulness of accounting ratios. Explain what is meant by the following:

Gross profit ratio;
Net profit ratio;
Return on net worth;
Current ratio;
Acid test ratio;
Average collection period;
Rate of stock turnover.

4 'There is not one but several concepts of profitability.' Comment.

5 Enumerate the most important operating ratios that would be of value in:

(a) a hotel;
(b) a restaurant;
(c) a luncheon club.

6 Explain the importance of working capital. What are the main factors determining the amount of the working capital required by hotel and catering establishments?

7 The following is the balance sheet of a small hotel, drawn up as at 31st December, 19...

Balance sheet

			£			£
Capital				*Fixed assets*		
Black		120 000		Leasehold hotel	200 000	
Rose		100 000		*Less* Depreciation	40 000	
			220 000			160 000
Current liabilities				Furniture	60 000	
Trade creditors		8 000		*Less* Depreciation	12 000	
Expense creditors		4 500				48 000
Advance bookings		500		Glass, china, etc.	8 000	
Current accounts:				*Less* Depreciation	3 000	
Black	1 250					5 000
Rose	1 750	3 000		*Current assets*		
			16 000	Stocks—food	4 200	
				—liquor	8 300	
				Debtors	8 500	
				Cash	2 000	
						23 000
			£236 000			£236 000

You are also given the following information:

(a) Sales for the year ended 31st December, 19.. were £800 000, of which

room sales	£400 000
food	250 000
liquor	150 000

(b) Purchases in the same period amounted to £200 000; of the total purchases cash purchases were £20 000.

(c) The net profit of the hotel was £30 000.

Comment on the financial position of the hotel as disclosed by the above balance sheet.

8 The following information was extracted from the books of a restaurant:

	31 October, 19..	*30 November, 19..*	*31 December, 19..*
	£	£	£
Debtors	2 200	2 400	2 800
Creditors	7 700	8 400	9 600
Stocks	9 000	9 400	9 800
Cash at bank	9 200	8 100	6 200
Accrued expenses	1 200	1 600	1 700

You are required to:

(a) calculate the working capital of the restaurant at each of the above dates;

(b) calculate the acid test ratio for each of the above dates;

(c) comment on the liquidity position of the restaurant.

9 Below are the financial results of The Classic Hotel Ltd for the years 1977 and 1978. The hotel has been operating since 1970 and is accommodation sales biased.

Balance sheets as at 31st December, 19..

	1977		1978	
	£	£	£	£
Fixed assets (net)				
Freehold property		320 000		390 000
Equipment and furniture		70 000		100 000
		390 000		490 000
Current assets				
Stocks of food and beverages	20 000		75 000	
Debtors	12 000		50 000	
Cash	53 000	85 000	2 000	127 000
		475 000		617 000
Financed by:				
Ordinary Share capital		250 000		320 000
Retained profits		90 000		120 000
		340 000		440 000
10% Debenture (secured on property—1985)		60 000		60 000
Current liabilities				
Creditors	8 000		15 000	
Taxation	40 000		60 000	
Proposed dividend	25 000		30 000	
Overdraft	2 000	75 000	12 000	117 000
		475 000		617 000

Profit and Loss Accounts for Year ending 31st December, 19..

	1977		1978	
	£	£	£	£
Sales		500 000		700 000
Less Cost of sales		100 000		140 000
Gross profit		400 000		560 000
Less Labour	140 000		200 000	
Other expenses	180 000	320 000	240 000	440 000
Net profit before tax		80 000		120 000
Less Corporation tax (50%)		40 000		60 000
Net profit after tax		40 000		60 000
Less Proposed ordinary share dividend		25 000		30 000
Retained profits for the year		15 000		30 000

You are requested to:

(a) calculate six key accounting ratios for 1977 and 1978; and

(b) comment on the strengths and weaknesses revealed by the ratios and any other information you consider relevant.

State clearly any assumptions you make.

(H.C.I.M.A.)

10 The following information relates to the Chatsworth Restaurant, a sole owned establishment in a provincial city:

Balance sheet as at 31 May, 1980

	Cost	Total deprn.	Net
	£	£	£
Fixed assets			
Leasehold building	80 000	4 000	76 000
Kitchen equipment	15 000	1 500	13 500
Restaurant furniture	10 000	1 000	9 000
Loose equipment (china, etc.)	4 000	500	3 500
	109 000	7 000	102 000
Current assets			
Food and beverage stocks		3 000	
Trade debtors		2 500	
Prepaid expenses		500	
Cash at bank		1 700	
Cash in hand		300	8 000
			110 000
		£	£
Capital on 1 June, 1979		90 200	
Add Net profit for year		19 000	
		109 200	
Less Proprietor's drawings		3 500	105 700
Current liabilities			
Trade creditors		2 800	
Advance reservation deposits		350	
Accrued expenses		1 150	4 300
			110 000

Additional information:

1 The owner/manager has been paid a salary of £7 000, which has already been charged against profits.

2 Sales for the year were:

Cash	£65 000
Credit	28 000
	93 000

3 Purchases for the year were all on credit and totalled £24 600.
4 On 1 June, 1979 food and beverage stocks, trade debtors and trade creditors were valued at £4 400, £3 100 and £3 600 respectively.
5 The restaurant is open 312 days per year.
6 This type of establishment is expected to achieve a 16% return on capital employed.

You are requested to examine the above data through the eyes of a prospective purchaser for profitability and liquidity and state, giving reasons supported by relevant calculations, if the restaurant would be a viable proposition at an asking price of £120 000.

Ignore income tax and VAT.

(H.C.I.M.A.)

CHAPTER 18

Departmental accounting

Definition and objects

Departmental accounting may be described as a method of book-keeping and accounting, the purpose of which is to find how much profit (or loss) is produced by each section or department of a business. In this context the term 'department' means a revenue-producing department, as trading results cannot be obtained for non-revenue-producing departments such as wash-up, stores, cellars, etc.

In a business consisting of several departments, it is clearly, necessary to find the separate results of each department. Otherwise, the fact that some departments are being operated at a loss will not be revealed, and over a long period the position might be as shown in Figure 198.

A. B. C. Catering Ltd

	Department A	Department B	Department C	Total
Sales	£10 000	£20 000	£25 000	£55 000
Less Costs	6 000	14 000	26 000	46 000
+Profit/ −Loss	+4 000	+6 000	−1 000	+9 000

Figure 198

Note: The overall profit on sales, viz. £9 000 on a turnover of £55 000 is probably quite satisfactory; yet in the absence of departmental accounting the loss incurred by department C would not be revealed.

Book-keeping records

In order to be able to ascertain the profit (or loss) of each department, suitably analysed records—subsidiary books and ledger accounts—must be kept. The exact analysis of income and expenditure depends on the particular circumstances of each business and on the degree of departmentalization desired. The following analytical records (Figures 199 and 200) show how an analysis may be kept in the case of a large licensed restaurant. It is assumed that the restaurant has three revenue-producing departments, namely, food, drink and tobaccos.

PURCHASES DAY BOOK

Date		Led Fol	Inv. No	TOTAL	FOOD	BEV.	TOBACCO
19..							
Jan 1	A. B. Brown & Co. Ltd.	16	001	160	160		
" 2	Irish Whiskey Ltd.	27	002	280		280	
" 3	N. O. Nicotine Ltd.	53	003	90			90
" 4	B. M. Grocer & Sons	19	004	240	240		
	etc.						
" 31	Trans. to Purchase A/c	116		16,000	11,000	4,000	1,000

Figure 199

PURCHASES ACCOUNT

Date		Total	Food	Bev.	Tobac.	Date		Total	Food	Bev	Tobac.
19..											
Jan 31	Sundries	16,000	11,000	4,000	1,000						

Figure 200

In addition to the purchases, sales and stocks, possibly other items would have to be analysed and recorded in the same manner.

Departmental trading and profit and loss account

There are three main methods by which departmental final accounts may be prepared. These may be described as the:

(a) gross profit method,
(b) departmental profit method, and
(c) net profit method.

Gross profit method This is the method most commonly used in hotel and catering establishments. It entails an analysis of purchases, sales and stocks only, i.e. items affecting the gross profit of each department. Its aim is to control the gross profit (kitchen profit, bar profit, etc.) of each department. Expenses such as wages, salaries, gas, electricity, etc. are not analysed and are debited in the profit and loss account against the total of gross profit plus any other income such as room sales, discounts received, and investment income.

The main advantage of this method is its simplicity. Its disadvantages are: firstly, no attempt is made to control departmental expenses such as wages, salaries, lighting, heating, etc.; and secondly, a department may earn a high percentage of gross profit yet, if its overheads are high, contribute little to the net profit of the business.

The application of the gross profit method is illustrated in Figuro 201 by the trading, profit and loss account.

THE MAGIC CARPET RESTAURANT

Trading and Profit & Loss Account for year ended 31st December, 19..

	FOOD	BEV.	TOBACCO	TOTAL		FOOD	BEV.	TOBACCO	TOTAL
	£	£	£	£		£	£	£	£
Opening Stocks	2,500	3,900	600	7,000	Sales	120,000	70,000	10,000	200,000
Purchases (net)	60,000	40,200	9,800	110,000					
	62,500	44,100	10,400	117,000					
Less Closing Stock	3,500	3,700	800	8,000					
Cost of Goods Sold	59,000	40,400	9,600	109,000					
Gross Profit c/d	61,000	29,600	400	91,000					
	120,000	70,000	10,000	200,000		120,000	70,000	10,000	200,000
Wages and Salaries				49,000	Gross Profit b/d				91,000
Rent and Rates				9,600	Discounts Received				2,000
Lighting and Heating				6,300					
Depreciation				5,000					
Repairs and Replacements				3,500					
Printing and Stationery				3,000					
Miscellaneous Expenses				600					
Net Profit - transfer to Capital A/c				16,000					
				93,000					93,000

Figure 201

Departmental profit method This second method, excellent as it is, requires a rather elaborate set of records and a high degree of departmentalization, and therefore can only be applied in large hotel and catering units. The aim of this method is to ascertain and control the departmental (controllable) profit of each section of a business. Departmental profit may be defined as the total revenue of a department *less* the cost of goods sold (if any), departmental wages, salaries and any other expenses attributable to (and controllable by) that department. All other expenses—those incurred on behalf of the business as a whole—such as rent, rates, advertising, etc. are debited against the total of departmental profits in the general profit and loss account.

A specimen general profit and loss account, illustrating this particular method, is shown in Figure 202.

GRAND HOTEL LIMITED
General Profit and Loss Account
for year ended 31st Dec., 19..

DEPARTMENT	NET SALES	COST OF SALES	DEPARTMENTAL EXPENSES	DEPARTMENTAL PROFIT
	£	£	£	£
Room Sales	480,000		172,000	308,000
Food Sales	320,000	140,000	110,000	70,000
Bev. Sales	120,000	48,000	26,000	46,000
Other Sales	30,000	20,000	8,000	2,000
Total	950,000	208,000	316,000	426,000
ADD: Other Income –				
Rents Receivable		24,000		
Miscellaneous Income		10,000		34,000
				460,000
LESS: Unapportioned Expenditure:				
Rent and Rates		55,000		
Repairs and Maintenance		27,000		
Depreciation		89,000		
Heat, Light and Power		12,000		
Advertising		52,000		
Administration Expenses		85,000		
Miscellaneous Expenses		34,000		354,000
NET PROFIT				106,000

Figure 202

In addition to the general profit and loss account, it is usual to prepare for each revenue-producing department a separate departmental profit and loss account,

Thus, in respect of room sales the following (more detailed) profit and loss account would be prepared:

Room Sales
Departmental Profit and Loss account
for the year ended 31st December, 19..

Total Room Sales		£490,000
Less allowances		10,000
Net Room Sales		480,000
Less Departmental Expenses:		
Wages and salaries	£120,000	
Staff meals	10,000	
Uniforms	4,000	
Laundry	12,000	
Linen	6,000	
Cleaning materials	3,000	
China and Glass replacements	3,000	
Commissions payable	8,000	
Miscellaneous expenses	6,000	172,000
Departmental Profit		308,000

Figure 203

Similar departmental profit and loss accounts would also be prepared for the other departments of the hotel.

It will be appreciated that this method is both good accounting and good management as, in effect, each departmental manager is made responsible for all income and expenditure he is capable of controlling. In order to produce an adequate amount of departmental profit, he must control not only the cost of goods he sells but also other expenses incurred by his department.

Net profit method

Under this method *all* expenses are debited to the revenue-producing departments in order to arrive at a figure of net profit for each of them.

Expenses which are attributable to or originate from a certain department are *allocated* to that department. Thus, the cost of kitchen wages would be debited against food sales; barmen's wages would be debited against bar sales, etc.

Expenses which are incurred on behalf of the business as a whole are *apportioned* (split) on some fair and reasonable basis as between the departments concerned. Thus, rent and rates could be apportioned on the basis of the floor space occupied by each department; general manager's salary could be apportioned on the basis of the turnover of each department, etc.

The net profit method is illustrated by the profit and loss account shown in Figure 204.

THE BOMBAY DUCK RESTAURANT

Trading and Profit & Loss A/c for year ending 31st December, 19..

	CEYLON ROOM	KASHMIR ROOM	AMERICAN BAR	TOTAL		CEYLON ROOM	KASHMIR ROOM	AMERICAN BAR	TOTAL
Opening Stocks	2,500	3,500	6,500	12,500	Sales	199,600	254,200	223,600	677,400
Purchases (net)	99,500	142,600	101,400	343,500					
	102,000	146,100	107,900	356,000					
Less Closing Stocks	2,000	3,100	6,400	11,500					
Cost of Goods Sold	100,000	143,000	101,500	344,500					
Gross Profits c/d	99,600	111,200	122,100	332,900					
	199,600	254,200	223,600	677,400		199,600	254,200	223,600	677,400
Wages & Salaries	46,500	64,100	22,100	132,700	Gross Profit	99,600	111,200	122,100	332,900
Rent & Rates	9,300	12,100	3,000	22,400					
Gas & Electricity	4,300	6,100	1,200	11,600					
Repairs & Renewals	8,100	12,400	6,700	27,200					
Depreciation	6,700	8,500	4,600	19,800					
Miscellaneous Exp.	5,300	6,200	1,300	12,800					
Net Profit	19,400	1,900	83,200	104,400					
	99,600	111,200	122,100	332,900		99,600	111,200	122,100	332,900

NOTE ON PROFIT AND LOSS ITEMS:

(1) Wages and Salaries – analysed and allocated
(2) Rent and Rates – apportioned on the basis of floor space occupied
(3) Gas and Electricity – metered consumption
(4) Repairs and Renewals – analysed and allocated
(5) Depreciation – analysed and allocated (depreciation of lease as in (2) above
(6) Miscellaneous Expenses – analysed and allocated

Figure 204

Arguments in favour of this method are:

(i) expenditure which has to be apportioned benefits all the departments concerned; each department should, therefore, be charged with a fair proportion of the total;

(ii) a department may produce a large amount of gross profit, yet, if its fixed expenses are high, show little or no net profit;

(iii) the main purpose of business is to make profit; an attempt should, therefore, be made to find how much net profit has been made by each department.

Arguments against this method are:

(i) whatever method of apportionment is chosen it is always an arbitrary method;

(ii) apportioned (indirect) expenses are incurred to benefit the business as a

whole—if a particular department were closed down many of these expenses would remain unchanged;
(iii) the apportionment of expenses may give a misleading picture of the results achieved by departments.

The net profit method is shown here simply to explain how it is applied in what is hoped is a small minority of establishments. Most certainly, the intention is not to recommend it as good accounting practice.

Balance sheet Whatever method of departmental accounting is in use the balance sheet of the business is not affected, except that it is usual to show separately the stocks of each department.

Problems

1 Write short explanatory notes on the following methods of departmental accounting: (a) gross profit method; (b) departmental profit method; (c) net profit method.

2 Distinguish between the allocation and the apportionment of expenditure.

3 What method of apportionment would you use in respect of the following; (a) rent and rates; (b) depreciation of premises; (c) depreciation of equipment; (d) general manager's salary; (e) advertising; (f) administration expenses?

4 Explain the purposes of departmental accounting and state what modifications it entails in the layout of the subsidiary books and the ledger.

5 The following balances were extracted from the accounts of the Blue Moon Restaurant at 31st December, 19..

Stocks at 1st January, 19..:	food	£10150
	beverages	8350
	cigarettes	1540
Purchases: food		197350
beverages		94710
cigarettes		12300
Sales: food		423740
beverages		236250
cigarettes		14070
Wages and salaries		149530
Light and heat		19470
Cleaning materials		3190
Postage and stationery		1560
Laundry		4940
Rates		8730
Advertising		5000
Repairs and replacements		1340
Depreciation		14260

You are required:
(a) To prepare the restaurant's trading, profit and loss account for the year ended 31st December, 19... The form and presentation of the account must be such as to convey the maximum information to the proprietor.
(b) To comment on the trading results of the restaurant on the basis of the information available.

(continued)

Stocks at 31st December, 19.. were valued as follows: food—£8 450, beverages—£6 340; cigarettes—£1 260. You are informed that the capital invested in the restaurant amounts to £400 000.

6 The following figures relate to a factory canteen for the six months ending 31st March, 1982. Prepare, in tabular form, a trading and profit and loss account, showing the contribution each type of sale makes towards the general expenses and profit.

	£
1st October, 1981. Opening stocks	
food	3 630
minerals	580
tobacco	1 640
Purchases for the six months	
food	7 150
minerals	1 690
tobacco	3 150
31st March, 1982. Closing stocks	
food	2 980
minerals	490
tobacco	1 480
Fuel	1 010
Wages: kitchen	4 030
counter and clerical	3 380
Receipts:	
food	19 220
minerals	2 010
tobacco	3 580
General expenses	530

M.H.C.I. (Modified)

7 The Supreme Hotel is owned by J. Smythe and T. Brown, and their capitals are £200 000 and £150 000 respectively. The following balances have been extracted from their books at 31st December, 19...

	£	£
Stock—1st January, 19..		
provisions	8 400	
liquor	21 000	
cigarettes and tobacco	3 500	
sundries	2 400	
Purchases for the year:		
provisions	528 000	
liquor	207 500	
cigarettes and tobacco	48 000	
sundries	17 000	
Wages	128 600	
National Insurance	12 400	
Discounts	780	2 750
Rates and water	9 600	
Fuels, etc.	28 200	
Lighting and heating	46 000	
Interest received		1 200
Partners' salaries paid during the year:		
J. Smythe	17 500	
T. Brown	18 000	
c/f	1 096 880	3 950

		£	£
	b/f	1 096 880	3 950
		61 500	
Office salaries		61 600	
Rent		77 500	
Printing and stationery		7 200	
Dividends received			2 000
Advertising		9 400	
Cleaning materials		6 900	
Laundry		11 000	
Drawings:			
J. Smythe		52 000	
T. Brown		45 000	
Income			
apartments			786 800
restaurant			239 600
liquors			258 300
cigarettes and tobacco			65 280

You are required to prepare:
(a) a trading and profit and loss account for the year, and
(b) the partners' current accounts as they would appear in the ledger, taking into account the following additional matters:
(1) Partners share profits and losses in proportion to their capitals.
(2) Partners are entitled to interest on capital at 5 per cent per annum.
(3) Partners are entitled to salaries as follows:
J. Smythe—£25 000 per annum
T. Brown —£20 000 per annum
(4) J. Smythe has loaned the firm £50 000 and is entitled to interest on this at 5 per cent per annum.
(5) On 1st January, 19.., the credit balances on current accounts were:
J. Smythe—£2 500, and
T. Brown —£1 000.
(6) The stocks at 31st December, 19.. were:

provisions	£7 600
liquors	30 000
cigarettes & tobacco	4 200
sundries	1 000

(7) Make provision for depreciation as follows:
premises (valued at £110 000) at 5 per cent per annum;
equipment (valued at £80 000) at 10 per cent per annum;
linen and cutlery £5 000 for the year.
(8) Provide £750 against doubtful debts.
(9) Accounts owing:
stationery £2 500
laundry £1 700
(10) Rates paid in advance £1 600. A.M.H.C.I. (Modified)

8 The Troika Catering Co. Ltd operates an establishment consisting of:
(a) restaurant,
(b) banqueting department,
(c) bar.

The Company operates a system of departmental accounts and, periodically, separate trading results are obtained for each department of the business.

(i) From the following information you are required to prepare the Company's departmental trading, profit and loss account for the year ended 31st December, 19...

(ii) If, having arrived at the net profit/loss for each department, you find that the results are misleading, suggest alternative method of arriving at the necessary departmental results.

Sales: restaurant	£500 000
banqueting	300 000
bar	200 000
Cost of food and beverages sold: restaurant	200 000
banqueting	100 000
bar	75 000
Wages and salaries: restaurant	145 000
banqueting	75 000
bar	15 000
Repairs and replacements: restaurant	21 000
banqueting	13 000
bar	4 000
Gas and electricity	30 000
Rent and rates	60 000
Depreciation	70 000
Postage and telephone	5 000
Advertising	40 000
Laundry and cleaning	6 000
Office and administration expenses	60 000

Note: Expenses which cannot be allocated to particular departments are apportioned as follows:

(a) gas and electricity: restaurant 60 per cent
banqueting 35 per cent
bar 5 per cent

(b) rent, rates and depreciation are apportioned on the basis of floor space occupied, viz:
restaurant 60 per cent
banqueting 30 per cent
bar 10 per cent

(c) all other expenses are apportioned on the basis of turnover.

CHAPTER 19

Interim and seasonal accounts

Interim accounts are those prepared before the end of an accounting period. They may cover periods of a week, a month, a quarter or some other relatively short period.

Seasonal accounts are usually prepared half-yearly and show separate trading results for the season and the off-season. As seasonal accounts cover a period shorter than the full accounting year they are, in fact, also interim accounts.

Interim and seasonal accounts are particularly valuable in smaller hotel and catering establishments, where more elaborate methods of control, e.g. costing or budgeting, are not usually operated. In such businesses interim accounts are the most important source of accounting information.

Objects and advantages

We said in a previous chapter that conventional annual accounts are not very helpful to managements in the day-to-day control of business operations. They cover too long a period and, as a result, when they are actually presented are of historical value only. The main objects and advantages of interim accounts may be summarized as follows:

(a) In all hotel and catering establishments interim accounts are a simple, but effective, method of control over the current progress of the business. They indicate what progress is being made (sales, costs, profit margins, etc.) and what control or corrective action is necessary. When interim accounts are prepared frequently enough, it is possible for the management to take the appropriate remedial action almost as soon as the cause for such action begins to operate.

(b) In seasonal hotel and catering establishments, interim accounts enable the management to ascertain how much profit (or loss) is made in the season and in the off-season. They also help the management to decide whether or not the business should be closed down in the off-season and, if so, for how long. Finally, interim accounts are an important aid to decision-making, and are of value in forecasting labour requirements, scheduling repairs and maintenance in relation to the volume of business, fixing reduced off-season rates, etc.

Method of preparation

In order to be of any value interim accounts must be reasonably accurate. They cannot normally be quite as accurate as the final audited accounts mainly because they necessitate rather more estimating than is the case with annual accounts. Quite clearly, however, provided that they are drawn up carefully, and on the basis of reasonably complete information, they can be almost as reliably accurate as any annual accounts.

Trading account

The preparation of the interim trading account is a simple matter where there is sufficiently frequent stock-taking to enable the calculation of the cost of sales for the period concerned to be made. There are, however, some hotel and catering establishments where stock-taking is undertaken infrequently, e.g. quarterly or half-yearly. Where that is so, the presentation of a weekly or monthly trading account is, obviously, more difficult.

The weekly or monthly cost of sales may, however, be calculated fairly accurately even in the absence of a stock-taking, provided that there is some system of stock records in use. An accurate estimate of the cost of sales may be obtained by pricing the stores requisitions for the period, and listing the suppliers' invoices in respect of any perishables received.*

Profit and loss account

The preparation of the interim profit and loss account is rather more difficult mainly because there are usually several items of expenditure, the size of which must be estimated. There are several more or less distinct groups of expenses, each requiring rather different treatment.

First, there are the fixed charges such as rent, rates and insurance. Particulars of such items are usually well known in advance and, for the purpose of interim accounts, all that is necessary is to divide the annual cost of such items by an appropriate number. Thus for monthly accounts, if the annual rent is £30 000

$$\frac{\text{annual rent £30 000}}{12} = \text{£2 500 (monthly charge)}$$

Secondly, there are the items which are in the nature of long-term estimates, such as depreciation of kitchen plant and furniture, repairs and advertising. All such items would be dealt with in the same manner as the fixed charges discussed above.

Next, there is the group of expenses, incurred frequently, such as wages, salaries, postage and floral decorations. The actual cost of such expenses is usually easily available and no estimating is, therefore, necessary. Finally, there is a group of items in respect of which estimates have sometimes to be made, e.g. gas, electricity, kitchen fuel, breakages, replacements, etc. As far as gas and electricity are concerned, it is possible to take readings of the appropriate meters and calculate the cost quite accurately. Where this is not possible, an intelligent estimate based on past records should be made.

Balance sheet

Where interim accounts are prepared frequently they usually consist of the trading, profit and loss account only. Where, on the other hand, they are prepared quarterly or half-yearly, an interim balance sheet is sometimes also drawn up.

Interim accounts and double entry

It should be pointed out that the preparation of interim accounts does not normally call for any actual entries in the ledger. Interim accounts are in the nature of financial statements, which are prepared on the basis of accounts but do not form part of the system of double entry.

Example 1

The financial year of the Cresta Restaurant ends on 31st March. The following information has been extracted from the books of the restaurant in respect of April and May, 19.., and you are required to prepare an interim trading, profit and loss account for May, 19... Your account should show the results for May as well as the position to date.

---

* This is explained in more detail in Chapter 3 of the author's *An Approach to Food Costing* (Barrie and Jenkins).

	April, 19..	May, 19..
	£	£
Sales	132 000	138 000
Monthly cost of perishables	29 000	31 000
„ „ „ non-perishables	19 000	18 000
Wages and salaries	28 500	29 500
Rent: £24 600 per annum		
Light and heat	4 800	4 200
Insurance: £1 920 per annum		
Printing and stationery, estimated £3 600 per annum		
Cleaning materials	450	500
Depreciation: £38 400 per annum		
Advertising: estimated £9 000 per annum		
Postage and telephone: estimated £2 880 p.a.		
Repairs and renewals: estimated £5 760 p.a.		
Miscellaneous expenses: estimated £6 000 p.a.		

CRESTA RESTAURANT
Trading, Profit and Loss Account
for May, 19..

	MAY		TO-DATE	
	£	£	£	£
Sales		138,000		270,000
Less Cost of Sales - Perishables	31,000		60,000	
- Non-Perishables	18,000	49,000	37,000	97,000
Gross Profit		89,000		173,000
Less Operating Expenses				
Wages and Salaries	29,500		58,000	
Depreciation	3,200		6,400	
Repairs and Renewals	480		960	
Light and Heat	4,200		9,000	
Rent	2,050		4,100	
Insurance	160		320	
Printing and Stationery	300		600	
Postage and Telephone	240		480	
Advertising	750		1,500	
Cleaning Materials	500		950	
Miscellaneous Expenses	500	41,880	1,000	83,310
Net Profit		47,120		89,690

Figure 205

Note: In order to make the above account more informative appropriate percentages could be added. Similarly, corresponding figures for the same period of the previous year could be given.

Example 2 The Two Seasons Restaurant is a seasonal establishment, and its accounts are prepared twice a year as at 30th September and 31st March. The following information is extracted from the books of the restaurant in respect of the year ended 31st March, 19...

	Season	*Off-season*
	£	£
Food sales	500 000	200 000
Cost of food sales	200 000	90 000
Bar sales	200 000	100 000
Cost of bar sales	70 000	35 000
Wages and salaries	180 000	85 000
Proprietor's salary	8 000	8 000
Rent and rates: £60 000 per annum		
Depreciation: lease—£80 000 per annum		
Depreciation: other—£40 000 per annum		
Light and heat	5 000	7 000
Laundry and cleaning materials	4 000	3 000
Postage and stationery	3 000	2 000

(a) Prepare the restaurant's trading, profit and loss account for the year ended 31st March, 19.., showing separate results for each half-year.

(b) If your accounts show that a net loss is incurred in the off-season, state whether or not the restaurant should be closed down in that half-year.

Proceed as shown in Figure 206.

THE TWO SEASONS RESTAURANT
Trading, Profit and Loss Account
for year ended 31st March, 19..

	SEASON	OFF-SEASON		SEASON	OFF-SEASON
Cost of Restaurant Sales	200,000	90,000	Sales - Restaurant	500,000	200,000
" " Bar "	70,000	35,000	- Bar	200,000	100,000
Gross Profits c/d	430,000	175,000			
	700,000	300,000		700,000	300,000
Wages and Salaries	180,000	85,000	Gross Profit b/d	430,000	175,000
Proprietor's Salary	8,000	8,000	Net Loss		20,000
Rent and Rates	30,000	30,000			
Depreciation - Lease	40,000	40,000			
" - Other	20,000	20,000			
Light and Heat	5,000	7,000			
Laundry and Cleaning	4,000	3,000			
Postage and Stationery	3,000	2,000			
Net Profit	140,000				
	430,000	195,000		430,000	195,000

Figure 206

In order to prove that the restaurant should be closed in the off-season one would have to show that this would:
Either (a) reduce the net loss in the off-season;
or (b) increase the total net profit for the whole year.

Now, regarding the loss in the off-season, the position is this; the loss at present is £20 000; if the restaurant were closed, the net loss in that period would be equal to the fixed expenses which have to be paid in any case. These are:

Proprietor's salary	£8 000
Rent and rates	30 000
Depreciation: lease	40 000
Depreciation: other ($\frac{1}{2}$)	10 000
Total	£88 000

Note: It is assumed that 'other' fixed assets depreciate at half the usual rate when not actually used.

From the above calculation it is clear that the restaurant would be worse off by closing down in the off-season to the extent of (£88 000 less £20 000) £68 000.

Looking at the net profit of the restaurant for the whole year, if it closes down in the off-season the position is as follows:

Loss of income (gross profit)	£175 000
The resulting saving of expenses would be:	
Wages and salaries	£85 000
Depreciation 'other' assets ($\frac{1}{2}$)	10 000
Light and heat	7 000
Laundry	3 000
Postage and stationery	2 000
Total saving	£107 000
Therefore: Loss of income	175 000
Less Saving of expenses	107 000
Restaurant worse off by	£68 000

In addition to the considerations stated above one would also have to take into account other factors before finally deciding one way or the other. Considerations which are relevant are: the effect of the closure on the volume of trade in the season; the possibility of not finding competent staff at the beginning of the season; the proprietor's ability to obtain income (e.g. take up employment) in the off-season, etc.

Problems

1 (a) What are the objects of interim and seasonal accounts?
(b) Of what value are interim accounts in seasonal hotel and catering establishments?

2 Describe how you would prepare a monthly estimated profit and loss account stating briefly how the figures are obtained.

A.M.H.C.I.

3 Jax Café is a seasonal establishment. The proprietor informs you that his takings are satisfactory between the beginning of April and the end of September, but that the rest of the year is very slack. He thinks his business makes a net loss in the off-season and asks you whether he should close down between October and March. He further explains that if he closed down in the off-season he would be able to work in his brother's business for a period of three months at a salary of £120 per week.

On checking his accounts you find that his sales and expenses for the past year were:

	Total	April to September	October to March
	£	£	£
Sales	101 000	72 000	29 000
Cost of food used	40 650	28 750	11 900
Wages and National Insurance	25 950	18 250	7 700
Gas and electricity	7 600	3 250	4 350
Depreciation: lease	8 200		
Depreciation: other assets	2 000		
Other expenses: rates, insurance, accountant's fees, telephone, etc.	7 300		

Advise the proprietor.

4 The Ebb-n-Flow Restaurant is a seasonal establishment in a seaside resort. It was opened on 1st January, 19.., and at the end of its first year's operation the following analysis of its trading results was prepared:

	January February	March April	May June	July August	September October	November December
	£	£	£	£	£	£
Sales	24 000	32 000	36 000	48 000	38 000	30 000
Less Cost of sales	9 600	12 800	14 400	19 200	15 200	12 000
Gross profit	14 400	19 200	21 600	28 800	22 800	18 000
Wages	10 000	11 000	12 000	16 000	14 000	12 000
Rent and rates	1 200	1 200	1 200	1 200	1 200	1 200
Advertising	600	600	600	600	600	600
Depreciation: lease	3 200	3 200	3 200	3 200	3 200	3 200
Depreciation: other	1 400	1 400	1 400	1 400	1 400	1 400
Repairs and replacement	300	300	400	500	400	300
Light and heat	700	700	600	500	600	600
Miscellaneous expenses	100	100	100	100	100	100
Total expenses	17 500	18 500	19 500	23 500	21 500	19 400
Profit		700	2 100	5 300	1 300	
Loss	3 100					1 400

Notes on allocation and apportionment of expenditure:
(i) Rent and rates are apportioned on a time basis;
(ii) Advertising is a fixed annual allocation;
(iii) Depreciation of lease is apportioned on a time basis; other depreciation is regarded as 50 per cent variable;
(iv) Wages—actual cost is allocated to each period;
(v) Repairs and replacements: this contains a fixed element of £200; the balance is regarded as variable;
(vi) Light and heat metered consumption allocated to each period;
(vii) Miscellaneous expenses: this consists of a large number of small items and is treated as a fixed cost.

The proprietors are of the opinion that the trading results for the second year should not materially differ from those for the first year. They are, however, concerned about the losses incurred in the off-season. Advise them as to whether or not it is desirable to close the restaurant during any particular part of the year.

5 J. Johnson is proprietor of the Full Moon Restaurant—a seasonal establishment open all the year. The accounting year of the restaurant ends on 31st March and the books are kept so as to enable the compilation of half-yearly trading and profit and loss accounts.

At 31st March, 1982, the following information was extracted from the books of the restaurant.

	Total	Season	Off-season
	£	£	£
Sales		198 620	100 106
Purchases		81 120	39 760
Wages and salaries		44 950	34 720
Rent	12 000		
Rates	4 120		
Insurance	1 920		
Depreciation	24 300		
Gas and electricity		5 060	2 060
Postage and stationery		2 400	1 280
Replacements and renewals		3 210	1 300
Sundry expenses		5 060	4 000

Notes:
(i) Rent, rates and insurance are to be apportioned on a time basis;
(ii) Debit 40 per cent of depreciation to the off-season;
(iii) Stocks were valued as follows:

31st March 1981	£4 160
30th September, 1981	£4 280
31st March, 1982	£3 960

Prepare the restaurant's trading, profit and loss account for the year ended 31st March, 1982, in a manner which you think appropriate and comment on your results.

6 The X Hotel Co. Ltd, is the proprietor of a large seaside hotel which is open all the year. The company's financial year ends on 31st March and the accounts are arranged to provide for the compilation of half-yearly trading and profit and loss accounts. At 31st March, 1982, the following information for each half-year was extracted from the books of the company:

	Half year to 30th September, 1981	Half year to 31st March, 1982
	£	£
Stocks at 1st April, 1981		
provisions	6 000	
liquors	18 000	
cigarettes and tobaccos	3 000	
sundries	1 500	
Purchases:		
provisions	165 000	76 000
liquors	120 000	35 000
cigarettes and tobaccos	12 000	6 000
sundries	7 000	3 200
wages	94 000	76 000
National Insurance	2 750	1 700
rates	4 000	4 000
lighting and heating	1 500	9 000
fuel and power	26 000	18 450
cleaning materials	9 000	6 000
office salaries	7 800	6 900
National Insurance	350	300
office expenses and stationery	6 000	5 000
postage and telephones	4 900	2 900
laundry	18 200	8 700
Receipts from:		
residents	360 000	183 000
restaurant: chance meals	82 000	14 000
liquors	146 000	69 200
sundries	7 200	3 600
cigarettes and tobaccos	14 000	6 800

(a) Prepare trading and profit and loss accounts for each half-year.

The following items must be brought into account:

	30th September, 1981	31st March, 1982
	£	£
Stocks on hand:		
provisions	6 000	7 000
liquors	17 000	18 000
cigarettes and tobaccos	2 500	3 250
sundries	1 250	1 750

Provision must be made for:
One year's interest on £100 000 debentures at 6 per cent.
Directors' fees £12 500
Depreciation on:
(1) kitchen equipment valued at £90 000 at 10 per cent per annum;
(2) furnishings and fittings valued at £120 000 at 15 per cent per annum;
(3) cutlery and linen, £10 000 for the year.

Note: The above provisions must be charged to each half-year in equal amounts.

(b) State briefly the conclusions you would draw from the accounts you have prepared. In particular state, with reasons for your opinion, if you think the hotel should be closed during the winter.

A.M.H.C.I. (Modified)

7 The El Peso Restaurant is a seasonal establishment. Its accounts are prepared twice yearly at 30th September and at 31st March. The following information is extracted from the books of the restaurant in respect of the year ended 31st March, 19...

	Season (half year to 30th September)	Off-season (half year to 31st March)
	£	£
Restaurant sales	228 070	104 960
Bar sales	71 940	34 050
Cost of restaurant sales	91 510	43 490
Cost of bar sales	27 460	12 620
Wages and salaries	106 030	63 510
Rent and rates	15 000	15 000
Depreciation: lease	16 000	16 000
Depreciation: other assets	9 000	6 000
Lighting and heating	2 600	8 000
Cleaning materials	3 060	2 500
Postage and stationery	2 540	1 490
Laundry	5 810	4 520
Fire insurance, etc.	1 000	1 000
Sundry expenses	2 000	1 500

You are required to prepare a trading and profit and loss account for the year ended 31st March, 19.., showing a separate result for each half year. State whether or not, in your opinion, the restaurant should be closed down in the off-season.

CHAPTER 20

Fixed and variable costs

Nature of costs

The costs of a business may be considered from two main points of view: their nature and their behaviour. From the point of view of their nature, we may distinguish three groups, often referred to as the 'elements of cost'. They are:

(1) Materials—in hotel and catering establishments include food, drink, cigarettes and tobaccos.

(2) Labour—includes the remuneration of the staff employed and consists of wages, salaries, employer's national insurance and graduated pension contributions, staff meals, bonuses, etc.

(3) Overheads—includes all other costs, such as rent, rates, depreciation, gas, electricity, licences, etc.

The division of total cost into materials, labour and overheads has been used in hotel and catering establishments for a long time. It is useful for some purposes but it does not take into account the dynamics of business, i.e. the effect on costs of changes in the volume of turnover.

Behaviour of costs

When we consider costs from the point of view of their behaviour in response to changes in turnover, we may divide all costs into three groups.

(1) Fixed—these costs tend to remain constant irrespective of changes in the volume of business, e.g. rent, rates, insurance, depreciation of premises, licences, etc. A characteristic feature of fixed costs is that they accrue with the passage of time; hence, they are sometimes described as 'period costs'.

(2) Semi-fixed—(also described as semi-variable costs). They move in sympathy with, but not in proportion to, the volume of sales. Examples of semi-fixed costs are: gas, electricity, cleaning materials and breakages and replacements. When the turnover of a business increases by 50 per cent it is quite certain that the cost of kitchen fuel will also increase; the increase will, however, be much less than 50 per cent.

(3) Variable—these tend to move in proportion to sales and include all commodity costs such as food, drink, tobaccos, etc. Provided that a close check is kept on the gross profit margins, all these costs will move almost in direct proportion to any changes in the volume of business.

Turnover, costs and profits

An appreciation of the relationship between the volume of turnover, costs and profits is indispensable to those responsible for the running of a business. For, as will have been appreciated, a given change in sales will not affect all costs in the same manner: some will remain constant; some will change less proportionately; others will change in proportion.

Example 1 Let us assume that the turnover, costs and profits of two restaurants are as shown below:

	Restaurant A	Restaurant B
Variable costs	£500 (50%)	£300 (30%)
Fixed costs	400 (40%)	600 (60%)
Net profits	100 (10%)....	100 (10%)
	£1 000 (100%)	£1 000 (100%)

Let us now assume that the turnover of both restaurants decreases by 10 per cent. The effect on the trading results of the restaurants will be as follows:

	Restaurant A	Restaurant B
Variable costs	£450 (50·0%)	£270 (30·0%)
Fixed costs	400 (44·4%)	600 (66·7%)
Net profits	50 (5·6%)	30 (3·3%)
	£900 (100·0%)	£900 (100·0%)

It may be seen that the relatively small decrease in the sales of the restaurants of 10 per cent has reduced the net profit of Restaurant A by 50 per cent (i.e. from £100 to £50) and the net profit of Restaurant B by 70 per cent (i.e. from £100 to £30).

A consideration of the figures given in this example enables us to draw the following conclusions:

(1) A given change in turnover will *not* result in a proportionate change in costs.

(2) When sales increase net profit tends to increase more than in proportion, and vice versa.

(3) The higher the proportion of fixed costs the greater the effect on net profit (or net loss) of any given change in turnover.

Turnover and unit costs

Changes in the turnover of a business affect unit costs in the same manner as they do the costs of the establishment as a whole.

An increase in sales increases the total variable cost of the establishment, but the variable cost per unit remains constant. Thus when the number of meals sold increases from 1 000 to 1 500 per week, the variable cost (food cost) increases by 50 per cent, yet the cost of food per meal served remains the same.

On the other hand, whilst an increase in sales will not affect the fixed costs of a restaurant, the fixed cost per unit will be decreased. The total fixed cost is now spread over a larger number of meals sold.

As a result, every increase in turnover will have the effect of reducing unit costs and thus increasing the net profit per unit sold.

Example 2 The fixed costs of the Old City Restaurant amount to £6 000 per week. The restaurant serves between 1 800 and 2 600 meals weekly and the average amount spent by the customers is £5.00 per meal. The variable cost (food cost) per meal is £2.00.

Find the total cost per meal served and the net profit or loss per meal when the restaurant serves 1 800, 2 000, 2 200, 2 400 and 2 600 meals per week.

Total cost and net profit per meal

	No. of meals served per week				
	1 800	2 000	2 200	2 400	2 600
Price per meal	£5.00	£5.00	£5.00	£5.00	£5.00
Variable cost per meal	£2.00	£2.00	£2.00	£2.00	£2.00
Fixed cost per meal	£3.33	£3.00	£2.72	£2.50	£2.30
Total cost per meal	£5.33	£5.00	£4.72	£4.50	£4.30
Net profit per meal	—	—	28p	50p	70p
Net loss per meal	33p	—	—	—	—

Break-even charts

The purpose of a break-even chart is to show how much profit or loss will be made by a business at different levels of turnover. The term 'break-even chart' is unfortunate in that it stresses a particular—and not necessarily the most important—purpose of the chart, i.e. the ascertainment of the break-even point. It should be appreciated that the object of a break-even chart is to project the profitability of a business *vis-a-vis* changes in its turnover and not merely to find the turnover which results in a condition where all costs are covered and no profit is achieved.

In order to construct a break-even chart the costs of a business must be divided according to their behaviour in response to changes in the volume of turnover, viz. into fixed, semi-fixed and variable costs.

Example 3 The Belle Vue Restaurant serves up to 2 000 customers per week. The average spending power is £5.00.

The costs of the restaurant are:

(1) fixed costs (rent, rates, insurance, wages and salaries) £2 500 per week;

(2) variable costs (food and beverages) 50 per cent of sales.

Calculaate:

(a) the amount of profit/loss per week when the restaurant serves 400, 800, 1 200, 1 600 and 2 000 customers per week.

(b) the break-even point of the restaurant.

The relationship between the turnover of the restaurant, its costs and profits may be represented in two ways: by means of a simple tabular statement or by means of a break-even chart.

The tabular statement could be drawn up as follows:

Belle Vue Restaurant

Weekly profit/loss at different levels of turnover

NOC	Sales	Fixed Costs	Variable Costs	Total Cost	+ Profit – Loss
	£	£	£	£	£
400	2 000	2 500	1 000	3 500	−1 500
800	4 000	2 500	2 000	4 500	− 500
1 200	6 000	2 500	3 000	5 500	+ 500
1 600	8 000	2 500	4 000	6 500	+1 500
2 000	10 000	2 500	5 000	7 500	+2 500

The break-even chart of the restaurant could be prepared either from the tabular statement given above or from the information shown in Figure 207.

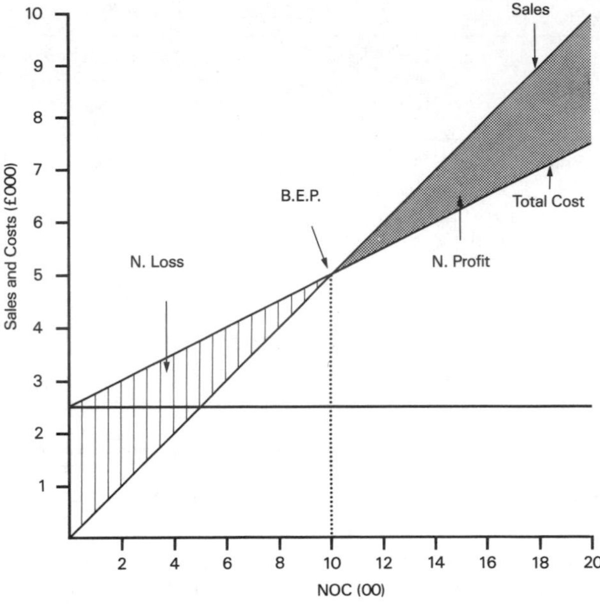

Figure 207

By reference to the break-even chart, it may be seen that:

(1) No profit can be made by the restaurant unless it serves 1 000 customers per week.

(2) When the restaurant serves 2 000 customers per week, its net profit is £2 500 per week.

(3) Once the break-even point (1 000 customers) has been reached, every increase of 100 customers increases the net profit of the restaurant by £250 per week.

Margin of safety An interesting and useful concept connected with break-even analysis is that of the margin of safety. This may be defined as the range of output over which a net profit must be made, i.e. the range of output between the break-even point and the total of sales possible.

Where the margin of safety is narrow a small drop in sales will reduce profits considerably or convert any net profit made into a loss. When, on the other hand, the margin of safety is wide, a considerable decrease in turnover has to take place for the business to incur a loss. In general, the higher the ratio of fixed costs to variable costs the narrower the margin of safety, and vice versa.

Example 4 The capital invested in the Pagoda Restaurant is £150 000. The proprietors' policy is to aim at a net profit target of 20 per cent on all restaurant sales.

The restaurant has a seating capacity enabling it to serve up to 5 000 customers per month, i.e. a maximum of 60 000 customers per annum. The A.S.P. of the restaurant is £5.00. Fixed costs amount to £90 000 p.a. and variable costs account for 40 per cent of the sales revenue. From this information a break-even chart is prepared as shown in Figure 208. This indicates:

(a) the break-even point;

(b) the margin of safety;

(c) the volume of sales required to achieve the net profit target.

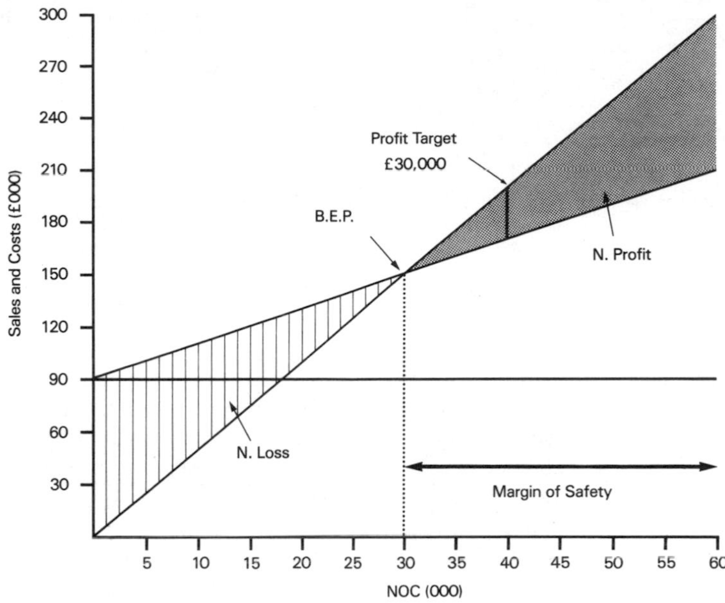

Figure 208

Profit estimates Another useful application of the division of costs into fixed, semi-fixed and variable is the estimating of future profits. Profit estimates are necessary in various circumstances, e.g.:

(1) when planning the operations of a business for a future period;
(2) when commencing a new business;
(3) when planning to extend the premises;
(4) when planning to take over a business as a going concern;
(5) when contemplating a change in the type of service, e.g. from self-service to waiter service.

The method to be applied in profit estimates is illustrated below.

Example 5 The following is a summary of the trading results of the Ajanta Restaurant for the quarter ended 31st March, 19...

Ajanta Restaurant
Trading results for the quarter ended 31st March, 19..

Sales: Restaurant		£160 000
Bar		90 000
		250 000
Less Variable costs		
Cost of food sold	£72 000	
Cost of beverages sold	36 000	108 000
Gross profit c/f		142 000

		Gross profit b/f		£142 000
Less Fixed costs:				
	Wages and salaries		£65 000	
	Rent and rates		15 000	
	Light and heat		8 000	
	Depreciation		12 000	
	Repairs and replacement		6 000	
	Advertising		5 000	
	Other costs		7 000	118 000
		Net profit		£24 000

The turnover of the restaurant has remained constant in the last two years, and the proprietors think that by eliminating waste and by improving menu planning the cost of food sold could be decreased from the usual 45 per cent to 40 per cent of the respective figure of sales. They also consider that an increase in press advertising costing £20 000 should raise the turnover for the next quarter to £300 000.

You are required to prepare:

(a) A summary of the estimated trading results for the next quarter on the assumption that the cost of food sold is decreased to 40 per cent of restaurant sales, but that no increase in press advertising takes place.

(b) A summary of the estimated trading results for the next quarter on the assumption that the cost of food sold is reduced and that the proposed increase in press advertising does take place.

Ajanta Restaurant

Estimated trading results—(a) for quarter ended 30th June, 19..

Sales: Restaurant				£160 000
Bar				90 000
		Total		250 000
Less Variable costs:				
	Cost of food sold		64 000	
	Cost of drink sold		36 000	100 000
		Gross profit		150 000
Less Fixed costs				118 000
		Net profit		£32 000

Ajanta Restaurant

Estimated trading results—(b) for quarter ended 30th June, 19..

Sales: Restaurant				£192 000
Bar				108 000
		Total		300 000
Les Variable costs:				
	Cost of food sold		£76 800	
	Cost of drink sold		43 200	120 000
		Gross profit		180 000
Less Fixed costs				138 000
		Net profit		£42 000

It seems, therefore, that as a result of the two proposed measures the net profit of the restaurant may be improved considerably, i.e. by £18 000. Of the total increase in net profit £8 000 is due to the reduction in the cost of food sold and £10 000 is due to the effect of the proposed advertising.

Pricing

The usual method of fixing prices in the hotel and catering industry is to calculate the variable cost (e.g. food cost) and increase it by a percentage of gross profit. The gross profit added to the variable cost must be sufficient to cover all other expenses such as labour costs and overheads and leave a satisfactory margin of net profit. Thus, another way of defining selling price is:

TOTAL COST + NET PROFIT = SELLING PRICE.

There are, however, particular circumstances which may justify selling at a price below total cost, and this is illustrated below.

Example 6 The Montrose Restaurant is divided into three separate sections; self-service, waitress service and banqueting. The annual fixed costs of the banqueting section are:

Proportion of rent and rates	£16 500
Depreciation	8 400
Repairs and maintenance	3 600
Salaries and wages	41 000
Other fixed costs	3 500
	£73 000

The banqueting section is open all the year round and the fixed cost per day is therefore:

$$\frac{£73\,000}{365} = £200$$

Taking into account the fixed cost per day and the variable cost (see below) in respect of a menu already agreed with your clients, calculate the charge per cover. Assume that a net profit of 20 per cent is required on all banqueting sales.

Variable costs for 100 covers

Food cost		£330
Extra labour (waiting staff)		110
Variable overheads—(linen, laundry, electricity, gas, etc.)		60
	Total variable cost	£500
The charge per cover is:		
Fixed cost		£200
Variable cost		500
	Total cost of banquet	£700

$$\frac{\text{TOTAL COST OF BANQUET}}{\text{NUMBER OF COVERS}} = \frac{£700}{100} = £7.00 = \text{Total cost per cover}$$

$$\frac{£7.00 \times 100}{80} = £8.75 = \text{Selling price per cover}$$

Let us now assume that, for one reason or another, it is necessary to offer the above banquet at a reduced price, and that if the banquet is not undertaken no other banqueting business can be secured for that particular day:

The position then is this:

(1) if the banquet is not undertaken the banqueting section will suffer a net loss equal to its fixed cost per day, i.e. £200;
(2) if a reduced charge is made the banqueting section may cover its variable costs and some of its fixed costs, and in this way suffer a loss of less than £200. This second alternative is, clearly, preferable to the first.

The minimum charge per cover—which will recover all variable costs and leave no contribution to fixed costs—is calculated as follows:

$$\frac{\text{TOTAL VARIABLE COST}}{\text{NUMBER OF COVERS}} = \frac{£500}{100} = £5.00$$

Assuming that a charge of £6.50 per cover is made, then

Sales 100 @ £6.50	£650
Less variable cost	500
Contribution to fixed costs	£150

As a result, the net loss of the banqueting section for that day will be £50 (£200 less £150).

Problems

1 Explain what is meant by: (a) fixed cost; (b) semi-fixed cost; (c) variable cost.

2 The following are the trading results of a restaurant in respect of Year 1.

Sales		£400 000
Less:		
(1) Fixed costs (rent, rates, insurance, salaries, etc.)	£100 000	
(2) Semi-fixed costs (fuel, light, telephone, laundry, etc.)	100 000	
(3) Variable costs (food, beverages, tobacco, etc.)	160 000	360 000
Net profit		£40 000

It is estimated that in Year 2 the sales of the restaurant will increase by 10 per cent. It is also estimated that semi-fixed costs will rise by $2\frac{1}{2}$ per cent. It is intended to keep the variable costs in the same ratio to sales as in Year 1.

Prepare an estimate of the trading results for Year 2.

3 The capital invested in the Norus Hotel is £1 000 000 and the following are the sales and costs of the hotel at different rates of occupancy.

	Occupancy			
	65%	75%	85%	95%
Sales	£630 000	£740 000	£850 000	£960 000
Total cost	580 000	640 000	700 000	750 000

(a) Comment on the relationship between sales, total cost and the net profit of the hotel.
(b) Calculate the return on the capital invested in the hotel in relation to each rate of occupancy given above.
(c) Comment on your results in (b) above.

4 The Provincial Catering Co. Ltd operates three restaurants, A, B and C. The following is a summary of the trading results of Restaurant A:

Restaurant A

Sales			£20 400
Less Cost of sales			8 160
	Gross profit		12 240
Less Labour costs		£6 000	
Overheads		4 200	10 200
	Net profit		£2 040

Other information:

(a) Net profit	10 per cent
(b) Gross profit	60 per cent
(c) Average sales per waitress	£3 400
(d) Average spending power	£4.10

You are informed that the turnover of Restaurant A is increasing and that the six waitresses already employed are finding it difficult to cope with the existing volume of business.

It is estimated that the employment of an additional waitress at a cost of £250 per month would result in an increase in turnover of £600 per month and an increase in overheads of £50 per month.

State, giving reasons, whether or not the seventh waitress should be employed.

5 Vitamins Ltd operate a works canteen for the provision of meals to their employees. They serve an average of 500 meals per day, 5 days per week for 50 weeks of the year, several choices being offered each day.

The annual cost of food is £93 750, wages £62 500, overheads £78 120. The company wish to provide meals at an average charge of £1.25 each and are willing to subsidise the canteen to the extent of £50 000 per annum.

The company occupying an adjoining factory have approached Vitamins Ltd and asked if they would be prepared to serve their employees with meals (400 per day) of the same quality at £1.25 each. They are prepared to take the meals at a different time to the Vitamins employees, so there would be no difficulty regarding accommodation. Additional labour costing £25 000 per annum would be required in the canteen.

As canteen manager, you are asked to suggest a pricing policy (i.e. the percentages to be added to the cost of each dish) and give your recommendation as to whether the company should be prepared to supply the meals to the neighbouring firm on the terms suggested.

You should supply detailed figures to support your recommendation.

M.H.C.I.

6 A catering company owns a number of medium-priced, small restaurants. The following are average monthly trading results of one of them:

Trading results

Sales			25 000
Less Cost of sales			10 000
	Gross profit		15 000
Less Labour costs		£7 000	
Overheads		5 000	12 000
	Net profit		£3 000

You are informed that the turnover of this restaurant is increasing and that the directors of the company are considering the desirability of taking over the remainder of an adjoining lease which has been offered to the company at a price of £60 000. The lease has ten more years to run.

It is estimated that, given the above additional space, the sales of the restaurant could be increased by £5 000 per month. In addition to the cost of the lease, further equipment and furniture would have to be acquired at a cost of £24 000. In order to cope with the increased volume of business further labour would have to be employed at a cost of £800 per month.

Finally, it is estimated that the increase in sales would cause a rise in semi-fixed costs of £400 per month and an increase in food stocks held of £1 000.

The directors are of the opinion that, because of limited internal resources, and current investment opportunities, any additional investment of capital must yield a net return of at least $12\frac{1}{2}$ per cent.

Advise the directors whether or not the premises should be extended.

7 High-class and Low-class are two restaurants with an identical volume of turnover.

From the information given below you are required to:

(a) prepare a break-even chart of each restaurant;

(b) explain which restaurant is likely to earn greater profits in conditions of:

(i) heavy demand, and (ii) low demand.

		High-class		Low-class
		£		£
Sales		200 000		200 000
Less Fixed costs	120 000		60 000	
Variable costs	60 000	180 000	120 000	180 000
Net profit		20 000		20 000

8 (a) Explain what is meant by fixed, semi-fixed and variable costs.

(b) A canteen serves between 1 800 and 2 200 main meals weekly. Its fixed costs (labour costs and overheads) are £1 300 per week and it operates at a gross profit of 50 per cent. The charge per main meal is fixed at £1.25. You are required to find:

(1) How many main meals the canteen has to serve each week to break even;

(2) The net profit/loss when 2 000 main meals are served weekly.

(c) Explain the relationship between the volume of sales and the net profit/loss of a business by reference to the information given in (b) above.

9 The Acropolis Restaurant serves between 3 000 and 4 000 customers per month. The average spending per head is £5.00. The restaurant operates at a fixed margin of gross profit of 60 per cent. Its fixed costs are as follows:

Wages, salaries, National Insurance, etc.	£5 200
Proportion of rent, rates and depreciation	2 400
Postage, telephone and stationery	1 000
Other fixed costs	1 900

You are required to:

(a) prepare a break-even chart for the restaurant;
(b) explain the significance of the break-even point;
(c) comment on the 'margin of safety' of the restaurant.

10 Hyfix and Lofix are two restaurants with an identical volume of turnover. The estimated profits and loss accounts of the restaurants are:

		Hyfix		Lofix
		£		£
Sales		400 000		400 000
Less Fixed costs	240 000		120 000	
Variable costs	120 000		240 000	
		360 000		360 000
Net profit		40 000		40 000

(a) Calculate the break-even point of each restaurant;
(b) comment on their respective 'margins of safety'.

11 Dix Catering Co. operates at a gross profit of 60 per cent. Its fixed expenses are £60 000.
Calculate: (a) the volume of sales required for the company to break-even;
(b) the volume of sales required for the company to achieve a net profit of £15 000.

12 Barnardo's Snack Bar operates at a gross profit of 60 per cent. Its fixed expenses are £50 000.

Find the volume of sales required for the snack bar to cover its fixed and variable costs only, also find the volume of sales necessary to give the snack bar a net profit of £20 000.

13 (a) How important is the distinction between fixed and variable costs?
(b) From the information given below calculate the charge per cover in respect of a menu already agreed with your clients.

Costs for 50 covers

Food stores:	£40
fishmonger	60
butcher	70
dairy	10
greengrocer	20
Other costs: proportion of fixed salaries	30
wages of part-time labour	90
proportion of fixed overheads	80
variable overheads	60

Your intention is to achieve a net profit of 10 per cent on all sales.
(c) From the information given above, calculate the lowest acceptable charge per cover, assuming that there is not alternative business for that day.

14 Pharmaceuticals Ltd operates a staff dining hall for the provision of meals to its employees and provides 900 meals per day, 5 days a week for 50 weeks of the year.

The current year's costs with respect to employee feeding are expected to be:

	£
Food	87 750
Labour	80 000
Overheads	47 250

In future the directors would like to provide meals at an average selling price of £0.60 each and are prepared to subsidise the eating facilities to a limit of £50 000 per annum.

Surgical Ltd, which occupies an adjoining factory, has recently approached Pharmaceuticals Ltd to inquire if they would be willing to provide similar meals each day to their 500 employees at the same price. They have offered to take their meals at a different time, thus avoiding capacity problems and are prepared to pay £16 000 per annum for the use of the facilities.

Pharmaceuticals Ltd has estimated that the additional labour and overhead costs of providing the extra meals would be £8 000 and £3 250 per annum respectively.

Required (a) Bearing in mind the above information, you have been asked to recommend to the directors of Pharmaceuticals Ltd whether they should, on financial grounds, provide meals to the employees of Surgical Ltd.
(b) Based on your recommendation in (a) above, you are further requested to suggest a pricing policy in terms of the average percentage to be added to the cost of each dish in order to recover the associated costs.
(c) List factors, other than financial aspects, that should be considered prior to making a final decision in this kind of circumstance.

H.C.I.M.A.

CHAPTER 21

Budgetary control

Definitions and objectives

More and more attention is being attached to budgeting in the hotel and catering industry. Whilst fifteen or twenty years ago only a few catering establishments operated some system of budgeting, there are now numerous hotels, restaurants, industrial canteens, etc. using this system of control.

A budget is a plan, expressed in monetary or other terms, which governs the operation of a business over a predetermined period of time. Whereas most budgets (e.g. sales budget, labour cost budget) are expressed in terms of money, some are expressed in terms of units or percentages. A personnel budget may be expressed in terms of numbers of employees to be replaced or engaged over a period of time. A sales budget invariably shows the budgeted value of sales; it may, in addition, show the budgeted number of covers or the budgeted rate of room occupancy.

Budgetary control is a means of control by which responsibility for various budgets is assigned to the managers concerned, and a continual comparison is made of the actual results with the budgeted results. Where there are discrepancies between the two, appropriate corrective action is taken.

From the definitions given above it will be realized that a budget is the plan on which a system of budgetary control is based. The budget sets standards of performance (targets) for the managers of a business. Budgetary control is a means of ensuring that the objectives set for the managers are fulfilled.

The main objectives and the consequent advantages of budgeting may be summarized as follows:

(a) The budget is a detailed plan of action which guides and regulates the progress of a business.

(b) Budgeting results in a better co-ordination of all activities of a business.

(c) The budget sets standards against which the performance of those responsible may be measured and assessed.

(d) Budgeting is an important method of expense control; it establishes clear lines of cost responsibility and promotes cost consciousness.

(e) Budgeting ensures an economical utilization of the resources of a business and thus helps to maximize profits.

Formulation of the budget

Budget Committee

Where there is a system of budgeting control in operation there is invariably constituted a budget committee. This consists of the senior executive of the business (managing director or general manager), several senior managers (e.g. the food and beverage manager, executive chef, executive housekeeper, banqueting manager) and the accountant. The senior executive usually acts as chairman and the accountant as secretary of the budget committee.

Before any budgets are drawn up the budget committee must decide how the overall system of budgeting will fit into the existing structure of the business. This entails a review of the organizational structure of the business and a definition of each manager's authority and responsibility. It is only when this preliminary work has been done that it is possible to draw up the necessary budgets for the various departments of the business. The departmental, as well as other, budgets will set appropriate targets expressed in terms of turnover, profit margins, operating ratios and cost limits.

The main function of the budget committee is to prepare budget proposals (draft budgets) for submission to the board of directors. When preparing the budget proposals the budget committee will take into account the following:

(a) Past performance—this entails a thorough analysis of past income, expenditure, trends in income and expenditure, etc.

(b) Current trends—this necessitates a review of the current position with regard to the items mentioned in (a) above.

(c) Other information—would include a consideration of the prosperity of the particular section of the hotel and catering industry, the condition of local industries, the degree of unemployment, if any, and the degree of competition.

The budget period

Another function of the budget committee is to choose an appropriate budget period. This, in most hotel and catering establishments, is one calendar year.

The most appropriate length of the budget period can only be determined by reference to the particular circumstances of each business. Businesses requiring a large amount of fixed capital tend to have a long budget period extending over several years. On the other hand, seasonal businesses and those subject to frequent and substantial changes in turnover tend to adopt a rather shorter budget period. Finally, a particular business may use more than one budget period. A hotel may budget for its income and expenditure a year in advance but, at the same time, plan its capital expenditure up to five years in advance.

The review period

In addition to determining the budget period the budget committee must choose the most appropriate review period (also referred to as 'control period').

As already mentioned an essential part of budgetary control is the continual comparison of the actual with the budgeted results. Ideally, the two sets of results should be compared daily, as actual results take place. In practice, however, this is not normally possible, and it is quite usual for most hotel and catering establishments to adopt a review period of one week or one calendar (or four-weekly) month.

Kinds of budgets

There are several kinds of budgets used in hotel and catering establishments.

From the point of view of the subject-matter budgeted for we may distinguish:

(1) Capital budgets—these are budgets dealing with the assets and the capital funds of a business. Examples of capital budgets are budgets dealing with equipment and plant, cash, any proposed issue of shares or debentures.

(2) Operating budgets—these are budgets concerned with the day-to-day running of the business. Examples of operating budgets are those dealing with sales, purchases, labour costs, office and administration expenses, maintenance, etc.

From the point of view of the comprehensiveness of budgets, we may distinguish:

(1) Master budgets—a master budget may be a budgeted profit and loss account, incorporating all income and all expenditure of a business; it may also be a budgeted balance sheet, incorporating all assets and liabilities of a business.

(2) Departmental budgets—these are concerned with particular departments of a business. Examples of such budgets are: banqueting budget, maintenance budget, housekeeping budget.

From the point of view of the level of sales assumed we may distinguish:

(1) Fixed budgets—these remain unchanged irrespective of the level of sales achieved. Thus a sales promotion budget may be a fixed budget in that the expenditure (press advertising, printing of brochures, etc.) may be a fixed amount allocated before the commencement of the budget period.

(2) Flexible budgets—a flexible budget predetermines costs in relation to several possible volumes of sales. The cost of sales budget of a resort restaurant relying on day trippers—and therefore dependent on weather conditions—will normally be a flexible budget. In seasonal hotels the labour cost budget will also be a flexible budget in that the budgeted labour costs will be planned in relation to the changing rate of occupancy.

It is pointed out that a particular establishment may have some fixed and some flexible budgets. A hotel may have a flexible labour cost budget and fixed budgets for sales promotion, maintenance and office and administration expenses. Secondly, students should realize a particular budget does not necessarily fall under one of the types given above. A labour cost budget is an operating budget but it may also be a departmental budget and a flexible or fixed budget.

The limiting factor

The first step in the preparation of a budget is to forecast the volume of sales, as it is this that affects most other parts of the budget. Thus, the forecast volume of sales will determine the level of all variable and semi-fixed costs; also it will affect the cash position of the business which, in turn, may determine the amount of capital expenditure planned for the period concerned.

When forecasting the future volume of sales it is important to remember what is known as the 'limiting factor' (also referred to as the 'key factor', 'governing factor' and 'principal budget factor'). This is the factor that limits the volume of sales and makes a further increase in sales impossible.

The following limiting factors will be found operating in hotel and catering establishments:

(1) Accommodation available—this operates in residential establishments, viz, hotels, motels, hostels, etc. Once all the accommodation available has been let it is impossible to increase the volume of sales except by raising prices.

(2) Seating capacity—this applies particularly to restaurants, the seating capacity of which is fixed; also to banqueting sales, as insufficient seating capacity may well result in loss of potential sales.

(3) Insufficient capital—in a multiple catering business an expansion of sales through the acquisition of further units may be impossible due to insufficient capital.

(4) Shortage of efficient labour—many hotel and catering establishments could increase their sales by improving the efficiency of their labour. Thus the speed with which cash is taken by the cashier in a self-service restaurant has an important bearing on the volume of sales; similarly, the speed with which waiters serve customers can affect the volume of sales considerably. The ability of the chef and other kitchen staff are equally important in this respect.

(5) Shortage of efficient executives—this, obviously, is even more important than a shortage of efficient labour. Inefficient management makes an expansion of sales difficult through bad organization, unimaginative menu planning and failure to take advantage of any opportunities to increase sales that may present themselves.

(6) Management policy—an increase in sales may be impossible as a result of the deliberate policy of a business. Thus a restaurant may discourage the 'wrong' type of customer; a hotel may refuse to accept coach tour business, football teams, etc.

(7) Consumer demand—this is a limiting factor the operation of which is most

difficult to remove. Consumer demand may be limited in several ways: by the prices charged; through competition, as a result of a fixed potential demand—e.g. in industrial canteens.

When an increase in sales proves difficult it is important to identify the limiting factor(s). The nature of the limiting factor will then indicate the most appropriate method of dealing with the problem.

Operating budgets

A full and detailed description of all the operating budgets used in hotel and catering establishments is, clearly, outside the scope of this text book. We will, therefore, deal with one operating budget (sales budget) at some length and only refer in a general way to other operating budgets.

Sales budget

This is the most important and the most difficult budget to prepare. It is the most important budget because it affects the accuracy of most other budgets. Thus, if budgeted sales are forecast inaccurately, budgeted variable and semi-variable costs will also be inaccurate. Similarly, the cash budget—which is obviously affected by the volume of sales—will be inaccurate. It is difficult to produce as, naturally, there are many external and therefore uncontrollable factors that influence the actual level of sales.

The sales budget is prepared on the basis of the following:

Past performance: (a) actual sales of previous periods; (b) sales mix; (c) trends in sales and sales mix.

Current trends: (a) state of sales, sales mix and trends; (b) bookings received for accommodation, banquets, etc.

Limiting factors: Where the increase in sales is considered inadequate, limiting factors should be identified and dealt with accordingly.

Other information: (a) condition of local industries; (b) state of employment and prosperity in the locality concerned; (c) political situation, government policy, etc., and their effect on future turnover.

Example 1

The Essex Restaurant is a large, licensed establishment and budgets its sales a year in advance; actual sales are reviewed in the light of the budgeted figures at the end of each 4-weekly period. The sales of the restaurant for the past three years have been as follows:

Analysis of past sales

	1981	*1982*	*1983*
	£	£	£
Restaurant sales	179 500	186 500	190 200
Percentage increase on previous year	7%	4%	2%
Bar sales	91 000	95 500	102 200
Percentage increase on previous year	4%	5%	7%
Sundry sales	30 500	32 000	34 000
Percentage increase on previous year	5%	5%	6%
Total sales	301 000	314 000	326 400
Percentage increase on previous year	6%	4.3%	4%

The following supplementary information is also made available:

(1) Restaurant sales: The rate of increase in this section of the turnover is falling off. This is due to the limited dining room space available. It is thought that, in the circumstances, little increase in sales is possible.

(2) Bar sales: The turnover has been rising satisfactorily but in view of the limiting factor restricting restaurant sales a higher rate of increase cannot be expected.
(3) Sundry sales: This is expected to increase at least as well as in 1983.

Determination of sales target

Having due regard to the past trends in sales and all other relevant factors the following sales targets are set for 1984.
(1) Restaurant sales—it is decided that these ought to be increased by 4 per cent. In view of the limited space available the increase in sales is to be achieved through increased prices. To this end, all restaurant prices are to be revised early in the year.
(2) Bar sales—these ought to show an increase of 7 per cent on the previous year.
(3) Sundry sales—in view of the past trend, an increase of 7 per cent should be aimed at.

The budgeted sales for 1984 are therefore:

Restaurant sales –	£190 200 + 4 per cent thereof	– £197 800
Bar ,, –	102 200 + 7 ,, ,, ,,	– 109 350
Sundry ,, –	34 000 + 7 ,, ,, ,,	– 36 380
		– £343 530

The budgeted sales for each 4-weekly period are:

Restaurant sales	$\frac{£197\,800}{13}$ = £15 210	—say	£15 200
Bar ,,	$\frac{£109\,350}{13}$ = £8 410	—say	8 400
Sundry ,,	$\frac{£36\,380}{13}$ = £2 790	—say	2 800
	Total monthly sales		£26 400

At the end of each 4-weekly period the actual sales would be compared with budgeted sales; any discrepancies (variances) would then be investigated and the necessary corrective action would be taken.

The following is a monthly sales report, based on the figures given above:

Essex Restaurant
Monthly sales report
for 4 weeks ended 28th January, 1984

To: 1. Managing director
2. General manager
From: Catering controller

	Budgeted sales	Actual sales	Variances + or –
Restaurant sales	£15 200	£14 400	– £800
Bar ,,	8 400	8 500	+ 100
Sundry ,,	2 800	2 950	+ 150
Total	26 400	25 850	– 550

Note: Only a partial revision of restaurant prices has taken place; a complete revision is called for.

Labour cost budget

This would be evolved in relation to the budgeted volume of sales. When an increase in sales is budgeted for it is necessary to establish how much of the increase can be dealt with by the existing staff of the establishment. A labour cost budget cannot be realistic unless it is based on a detailed analysis of the staffing of each department *vis-a-vis* the budgeted turnover. The budget will have to take into account the following:

(a) The number and grades of staff in each department;
(b) The current rates of pay for each grade of staff;
(c) Casual labour and authorized overtime;
(d) Proposed changes in staffing, rates of pay and grading of staff;
(e) Staff meals, holiday pay and other labour costs.

Overhead cost budget

Whilst a smaller hotel or catering establishment would tend to have an overhead cost budget covering all overheads, larger establishments would tend to have separate budgets for the various component parts of overhead expenditure, e.g. maintenance, office and administration costs, advertising, etc.

The overhead cost budget is also evolved in relation to the budgeted sales. It must, therefore, clearly distinguish between fixed overheads (rates, depreciation of premises, licences, etc.) and variable and semi-variable overheads (gas, electricity, telephone, laundry, cleaning materials, etc.).

Office and administration budget

This budget will tend to change little from one year to another. The most important items covered by the office and administration budget are: (a) office salaries; (b) depreciation of office equipment; (c) telephone; (d) printing and stationery; (e) insurances, bank charges and audit fees.

As with all other budgets the office and administration budget will distinguish between fixed and variable costs. This is particularly important in seasonal establishments.

Maintenance budget

Whilst most smaller hotel and catering establishments include maintenance costs in a total expense budget or overhead cost budget, larger units tend to have a separate maintenance budget.

A well-prepared maintenance budget will do two things: first, it will predetermine the maintenance costs; secondly, it will show the sequence of the work to be done over the budget period.

Budgeted maintenance costs will be arrived at by reference to: (a) the state of the premises, kitchen plant, furniture and other equipment, (b) the standard of comfort which it is necessary to provide, having regard to the type of customers catered for and (c) the current availability of funds.

The costs which have to be taken into account are:

(a) Maintenance materials and supplies—items such as paints, wallpaper, electrical components, loose tools and other supplies required by the maintenance department.

(b) Maintenance labour costs—this includes all wages and salaries payable to the maintenance staff.

(c) Other costs—such as depreciation of maintenance department's equipment, stationery, office supplies, etc.

The sequencing of maintenance work is necessary to ensure that it does not interfere with current operations (e.g. the letting of rooms, banqueting business) and that all budgeted maintenance work is completed in a thought-out, logical manner.

Finally, when planning a maintenance budget it is necessary to distinguish between and itemize separately (a) routine maintenance work (b) maintenance work to be carried out by outside parties in respect of any maintenance contracts;

provision must also be made for emergency repair work which, though quite unpredictable, always presents a claim on the staff of the maintenance department.

Housekeeping budget This, like other budgets, will be evolved in relation to the budgeted turnover of the hotel and in relation to the budgeted rate of occupancy in particular. The costs which it has to include are:

(a) Wages and salaries—this would include all labour costs of the housekeeping department and cover housekeeping staff such as housekeepers, chambermaids, cleaners, house porters, linen keepers and valeting staff.

(b) Linen and laundry costs—this would include the laundering of sheets, pillow cases, towels; the cleaning of furnishings, etc.

(c) Other housekeeping costs—under this heading would be cleaning materials, floral decorations, first aid, replacements of loose housekeeping equipment, etc.

Capital budgets

Capital budgets, as already explained, are budgets concerned with the assets and capital funds of a business. More specifically, they are budgets in respect of matters such as: capital expenditure on new fixed assets, cash, debtors, stocks; the raising of fresh capital by the issue of shares or debentures, etc. In practice, the most important of such budgets is the cash budget.

Cash budget This is prepared from the various operating and capital budgets. Particulars of cash receivable over the budget period will be obtained from the sales budget and other sources. Particulars of cash payable over the budget period will be extracted mainly from the operating (expense) budgets and budgets in respect of any planned acquisition of fixed assets.

Example 2 From the information given below prepare a cash budget for the six months commencing 1st April, 19...

Month	Food sales	Drink sales	Food purchases	Drink purchases	Labour costs	Overheads
	£	£	£	£	£	£
February	30 000	9 000	12 000	4 400	12 000	10 400
March	31 000	9 600	12 200	4 800	12 400	10 400
April	34 000	10 400	13 600	5 400	13 000	10 800
May	35 600	12 600	14 000	6 400	13 800	11 200
June	46 000	13 800	14 600	6 800	15 000	11 600
July	50 000	16 200	16 600	8 200	14 800	11 400
August	45 000	14 200	14 600	7 200	13 400	10 600
September	40 800	13 000	14 200	6 400	12 200	10 200

Notes:

(i) Assume that all sales are cash sales;

(ii) The annual interest on the company's investments, £1 600, will be received in July;

(iii) The time lag in the payment of suppliers is two months; in the payment of overheads the time lag is one month; in the case of the labour costs it is nil;

(iv) New kitchen plant costing £10 000 will be purchased in May and paid for the following month;

(v) The bank balance of the company on 1st April, 19.. was £30 000.

The cash budget would be drawn up as shown in Figure 209.

CASH BUDGET
for Six Months ending 30th Sept., 19..

	April	May	June	July	August	September
	£	£	£	£	£	£
Opening Balance	30,000	35,000	41,600	46,200	67,200	80,200
SOURCES OF CASH:						
Food Sales	34,000	35,600	46,000	50,000	45,000	40,800
Beverage	10,800	12,600	13,800	16,200	14,200	13,000
Other Receipts				1,600		
Total	74,800	83,200	101,400	114,000	126,400	134,000
APPLICATIONS OF CASH:						
Food Purchases	12,000	12,200	13,600	14,000	14,600	16,600
Beverage	4,400	4,800	5,400	6,400	6,800	8,200
Labour Costs	13,000	13,800	15,000	14,800	13,400	12,200
Overheads	10,400	10,800	11,200	11,600	11,400	10,600
Other Payments			10,000			
Total	39,800	41,600	55,200	46,800	46,200	47,600
Closing Balance	35,000	41,600	46,200	67,200	80,200	86,400

Figure 209

Notes on cash budget:

(1) The data shown in the cash budget are extracted from the operating and capital budgets.

(2) As all the sales are cash sales, the sales for each month represent an immediate cash inflow for that month. Where there are credit sales (e.g. in respect of banqueting) there is a time lag of a month or more between the sales and the receipt of cash for such sales.

(3) From the cash budget it is possible to determine whether or not the future cash position is going to be satisfactory. It is also easier to plan capital expenditure and, generally, ensure a more economical use of the cash resources of the business.

Master budgets

When all the operating and capital budgets have been completed it is possible to prepare the master budgets of the business, i.e. the budgeted profit and loss account and the budgeted balance sheet.

The budgeted profit and loss account will incorporate the sales budget, all the expense budgets and will show the budgeted net profit.

The budgeted balance sheet will be compiled by reference to the last balance sheet (to ascertain the state of affairs at the beginning of the budget period), the capital budgets (with regard to any new acquisitions of assets) and the expense budgets (with regard to budgeted amounts of depreciation).

Problems

1 Explain what you understand by: (a) budget; (b) budgetary control.

2 What are the objectives and advantages of budgetary control?

3 Write short explanatory notes on: (a) budget committee; (b) budget period; (c) review period.

4 Distinguish clearly between the following: (a) operating budgets and capital budgets; (b) departmental budgets and master budgets; (c) fixed budgets and flexible budgets.

5 Explain what you understand by 'limiting factor'.

6 Write short notes on how you would prepare the following: (a) sales budget; (b) cash budget; (c) maintenance budget; (d) housekeeping budget; (e) budgeted balance sheet.

7 The Leaning Tower Restaurant is a large, unlicensed restaurant and operates a system of budgetary control. Its bank balance on 1st April, 19.. is £16 000. From the information given below you are to prepare a cash budget for the quarter ending 30th June, 19..

Budgeted sales

	February	March	April	May	June
Cash sales	12 000	13 000	15 600	17 200	20 400
Credit sales	6 400	7 000	8 400	8 800	9 000
Total	18 400	20 000	24 000	26 000	29 400

Notes: You are informed that 80 per cent of credit sales are settled by clients within one month; the balance of 20 per cent is settled with a time lag of two months.

Budgeted food cost

The restaurant operates at a food cost of 40 per cent. Thirty per cent of food cost represents current cash purchases. Seventy per cent of food cost is purchased on credit and settled in the month following purchase.

Budgeted labour costs

	April	May	June
Kitchen staff	£2 430	£2 830	£3 350
Waiting staff	1 870	2 150	2 470
Other	1 100	1 220	1 220
	£5 400	£6 200	£7 040

Note: The time lag in the payment of labour costs is nil.

Budgeted overheads

	January	February	March	April	May	June
	£	£	£	£	£	£
Rent				1 400	1 400	1 400
Rates				700	700	700
Depreciation				1 640	1 640	1 640
Insurance				20	20	20
Gas	150	150	160	160	170	180
Electricity	150	100	80	70	80	90
Telephone	20	20	30	30	30	40
Total				4 020	4 040	4 070

Note:

(a) The rent of the restaurant is payable in two half-yearly instalments, each March and September;

(b) Half-yearly demand notes in respect of rates are received each April and October;

(c) The full annual insurance premium is payable on 17th April;

(d) The gas, electricity and telephone accounts are payable quarterly each January, April, July and October;

(e) The time lag is the payment of overheads is one month; this does not apply to the insurance premium.

8 From the following information prepare a cash budget for the months of June, July, August and September, 19..

	£
1st June, 19.. bank balance	51 269
sales for April, 19..	31 465
sales for May, 19..	29 658
Estimated sales for June, 19..	42 147
,, ,, ,, July, 19..	58 393
,, ,, ,, August, 19..	61 215
,, ,, ,, September, 19..	52 147
Investment income due 30th June, 19.., £1 000—receivable in July, 19...	
Estimated expenses for June, 19.. (including wages and salaries)	10 213
Estimated expenses for July, 19..	10 869
,, ,, ,, August, 19..	11 019
,, ,, ,, September, 19..	10 542
Purchases for May, 19..	49 251
Estimated purchases for June, 19..	52 375
,, ,, ,, July. 19..	19 142
,, ,, ,, August, 19..	11 641
,, ,, ,, September, 19..	16 842
Rent payable on 30th June, 19..	1 200
Rent payable on 30th September, 19..	1 200

Interim dividend of 5 per cent on capital of £50 000 payable on 1st July, 19..

Allow for 2 months' credit on sales.

Allow for 1 month's credit on purchases.

Discuss briefly the use of such a cash budget.

M.H.C.I.

9 From the following forecasts of income and expenditure prepare a cash budget for the six months commencing 1st April, 19...

Notes:

(a) Assume that all sales are on a cash basis;

(b) The time lag in the payment of suppliers' accounts is two months;
(c) The time lag in the payment of overheads is one month; in the case of labour it is nil;
(d) New furniture, costing £6 000, will be purchased in June and paid on delivery;
(e) The annual interest on the company's investments will be received in August; the amount is £1 000.

Month	Sales		Purchases		Labour	Overheads
	Food	Beverages	Food	Beverages		
	£	£	£	£	£	£
February	20 000	6 000	8 000	3 000	8 000	7 000
March	22 000	6 200	8 800	3 100	8 400	7 000
April	24 000	7 200	9 600	3 600	8 400	7 200
May	28 000	8 400	11 200	4 200	9 200	7 200
June	32 000	9 600	12 800	4 800	10 000	7 400
July	36 000	10 800	14 400	5 400	10 000	7 400
August	32 000	9 600	12 800	4 800	9 600	7 400
September	26 000	7 800	10 400	3 900	8 800	7 200

You are informed that the company's bank balance on 1st April, 19.. was £20 000.

10 A large, licensed seasonal restaurant is managed by two partners, A and B. The restaurant was opened on 1st January, 19.., and at the end of the first year of its operation, the following accounts were prepared:

Trading, profit and loss appropriation account
for the year ended 31st December, 19..

Cost of sales			Sales:		
Food	134 000		Food	330 000	
Beverages	56 000		Beverages	170 000	
		190 000			500 000
Gross profit c/d		310 000			
		500 000			500 000
Wages and salaries		148 000	Gross profit b/d	310 000	5 000
Rates		24 000	Rent receivable		
Insurance		2 000			
Advertising		8 000			
Printing and stationery		5 000			
Laundry and cleaning		4 000			
Depreciation		32 000			
Repairs and renewals		11 000			
Light and heat		12 000			
Miscellaneous expenses		2 000			
Net profit		67 000			
		315 000			315 000

(continued)

Salary:			Net Profit	67 000
A	15 000			
B	15 000			
		30 000		
Net profit:				
A—½	18 500			
B—½	18 500			
		37 000		
		67 000		67 000

Balance sheet
as at 31st December, 19. .

Capital accounts			Fixed assets		
A	125 000		Leasehold	150 000	
B	125 000		Kitchen plant	40 000	
		250 000	Furniture	50 000	
			China and cutlery	5 000	
Current accounts					245 000
A	6 500				
B	6 500		Current assets		
		13 000	Stocks	7 500	
Current liabilities***			Debtors*	4 000	
Creditors	4 000		Prepayments**	6 500	
Accrued advertising	3 000		Cash at bank	7 000	
		7 000			25 000
		270 000			270 000

* *Receivable in month 1*
** Consists of prepaid rates £6 000 and prepaid insurance £500.
*** Payable in month 1.

The partners are anxious to introduce from the beginning of the following year a simple system of budgetary control. They have prepared the following sales budget for the year commencing 1st January, 19...

Sales Budget

	Food	Beverages
	£	£
Month 1	10 000	5 000
,, 2	15 000	7 500
,, 3	20 000	10 000
,, 4	30 000	15 000
,, 5	40 000	20 000
,, 6	55 000	27 500
,, 7	55 000	27 500
,, 8	50 000	25 000
,, 9	45 000	22 500
,, 10	35 000	17 500
,, 11	20 000	10 000
,, 12	15 000	7 500
,, 13	10 000	5 000
	400 000	200 000

Notes on sales budget:
(1) All beverage sales are on a cash basis.
(2) Half the food sales are cash sales: the other (credit) sales are settled by customers with a time lag of one month.

You are required by the partners to prepare the following draft budgets for their consideration:
(1) An expense budget;
(2) A cash budget (showing the balance available at the end of each month);
(3) A budgeted profit and loss account;
(4) A budgeted balance sheet.

You are given the following information on the various draft budgets you are to prepare:
Expense budget: This, as well as the cash budget, is to cover the ensuing financial year of twelve calendar months.
Wages and salaries: The partners intend to employ additional labour to cope with the budgeted increase in sales and, having analysed the staffing of the restaurant, inform you that the budgeted cost of wages and salaries for the coming year should be:

Month	1	£9 000
,,	2	9 000
,,	3	11 000
,,	4	12 000
,,	5	12 000
,,	6	14 000
,,	7	16 000
,,	8	14000
,,	9	12 000
,,	10	12 000
,,	11	12 000
,,	12	10 000
,,	13	9 000
	Total	£152 000

All wages and salaries are paid by the restaurant weekly.
Rates: The rate in the £ is expected to remain constant in the coming year. The rates are paid half-yearly in advance each month 4 and month 10.
Insurance: This will remain unchanged. The premiums are paid half-yearly in advance—in months 3 and 9.
Advertising: This consists of press advertising only. The partners have decided to spend the same amount as in the previous year. Of the £8 000 one-half will be spent in month 3 and £2 000 will be spent in months 4 and 5 each.
Printing and stationery: Owing to an increase in printing costs and the partners' intention to introduce more attractively printed menus the budgeted expenditure on this item is expected to increase by £1 000. Of the £6 000 one-half will be spent in month 1 and the rest of the expenditure will be incurred in the remaining months.
Laundry and cleaning: The amount budgeted by the partners for this item is £4 500. In months 6, 7 and 8 the cost of this item will be £500 per month, in the remaining ten months it will be £300 per month. The time lag in the payment of this expenditure is one month.
Depreciation: This will remain as in the previous year, i.e.

Leasehold	£19 000
Kitchen plant	7 000
Furniture	6 000

Repairs and renewals: The partners budget to spend £13 000 on this item. Of this £6 000 is to be paid out in month 3 in respect of urgent external repairs and the balance is to be made available for other repairs to be carried out towards the close of the season and paid out in month 12.
Light and heat: It is anticipated that as a result of the additional volume of sales the budgeted amount for this item should be £12 500. The cash payments will be as follows:

Month 4	£3 500
,, 7	3 000
,, 11	2 500
,, 13	3 500
Total	£12 500

Miscellaneous expenses: This item consists of a large number of small items. The budgeted amount for the ensuing year is £2 600 and, you are informed, there is no time lag in the payment of these items.
Cash budget: The partners have decided to leave the balances owing to them (see current accounts) until month 6, when they hope the cash position of the restaurant will warrant withdrawing these sums.

They also intend to draw cash from the business in anticipation of profits at the rate of £1 000 each, commencing in month 7.

The rent receivable is in respect of the premises sub-let to a travel agency and is payable in full at the end of each year calendar year.
Budgeted profit and loss account: It is intended by the partners that the restaurant should operate at an overall gross profit margin of 60 per cent.

It is planned that half the cost of sales for any one period should be cash purchases, the other half being credit purchases to be settled the month following purchase.

The net profit of the restaurant is to be divided between the partners in the same manner as in the previous year.
Budgeted balance sheet: No new acquisitions of fixed assets are planned by the partners.

It is intended that the stocks should be maintained at the same level as at the end of the first year of operation.

CHAPTER 22

Assessment of Capital Projects

Introduction The main purpose of the present chapter is to explain and illustrate the main methods of assessing the commercial viability of capital expenditure.

The hotel and catering industry is not only labour-intensive but also capital intensive. This is particularly so in the case of hotels, where the capital cost per bedroom has risen very substantially in recent years. In all sectors of the industry the acquisition of kitchen plant, furniture and other assets entails large capital outlays. Quite clearly, therefore, unless we are familiar with appropriate techniques of assessing capital projects we are not going to make the best use of available resources.

Funds available are always limited; and there are at all times numerous investment opportunities. Hence, the central problem here is to decide how best to invest the limited resources of the business in relation to the investment opportunities that present themselves. Thus a hotel may have accumulated cash balances of £250 000 which are not needed for current operational purposes. The hotel may be short of bedroom accommodation and have sufficient space to build an extension. Another possible outlet for the cash balances might be to take over an existing hotel. It may well be that the existing facilities (bedrooms, public rooms, dining rooms etc.) are in need of modernisation. Finally, the cash available may be invested outside, either in the hotel and catering industry or in some other industry.

Certainly where the choice is as wide as indicated above it is a difficult problem to decide in which direction the cash resources should be channelled. The starting point for the complex process of decision-making must surely be the objectives of the business. We must, first of all, define the main objectives to the business and then decide how we can best use what resources are available to achieve these objectives. In the case of a hotel or restaurant the main objective will naturally be maximum long-run profitability. Hence, other things being equal, all resources should be directed to investment opportunities which help to maximize profit in the long run.

In addition to profitability a business may have other, on occasion, equally important objectives. A new business may, in the first year or two, concentrate on building up its clientele and its turnover and, during this early stage of its growth, regard profitability as of lesser importance. In such circumstances expenditure which is likely to increase turnover might be given some priority over expenditure designed specifically to increase profitability. Similarly, a well-established business may find itself facing increasing competition from nearby competitors, in which event retention of its share of the market might be regarded as the prime objective.

Finally, it should be realized that expenditure on capital projects commits the resources of the business for a long period of years. Once an extension to a hotel/restaurant has been built the resources of the business have been committed for a long time. Hence, the larger the amount involved and the longer the period of investment the more carefully a project should be examined before a final decision is made.

There are three main methods of assessing capital projects: the pay-back method, the return on investment method and the discounted cash flow (D.C.F.) method.

Pay-back method The pay-back method looks at the number of years (i.e. the pay-back period) in which a project will pay for itself out of savings in expenditure or additional profits. It should be noted that we are concerned with two elements here: time and cash; time, because the stress is on the speedy recovery of the initial cash outlay, and cash because this particular method is concerned with cash rather than profits.

The formula for calculating the pay-back period is simple. One divides the cost of the project by the cash profits or savings in cash costs and thus obtains the pay-back period for each project. Other things being equal, one chooses the project with the shortest pay-back period. In some cases the annual cash profits or savings in cash expenditure are not constant over a period of time. The pay-back period would, in such circumstances, be arrived at by accumulating cash profits or cash savings until one reached a figure equal to the cost of the project.

Example The annual cost of running the bill office of a hotel is as follows:

Supervisor	£12 000
3 Clerks @ £8 000	24 000
Stationery	2 000
Total	£38 000

The manager proposes to mechanize the bill office and, to this end, purchases two billing machines costing £10 500 each and having an estimated life of seven years. He estimates that the cost of the new system will be as follows:

Supervisor	£12 000
2 Clerks @ £8 500	17 000
Depreciation	3 000
Stationery, maintenance, etc.	4 000
Total	£36 000

The cost of the project (immediate cash outlay) is £21 000. The savings of cash expenditure are:

Cost of old system	£38 000
Less cost of new system (£36 000 less £3 000 depreciation)	33 000
Cash costs saved p.a.	£5 000

Therefore the pay-back period is:

$$\frac{£21\,000}{£5\,000} = 4.2 \text{ years.}$$

In other words the loss of cash resources (£21 000) following the acquisition of the billing machines will be recovered from savings in cash expenditure in about four years and two months.

The main advantages of the pay-back method are its simplicity and ease of application. It is for these reasons that this method is liked by businessmen. The method has, however, some serious disadvantages. Firstly, the orientation of the method is wrong: it stresses the recovery of capital expenditure whilst the main objective of business activity is profitability. Secondly, the pay-back method ignores the element of time and assumes that £1 in the future is worth as much as £1 now. Finally, the method looks at the pay-back period and, often, what happens after the pay-back period is more important than the duration of the pay-back period itself.

Example A catering company considers two alternative capital projects, A and B, each costing £10 000 and having an estimated life of ten years. Given below are the estimated cash profits from the two projects.

Year	*Estimated cash profits:* A		B	
1	£4 000		£2 000	
2	3 000		2 000	
3	3 000	£10 000	3 000	
4	2 000		3 000	£10 000
5	2 000		4 000	
6	2 000		4 000	
7	1 000		5 000	
8	1 000		5 000	
9	1 000		6 000	
10	1 000		6 000	
	£20 000		£40 000	

Project A has a pay-back period of 3 years and project B has a pay-back period of 4 years. Yet the cash profits from project B are twice those from project A. It is obvious that in such circumstances the duration of the pay-back period would not be the sole criterion for the final choice between A and B.

In spite of the foregoing deficiences of the pay-back method, it is one which is useful to apply particularly in conjunction with the other methods discussed below.

Return on investment method

This method concentrates on the percentage return (net profit) in relation to the capital cost of a project. Where there are several capital projects being considered then, according to this approach, the project showing the highest return is chosen.

The percentage return on investment is obtained by relating the net profit from a project to half the capital cost of the project, e.g.:

$$\frac{\text{Net profit}-£1\,000}{\text{Cost of project}-\frac{1}{2}\text{ of }£10\,000} = 20\%$$

The reason for taking only one-half of the capital cost of the project is this. After the purchase of an asset depreciation is written off and, in this way, the capital cost of the asset is recovered via the profit and loss account. As a result, the net amount invested in the asset is diminishing throughout the life of the asset until, at the end of its effective life, it is nil.

Let us assume that £5 000 is invested in an asset having an estimated life of 5 years: also, that depreciation is written off on the straight-line method. The average annual investment in the asset and the average investment over the life of the asset will be as shown in Figure 210.

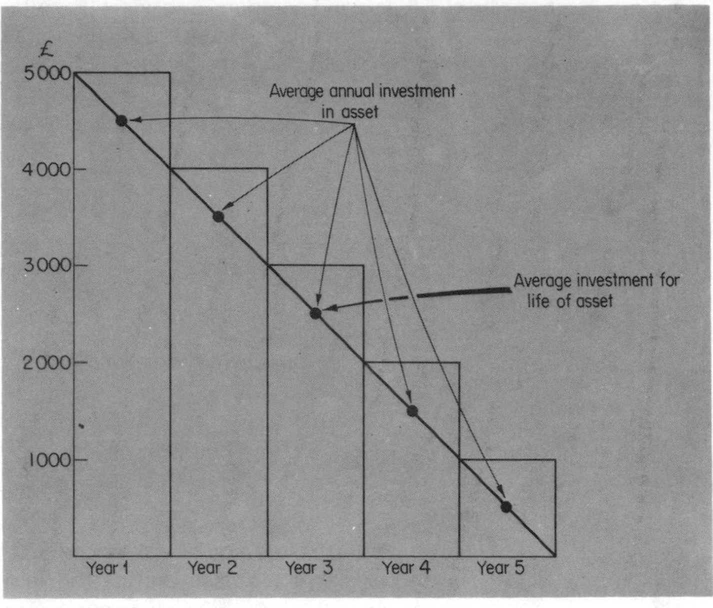

Figure 210

Example A hotel company is considering two mutually exclusive projects, A and B, costing £20 000 each and having an estimated life of five years, as shown below:

	Project A	Project B
Cost of project	£20 000	£20 000
Estimated profits:		
Year 1	£3 000	£1 000
Year 2	2 000	1 000
Year 3	1 000	2 000
Year 4	1 000	2 000
Year 5	1 000	3 000
Total	£8 000	£9 000
Average profits p.a.	£1 600	£1 800
Return on investment ($\frac{1}{2}$ of £20 000)	16%	18%

The advantages of this method are clear: it is easy to understand, simple to apply and it has the correct orientation (it looks at profitability). However, a major disadvantage of this method is that it ignores the timing of revenue inflow. Although the return on project B is somewhat higher than that on project A, it may be seen that the 'earnings profile' of project B is less favourable, as more than half the projected profits are made in the last two years of the life of the project. Clearly, however, profits in year 1 are preferable to profits in later years. This the return on investment method ignores.

Discounted cash flow (D.C.F.) method

The present value concept

The element of time as a complicating factor in the assessment of capital projects has already been mentioned. The two methods already described assume that £1 in the future is equivalent in value to £1 now. Quite obviously, this assumption is incorrect.

Let us take an example. £100 invested today at 10 per cent will increase to £110 in a year's time. Over a period of two years the initial sum (£100) will increase to £121. Hence, given that the rate of interest is 10 per cent, the value of £100 receivable in a year's time is $\frac{£100}{£110} = £90.91$. The present-day value of £100 receivable in two year's time is only $\frac{£100}{£121} = £82.64$. The general rule then is this: given a particular rate of interest the more distant (in time) the cash the lower its present-day value, and vice versa. Secondly, the higher the rate of interest the lower its present-day value of any sum receivable in the future. This is illustrated in Figure 211.

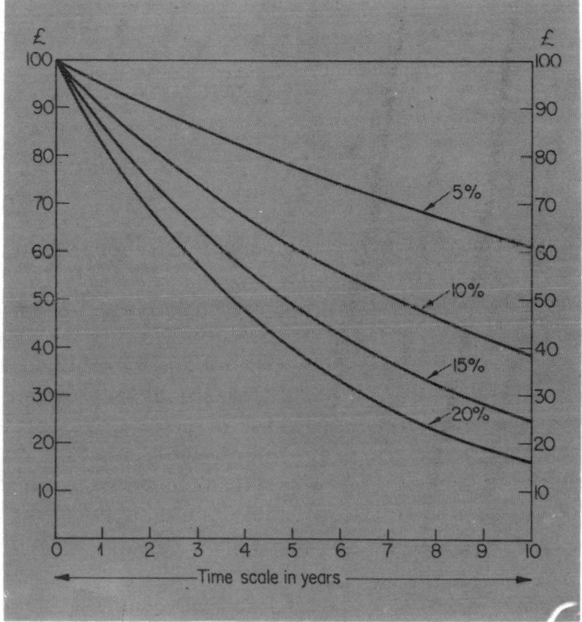

Figure 211

As may be seen from Figure 211 £100 receivable in ten year's time has (given interest at 5 per cent) a present-day value of just over £61. Assuming that the appropriate rate of interest is 20 per cent, the present-day value of £100 receivable in ten year's time is just over £16. It should be appreciated that the process of discounting is the opposite of the process of compounding. Hence, £61.39 invested at 5 per cent compound interest will, over ten years, increase to £100. Similarly, £16.15 invested at 20 per cent (compound interest) will in ten years grow to reach £100. This is illustrated in Figure 212.

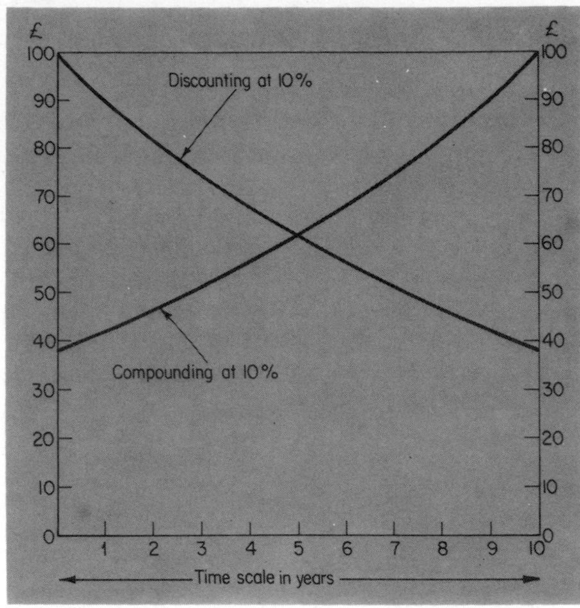

Figure 212

Mechanics of D.C.F. Under the D.C.F. method this approach to the assessment of capital projects is this. When a project is undertaken there is an immediate cash outflow (cost of project). Subsequently, each year over the life of the project there is some cash inflow. As cash in the future is less valuable than cash now, it is necessary to 'discount' these future cash flows to find their present-day value. When the discounting has been done it is possible to compare the cost of the project with the present-day value of the sum total of the future cash inflows.

Where the total of the discounted cash inflows is less than the cost of the project, there is clearly no point in undertaking the project as a loss would be incurred. Naturally, the greater the excess of the discounted cash flows over the cost of the project the more profitable the project.

The conversion of future cash flows to present-day values is easiest with the aid of a D.C.F. interest table, which shows the present-day value of £1 discounted for different numbers of years and at different rates of interest. Thus, the conversion factor for 10 per cent over 5 years is 0·6209. This means that, assuming interest at 10 per cent, the present-day value of £1 receivable in 5 years is approximately 62p. It also means that, at this rate of interest, £10 000 receivable in 5 years is equivalent in value to £6 209 today as the latter sum invested at 10 per cent will increase to £10 000 in 5 years' time (see D.C.F. table, p. 342).

Example 1 A hotel is considering a capital project costing £50 000. The projected cash inflow over the life of the project is given below. Let us assume that the appropriate rate of interest is 10 per cent.

Year	Cash inflow	Conversion factor	Present value
1	£5 000	0·9091	£4 546
2	5 000	0·8264	4 132
3	6 000	0·7513	4 508
4	7 000	0·6830	4 781
5	9 000	0·6209	5 588
6	10 000	0·5645	5 645
7	10 000	0·5132	5 132
8	10 000	0·4665	4 665
	£62 000		£38 997

The actual cash inflow over eight years will be £62 000. The present-day value of the £62 000 receivable in the future is only £38 997. As the cost of the project is £50 000 there is no point in going ahead with it and, in effect, exchanging £50 000 now for £62 000 in the future worth only £38 997 now.

Example 2 A catering concern is considering two possible projects, costing £14 000 each as shown below:

	Project X	Project Y
Cash inflow:		
Year 1	£2 000	£6 000
,, 2	3 000	5 000
,, 3	4 000	4 000
,, 4	6 000	3 000
,, 5	6 000	2 000
	£21 000	£20 000

Let us assume that the rate of interest appropriate in this case is 11 per cent. The D.C.F. calculations are given below.

Year	Conversion factor	X		Y	
1	0·9009	£2 000 =	£1 802	£6 000 =	£5 405
2	0·8116	3 000 =	2 435	5 000 =	4 058
3	0·7312	4 000 =	2 925	4 000 =	2 925
4	0·6587	6 000 =	3 952	3 000 =	1 976
5	0·5935	6 000 =	3 561	2 000 =	1 187
		£21 000 =	£14 675	£20 000 =	£15 551

The calculations above suggest that:

(a) Both projects are likely to be profitable as they both show some 'net gain', i.e. excess of the total of discounted cash flows over the cost of the project.

(b) Project X will generate a greater cash inflow in the future than project Y, but the present-day value of the £20 000 (for Y) is higher than the present-day value of the £21 000 (for X).

(c) The cash inflow profile of project Y is more favourable as relatively more cash is likely to flow into the business in the early years of the project. This is another reason why, on balance, project Y is to be preferred to project X. It should be stressed that the calculation of future cash flows entails numerous forecasts (e.g. turnover, cost levels, etc.). The more distant the future the less certain we are about the accuracy of such forecasts. Hence the cash inflow profile is an important criterion in this kind of decision-making.

Meaning of cash flow

Cash flow is not synonymous with profits. It may be defined as net profit before depreciation less tax.

It will be appreciated that depreciation, although properly chargeable in financial accounts, is a non-cash expense; that is to say, it is debited in the profit and loss account but it does not entail a cash outflow. Hence, when calculating the cost flow resulting from a capital project depreciation must be ignored.

Any tax paid on the profits generated by a capital project represents an actual cash outflow. Tax must, therefore, be deducted to obtain the figures for D.C.F. purposes. In order to obtain accurate figures of cash flow it is essential to ascertain the timing of the payment of tax liabilities as, invariably, tax is paid some time after the earning of profits.

Choice of rate of interest

It is difficult to suggest a simple formula for the choice of an appropriate rate of interest at which to discount future cash flows. The circumstances of each business will differ somewhat; also the source of funds for a project will differ from one case to another. It is, therefore, only possible to suggest some general principles which affect the choice of the rate of interest.

Briefly, any investment in a capital project should be regarded as follows: one invests a certain amount of resources (capital) which have a cost (rate of interest) in order to secure earnings in excess of that cost. The choice of the rate of interest for discounting future cash flows must, therefore be based on cost of securing the necessary funds for the project concerned. Hence, it is essential to adopt a 'cost of capital approach.

Where a project is financed by a bank loan then future cash flows should be discounted at the same rate of interest as is payable on the loan. When the funds are obtained by the issue of debentures the rate for discounting cash flows should be based on the rate of interest payable to debenture holders. Where a project is financed with internal resources then, it is suggested, the rate of interest should reflect the average cost of capital to the business over a period of time. In the case of a company which has obtained its capital through the issue of ordinary shares, preference shares and debentures the cost of capital would not be readily apparent and would require rather detailed calculations. Many companies establish a long-run internal rate of interest for D.C.F. purposes. This reflects the long-run cost of capital to the company and is applied to all proposed capital projects.

Capital projects with indeterminate profitability

Our consideration of the methods of assessment of capital projects has, so far, centred around projects which have measurable consequences on the profitability of the business. There are, however, many projects which have a measurable cost but whose consequences on the earnings of the business are almost impossible to assess.

Education and training projects are, no doubt, in this category. The cost of a proposed training department is fairly easy to calculate. There is often no doubt that the introduction of a training programme is highly desirable and likely to lead to greater efficiency. However, the precise effect of improved efficiency on turnover, operating costs and profitability is not, by any means, certain.

The provision of improved canteen facilities in a factory is certainly likely to have a positive effect on the morale and health of the employees. To what extent this is going to improve the earnings of the business is quite uncertain. Many prestige projects are in this category: expensive cars for company executives, big executive desks, expensive carpets in offices, etc.

In all these cases an assessment of the proposed capital expenditure is diffciult. Yet whenever resources are to be committed a decision one way or another must be made. One possible solution is to rely on the collective value judgment of the decision-makers (e.g. board of directors, budget committee). When there are several such projects possible, the individuals concerned should be asked to indicate their respective preferences as between the various projects and to state their degree of preference (e.g. essential, desirable, possible). It is then possible to quantify the general opinion and express it in terms of a collective and definite decision.

Problems

1 'Resources are always scarce in relation to investment opportunities.' Discuss.

2 'All resources should be directed to investment opportunities which help to maximize long-run profits.' Explain.

3 Explain the pay-back method of assessing capital projects and enumerate its main limitations.

4 What do you understand by 'return on investment', in relation to the assessment of capital projects? Explain the main advantages and disadvantages of this method.

5 Explain what you understand by: (a) discounting, and (b) compounding.

6 What is 'cash flow'?

7 'There are many capital projects which have a measurable cost but whose consequences on the earnings of the business are impossible to assess.' Explain.

8 Discount the following cash flows at 10 per cent and comment on your results.

Year		Project A	Project B
1		£2 000	£5 000
2		3 000	4 000
3		4 000	3 000
4		5 000	2 000
	Total cash flows	£14 000	£14 000

9 A hotel company is considering two projects, A and B

	A	B
Cost of project	£100 000	£160 000
Cash flow: year 1	£20 000	£30 000
2	25 000	35 000
3	30 000	35 000
4	30 000	55 000
5	25 000	45 000
	£130 000	£200 000

(a) Assess the relative profitability of each project.
(b) Comment on the relevance of the size of the project to the final investment decision.

10 Using appropriate graphical methods, show:
(a) the effect of compounding £42.24 at 9 per cent over 10 years;
(b) the effect of discounting £100.00 at 18 per cent over 10 years.

11 Two alternative projects, costing £20 000 each, are being considered. The projected cash flows are given below.

Year	Project A	Probject B
1	£8 000	£4 000
2	7 000	6 000
3	6 000	7 000
4	5 000	7 000
5	4 000	8 000
	£30 000	£32 000

Assuming that interest at 11 per cent is appropriate in this case, state which project should be preferred.

12 A company is considering a capital project costing £40 000. The sales forecast and the relevant costs are given below.

Year	Sales	Cost of sales	Other vble costs	Fxd costs excl deprctn	Depreciation
1	£20 000	£6 000	£2 000	£3 000	£10 000
2	30 000	9 000	3 000	3 000	10 000
3	40 000	12 000	4 000	3 000	10 000
4	30 000	9 000	3 000	3 000	10 000
	£120 000	£36 000	£12 000	£12 000	£40 000

You are required to:
(a) calculate the pay-back period for the project;
(b) calculate the return on this investment;
(c) assess the project by means of the D.C.F. method; assume that the appropriate rate of interest is 10 per cent;
(d) prepare a break-even chart for the above project and comment appropriately.

13 A company is considering a capital project costing £50 000 and having an effective life of five years. Given below are preliminary forecasts of sales of costs.

Year	Sales	Cost of sales	Depreciation	Other costs
	£	£	£	£
1	20 000	7 000	10 000	4 000
2	20 000	7 000	10 000	4 000
3	30 000	9 000	10 000	5 000
4	30 000	9 000	10 000	6 000
5	50 000	13 000	10 000	6 000

You are required to:
(a) calculate the payback period for the project;
(b) calculate the return on this investment;
(c) assess the project by means of the D.C.F. method, assuming that the appropriate rate of interest in this case is 11 per cent.

14 It is proposed to mechanize a department of a hotel. The cost of the necessary machines and equipment is £38 000, and installation costs will amount to £2 000. The estimated life of the new assets is six years, at the end of which they will have a nil scrap value. All work in the department is at present done manually and the annual costs for the next six years are estimated as follows:

Year	1	2	3	4	5	6
	£	£	£	£	£	£
Labour costs	22 000	23 000	24 000	25 000	26 000	28 000
Supplies	400	500	500	600	600	700
Total cost	22 400	23 500	24 500	25 600	26 600	28 700

The cost of the mechanized operation is projected as follows:

Year	1	2	3	4	5	6
	£	£	£	£	£	£
Labour costs	10 000	11 000	12 000	13 000	14 000	14 000
Electric power	400	400	500	500	600	600
Supplies	600	600	700	700	800	900
Repairs	—	—	200	200	300	400
Total cost	11 000	12 000	13 400	14 400	15 700	15 900

You are required to calculate:
(a) the pay-back period;
(b) the net present value of the project, assuming that the appropriate rate of interest is 10 per cent.

CHAPTER 23

Uniform accounts and inter-firm comparison

Uniform accounts

Uniform accounts are by no means a new concept in accounting practice. Several dozen schemes of uniform accounts have been devised in the last few decades, and some of these have now been in use for a long time in a variety of industries.

A scheme of uniform accounts must satisfy several conditions. Firstly, there is the necessity for uniformity in accounting records. Both subsidiary books and ledger accounts kept by the participants must be uniform in layout and enable the recording of all transactions in a pre-determined manner.

Secondly, a scheme of uniform accounts necessitates a high degree of standardization in the recording of all income and expenditure. Thus the scheme must identify the main functions or divisions of business (e.g. apartments, food, drink etc.), and lay down procedures for systematic and consistent recording of all income and expenditure in relation to each function of the business. This, in turn, necessitates some system of coding of accounts to ensure that all businesses participating in the scheme treat particular items of income and expenditure in the same manner.

Finally, uniform accounting necessitates uniformity of accounting practice in matters such as valuation of fixed assets, methods of depreciation, valuation of stocks, apportionment of fixed expenses to departments, etc.

Quite clearly a scheme of uniform accounting offers many advantages to an industry. The accounting procedures laid down by such a scheme are invariably based on the best practice in the industry. There follows, as a result, a general improvement in accounting methods and procedures in the business concerned. As there is uniformity in the recording of income and expenditure there is also more uniformity in the preparation of cost estimates, pricing methods, quotations etc.

Uniform accounting is often linked with a system of inter-firm comparison. When that is so, the participants are able to compare their own trading results with those of competitors similarly placed and thus initiate, where required, corrective measures.

It must not be assumed that the introduction of uniform accounting is easy. Standardization of accounting methods and procedures is always difficult, and not only because it implies a change from existing practice. It is certainly true to say that standardization of accounts is particularly difficult in the case of a heterogeneous industry like the hotel and catering industry. Clearly, it would be impossible to have one system of uniform accounts for all the different types of establishment (hotels, restaurants, canteens, etc.). Even within a particular sector of the industry (e.g. hotels) there are great differences from one unit to another. Hotels differ in price, size, location, sales mix, etc. All these factors militate against the easy adoption of uniform accounting, however desirable the latter may be.

The full benefit of uniform accounting can only be derived when a business adopts the scheme and takes part in a related scheme of inter-firm comparison. Many businessmen feel that they do not wish to part with what they regard as confidential information and, as a result, have little inclination both to adopt uniform accounts and participate in inter-firm comparison.

In August, 1969, the Economic Development Committee for Hotels and Catering published a scheme of uniform accounts for hotels. This is known as the 'Standard System of Hotel Accounting'. It is certainly desirable that the scheme should be accepted by the hotel sector of the industry. However, its degree of popularity will only be apparent over a period of years, when hoteliers have had the opportunity to acquaint themselves with the standard system.

Standard system of hotel accounting

The purpose of this section is to explain some of the main features of the standard system of hotel accounting. For a detailed description of the system the student is referred to the manual itself.

The standard system provides for a basic classification of accounts as follows:

(a) classification of profit and loss accounts;
(b) classification of balance sheet accounts.

In addition the manual gives examples of operating statements and a summary balance sheet; also there is an alphabetical list of accounts in the basic classification.

Profit and loss accounts

The system distinguishes three 'operated departments':

(i) rooms;
(ii) food;
(iii) liquor and tobacco.

These are departments which 'with a measurable use of labour, engage directly in the services and commodities provided for hotel guests'.

In order to control the financial operation of the hotel several 'control levels' are suggested by the system. These are illustrated below.

Operated Department's Net Sales
less Cost of Sales
equals Departmental GROSS PROFIT

Gross Profit
less Wages and Staff Costs
equals Departmental NET MARGIN

Net Margin
less Allocated Expenses
equals Departmental OPERATING PROFIT

Departmental Operating Profit
plus Other Income
equals Hotel OPERATING INCOME

Hotel Operating Income
less Service Departments and General Expenditure
equals Hotel OPERATING PROFIT

Hotel Operating Profit
less Repairs, Plant and Property Expenses
equals Hotel NET OPERATING PROFIT

Thus there are six basic control levels at which it is possible to evaluate the financial progress of the hotel.

Figure 213 shows the recommended layout of a Summary Operating Statement for the operated departments.

THIS PERIOD						*YEAR TO DATE*			
BUDGET		*ACTUAL*			*ACCOUNT*	*ACTUAL*		*BUDGET*	
£	%	£	%	*CODE*	*DETAIL*	£	%	£	%
					OPERATED DEPARTMENTS				
					Net sales				
5,000	35.7			01	Rooms				
6,000	42.9			02	Food				
3,000	21.4			03	Liquor & tobacco				
14,000	100.0				TOTAL NET SALES				
					Gross profit				
5,000				01	Rooms				
4,010	66.8			02	Food				
1,140	38.0			03	Liquor & tobacco				
10,150	72.5				TOTAL GROSS PROFIT				
					Wages & staff costs				
1,300	26.0			01	Rooms				
1,800	30.0			02	Food				
460	15.3			03	Liquor & tobacco				
3,560	25.4				TOTAL WAGES & STAFF COSTS				
					Net margin				
3,700	74.0			01	Rooms				
2,210	36.8			02	Food				
680	22.6			03	Liquor & tobacco				
6,590	47.0				TOTAL NET MARGIN				
					Department operating profit				
3,400	68.0			01	Rooms				
1,810	30.1			02	Food				
530	17.7			03	Liquor & tobacco				
5,740	41.0				TOTAL DEPARTMENT OPERATING PROFIT				
500				09	OTHER INCOME				
6,240	44.5				HOTEL OPERATING INCOME				
					Service departments & general expenditure				
1,250	8.9			11	Administration				
550	3.9			12	Sales advertising & promotion				
520	3.7			13	Heat, light & power				
1,150	8.2			19	General expenditure				
(550)	(3.9)			159	Staff accommodation adjustment				
2,920	20.9				TOTAL SERVICE DEPARTMENTS & GENERAL EXPENDITURE				
3,320	23.7				HOTEL OPERATING PROFIT				
400	2.8			21	Repairs & maintenance				
450	3.2			22	Plant & machinery				
450	3.2			23	Property				
1,300	9.2								
2,020	14.5				HOTEL NET OPERATING PROFIT				
(60)				31	Non-operating income & expenditure				
1,960	14.0				NET PROFIT, before TAX				

Figure 213

In addition to the Summary Operating Statement a departmental operating statement would be prepared for each of the operated departments. An example for the Food Department is given below in Figure 214. It will be observed that the departmental operating statements take the income and expenditure only to the level of departmental operating profit.

THIS PERIOD						*YEAR TO DATE*			
BUDGET		*ACTUAL*			*ACCOUNT*	*ACTUAL*		*BUDGET*	
£	%	£	%	*CODE*	*DETAIL*	£	%	£	%
5,500				011	Restaurant sales				
550				031	Banquets				
6,050					*TOTAL SALES*				
50				091	Allowances to guests				
6,000	100.0				*NET SALES*				
2,500				101	Food purchases				
120				109	Food stock inc/Dec				
20				125	Stock losses				
(40)				126	Sale of kitchen waste (Cr)				
(610)				127	Cost of staff meals & liquor (Cr)				
				128	Cost of entertaining (Cr)				
1,990	33.2				*COST OF SALES*				
4,010	66.8				*GROSS PROFIT*				
1,200				131	Gross pay				
40				132	GPF				
60				133	NI & SET				
50				134	Holiday pay				
250				135	Staff meals & liquor				
200				136	Staff accommodation				
1,800	30.0				*TOTAL WAGES & STAFF COSTS*				
2,210	36.8				*NET MARGIN*				
60				201	Department supplies				
60				202	Flowers & decor				
20				211	Printing & stationery				
40				232	Kitchen fuel				
40				271	Laundry & dry cleaners' charges				
20				272	Cleaning contracts				
80				282	Music & entertainers				
10				324	Trade licences				
20				411	Linen				
10				412	Uniforms				
10				413	Plate & cutlery				
20				414	Glass & china				
10				415	Utensils				
400	6.7				*TOTAL ALLOCATED EXPENSE*				
1,810	30.1				*DEPARTMENT OPERATING PROFIT*				

Figure 214

Balance sheet The standard system also recommends a form of vertical balance sheet. This is intended for internal use (i.e. not for publication). A specimen Summary Balance Sheet is shown in Figure 215 below.

Category Code		*Balance as at:* End of last period	End of this period	*Increase/ decrease*
	FIXED ASSETS			
51	Property			
52	Plant & machinery			
55	General equipment			
56	Investments & loans			
58	Goodwill			
	(Net of depreciation)			
	TOTAL FIXED ASSETS	£		
59	*OTHER ASSETS*			
	TOTAL FIXED & OTHER ASSETS	£		
	CURRENT ASSETS			
61	Stocks			
65	Debtors			
68	Current investments			
69	Bank balances & cash			
		£		
	Less: *CURRENT LIABILITIES*			
71	Creditors			
79	Bank overdrafts			
	WORKING CAPITAL	£		
	TOTAL	£		
	Less: *PROVISIONS*			
81	for renewal of fixed assets			
82	Other provisions			
89	*DEFERRED LIABILITIES*			
		£		
	CAPITAL & RESERVES			
91	Share capital			
92	Reserves			
93	Loan capital			
		£		

Figure 215

Coding of accounts In order to enable hotels to record all income and expenditure in a uniform manner the standard system provides for detailed coding of accounts.

Thus:	Rooms are code	01
	Food is code	02
	Liquor and tobacco is code	03
	Other income is code	09

The item Stock Losses is code 125. When there are losses in food stocks the combined code is 02 125; when there are losses of liquor and tobacco, the combined code will be 03 125.

Gross pay is code 131. Thus gross pay in respect of the rooms department will be 01 131; gross pay in respect of the food department will be 02 131.

In the case of the balance sheet accounts there is a category code for each main kind of asset and liability. The category code for plant and machinery is 52. Under this main code we find:

52 621	Machinery
52 622	Depreciation of Machinery
52 625	Furniture
52 626	Depreciation of Furniture
52 631	Fixtures and Fittings
52 632	Depreciation of Fixtures and Fittings
52 635	Motor Vehicles
52 636	Depreciation of Motor Vehicles

It will be appreciated that the coding of accounts offers several advantages. It ensures a consistent recording of all income and expenditure; it enables a logical physical arrangement of all accounts kept; finally, it enables a consistent treatment all items of capital and revenue in the final accounts and thus enables inter-unit comparison in the hotel sector of the industry.

Inter-firm comparison

Inter-firm comparison in the hotel and catering industry is still in its infancy. Only a small number of organizations have participated in the schemes that have been evolved. It seems that two main factors have operated against inter-firm comparison in this industry: the heterogeneity of firms and the traditional unwillingness to part with information relating to turnover, cost levels, profit margins, etc.

A scheme of inter-firm comparison works as follows. It is necessary to set up a central agency for the collection and processing of data from the participants. The central agency will periodically (monthly, quarterly, annually) receive returns from the participating members. The returns will cover a variety of matters: revenue, sales mix, departmental operating costs and a number of operating and accounting ratios. The information must then be processed in accordance with certain predetermined criteria. Thus comparisons may be made according to the location of participants, size of business, level of establishment, etc.

Clearly, in the case of hotel and catering establishments it is imperative to divide the participants into several distinct categories. There is little point in comparing the costs of an inexpensive seasonal hotel with those of a luxury London hotel; similarly, no useful purpose will be served by comparing the sales mix of a country inn with that of a large city hotel. It follows, therefore, that much careful thought is required if one is to ensure that the feed-back to the participants is both meaningful and fair.

Finally, after the necessary processing of the data has been completed it is essential to provide for an adequate feed-back to the participants. The latter must be informed not only whether or not their results are different from those of their competitors but also why their results are different.

After the central agency has been in operation for some years it should be in a position to establish a series of 'norms' for the use of the participating firms. The norms often take the form of operating and accounting ratios, which have been found to be typical in the industry.

Inter-firm comparisons offer many advantages to the participating firms. Firstly, they are able to compare their own results with those of other firms similarly placed. This enables the participants to examine their operating costs, profit margins, trends in sales, etc. in relation to those prevailing in other firms. Where there are substantial differences between a particular participant's results and those of the other firms a detailed investigation is required to establish the causes of such differences. It is as a result of detailed perusal of the returns from the central agency that much expense may be saved and trading results improved.

Problems

1 Explain what is meant by uniform accounting. What conditions must be satisfied by a scheme of uniform accounting?

2 What are the main factors which make the introduction of uniform accounting difficult in the hotel and catering industry?

3 In connection with the standard system of hotel accounting, explain what is meant by each of the following:

(a) gross profit;
(b) net margin;
(c) operating profit;
(d) operating income;
(e) hotel operating profit;
(f) net operating profit.

4 What are the main advantages of inter-firm comparison?

5 Explain how a scheme of inter-firm comparison works and enumerate the main advantages of such schemes for the participating members.

6 State what information you would expect to receive from the central agency as a participant in a scheme of inter-firm comparison.

CHAPTER 24

Revenue accounting

During the last few years it has been possible to identify some of the special characteristics of hotel and catering establishments. Amongst the principal characteristics is the heavy dependence of hotels, restaurants, etc. on market demand. This particular characteristic has a most pervading and, indeed, dominant influence on many aspects of hotel and catering operation including profitability.

The sector of the hotel and catering industry which is very dependent on market demand is here described as 'market oriented'. Included in the market oriented sector are units such as hotels, motels, conference centres and restaurants. Industrial canteens, hospital and college catering, etc., are, on the other hand, described for our purpose as 'cost oriented'.

The easiest way to identify the orientation of an establishment is to subject it to *profit sensitivity analysis* (PSA). The description of this technique is offered in this chapter not because PSA is seen as an integral part of the concept of revenue accounting but, simply, because it indicates the correct approach to accounting and control methods. As will be gathered later in this chapter, the correct approach to accounting and control is one which gives adequate prominence to the revenue, rather than cost, side of the business. This, briefly, is what is meant by the concept of revenue accounting.

Introduction to PSA

The main aim of profit sensitivity analysis is to identify the 'key factors' which influence profitability (e.g. occupancy, average spending power, food and beverage costs, labour costs, etc.) and quantify their impact on the net profit of the business. As explained in Example 1 below, key factors which have high profit multiplier values have more impact on profitability than those which have low profit multiplier values.

When the key factors have been identified and the P.M. values calculated, we can look at the profile of the P.M. values and draw appropriate conclusions. One of the main conclusions that may be drawn relates to the orientation of the business. In other words, we are able to decide whether the business is cost oriented or market oriented.

Example 1 Given below is the summary of the quarterly trading results of a small restaurant.

Trading results

No. of covers		10 000
Average price		£5.00
Sales		£50 000
Less Food cost	£20 000	
Fixed labour	10 000	
Variable labour	5 000	
Fixed overheads	10 000	
		45 000
Net profit		£5 000

The key factors which influence the net profit of the restaurant are shown in Figure 216.

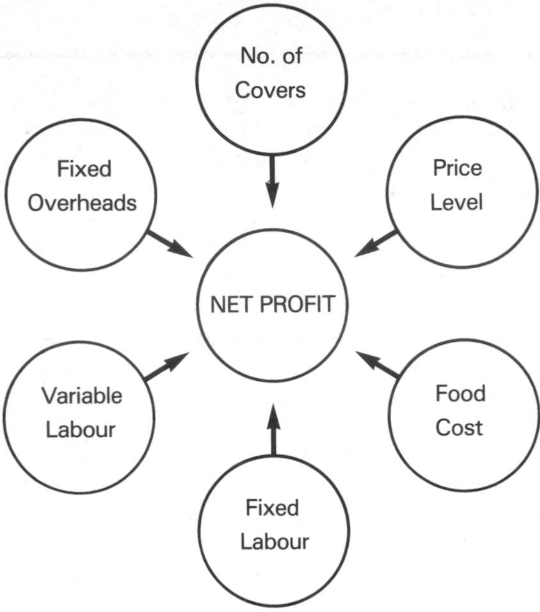

Figure 216

A change in any one of the key factors will have some effect on the net profit. Thus if fixed overheads increase (and there is no other change at the same time) net profit will decrease. If food cost is decreased and, again, there is no other change, net profit will increase.

Now that we have identified the key factors let us quantify the impact of each key factor on the net profit of the restaurant. The procedure is this. We assume a small change in a key factor and, holding other factors constant (except, of course, for consequential changes such as an increase in food costs resulting from a larger number of covers, etc.), we trace the effect of the small change on net profit. If, for instance, we assume an increase in the price level of 10 per cent and this has the effect of increasing the net profit by 50 per cent, we have, dividing one percentage by another, a profit multiplier of 5.0 A P.M. value of 5.0 means that every 1 per cent change in the price level results in a 5 per cent change in net profit. Thus, if we had a P.M. value of 3.00 for food cost, and decreased it (the food cost) by 2 per cent, the effect would be an increase in net profit of 6 per cent.

Let us now calculate the P.M. values for the restaurant in Example 1. For ease of calculations we shall assume a change of 10 per cent in each case.

Price level:

Sales	£55 000
Less total cost	45 000
Net profit	£10 000

Only the price level has changed here and there is no change on the cost side. Total cost is, therefore, unchanged at £45 000. The net profit has increased from

£5 000 to £10 000, which is an increase of 100 per cent, following a 10 per cent change in the price level. Our P.M. value is, therefore, 10.0, which suggests that net profit is very sensitive to changes in the price level: every 1 per cent change in the price level results in a 10 per cent change in net profit.

No. of covers:

Sales	£55 000
Less total cost	47 500
Net profit	£7 500

It will be observed that total cost has increased by £2 500. This is due to the consequential increases of 10 per cent in food cost, £2 000 and variable labour, £500. The increase in net profit is (from £5 000 to £7 000) 50 per cent and this gives us a profit multiplier of 5.0.

Food cost:

Sales	£50 000
Less total cost	47 000
Net profit	£3 000

In this calculation there is a change of only 10 per cent in food cost and, of course, no consequential changes. The result is for the restaurant to lose £2 000 of its net profit and this represents 40 per cent of the original net profit. The P.M. value is therefore 4.0. (Strictly speaking it is – 4.0, as we have divided a negative figure by a positive figure. However, the minus sign is of no practical consequence in P.S.A. and is, therefore, ignored.)

Fixed labour:

Sales	£50 000
Less total cost	46 000
Net profit	£4 000

The 10 per cent increase in this key factor has resulted in a loss of 20 per cent of the net profit. Our P.M. value is 2.0.

Variable labour:

Sales	£50 000
Less total cost	45 500
Net profit	£4 500

We have lost 10 per cent of our net profit following the 10 per cent increase in variable labour. This results in a P.M. value of 1.0.

Fixed overheads:

Sales	£50 000
Less total cost	46 000
Net profit	£4 000

The net profit has decreased by 20 per cent and the profit multiplier is 2.0.

We have now calculated all the necessary profit multipliers and their impact on net profit may be shown as in Figure 217.

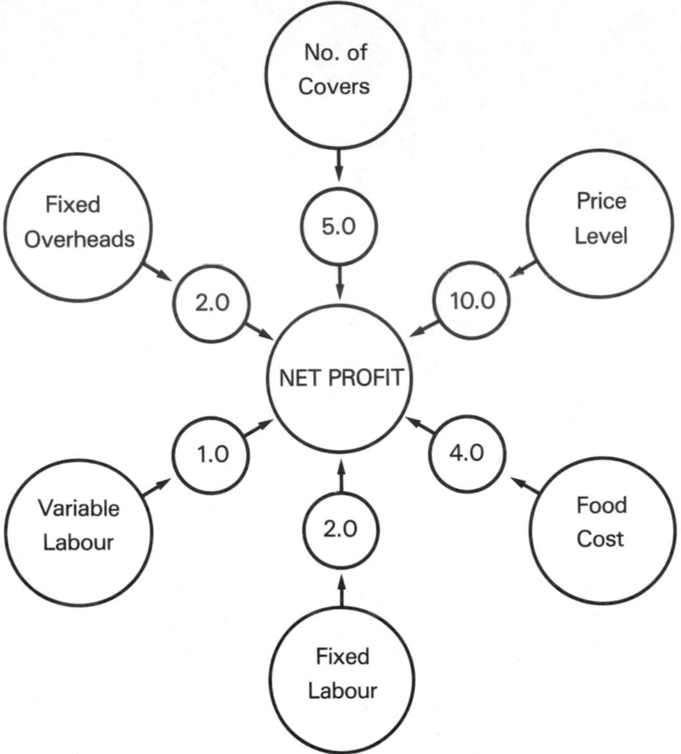

Figure 217

From Figure 217 it may be seen that different key factors have a different degree of impact on profitability. Some of the key factors have very high P.M. values (e.g. price level); others (e.g. variable labour) have a relatively minor effect on net profit.

Ranking of profit multipliers

We may now rank our profit multipliers and, subsequently, by looking at their profile, draw appropriate conclusions.

Ranking

Key factor	*P.M.*	*C/U**
Price level	10.0	C
No. of covers	5.0	C
Food cost	4.0	C
Fixed labour	2.0	U
Fixed overheads	2.0	U
Variable labour	1.0	C

It is necessary to point out that whilst some key factors may have high P.M. values, this may be of little practical value in the short term. In this example fixed labour and fixed overheads are largely uncontrollable. Even if these P.M. values were much

* Denotes controllable and uncontrollable key factors.

higher they would not be of much consequence in the context of profit management from one period to another.

Conclusions

The main conclusions which we may draw from the table ranking the profit multipliers are as follows.

The two revenue based profit multipliers have the highest values and hence appear right at the top of the list. This indicates that it is the revenue side of the business that has the stronger impact of profitability. Even small changes in the price level and the N.O.C. will result in substantial changes in net profit. As the price level profit multiplier is 10.0, every 1 per cent increase in the restaurant's menu prices will, other things being equal, result in a 10 per cent increase in net profit. With the exception of the profit multiplier for food cost, the cost side of the restaurant is represented by low P.M. values—some of which are, in any case, uncontrollable over short periods of time. From this profile of P.M. values we must conclude that the restaurant is market rather than cost oriented.

Our principal second conclusion is this. As the restaurant is market oriented and its profitability is mainly influenced by factors operating on the revenue side of the business, we must have a revenue accounting approach in our efforts to secure adequate profitability. This, briefly, means that whilst controlling the food costs, the greatest efforts should be made to control the revenue of the restaurant. To be more specific, we must pay particular attention to the sales volume, sales mix, gross profit and differential profit margins, average spending power, restaurant occupancy and, finally, matters like pricing methods and periodic reviews of menu prices.

Profit multipliers: significance and applications

From Example 1 students will appreciate that high P.M. values mean that net profit is very sensitive to changes in the relevant key factors. We may thus associate low P.M. values with profit stability and high P.M. values with profit instability. Quite clearly, if a business operates at a price level profit multiplier of 10.0 or 15.0 and a sales volume profit multiplier of over 5.0, even minute changes in these key factors will have a powerful impact on net profit. We must conclude, therefore, that when planning a new operation it is essential to arrange the price structure, cost levels and profit margins in such a manner as to secure a generally low level of P.M. values and, in this way, assure a reasonable degree of profit stability.

In the above example the revenue based profit multipliers were at the top, i.e. had the highest values. Where this is so, we have a clear indication that the business is market oriented. This characteristic of market orientation has, in turn, certain implications for business strategy as well as the choice of accounting methods and control procedures. In a market oriented business most problems relating to profitability relate to market demand and its consequences in terms of the sales revenue of the business. The correct solutions to such problems will not normally be found in the area of cost control: a market oriented solution will usually have to be provided.

A cost oriented business will, amongst others, have a high proportion of variable/controllable costs. Where that is so cost control procedures constitute an effective tool in the management of profitability. In market oriented businesses there is generally a high proportion of fixed/uncontrollable costs and, as a result, the scope for cost control is limited. The correct approach in this situation is to concentrate on revenue oriented accounting and control methods. In most hotels it will be found that the highest profit multipliers relate to the price level, occupancy and the (generally fixed) unapportioned operating expenses. The latter offer little scope in terms of cost control and, therefore, the most effective way of ensuring the right level of net profit is to concentrate on the management of the revenue inflow of the hotel.

Numerous operating ratios may be used by hotel and catering managers in controlling a business from one week/month to another. Many managers find it difficult to decide which ratio is more important or significant than another. From the point of view of P.S.A. the answer to this problem lies in the respective P.M. values attaching to the various operating ratios. Thus the average room rate will have a higher P.M. value than the cost of food or beverages consumed. More importance should, therefore, be attached to the former than to the latter. By the same token, more attention should be paid to A.S.P. statistics than to the food cost percentage—though, of course, no-one would wish to dispute the importance of food control. Ideally, a manager should control all aspects of his business. But, as the time available for control is limited, it is essential that it should be allocated in a manner which reflects the relative importance of each aspect of control as measured in terms of its impact on profitability and other business objectives. The best guide to this allocation of time are the relevant P.M. values.

Example 2 Given below are the summarised budgeted results of two catering establishments, Imperial Restaurant and Jax Café.

	Imperial	*Jax*
No. of covers	2 000	10 000
Price per cover	£5.00	£1.00
Sales	£10 000	£10 000
Food and beverage cost	3 000	5 000
Other costs—fixed	5 000	2 000
Other costs—variable	1 000	1 000
Net profit	1 000	2 000
	£10 000	£10 000

You are required to:
(a) calculate the P.M. values for both units;
(b) rank the profit multipliers;
(c) comment generally on the two sets of profit multipliers.

Here again we shall assume a change of 10 per cent in each key factor for the purpose of calculating the profit multipliers.

Imperial Restaurant

Key factor	Sales	Total cost	Net profit	P.M.
	£	£	£	
Price level	11 000	9 000	2 000	10.0
No. of covers	11 000	9 400	1 600	6.0
Foof & beverage costs	10 000	9 300	700	3.0
Other costs—fixed	10 000	9 500	500	5.0
Other costs—variable	10 000	9 100	900	1.0

Jax Café

Key factor	Sales	Total cost	Net profit	P.M.
	£	£	£	
Price level	11 000	8 000	3 000	5.0
No. of covers	11 000	8 600	2 400	2.0
Foof & beverage costs	10 000	8 500	1 500	2.5
Other costs—fixed	10 000	8 200	1 800	1.0
Other costs—variable	10 000	8 100	1 900	0.5

We may now show the ranking of the profit multipliers for the two establishments as follows.

Ranking

Imperial Restaurant		*Jax Café*	
Key factor	P.M.	Key factor	P.M.
Price level	10.0	Price level	5.0
No. of covers	6.0	Food & beverage costs	2.5
Other costs—fixed	5.0	No. of covers	2.0
Food & beverage costs	3.0	Other costs—fixed	1.0
Other costs—variable	1.0	Other costs—variable	0.5

In the case of the Imperial Restaurant we have a clear indication of the characteristic of market orientation: both the revenue based key factors have the highest P.M. values. In the case of Jax Café, the position is not quite clear: the price level P.M. is immediately followed by that for food and beverage costs. From this it is clear that food and beverage control should in Jax Café be given more importance than in the other establishment.

P.M. values, margin of safety and profit stability

It was explained in Chapter 20 that the margin of safety is a measure of the stability of profits: the wider the MOS, the greater the degree of profit stability, and vice versa. In the present chapter we have introduced the concept of the profit multiplier and explained the high profit multipliers operate to produce a degree of profit instability, and vice versa. From this students will guess that there should be some general relationship between the level of P.M. values and the width of the margin of safety. In Figure 218 we show the break-even charts for the two establishments in Example 2.

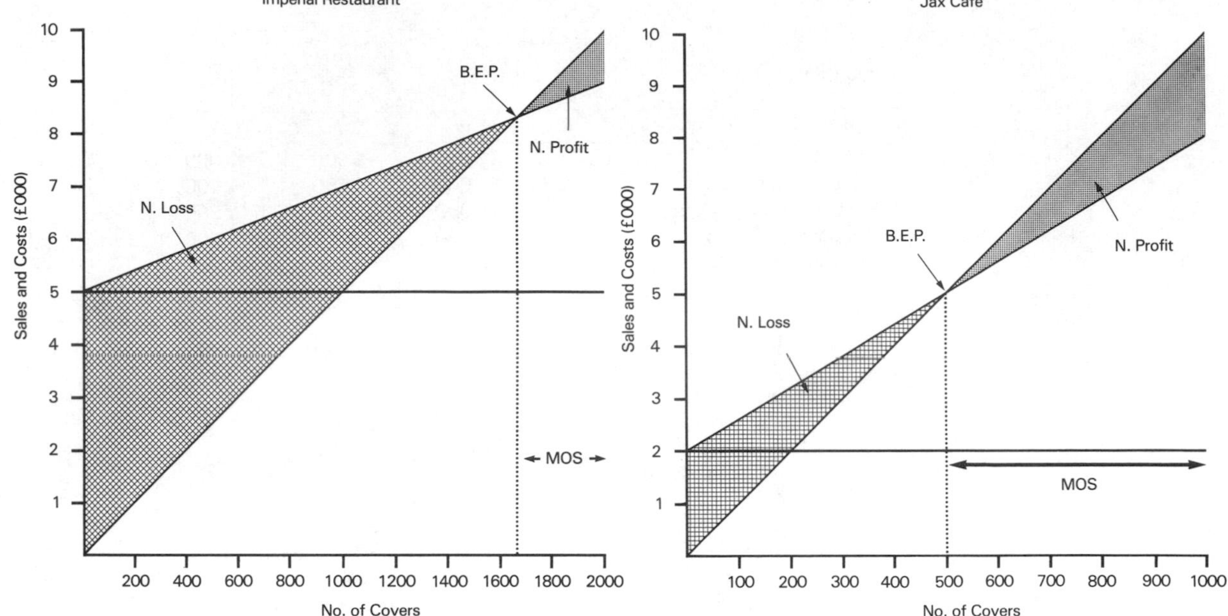

Figure 218

Imperial Restaurant, which operates at a generally higher level of profit multipliers, has a narrow margin of safety. Jax Café has quite low profit multipliers and a very wide margin of safety. We may thus associate high P.M. values with a narrow margin of safety and profit instability and, conversely, low P.M. values with a wide margin of safety and profit stability.

Example 3 In this third example it is intended to show another possible application of profit multipliers; their use in profit planning and pricing decisions.

Given below is the draft budgeted profit and loss account of a restaurant prepared by the accountant of the business.

Budgeted Profit & Loss A/c – Draft

Sales	Sales mix	Sales Value	Gross Profit	Gross Profit
	%	£	%	£
Soups and Appetizers	13	65,000	75	48,750
Meat, Fish and Poultry	45	225,000	55	123,750
Vegetables	17	85,000	75	63,750
Sweets	15	75,000	70	52,500
Teas and Coffees	10	50,000	80	40,000
	100%	£500,000	–	£328,750
Less Operating Expenses:			£	
Payroll			135,000	
Administration Expenses			35,000	
Advertising and Promotion			20,000	
Heat, Light and Power			20,000	
Repairs and Replacements			12,000	
Depreciation			24,000	
Laundry and Cleaning			6,000	
Sundry Expenses			16,750	268,750
Net Profit				£ 60,000

Figure 219

The directors of the restaurant are not satisfied with the level of the budgeted net profit and insist that the business should aim at not less than £66 000 during the forthcoming year. They would like to know what price increases are necessary in order to achieve the additional 10 per cent net profit. It may be assumed for this purpose that small changes in the price level of up to 5 per cent will not have an adverse effect on the number of covers or the operating expenses of the restaurant.

We may provide an analysis of the P.M. values relating to the sales mix of the restaurant. Again, for ease of calculations, we shall assume a change of 10 per cent in each element of the sales mix.

Effect of changes in sales mix prices on total net profit

Sales Mix	Net Profit Base	Sales mix value	10% of S.M. value	Increased Net Profit	P.M.	% increase required to raise net profit by 10%
	£	£	£	£		%
Soups and appetizers	60 000	65 000	6 500	66 500	1.11	9.01
Meat, fish & poultry	60 000	225 000	22 500	82 500	3.75	2.67
Vegetables	60 000	85 000	8 500	68 500	1.42	7.04
Sweets	60 000	75 000	7 500	67 500	1.25	8.00
Teas and coffees	60 000	50 000	5 000	65 000	0.83	12.00

In the first column we have our base—the £60 000 net profit from the Budgeted Profit and Loss Account. The sales mix value of soups and appetizers is £65 000; and if, holding all other factors constant, we just increase all prices of this element of the sales mix by 10 per cent, we shall add £6 500 to our total net profit. Our net profit will thus be raised to £66 500, which is 110.8 per cent of the profit base and this results in a price level profit multiplier for this element of the sales mix of 1.11. Also, as may be seen from the figures given in the above tables, we require a rise of 9.01 per cent in the prices of soups and appetizers to raise the total budgeted net profit to £66 000. The 9.01 per cent increase in prices multiplied by the P.M. value of 1.11 will result in a 10 per cent increase in total net profit.

Profit planning: the pricing options

Now that we have calculated the P.M. values for all the elements of the sales mix, we are able to suggest to the directors a variety of possible solutions relating to price revisions. Some examples are given below.

(a) As the overall price level P.M. is 8.36 (sum total of the individual P.M. values) in order to secure an increase in net profit of 10 per cent all menu prices have to be increased by just 1.2 per cent.

(b) If we raise all prices of the sweets on the menu by 5 per cent, this multiplied by the relevant P.M. value of 1.25 will increase net profit by 6.25 per cent. If, in addition, we raise the prices of meat, fish and poultry by 1 per cent, then through the relevant profit multiplier of 3.75, we shall, additionally, raise the net profit by 3.75 per cent. In this way we will achieve a total increase in the net profit of the restaurant of 10 per cent.

(c) If we raise the prices of meat, fish and poultry by 2 per cent, this through the P.M. value of 3.75 will add 7.50 per cent to total profit. If additionally we provide for an increase of 2 per cent in the prices of sweets, we will secure—again through the relevant profit multiplier of 1.25—a 2.50 per cent increase in net profit. Both these modest price increases will add a total of 10 per cent to the budgeted net profit.

As will have been gathered by now, there is a large number of ways in which menu prices may be increased to secure the 10 per cent increase in the net profit of the restaurant. It is now for the directors to decide which of the various price increases are most appropriate.

Profit and loss account: revenue accounting approach

From the examples given so far students will have realised the importance of the revenue based profit multipliers. The operation of such profit multipliers in a market oriented business is very strong indeed; and this enjoins a particular approach to the preparation of the profit and loss account. As the influence on net profit of the revenue side of the business is strong, it is essential to give the sales revenue more prominence than would be necessary in a cost oriented business. Quite frequently one sees a method of presentation such as shown in Figure 220.

Profit & Loss A/c

	Sales	Cost of Sales	Gross Profit
	£	£	£
Food Sales	400,000	160,000	240,000
Beverage Sales	200,000	87,500	112,500
Total Sales	600,000	247,500	352,500
Less Operating Expenses:			
Payroll	145,000		
Employers' Insurance	13,500		
Employee Benefits	9,500	168,000	
Office Expenses	27,000		
Advertising and Promotion	14,000		
Laundry and Cleaning	9,000		
Heat, Light and Power	13,000		
Repairs & Replacements	21,000		
Depreciation	24,000		
Sundry Expenses	15,000	123,000	291,000
Net Profit			£ 61,500

Figure 220

The information relating to the sales revenue is very scant indeed. Either more detail relating to profit margins, A.S.P., etc. has to be built into the profit and loss account, (e.g. as in the trading account in Figure 222), or such information could be given in additional schedules, as illustrated below.

Food Sales Statistics :

	Sales mix %	Sales mix £	Gross Profit %	Gross Profit £
Soups and Appetizers	10	40,000	60	24,000
Meat, Fish and Entrées	50	200,000	55	110,000
Vegetables	15	60,000	70	42,000
Sweets	15	60,000	60	36,000
Teas and Coffees	10	40,000	70	28,000
	100%	£400,000	60%	£240,000

Beverage Sales Statistics :

	Sales mix %	Sales mix £	Gross Profit %	Gross Profit £
Spirits	25	50,000	70	35,000
Fortified Wines	15	30,000	65	19,500
Table Wines	30	60,000	55	33,000
Beers	25	50,000	40	20,000
Minerals	5	10,000	50	5,000
	100%	£200,000	56·3%	£112,500

Figure 221

In Figure 222 we present a trading account which includes most of the revenue based information that is relevant. The trading account shows not only the departmental sales volumes but also their determinants (A.S.P. and N.O.C. figures) both of which have to be controlled from one trading period to another. The trading account shows neither the stock levels nor the cost of sales; and this is in accordance with the practice of many establishments in the industry which are beginning to adopt a revenue accounting approach in the presentation and layout of accounts.

Trading Account
for six months ended 30 Sept., 19..

	Grill Room	Snack Bar	Banqueting	Private Bar	TOTAL
No of Covers	13,000	8,000	4,000	6,000	31,000
	£	£	£	£	£
Food Sales	93,600	15,200	16,800	1,200	126,800
Beverage Sales	41,600	6,400	8,400	5,400	61,800
Total Sales	135,200	21,600	25,200	6,600	188,600
	%	%	%	%	%
Sales Mix: Food	69·2	70·4	66·7	18·2	67·2
Beverages	30·8	29·6	33·3	81·8	32·8
Total	100·0	100·0	100·0	100·0	100·0
	£	£	£	£	£
ASP: Food	7.20	1.90	4.20	0.20	–
Beverages	3.20	0.80	2.10	0.90	–
Total	10.40	2.70	6.30	1.10	–
	£	£	£	£	£
Gross Profit: Food	60,840	10,336	12,096	888	84,160
Beverages	24,960	3,712	5,460	3,348	37,480
Total	85,800	14,048	17,556	4,236	121,640
	%	%	%	%	%
Gross Profit %: Food	65·0	68·0	72·0	74·0	66·4
Beverages	60·0	58·0	65·0	62·0	60·7
Total	63·5	65·0	69·6	64·1	64·5

Figure 222

Revenue accounting: basic records

From the last few examples given in this chapter it will be realised that the preparation of revenue oriented accounting and control statements necessitates the maintenance of appropriate records. Such records have to be maintained in respect of sales mix, gross profit levels, differential profit margins, the number of covers and occupancy. A few examples are given below.

Sales Mix Analysis : Total Sales

Week No	Food £	Food %	Beverages £	Beverages %	Sundries £	Sundries %	Total £	Total %
1	2,477	61	1,137	28	446	11	4,060	100
2	2,653	62	1,156	27	471	11	4,280	100
3	2,778	63	1,147	26	485	11	4,410	100
etc								

Figure 223

Sales Mix Analysis : Food Sales

Week No	Starters £	Starters %	Meat and Fish £	Meat and Fish %	Vegetables £	Vegetables %	Sweets £	Sweets %	Teas and Coffees £	Teas and Coffees %	Total £	Total %
1	272	11	1,238	50	371	15	372	15	224	9	2,477	100
2	265	10	1,328	50	398	15	424	16	238	9	2,653	100
3	250	9	1,389	50	417	15	472	17	250	9	2,778	100
etc												

Figure 224

Sales Mix Analysis : Beverage Sales

Week No	Spirits £	Spirits %	Fortified Wines £	Fortified Wines %	Table Wines £	Table Wines %	Beers £	Beers %	Minerals £	Minerals %	Total £	Total %
1	295	26	171	15	341	30	273	24	57	5	1,137	100
2	278	24	185	16	358	31	266	23	69	6	1,156	100
3	286	25	195	17	368	32	241	21	57	5	1,147	100
etc												

Figure 225

Figures 223, 224 and 225 show a complete weekly analysis of the food and beverage sales mix. These basic records have two main functions. They show, from one week to another, the trends that develop within the food and beverage sales mix. Thus Figure 224 shows that the sales of starters are showing a downward trend and that the reverse applies in the case of sweets. If the establishment operates at different percentages of gross profit on these two elements of the sales mix, then these trends could have an important effect on total gross profit.

Similar trends may be observed in the case of beverage sales. Fortified wines and table wines are showing an upward trend; and these, normally, have a higher gross profit loading than beers which attract a much lower gross profit and, over the three weeks, are showing the opposite trend. The effect of these changes must be beneficial in terms of gross profit performance.

Finally, these records are essential for the preparation of revenue oriented periodic accounting statements, e.g. trading accounts, profit and loss accounts, budget reports, etc.

ASP Analysis : Total Sales

Week No	Total Sales	NOC	ASP			
			Total	Food	Bev.	Sundries
1	£4,060	510	£7·96	£4·86	£2.23	£0·87
2	4,280	529	8·09	5·02	2·18	0·89
3	4,410	543	8·12	5·12	2·11	0·89
etc						

Figure 226

In Figure 226 we show a weekly analysis of the average spending power. The A.S.P. profit multiplier is normally lower than that in respect of the price level, but it is one of the highest P.M. values in a market oriented business. The A.S.P. statistics must, therefore, be monitored very carefully as they are one of the main indications of the general trend of business and have an important bearing on profitability. The food and beverage controller would certainly want to establish the reason for the downward trend in the A.S.P. on beverages before deciding what corrective action was required.

We have now shown some of the principal basic revenue accounting records. In a short chapter like the present it is impossible to show all the records in detail. Apart from those included here; records should be kept for gross profit performance, both in terms of overall gross profit levels achieved on food and beverages and the differential profit margins.

Problems

1 Explain what you understand by the terms: 'cost oriented' and 'market oriented'.

2 Write short, explanatory notes on:
(a) P.S.A.;
(b) profit multipliers;
(c) key factors.

3 Enumerate the practical applications of P.S.A.

4 Explain the relationship between the P.M. values, the margin of safety and profit stability.

5 State briefly what you understand by 'revenue accounting'.

6 What are the main revenue accounting records? Why are they maintained?

7 Given below is a summary of the trading results of an establishment.

Trading results

No. of covers		10 000
Average price		£10.00
Sales	£100 000	
Less Food cost	£40 000	
Variable labour	10 000	
Fixed labour	20 000	
Fixed overheads	20 000	
		90 000
Net profit		£10 000

You are required to:
(a) identify the key factors;
(b) calculate the P.M. values;
(c) rank the key factors;
(d) suggest what conclusions may be drawn from (c) above.

8 Given below are particulars relating to two restaurants.

		A	B
N.O.C.		10 000	10 000
Average price		£4.00	£8.00
Sales		£40 000	£80 000
Food and beverage costs		18 000	32 000
Other variable costs		6 000	8 000
Fixed costs		12 000	24 000
Net profit		4 000	16 000
	Total	£40 000	£80 000

Calculate the P.M. values for the key factors in A and B and suggest what conclusions should be drawn from them.

9 Given below is the half-yearly budgeted profit and loss account in summary form.

	Sales Mix	Sales Volume	Gross Profit	Gross Profit
	%	£	%	£
Starters	10	20 000	60	12 000
Main dishes	50	100 000	55	55 000
Vegetables	15	30 000	70	21 000
Desserts	15	30 000	60	18 000
Teas and coffees	10	20 000	70	14 000
	100%	£200 000	60%	£120 000
Less Fixed operating expenses				90 000
Budgeted net profit				£30 000

(a) From the information given above calculate the price level profit multipliers for the five elements of the sales mix.

(b) Assuming that small changes (of up to 5 per cent) in the price level have no effect on the number of covers or the operating expenses, find the effect on net profit of:

(i) increasing the prices of all the main dishes by 3 per cent.

(ii) increasing the prices of vegetables by 5 per cent and the prices of sweets by 5 per cent.

(iii) increasing the prices of the main dishes by 2 per cent and the prices of teas and coffees by 5 per cent.

(iv) increasing all menu prices by 3 per cent.

Appendix A:

Table I. Present value of £1.00 received in the future

Periods Hence	1%	2%	4%	6%	8%	10%	12%	14%	15%	16%	18%	20%	22%	24%	25%	26%	28%	30%	35%	40%
1	0.990	0.980	0.962	0.943	0.926	0.909	0.893	0.877	0.870	0.862	0.847	0.833	0.820	0.806	0.800	0.794	0.781	0.769	0.741	0.714
2	0.980	0.961	0.925	0.890	0.857	0.826	0.797	0.769	0.756	0.743	0.718	0.694	0.672	0.650	0.640	0.630	0.610	0.592	0.549	0.510
3	0.971	0.942	0.889	0.840	0.794	0.751	0.712	0.675	0.658	0.641	0.609	0.579	0.551	0.524	0.512	0.500	0.477	0.455	0.406	0.364
4	0.961	0.924	0.855	0.792	0.735	0.683	0.636	0.592	0.572	0.552	0.516	0.482	0.451	0.423	0.410	0.397	0.373	0.350	0.301	0.260
5	0.951	0.906	0.822	0.747	0.681	0.621	0.567	0.519	0.497	0.476	0.437	0.402	0.370	0.341	0.328	0.315	0.291	0.269	0.223	0.186
6	0.942	0.883	0.790	0.705	0.630	0.564	0.507	0.456	0.432	0.410	0.370	0.335	0.303	0.275	0.262	0.250	0.227	0.207	0.165	0.133
7	0.933	0.871	0.760	0.665	0.583	0.513	0.452	0.400	0.376	0.354	0.314	0.279	0.249	0.222	0.210	0.198	0.178	0.159	0.122	0.095
8	0.923	0.853	0.731	0.627	0.540	0.467	0.404	0.351	0.327	0.305	0.266	0.233	0.204	0.179	0.168	0.157	0.139	0.123	0.091	0.068
9	0.914	0.837	0.703	0.592	0.500	0.424	0.361	0.308	0.284	0.263	0.225	0.194	0.167	0.144	0.134	0.125	0.108	0.094	0.067	0.048
10	0.905	0.820	0.676	0.558	0.463	0.386	0.322	0.270	0.247	0.227	0.191	0.162	0.137	0.116	0.107	0.099	0.085	0.073	0.050	0.035
11	0.890	0.801	0.650	0.527	0.429	0.350	0.287	0.237	0.215	0.195	0.162	0.135	0.112	0.094	0.086	0.079	0.066	0.056	0.037	0.025
12	0.857	0.788	0.625	0.497	0.397	0.319	0.257	0.208	0.187	0.168	0.137	0.112	0.092	0.076	0.069	0.062	0.052	0.043	0.027	0.018
13	0.879	0.778	0.601	0.469	0.368	0.290	0.229	0.182	0.163	0.145	0.116	0.093	0.075	0.061	0.055	0.050	0.040	0.033	0.020	0.013
14	0.870	0.758	0.577	0.442	0.340	0.263	0.205	0.160	0.141	0.125	0.099	0.078	0.062	0.049	0.044	0.089	0.032	0.025	0.015	0.009
15	0.861	0.748	0.555	0.417	0.315	0.239	0.183	0.140	0.123	0.108	0.084	0.067	0.051	0.040	0.035	0.031	0.025	0.020	0.011	0.006

INDEX